Lady in the Labyrinth

Milton's *Comus* as Initiation

William Shullenberger

Madison • Teaneck
Fairleigh Dickinson University Press

© 2008 by Rosemont Publishing & Printing Corp.

All rights reserved. Authorization to photocopy items for internal or personal use, or the internal or personal use of specific clients, is granted by the copyright owner, provided that a base fee of $10.00, plus eight cents per page, per copy is paid directly to the Copyright Clearance Center, 222 Rosewood Drive, Danvers, Massachusetts 01923. [978-0-8386-4174-3/08 $10.00 + 8¢ pp, pc.]

Associated University Presses
2010 Eastpark Boulevard
Cranbury, NJ 08512

The paper used in this publication meets the requirements of the American National Standard for Permanence of Paper for Printed Library Materials Z39.48-1984.

Library of Congress Cataloging-in-Publication Data

Shullenberger, William.
 Lady in the labyrinth : Milton's Comus as initiation / William Shullenberger.
   p. cm.
 Includes bibliographical references and index.
 ISBN-13: 978-0-8386-4174-3 (alk. paper)
 1. Milton, John, 1608–1674. Comus. 2. Milton, John, 1608–1674—Characters—Women. 3. Milton, John, 1608–1674—Religion. 4. Milton, John, 1608–1674—Ethics. 5. Virtue in literature. 6. Chastity in literature. 7. Christianity in literature. 8. Ethics in literature. 9. Feminism in literature. 10. Initiation rites in literature. I. Title.
 PR3557.S58 2008
 822'.4—dc22
                                                                            2008008450

PRINTED IN THE UNITED STATES OF AMERICA

Lady in the Labyrinth

For Shannon, Lily, Isabel, and Morgan

Contents

Acknowledgments	9
Introduction: Milton's Portrait of a Lady	15
1. "Growing a Girl": The Masque of Passage	46
2. Singing Master of the Soul: The Attendant Spirit	82
3. Tragedy in Translation	109
4. Double Trouble: Comus and His Bloodlines	142
5. Girl Power: The Profession of Virginity	175
6. Milton's Lady and Lady Milton: Chastity, Gender, and Prophecy	203
7. Girl, Interrupted and the Changing Woman	226
8. Homecoming Queen	251
Notes	280
Bibliography	331
Index	348

Acknowledgments

MILTON'S SATAN SURPRISINGLY EXPLAINS TO HIMSELF AND TO US the paradox of a providential economy, that "a grateful mind / By owing owes not, but still pays, at once / Indebted and discharg'd; what burden then?" (*PL* 4.55–57). So it is that as I recollect the multitude of debts I owe for this book, I feel no burden, only gratitude. I should first acknowledge that the filiations of gratitude extend well beyond the names I mention specifically here, to include everyone whose work I cite, among them those with whom I have disagreed. I take Blake at his word, in *The Marriage of Heaven and Hell,* that "Opposition is true Friendship." The evidence for this is that I have certainly learned and been strengthened as much from the people I have taken issue with as from the people whose work has proved more consonant with my own way of thinking about Milton.

I learned my Milton from the blessed Kathleen Swaim, and I learned from her that being a Miltonist means much more than knowing the texts and the scholarship. This project, "long choosing, and beginning late" (*PL* 9.26), is a gift to her for all she has given me. I am grateful as well to the many rigorous and generous editors who have challenged and nourished parts of this work, in particular Roy Flannagan, Edward Jones, Beth Quitslund, and Andrew Escobido; Claude Summers and Ted-Larry Pebworth; Charles Durham and Kristin Pruitt; Catherine Martin; Arthur Kinney; and Ken Hiltner. I also want to thank Harry Keyishian and the editors and readers of Fairleigh Dickinson University Press, who have trusted enough in the public value of this experiment in Milton criticism to support its publication.

Teaching at Sarah Lawrence College, thanks to students and colleagues, is an ongoing exercise in thinking outside the box, which I hope this book will also encourage its readers to do. Many friends at Sarah Lawrence have been invaluable in sharing their wisdom and connecting me to essential ideas and resources about which I would otherwise know very little. In particular, I want to thank Elfie

Raymond, Michael Davis, Pauline Watts, Joseph Forte, David Castriota, Ann and Joe Lauinger, and Paula Loscocco. Peter Whiteley, formerly at Sarah Lawrence and now at the Museum of Natural History in New York, suggested some crucial anthropological texts that allowed me to frame and develop my argument in this book.

The Bogliasco Foundation for the Arts and Letters provided a stunning paradisal retreat overlooking the "Golfo Paradiso" in the Bay of Liguria, where much of this book had its inception. Sarah Lawrence College provided timely sabbaticals and release time, and its librarians were extraordinarily helpful in tracking down texts that I needed and sending them to me wherever in the world I found myself. Funds from the Dean's office and from the Joseph Campbell Chair in the Humanities helped to defray some of the publication costs of this book; I am most grateful to the donors who established the Campbell Chair. The Diocese of Western Newfoundland invited my wife Bonnie to serve as priest in the parish of Flowers Cove on the northern peninsula, and the English Church in Europe invited her to serve as visiting chaplain to the English congregation of the Erlöserkirche in Heidelberg, Germany. I came along as her parish secretary and general factotum, and crucial parts of this book had their gestation in these strange and wonderful places.

Bonnie, of course, is my soul mate and my spiritual director, and the primary reason I can write anything at all about the nature of love and of chastity, or anything else. We have gone to the ends of the world together, and they always feel like home. Our son Geoff, the combined Elder and Younger Brother of our own family romance, whom we have long called "the true intellectual of the family," has grown up with this project, bemused, curious, and critical. As Geoff and his wife Charlotte have been called to their own promising vocations and adventures in scholarship and teaching, I have tested every sentence in this book with the hope that they might learn from it and find it pleasing. But most of all, this book is for our daughter Shannon. I think the subjects of our writing choose us as much as we choose them, and so I think it is no coincidence that I started wondering about Milton's *Maske* as a rite of passage at just the time when Shannon was hitting adolescence, or adolescence was hitting her. Since then, she has survived many temptations, shocks, and hardships, and rejoiced in many blessings, especially her children and her work, with great integrity, intelligence, resilience, and capacity to love—with what the *Maske* thematizes as chastity. I remark of Milton's Lady in the introduction to this book, "we can find ourselves saying of her, with admiration, that this is, God willing (and Milton's God is always willing), what a human being is capable of being." That is how I feel about Shannon. This book is dedicated to her, and to our grandaughters, Lily, Isabel, and Morgan.

❧

Sections of chapter 3 appeared previously in "Into the Woods: The Lady's Soliloquy in *Comus*," *Milton Quarterly* 35, no. 1 (2001): 33–43; and in "Tragedy in Translation: The Lady's Echo Song," *English Literary Renaissance* 33, no. 3 (Autumn 2003): 403–23.

Sections of chapter 4 appeared previously in "Nietzsche for Girls," in *Milton's Legacy*, edited by Charles H. Durham and Kristin A. Pruitt (Selinsgrove, PA: Susquehanna University Press, 2005), 116–35; and in "Circe's Best Boy," in *Uncircumscribed Mind: Reading Milton Deeply*, edited by Charles H. Durham and Kristin A. Pruitt (Selinsgrove, PA: Susquehanna University Press, 2008).

An earlier version of chapter 5 appeared previously in "The Profession of Virginity in Milton's Ludlow *Maske*," in *Milton and Gender*, edited by Catherine Gimelli Martin (Cambridge: Cambridge University Press, 2004), 77–94.

Sections of chapter 6 appeared previously in "Milton's Lady and Lady Milton: Chastity, Prophecy, and Gender in *A Maske Presented at Ludlow Castle*," in *Faultlines and Controversies in the Study of Seventeenth-Century English Literature*, edited by Claude J. Summers and Ted-Larry Pebworth (Columbia: University of Missouri Press, 2002), 204–26.

Sections of chapter 7 appeared previously in "Girl, Interrupted: Spenserian Bondage and Release in Milton's Ludlow *Mask*," *Milton Quarterly* 37, no. 4 (2003): 184–204.

A section of chapter 8 appeared previously in "Milton's *Primavera*," in *Renaissance Ecology: Imagining Eden in Milton's England*, edited by Ken Hiltner (Pittsburgh: Duquesne University Press, 2008).

Lady in the Labyrinth

Introduction: Milton's Portrait of a Lady

1

A REMARKABLE THING HAPPENS IN MILTON'S LUDLOW *MASKE*, QUITE unlike anything I can think of in English theater. The *Maske,* which I will follow custom in sometimes referring to as *Comus,* initiates a real person into a new stage of her life. It is not only representational, but performative. It is not only *about* a young woman's passage from girlhood into womanhood; it ritually *accomplishes* that passage for a specific young woman. The Lady who performs the *Maske,* Alice Egerton, was the fifteen-year-old daughter of John Egerton, Earl of Bridgewater, and Egerton's installation and establishment of residence in Ludlow as Lord President of the Council of Wales and the West Marches was the institutional occasion for the *Maske*'s performance on September 29, 1634. Conventional masques in the Stuart period ceremonially marked, but did not make, the occasions for which they were commissioned. When either of James I's sons, Prince Henry or Prince Charles, commissioned or performed in a masque celebrating his virtue, the masque served the ideological purposes of dynastic monarchy, but it did not affect his status and duties as prince.[1] When Charles came into his own as king, the masques he commissioned and performed did not make him king, but celebrated and mythologized his already established social authority. Milton's *Maske* performs a double duty. It celebrates the Earl of Bridgewater's ceremonial accession to the seat of a political and judicial authority already invested in him, but it also makes of his daughter something she wasn't before the *Maske*'s performance: an articulate, temperate, sexually mature and responsible, socially conscientious and engaged, freedom-loving Christian woman. The imaginative attention of the *Maske* quite remarkably minimizes the importance of the earl's investiture as it stresses the Lady's ordeal and transformation. So the Lady in the *Maske* is a unique figure in Milton's writing, and indeed, if I am right, in the writing of English literature, and Alice Egerton is a unique performer. What happens to the character in the text happens to the performer of that character. As Alice performs the role inscribed for her in the *Maske,* it transforms her as a person. A woman emerges from the performance which she began as a girl. The kind of woman she becomes is, in turn, meant to be doctrinal and exemplary to a nation (*RCG* 2.669).[2]

We are all, in various ways, transformed by the roles we play. Pirandello made riddling existential drama of the impossibility of splitting the "real person" from the social or dramatic roles he or she plays out, and great movies have been made of the psychological traumas and transformations of actors by the roles they perform. But the change of the Lady in *Comus* is not a private personal event of this sort, a fatal shift in feeling and character that makes for great melodrama. Her transformation is staged as a publicly witnessed and publicly authorized event. The audience's participatory recognition and acknowledgment of her change is essential to the accomplishment of the change. So it is not just a matter of Alice's difference in feelings and attitudes toward herself, but the difference made in her position in the world, and the difference made in the world by this new positioning, that matters in the *Maske.*

This is not so much a matter for biographical assessment. One cannot say whether Alice Egerton literally became the kind of woman which the *Maske* prepared her to be. Even if the biographical materials were thick enough, it would take a reading of the heart that goes deeper than biography to estimate this. Alice had performed in previous masques, most recently Thomas Carew and Inigo Jones's spectacular *Coelum Britannicum,* the same year as *Comus.* One of Alice's sisters was enough of a Puritan rigorist to refuse a role in masques, and "several of the first Earl's daughters . . . ended up as Nonconformists," a social character we can assume that the Earl of Bridgewater would have supported and approved.[3] But to claim the *Maske* as a decisive element in Alice's personal development would be to read too much into its place in a more complex weave of social and family influences. Public records make possible an easier kind of assessment of whether Lord Brackley lived up to the image of progressive administrator whom the *Maske* appeals to and celebrates.[4] Although the boundaries between literary, historical, and political discourse become blurred over precisely such questions now, my interest in this book is not in the historical outcome of the *Maske*'s determination of Alice's character, for that would entail reading both the *Maske* and Alice's history and psychology too literally. My interest is in how, in initiating Alice, it reconfigures the cultural image and idea of womanhood that she incarnates and reconfigures mythical and psychological templates for this vital cultural formation. Although the *Maske* celebrated John Egerton's installation as Lord President, it did not in itself make him Lord President in the way that it made a woman, and a new kind of woman, of his daughter. The *Maske* observes the aristocratic and patriarchal protocols of its genre by framing itself to the occasion of his investiture, and it ends with a ritual gesture typical of the masque by restoring his children and redirecting its audience's attention to his protection and authority.[5] But by the time this has happened, Milton has managed to center our moral and political attention elsewhere, on the transformation, or, we might say, the "reformation" of his daughter.[6] We shall see that the privileged term that the *Maske* itself suggests for such momentous change is "translation" (242).

Although this reformation of character implies, as Angus Fletcher suggestively remarks, that "for the first time she has experienced her own presence," this is not primarily a private episode of self-recognition.[7] The Lady's representational position as a heroic exemplar of chastity makes her a kind of Everyman. She is representative of English Protestant aspiration in the way that Spenser's Redcrosse Knight and Britomart had been representative and in the way that Bunyan's Christian and Christiana would also be representative. How she manages to fend for herself in the wanton night world of Comus is not just a unique personal achievement, but a cultural achievement that stakes out moral ground for others. The *Maske* necessarily dramatizes the personal achievement in class-specific terms, but the cultural achievement approximates universality. There is just a slight element of snobbery about the Lady at some moments of her ordeal. She conducts herself with something of the defensive propriety and poise of England's titled classes, and she undergoes a ritual ordeal that is stylized according to the education, habits, assumptions, indulgences, prerogatives, and entertainments of those classes.[8] But the implication and opportunity of the virtue that she exercises presses toward universality, in the way that Christian and Christiana's will or Milton's Adam and Eve's will.[9] Unique among the ritually determined characters of Stuart masques, the Lady proves to be an initiate into a moral agency and political identity that do not owe their formation, legitimacy, or efficacy to the king and to the social hierarchy in which he is implicated and over which he is sovereign. As will be the case with Milton's other heroes, those who do not fall as well as those who do, the Lady has a specific integrity and consistency that marks her as a person, one of a kind. Yet we can find ourselves saying of her, with admiration, that this is, God willing (and Milton's God is always willing), what a human being is capable of being. This is what I mean by the approximate universality of her moral achievement. It is astonishing that Milton imagines the first of his fully developed ethical and poetic heroes as a Lady, and a very young one at that. It is equally astonishing that Milton identifies his own poetic, moral, and political intentions with her.

Because *Comus* is a masque, its ritual features have hardly been ignored, as its parallels, contrasts, and possible influences from other masques have been exhaustively traced and studied. I cannot claim to be the first to have noticed its initiatory structures either. Several of Milton's critics nod to the initiatory aspects of *Comus*. But because they read it as a literary text and wish to recoup it as a literary genre, they read it *as if* it were a rite of passage, that is, a literary imitation of one. This kind of poetry is the sort which, if I may borrow (respectfully) from Auden, "makes nothing happen."[10] The conventional court masque, at least in Ben Jonson's scripting, intends to be performative and transformative, choreographing its aristocratic performers in a dance of virtue that instructs them in the justice and honor that their privileges and training purportedly oblige them to exercise "in real life." Milton's *Maske* is a more ethically ambitious and explicit artifice, and it is doubly performative as a ritual. As a court masque, its general cultural task involves the reformation of the noble class that constitutes both its performers and its audience. As a rite of initiation, it is specifically committed to the formation of a child into an adult character. But the initiatory activity of the *Maske* radically reconfigures its traditional institutional bases and purposes: the chaste, morally intelligent and socially committed individual, rather than the king or his representative, emerges as the power source and exemplar of ethical authority, social health, and poetic creativity. Alice Egerton's initiation relocates the magic incanted by the masque, from the king as source and epicenter of power and virtue, to the chaste conscience of the emerging and autonomous Puritan self. By staging the emergence of a new kind of political and religious subject in the character of Alice as the Lady, Milton implies a reordering of both psychology and social relations, and he projects a dynamically innovative mythocosmic structure, designed to support the newly emergent self and answer to her will and desire.

Although several cogent recent critics have argued for the implicit radicalism of a masque released from royalist presumptions, they have not explicitly linked this recognition to the *Maske*'s unique fashioning of an ethically secure, articulate, sexually aware, and dynamic young woman as a model for the early modern subject. The central character of the initiation, and the incarnate human form that its virtue takes, is female, a surprise that seriously challenges the gender bias built into the masque form as well as other modes of seventeenth-century discourse. Milton's exemplary moral agent, who can speak for herself, envision and embody her own ethical ideals, hold out for a community that will recognize and honor them, and articulate and defend a just and charitable reprise to the world's offers of greediness, narcissism, and power, is a young woman: "Contrary to all expectation, in consequence of the moral and political imperatives of the text, the eloquence of a woman fuses word and Word, politics and religion, in a programme for personal virtue and the social organization of a Christian commonwealth."[11] As we will see in reviewing feminist and new historicist criticism relevant to the *Maske,* it is not difficult to contextualize this development in such a way as to minimize its social impact and consequences. But it seems to me that the social importance of the Lady as leading character and a morally free agent makes the *Maske* a founding and still challenging gesture of early modern liberal feminism. A claim like this may unsettle some of my Miltonist colleagues, for whom it will seem to be patently ahistorical and ideologically incoherent with contemporary critical conventions that assume and reconstruct variations on the image of Milton as "English literature's paradigmatic patriarch."[12] The ferocity of critiques and parodies of Milton, which frequently work their way into ongoing politicized and historicized criticism as controlling assumptions, probably issues in part from a need to defend against the unsettling radical possibilities in Milton's texts themselves.[13]

Let me preview here the features of this remarkable text as I propose to read it in the pages following. Milton makes the central character of his *Maske* a fifteen-year-old-girl. He does not defer to the king as the ultimate source of authority and ethical integrity in his text, but instead positions the Lady at the center of the text's reconfigured ethical and aesthetic force field. The Lady's rite of passage into maturity is staged as a rite of passage into the engaged social practice of prophetic poetry and political argument. The Lady thus represents Milton's own aspirations to be exemplary poet for a nation, and her passage represents his own self-conscious enactment of his passage into that role and responsibility. The Lady deflects aggressive male attention in the person of Comus and deflates his self-estimation, on the ground of her own integrity. She holds her ground against Comus, for all his rhetorical virtuosity and erotic charisma, and indeed rhetorically defeats and unmans him, until she can be physically released from her bondage to him. In doing so, she publicly demonstrates the capabilities and prospects of women as speakers and actors in the public sphere; and at the same time establishes room for the female voice in a literary tradition generated, in part, from the long-standing repression and silencing of such a voice. Her release comes not from the touch or kiss of intervening male heroes typical of fairy stories analogous to the *Maske,* but from a goddess whose own story prefigures hers and whose regenerative power is transmitted to her. When she returns to her parents and to her social world in the *Maske*'s final movements, the Lady is no longer a dependent child but a woman. At the conclusion of the performance, she carries with her into the revels that join together the players and the witnesses of the *Maske* the blessing power of a goddess, who reconstitutes in charity, health, justice, and energy the entire gathered community. In the 1634 performance of the *Maske,* the celebratory revels revolve around the Lady and depend upon her for completion. The visionary Epilogue that closes the *Maske* in its 1637 and 1645 published versions (976–1011) extends and explicates the symbolism of the revels, intimating that the initiation of the Lady into womanhood reforms not only the order of society, but the very conception of the Beyond upon which it is founded. Thus the Lady's triumphant return to her father's household, itself a social type of the celestial order, entails the radical transformation of both spheres.

Entertain, for a moment, a kind of thought experiment. If a manuscript called *A Maske Presented at Ludlow Castle,* identical to the dramatic poem in question in every respect except that it was written by a woman, were to surface in a British archive, would we give it a different reception and reading from that of the text written by John Milton?[14] My guess is that we would delight in recognizing in the plot and imagery of this hypothetical text a formidable parable about the cultivation, liberation, and sanctification of female energy, voice, identity, and initiative, and the social good that would issue therefrom. This imaginary text might seem startlingly sui generis and ahistorical, but we would try to account for that seeming ahistoricity not by qualifying or explaining away its achievement, but by revising both our understanding of its history and our understanding of imagination's power to expose, test, and reconceive the ideological premises of the very culture that generated it. Part of my project in this book is to read the text we do have, scripted by the poet whose college nickname was "the Lady," in a spirit of comparable openness to the discovery of emancipatory possibilities that might otherwise be neglected because of our contemporary presumptions about John Milton, and about what could be thought and projected about gender, virtue, and selfhood, in his historical period.

2

This book has been informed by and hopes to contribute to the ongoing academic project of describing what has been frequently called "the construction of the early modern subject," but my approach is less a politically driven and historicist one than an anthropological and psychological one. I hope thereby to avoid some of the rhetorical habits and conceptually restrictive conventions that seem to me to arise sometimes from the dogmatics of the new historicism and cognate critical practices. "Subject" itself is a doubly defining term, antithetical to itself, as it describes a kind of autonomous agency at the same time that it marks dependency and determining constraints: the early modern "subject" is understood to be capable of self-reflectively initiating significant actions on behalf of herself or himself and others, yet also is understood as "subject to" powers and discourses about which she or he is less likely to be conscious and over which she or he is unable to establish mastery.[15] Milton uniquely resolves this seeming paradox by dramatizing how self-conscious recognition of one's own contingency is the beginning of one's knowledge and exercise of power. Stanley Fish nicely defines this resolution in the Lady's discovery of the external source of a virtue that is nevertheless fully hers: "The mind finds, that is, the sustaining Other that founds it and authorizes a self-sufficiency that is blameless because it is a sufficiency of perfect dependence."[16]

A number of scholars have shown us how Jacobean tragedy—as well as the crisis poems of Donne, Herbert, and others—opens and ramifies the subject of "the subject" by experimenting with the full range of anguished contradictions realized by self-aware characters who come to know the extent of their own subjection.[17] John Rumrich argues that Milton distinguishes himself from this trend: "At certain moments, especially in his two final poems, Milton may reflect the increasing tendency toward modern contraction, opacity, and internalization of psychic life. But overall, this trend in early modern intellectual history, unlike so many others, he did not notably advance or anticipate. Although he figures as perhaps the greatest English poet of *individuality,* he did not have much to say about *interiority,* though these distinct notions are often confused."[18] One senses the distinction that Rumrich is proposing when one tries to compare how Milton's characters talk to themselves in soliloquy as compared to how Shakespeare's characters talk to themselves. But it is a problematic generalization to sustain. In light of the range of self-disclosing strategies afforded by the seventeenth-century dramatic soliloquy as an emerging type of poetic speech, do Milton's characters index interiority less vividly than Shakespeare's because they seem directed by more strenuous ethical self-reflection and self-determination? If dramatic silence is an index of inaccessible interiority, is the Lady's silence at the end of her ordeal any less mysteriously evocative of a soul's privacy than the more menacing silence of Iago at the end of *Othello?*

Milton as a Christian poet is disposed to resist the conclusions of tragedy—"After the final no there comes a yes, / and on that yes the future world depends"[19]—even as he stages tragedy as a wisdom-giving ordeal with which his subjects must engage. This is as true for the Lady, the first fully dramatized hero of faith in his poetry, as it will be for Adam and Eve, for the Jesus of *Paradise Regained,* for Samson, and for the poet himself outliving the descent of his blindness, the loss of his wives, the blighting of his political hopes. We better understand the depth and complexity of the Lady as subject if we consider her in relation to these other Miltonic characters, as well as in relation to her tragic prototypes on the Jacobean stage. She enters the space that previous dramatizations of character have created and transforms its possibilities. She shows how the subject can be opened, deepened, broadened, strengthened, and transformed by the experience of tragedy without being destroyed by it, and she thereby makes of tragic experience something else, which we might describe as the character-structure of the Miltonic sublime.

The subject and subjectivity have been variously and profitably mapped and interpreted, and they can be correlated with different historical and political developments, many of which have proven relevant to the study of Milton's *Maske:* radical populism or aristocratic republicanism, acquisitive bourgeois individualism, the rigorous self-monitoring of Puritan ethics, the Reformation's sanctification of chaste companionate marriage and its consequent restructuring of family life, the private domain circumscribed by the contractually organized modern state. These socially driven transformations coordinate with religious and philosophical discourses participating in the formation of the early modern subject. Interiority and self-consciousness coincide with the emerging psychodynamics of Protestant cultivation of individual conscience. Liberation of the individual from the mediating custody of medieval Roman Catholicism produced anxiety, what Kierkegaard would call religious dread: released from the labyrinth of externally administered and cyclically repetitive institutional sanctions, prohibitions, and penances, the self faced the abyss of its own self-aware and insecure loneliness before God.[20] Philosophy, in turn, secularized and psychologized this isolated interiority by analyzing thought's presence to itself as the foundation of modern self-conscious subjectivity. Although Descartes' cogito discovers itself in relation to a divine awareness that authorizes and constitutes it,[21] Descartes provides the basis for subsequent models of mental processing whose source is life experience rather than divine initiation and intercession and authorization.

However contextualized and defined, and however flexibly interpreted, different accounts seem to agree that something new and consequential develops in the definition of the "human" in the early modern period. The subject as we have come to think of it has an indeterminate and improvisatory nature, self-generative and self-divided, in comparison to the self-consistent collocation of attributes marking traditional ideas of human character. Certain features cluster about the idea of the emerging subject, to which Milton's writing contributes: interiority, self-consciousness, autonomy, dynamism, instability, crisis formation. The modern self becomes aware of itself as an independent private moral and political agency with a degree of determination of its own shape and nature. But the modern self typically has trouble understanding itself, as Hamlet most famously instantiates, and Freud most powerfully accounts for. The *theomachia* of the late medieval morality play, with the wayward but self-consistent character compelled and confused by forces external to itself, yields to the drama of the early modern self bewildered by eruptions of thought and feeling whose sources seem within, yet remain inaccessible to rational or theological explanation.

The type of the early modern subject is thus simultaneously a concentrated singularity—as the centroversion of Descartes' model of thinking would imply, and the powerfully individuated characters of Elizabethan and Jacobean theater and poetry vividly exemplify—and a bewildering multiplicity, because of its permeability to multiple influences and discourses, its distancing of itself from the constraints and supporting definitions of external authority, and its consequent multivocality. Conscience, conscientiousness, and integrity are qualities typifying the early modern subject, but they are twinned with self-doubt, ambivalence, and resistance. We notice the comparative differences between Shakespeare and Milton in their management of this duality. Shakespeare elaborates subjectivity on the basis of what we might call a literary version of the uncertainty principle, whereas Milton articulates subjectivity in commitment to what we might call a literary certainty principle. Shakespeare in his tragic soliloquies subjects his great tragic characters to the almost irresistible undertow and disintegrating pressure of intuitions, fantasies, wishes, anxieties, and compulsions over which they cede conscious, directive control. Thereby Shakespeare opens wide the prospect of the abyss of self-consciousness and creates a literary grounding effect for Freud's theorization of the unconscious. Milton acknowledges the potential for such a psychology, but his valorization of the heroic rationally directed conscience leads him to resist its development, except of course in the monumental Shakespearean anguish of Satan, and, movingly, in Samson's self-reckoning with betrayal and guilt. In the case of the Lady, we will study how her introductory soliloquy (170–229) and subsequent Echo Song (230–43) subject the momentum of the stricken self-conscious Shakespearean subject to the deliberative poise of rational conscience and the imaginative resources which form it and upon which it depends. The strength of the Lady's resolve, which will fortify her and defend her in the encounter with Comus, gathers itself out of the recognition of and resistance to her own potentially tragic ambivalences and insecurities. Her strength sublimates itself out of its own potential vulnerability. The energies that ultimately subvert and shatter the coherence of the Shakespearean tragic subject become the constructive source of Miltonic self-fashioning.

The early modern subject is a written subject, and its self-consciousness consequently a writerly one, coincident with the dissemination of printed texts and the expansion of literacy in the period, with the consequent emergence of new literary forms and types, and the increasingly complex self-awareness that the textual revolution both represented and fostered: "Constituted in *writing,* the discursive medium which governs the epoch and separates itself silently but efficiently from the spectacle, covering its own traces, the bourgeois subject substitutes for its corporeal body the rarefied body of the text."[22] Harold Bloom's declaration of Shakespeare's "invention of the human" perhaps shares more conceptually with critical modes that he claims to despise than he is willing to admit, for the models of the "human" that he claims Shakespeare most eminently scripts for us and bequeathes to us are of course the great modern "subject" types, both seemingly inexhaustible when fully themselves: the baffled, internally riven Hamlet and the ironic vitalist Falstaff.[23] The newly textualized self "reads" itself, and "reads" itself in relation to texts that have formed it and provide it interpretive models and narrative patterns for processing of personal experience and self-recognition—eminently the Bible as a totalizing typology in relation to which all lives are ambiguous shadows, but also classical literature, and, increasingly, history itself. We will see the degree to which the Lady reflects upon herself and the circumstances in which she finds herself by resort to such texts. What may have been schoolbook training for her in her girlhood takes on new meaning as she accesses, activates, and reinterprets it as imaginative and ethical resources for creative self-protection, self-fashioning, and self-transcendence.

Because the modern subject emerges from texts, reads itself and permits itself to be read, the self-consciousness of the written subject implicates the author in the project or projection of the text: in inevitable but obscured ways, the author stages the emergence of his or her own subjectivity. Leah Marcus remarks, "[Milton], as much as any other single historical figure of the English Renaissance, may be credited with having inaugurated a new way of situating the author within literary history, or rather, of asserting the author's resistance to or transcendence of historical contingency by incorporating history within his conception of individual authorship."[24] Milton signals his personal intervention and presence in the texts he creates more insistently and aggressively than Shakespeare, and he makes the textualization of the author's selfhood an explicit theme upon which he reflects with consistent urgency, not only in the great invocations of *Paradise Lost* but also in his prose:

> And long it was not after, when I was confirmed in this opinion that he who would not be frustrate of his hope to write well hereafter in laudable things, ought himself to be a true poem, that is, a composition and pattern of the best and honorablest things—not presuming to sing high praises of heroic men or famous cities, unless he have in himself the experience and the practice of all that which is praiseworthy. (*Apology for Smectymnuus*, 694)

> For books are not absolutely dead things, but do contain a potency of life in them to be as active as that soul was whose progeny they are;

nay, they do preserve as in a vial the purest efficacy and extraction of that living intellect that bred them. I know they are as lively and as vigorously productive as those fabulous dragon's teeth; and being sown up and down, may chance to spring up armed men. And yet, on the other hand, unless wariness be used, as good almost kill a man as kill a good book: who kills a man kills a reasonable creature, God's image; but he who destroys a good book, kills reason itself, kills the image of God, as it were, in the eye. Many a man lives a burden to the earth; but a good book is the precious lifeblood of a master spirit, embalmed and treasured up on purpose to a life beyond life. (*Areopagitica,* 720)

The poet's own projection into and participation in the text he invents is a consistent feature of Milton's poetry from the birth announcement of the Nativity Ode's Proem to the subliminal identification with Samson in his blindness and experience of defeat, providing a founding version and prototype for what Keats would diagnose as Wordsworth's greatness, the "egotistical sublime."[25]

But in the case of the *Maske,* critics have tended to tiptoe around the nature of Milton's authorial projections.[26] This is perhaps in part because the depersonalization of dramatic form excludes the possibility of a narrative "I" to represent the author. In resistance to character limitations built into its representational schema by generic convention, the *Maske* is surprising in respect to Milton's nearly Shakespearean dispersed identification with each of its characters and his endowment of each with the implied complexity and coherence of an autonomous ego or ego-in-formation. Each represents a certain imaginative and ethical position or stage, but the limitations upon them are primarily of the conceptual sort that requires a clear outline. This outline is partially bequeathed by masque convention, yet it anticipates and prepares for the fierce engagements of characters in Blake's visionary schematism. In Milton's case, the "schematic" nature of his character distribution is a characteristic mark of his analytic discipline and intellectual rigor. These qualities are themselves not unique writerly qualities so much as powerful personal inflections of cultural norms encoded in pedagogy and genre: the powerful and repetitive rhetorical training in analysis and invention of argument on behalf of competing values and positions, in which schoolboys and university students were thoroughly versed; and the generic practices of allegorical categorization and abstraction built into the masque as performance art. Given the standardizations and abstractions inevitable to masque invention, the degree to which Milton presses masque toward drama through detailed particularization of various arguments, with each argument implying a character arguing, is astonishing.[27]

Milton's positioning of the revised text of the *Maske* in his early collection of English and Latin poems, the 1645 *Poems of Mr. John Milton,* signals this awareness of the *Maske*'s dramatic uniqueness. Its final position in the English sequence seems to set it apart from both the shorter English and the Latin lyrics, by reason of its length and by contrast of its dramatic objectivity to their predominance of first-person lyric speakers. But it can also be read as a completion and fulfillment of the trajectory of the English lyrics, a personal bookend matching the bookend of the inaugural Nativity Ode. If the Proem of the Nativity Ode is a birth announcement not only for the newborn Christ but for the newly inspired prophetic poet, whose voice, like Isaiah's, has been "toucht with hallow'd fire" (28), the *Maske* stages publicly not only the Lady's but her author's initiation into imaginative and political maturity. The *Maske*'s positioning after "Lycidas" in the 1645 *Poems* perhaps sets it up as the fresh version of pastoral—"fresh Woods, and pastures new" (193)— toward which the swain of "Lycidas" looks in the conclusion of the great elegy. Having distanced himself from his own projected anguish in "Lycidas" with the narrative step back from immediate, present-tense first person (1–185) to the third-person past perfect tense of the elegy's conclusion (186–93), Milton prepares for the objectified, depersonalized, immediate dramatic action of the *Maske.* The poised objective voice and wide perspective that closes "Lycidas" finds its dramatic complement in the omniscient establishing shot provided by the Attendant Spirit in the *Maske*'s Prologue (1–92). In effect Milton disappears into the dramatis personae of his *Maske,* both everywhere at once and nowhere to be found in the poem.[28]

The lack of sustained attention to Milton's authorial self-representation in the *Maske* is also, I think, because of the embarrassment of trying to fathom Milton's enactment of his own initiation into poetic and political maturity through the vehicle of a female protagonist. Another feature of the early modern subject, typified by the Lady, is its gendered specificity and self-consciousness. So what are we to make of Milton's move to represent his first fully realized Christian hero as a young woman, in light of the masculinist biases of his culture and, as some have presumed and argued, of his own character? Milton's identification with his Lady is a critical commonplace, but it has tended to lead to a dead end. Those who go beyond the obligatory notice of the "Lady" of Christ College's identification with his leading character in the *Maske* tend either to read it as a sign of imaginative limit or disability, or as a sign of Milton's patriarchal presumption to speak for and through women.[29] These critical positions seem to me inadequate accounts of the startling instance of gender crossing in this moment of identification and the equally startling implication of a kind of mutual empowerment by the mirrored fictional subjects: the empowerment of the poet, as he is doubly represented by the Attendant Spirit and the Lady, the true poets of the entertainment; and the cultural and political empowerment of women as public speakers and moral agents, figured forth in the exemplary Lady. The Lady, as I argue more substantively elsewhere in this book, stands in for Milton as the emerging self-in-progress, which is also to say, the poet undergoing initiation into maturity, and enacting a conception of the subject that is continually open to innovation and self-transcendence, including the transcendence of fixed binary gender positions. She represents Milton's deepest commitments to the inviolable integrity of the ethical life as the source of poetic, prophetic vision. The Attendant Spirit, in turn, is the destination of the Lady's—and Milton's—imaginative aspirations. If the Lady represents Milton as he initiates himself into his maturing vocation as prophetic poet, the Attendant Spirit represents Milton's ego ideal, the commanding poet he would be when he achieves full attainment and integration of imaginative and moral power.

This way of sizing up Milton's authorial self-representation in the *Maske* contends with another critical commonplace, one that presumes that Milton's deepest imaginative and emotional affiliation is with the compelling antagonist of his *Maske,* Comus. The biographical speculation that Milton played Comus in the Ludlow production is tantalizing if unfounded,[30] but it underscores the imaginative vigor with which he both writes and subverts the sensuous brilliance and teeming erotic abundance and energy of his villain's script. Critics continue to argue that the *Maske* enacts a split in Milton's poetic character like that between the rigorous but imaginatively impoverished moralist and the antinomian, romantically inspired vitalist that Blake suggested, in *The Marriage of Heaven and Hell,* was both the fault and the saving strength of *Paradise Lost.* According to this argument, the seductive force of Comus's rhetoric of sensuality demonstrates that Milton was a true poet and of Comus's party without knowing it.[31] I think that the attractive power of Comus represents not a split in Milton's own subjectivity, but a Shakespearean capacity for identification, strengthened by rhetorical training, which we tend to misread in Milton because of his consistent interest in the moralization of character. Comus is no less cogent, no less particularized, because Milton intends a severe judgment against his moral and imaginative limitations. Paradoxically, Comus serves as the Lady's forceful and persistent tutor, albeit in adversarial form. If the Lady is to emerge from her initiatory ordeal with a power of identity that is credible, Milton knows that he must endow her antagonist and initiator, as he will endow the Satans of *Paradise Lost* and *Paradise Regained,* with a perverse rhetorical cogency and charisma of his own.

As a subject himself, Comus is strikingly familiar and fascinating to us, perhaps more immediately accessible and comprehensible as a type of early modern subject than the more disciplined and seemingly distant Lady appears to be. It is not surprising, but discouraging, to find one of the most learned and cogent readers of English Renaissance literature, Stephen Orgel, going to bat for Comus in a recent essay on the *Maske*.[32] In this essay, which argues the Lady's inevitable subjection to patriarchy and appreciates Comus's rhetorical brilliance, antinomian skepticism, and rejection of such oppressive constraints, Orgel concedes too much to Comus, which means conceding too much to the power of historical and economic imperatives that determine subjects and texts, and not enough to the prophetic power of poetry, which in the case of the *Maske* entertains a prospect of real, not imaginary, freedom for women in speech and in action. Readers familiar with recent scholarly accounts of the early modern formation of subjects may find the argument and the diction of my book somewhat "old-fashioned," different in diction and interpretative framing from accounts like that of Orgel. This is in part a consequence of the kinds of resources I have chosen to draw from, including the intrinsic resources of the *Maske,* an inexhaustible and formative meditation on poetic tradition, and in part a consequence of the kinds of claims that I think emerge from the *Maske* to challenge its readership. To describe these claims, which are aesthetic, ethical, and existential, and to engage with them, entails perhaps a breach of scholarly protocol, for modern scholarly writing typically sets such claims aside, for the sake of what seeks to be historical precision, abundant archival research, and impersonal, analytic detachment. But in a period when eminent scholars engage the question of "Why Milton Matters," a period in which Milton matters perhaps more than ever, scholarly protocol needs to be flexible and open enough to acknowledge and address challenges made by Milton's texts that may not be altogether confineable to academic journals and college classrooms.[33]

Accounts of the early modern formation of the subject tend to be posthumanist in their ideology, claiming for themselves the ideological sophistication of a methodologically rigorous historicism. They describe the subject and the humanist culture that produces it as the outcome and inscription of contending ideological and cultural discourses that reify, reiterate, and mystify networks of social power: in Milton's case, networks of power that valorize and in turn depend on the privatized, autonomous individual and household of early modern Europe, the basic economic and social units of emerging competitive, patriarchal, bourgeois Protestant culture. No wonder that the search for evidences of such cultural formations in the *Maske* leave its Lady, and its author, little room to move and grow. But Milton remains more radical as a politically engaged artist and intellectual than we tend to give him credit for. His writing continues to challenge his critics to be self-reflective and self-critical, to acknowledge and examine the ideological criteria that direct our reading of it. Several generations ago, humanist scholarship could claim a comparatively unexamined place for itself outside of politics and beyond ideology, but that position has been (legitimately, I think) exposed as impossible to sustain. Humanism became allied with the forces of the status quo, which reiterated and mystified the institutional and ethnocentric hegemonies of colonialist power networks, including the academy. But a reconsideration of the institution-challenging impetus of Milton's writing, even in a work as seemingly early, yet as fully mature, as the *Maske,* provides the basis for a revival of a dynamic humanism that challenges not only the complacencies of the traditional academy but also the orthodoxies of contemporary politically driven criticism. Thus I discovered in the course of reading, and of being read by, the *Maske,* that my account of Milton's subject formation in the figure of his Lady is serviceable not in the critique but in the furthering of such a progressive humanism, of the possibilities of imaginative, ethical, and political freedom that it fosters, and of the kinds of cultures that might be formed from the exercise of such freedoms. Old-fashioned as this intention may seem, I find it more compelling than most critiques of such a position, sophisticated as they may be, and so I hope it will not prove to be naive or obsolete. There is a performative power to the poetic faith that motivates the *Maske* that we ought not willingly let die.

The young author of the *Maske* sustained and enlarged his literary culture's optative commitment to poetry's power to transform character and society, a faith that he developed out of many sources, classical, biblical, and contemporary, among them, more recently and locally, Sidney's inspired descriptions of imagination's power to regenerate and transcend the world, Spenser's allegorical projections and testings of ethical ideals in his wayfaring heroes for the sake of fashioning "a gentleman or noble person in vertuous and gentle discipline," and Jonson's defenses of the ethics of masquing itself as an exercise of performative moral philosophy whose Neoplatonic activity substantializes the court's ideals.[34] A generation before Milton, Sidney argued the superiority of poetry to philosophy and history by reminding his readers how poetry accesses the strengths while escaping the limitations of her rival discourses. In Sidney's account, poetry has the sensuous concreteness of life vividly lived, appealing to human curiosity and pleasure in the senses and organizing desire more passionately and effectively than the abstractions of philosophy. Yet poetry has the moral purposiveness of philosophy, and thus can construct plots of possibility that transcend the determinism of historical narrative, representing "what may be, and should be,"[35] rather than what has been. The mimetic nature of humanity, which expresses itself in poetry even as it delights in poetry, is in turn the reason for poetry's affective impact and renovative power. We are what we read: we are fired by what we read to imitate the good and to detest evil.

For Milton as for Sidney, if it is possible to overcome the ruin of our first parents (*Of Education,* 631), it will be through our erected wit,[36] and that wit will be erected through learning, which will liberate the human spirit to "rove about until the bounds of creation itself no longer limit the divine magnificence of its quest. Then most happenings and events about us will become obvious so quickly that almost nothing can happen without warning or by accident to a man who is in possession of the stronghold of wisdom. . . . This is the way to live in all the epochs of history, Gentlemen, and to be a contemporary of time itself" (Prolusion 6, 625). To become a "contemporary of time itself," as Milton becomes in his writing, is to engage the future with the same insistence as he engages the past and the present, to read and confront the future in his readership. The emancipatory learning that he defends will be most deeply and compellingly mediated by poetry, "a kind of moral and social mnemonics."[37] This humanist conviction is not quite dead, although certainly attenuated and under suspicion in the materialist cultures and postmodern skepticisms of the academies of Europe and the Americas, in which poetry dissolves into discourse, discourse encodes and reiterates ideology, and ideology determines subjects.

In the face of such determinism, I would like to enlist the marxist

Louis Althusser, paradoxically, in a defense of the idealist interests of Milton's iconoclastic humanism against the materialist and radically historicizing critical practices that Althusser himself developed and influenced.[38] Althusser proposes that literary art stakes out for itself a different kind of discursive space and a different kind of political self-reckoning from more functionally determined public discourses and that thereby it "presupposes a *retreat,* an *internal distantiation*" from the very ideology that generates it, repressing yet exposing the contradictions of that ideology.[39] Literary texts can stage the ideologies to which they are indebted, but the very imaginative staging allows for author and attentive audience a critical relation to them that resists determinism.[40] What if Milton's commitment to a poetic practice that exposes and analyzes vice and generates virtue, which is for him the very ground of political freedom, provides such a critical edge to his work in the *Maske* and thereby engenders historical possibilities that the modern apotheoses of the discipline of history, new historicism and other materialist critical practices, if left to themselves, cannot anticipate or account for?[41] I think that, for all of our claims to methodological rigor and ideological self-awareness, many of us who are in the paradoxical position of professing literature, pragmatically and politically marginalized although (some of us) institutionally entrenched, probably do so out of some vestigial inspiration by a humanist faith in or nostalgia for the poetic word to become flesh and transform the world. Otherwise, we are just strutting our stuff, marking our exams, writing our essays, going to our conferences, collecting our wages and benefits, serving our time until our pensions kick in. Taking Milton at his word can give us the heart to risk more than this and to carry the humanizing—and truly revolutionizing—work of literature forward in good conscience.

3

There are many things that fascinate me about Milton's *Maske,* more than I can claim to be able to make sense of, certainly more than I can write competently about. Comus himself can be taken as a textual figure for this profusion of elusive, entangling curiosities. Comus is both the keeper of the labyrinth of the *Maske* and the beast at its heart. What seems required to enter and reemerge from the maze is both a willingness to wander—to become lost enough to find oneself, as the Lady and her brothers do—and a grasp on a sturdy but flexible analytic thread or set of threads to provide security during uncertainty and to guide the way down and out.[42] This kind of investigatory criticism enters the text with more questions than conclusions and lets the drift of the question determine the movement of a claim. When we set out to write, critics typically have points to prove about a text. This shapes our critical approaches either as necessarily selective processes, which pursue a single kind of evidence to the neglect of all others, or as totalizing arguments, which subject all available evidence to a primary terminology and thus streamline complexity, variety, and contradiction. But exegetical schemata are always neater—and more impoverished—than aesthetic data, especially in an overdetermined text like *Comus,* where the whole imagined cosmos resonates in every detail. The fluidity and richness of Milton's *Maske* defeated my efforts at this sort of exegetical reduction, and thus the book entertains "multiple points of entry," as one reader described it, even as it pushes toward thematic coherence, toward what I hope will be experienced as something of strange constancy.

Although I have organized this account of the *Maske* in self-contained, forward-moving chapters, focusing sequentially on comprehensive analyses of character structures, key dramatic crises, and poetic passages, I think of each chapter as a provisional clustering of evidence and exegesis around a specific topic, character, passage, or setting. The heading of each chapter serves as a kind of provisional signpost along the way, but it points in more directions than serially forward. When in the early 1990s my son Geoff and I used to run for pleasure (more than fitness) in Kampala, Uganda, with a whole crowd of crazy expatriates and Ugandans called the Hash House Harriers, the planners of each weekly run through the red clay alleyways, the potholed benzine-acrid boulevards, the soft dusty hills and glittering banana groves would provide a checkpoint, ephemerally marked by circles and crosses of maize meal, every kilometer or so in our mazy progress. The checkpoints were resting places for runners, joggers, and walkers to gather, catch their breath, and make sure that no one had got lost along the way. This fragile signifying system carried forward into our fortunate time in a reviving Uganda a still vivid remembrance of terror. When the Harriers had continued to run through Kampala in the 1970s and 1980s, to keep asserting the possibility of normalcy and continuity and solidarity and eccentricity through the periods of state terrorism and civil war, the checkpoints marked by maize meal were crucial temporary sanctuaries from the specter of violence, where runners would reconnoiter to ensure that none of their brave and crazy company had disappeared in the labyrinthine darkness, captured and carried off by agents of the brutal powers that dwelt there. Although this book claims nothing of the risk and the daring of such adventures, the provisional closure of each section of this book is intended to create a checkpoint in the reading progress. The opening of each succeeding section initiates a new direction of argument as it also picks up where previous sections may have left off. Within each section I try to pick up on new aesthetic cues within the text, link them to previously developed clusters of significance, and shift from one level of attention to another. Since this schema is as artificial as any other argumentative structure, I will not claim it is "organic" in its unity. Perhaps a more adequate contemporary analogy is provided by the availability of multiple files on the desktop of a computer, on which, with a mouse click, you can shift your attention from one window to another: a process of redirecting and rearranging levels of attention.

Insofar as medieval discoveries of the "four levels" of allegory nested within a text observe something of this kind of interpretive movement between zones of attention, I want to invoke a degree of traditional precedent and authorization for this process. The "four levels" whose windows I will be variously opening and minimizing can be construed as the cultural, the psychological, the aesthetic or textual, and the ethical, with the seemingly endless mythological resources invoked and reworked by Milton underwriting them all. I resist, although not entirely successfully, the kind of theologically structured hierarchy established by medieval hermeneutics: my very ordering of the sequence implies priorities. The various levels of this emerging allegoresis are mutually implicated in one another. When Milton constructs his fictive world, his *Maske* becomes the site of a ritual intersection between society, self, poetic artifice, and cosmos. Cultural protocols and rituals as well as political contexts order and inform the *Maske*'s drama. Mythic characters give form and outline to the psychic pressures upon and resources available to an emerging paradigm of virtuous identity. Poetic symbolization articulates a cosmic order and inserts both the culture and character in it. Cultural and generic protocols, mythic characters, and poetic symbols are themselves the stuff of Milton's intellectual and poetic inheritance. This makes his work an intentional project of literary reformation as much as it is one of social, psychological, and moral reformation: in order to "read" the emerging modern subject of his Lady and her subversive counterpartner Comus, Milton subjects the culturally formative mythological resources of European literary tradition to a powerful revisionary reading.

Each descriptive and exegetical mode intersects with and yields to another when it approaches a certain kind of interpretive limit. Anthropology can instruct us productively when we raise questions about the cultural structures and social implications of the *Maske* but must disqualify itself as a tutor when we want to think more about the psychology of the Lady as an emerging modern subject. Psychological formations, in turn, are based on aesthetic foundations in the *Maske*. The psychology of the *Maske* is less ideologically constructed than intertextually constructed, which requires that we study Milton's imaginative engagement with and deployment of previous texts—the Greek poets, Ovid, Spenser, Shakespeare, biblical narratives and prophecies—and anticipation of texts yet to be written-Blake, Keats, Nietzsche, Yeats, Stevens—in his representation of the emerging subject. But there is no art for art's sake in Milton, and nothing of the courtly dilettantism of his contemporaries, the libertine and cavalier poets. Strong poems are the offspring and embodiment of a strong conscience, and conscience gains its strength, in Milton's accounts of it, through worldly wayfaring and spiritual warfaring, which includes fierce and honest engagement with texts. And so aesthetics open into ethics in Milton's *Maske*. Virtue is not only an aesthetic posture and attitude toward reading projected by the *Maske,* or an ideological formation serviceable to the interests of dynamic early modern social classes, but an existential stance challenged and nourished by poetry, which the *Maske* both represents to and requires of its readers.

In chapter 1, "'Growing a Girl': The Masque of Passage," I investigate the *Maske*'s structural relation to two ritual paradigms: time-honored rites of passage for girls orchestrated in traditional societies and the masques that staged and celebrated monarchic power and aristocratic virtue in Stuart England. Although the two types of ritual and the cultures that staged them might initially seem incompatible and uncomparable, I coordinate and compare them in order to clarify the stages of the Lady's transformation from girl to woman in the process of the social drama and to highlight the radical revision Milton makes of the cultural work of masquing. In the conventional court masque, developed out of more archaic cultural dramas, the king was represented as both the source of transformational power and the end which it sought, the living totem of fertility, virtue, and social order. The three stages of the masque—antimasque, masque, and revels—reconsolidated and inculcated this absolutist myth of virtue through a Neoplatonic pantomime in which the whole court participates. This, I argue, is even the case with the "queen's masques" produced by Queen Anne in the early period of James's rule and by Henrietta Maria in the heydays of Charles's personal rule. Their spectacular celebrations of female virtue and power ultimately reinforce the aspirations toward patriarchal absolutism by the Stuart rulers. Milton performs a double reverse on conventional expectations of the genre. He represents virtue in a form that is independent, and implicitly critical, of royalist ideology. In the same stroke, by highlighting the Lady as the *Maske*'s representative of virtue's challenges and prospects, he feminizes both the discourse of virtue and the mythologized cosmos which supports it.

In "Singing Master of the Soul: The Attendant Spirit," my second chapter, I prepare the way for the study of the Lady's initiation by first assessing the complex multitasking role of the rite's master of ceremonies, the Attendant Spirit. The Attendant Spirit serves as the rite's omniscient elder and instructor. Nearly omnipresent and foregrounded through much of the *Maske,* exercising a rich variety of poetic registers and vividly evoking the several visionary landscapes of the *Maske*'s action, the Attendant Spirit is a poetic demiurge. He initiates the brothers within the *Maske* and the audience and readership of the *Maske* in the rites of imaginative and ethical reading. This chapter revisits the ongoing and unresolvable scholarly discussion of the protective herb Haemony and the healing goddess Sabrina in order to show how the Attendant Spirit prepares us to read poetic tradition itself as the ever-fresh but often neglected providential resource for the alerted critical and liberatory imagination. His response to the Lady's Echo Song exemplifies this resourcefulness; the harmonics created by a duet of voices, pupil and mentor, across the poetic text, testifies to the power of music and of poetry over the powers of nature and even of death.

The Attendant Spirit is a mediator not only within the poetic text but in more than one way between the poetic text and its historical and political moment. Played by the esteemed court musician Henry Lawes in the *Maske*'s original performance, the Attendant Spirit mediates between the aspiring poet and his father, a musician who is nevertheless skeptical of Milton's emerging dedication to poetry. A singing master who loves and practices poetry in the *Maske,* Lawes as the Attendant Spirit symbolically heals the division between Milton and his father by displaying the mutual enrichment of the twin vocations of poetry and music. Lawes's participation as court musician and composer certifies the *Maske* as conventional allegorical entertainment for its noble performers and audience, and his tutorial supervision of the Lady's two brothers forwards the proprietary interests of the occasion. He thus distracts the audience from potential suspicion of the *Maske*'s startling subversions of masque conventions and the royalist interests that they typically serve. But in a masque whose primary purpose is to initiate its Lady into womanhood, the Attendant Spirit remains at a strategic remove from her experience and has very little directly to do with or say to her. This chapter concludes by showing how his puzzling detachment from the Lady during her ordeal has to do, in ethical terms, with his commitment to the Miltonic principle that virtue must prove, strengthen, and know itself through trial, and in ritual terms, with Milton's tacit recognition that the Lady's initiation into female mysteries requires a female rather than a male sponsor and guide.

In chapter 3, "Tragedy in Translation," we turn to the Lady's Introit, her entry into the ritual space with soliloquy and song, swiftly beginning to improvise her way toward prophetic voice and ethical resilience by the discovery of the power of the word. This chapter offers exercises in close reading: the Lady's close reading of her own circumstances and our close reading of the stages of textual reflection and engagement by which she fashions the unassailable interiority that she hails as chastity. The Lady's complex opening soliloquy makes sense by comparison to its prototypes on the Stuart stage, for we can find nothing quite like this moment of self-reckoning in the dramatically thin ritual theater of the court masque. Resisting the entropic momentum of thought dramatized by the great tragic figures preceding her on the Jacobean stage, the Lady discovers in the commonplaces of her moral education a way of ordering her thought and action in a newly unstable and far more complicated world than she had known in the safe confines of her father's house, and her soliloquy beautifully engages her audience in the heightened perception of her emerging self-recognition.

The first fruits of this self-fashioning, her Echo Song demonstrates the Lady's creative revision, or "translation" (242) of the mythological materials that underwrite her ordeal. This "translation" exemplifies Milton's deployment of his mythic resources in the rest of the *Maske* and implicitly critiques standard Renaissance practices of allegorizing myth. Conventional allegoresis philosophically streamlines and moralizes mythic contents so as to neutralize and recuperate the erotic and psychological threat they carry. Milton reopens the myths and exposes the Lady to their dangers, so staging her ritual experience that she recalls and relives tragic stories of suffering, in order to reinterpret them in life-renewing ways. Her first and exemplary instance of such work of translation, the Echo Song secures the mutual identification of the Lady and of Milton as mythoclastic, visionary poets. Invoking and weaving allusions to several mythic victims—Ovid's Echo, Narcissus, and Philomela, and perhaps more subliminally, Sophocles' Oedipus—into her song, she begins to figure out who she is by reading her own situation in relation to myth. Recalling these violated and silenced selves without succumbing to their fates, she awakens a voice that has power to protect her from the tragic destinies she translates. Echo, no longer the baffled, invisible victim of Ovidian desire, but "Sweet Queen of Parley" (241), is the name that the Lady gives to that voice, which becomes through her translation a muse, and a providential projection of her own newly discovered and tested imaginative capacities.

Chapter 4 provides a detailed account of the Lady's ritual antagonist and ironic catechist, Comus. The second of the supernatural masquers to appear in the Lady's liminal ordeal, Comus takes on the role of the "mock bridegroom" in traditional rites of passage like those of the Bemba people of Zambia. Appropriate to a Caroline entertainment, Comus's ritually sanctioned harassment of the Lady partakes of the libertine extavagances that Milton intends to critique and reform. But Comus's character is curiously bipolar, which means double trouble for the Lady, thence the title of this chapter. Milton indexes this bipolarity by inventing as Comus's parents the Greco-Roman ecstasy god Bacchus, and the mind-melting sex goddess Circe. To make sense of the paternal inheritance, I take an excursus through the most powerful modern explanation of tragedy, Nietzsche's *The Birth of Tragedy,* which the *Maske* anticipates and proleptically answers in several respects. For Nietzsche, the kind of autonomous and integrated selfhood to which the Lady aspires is a necessary and beautiful illusion, fostered by the power of dream, vision, and poetry identified with the god Apollo. In Nietzsche's reading, in the tragic confrontation with the Dionysian depths of existence represented by Bacchus's son Comus, individuality of the type that the Lady aspires to is inevitably shattered. Milton knew the necessity for this confrontation as well as Nietzsche but scripted a different trajectory for selfhood. By surviving and triumphing over the Dionysian threat embodied in Comus, the Lady clears the ground for her own ethical maturity by working out a flexible, self-transcending poetic that opens itself to the tragic in order to rewrite its devastating outcomes into life-renewing possibilities.

Comus's ritual function in the *Maske* entails the complementary and perhaps more subtle threat of regression and dissolution in the mythic Mother Goddess, lusciously personified by his mother Circe. Latent in the apparitional dynamism of Comus's appeal to energy and gratification is a despairing wish to give over the burdens of selfhood, to return to the womb-world of maternal gratification and absorption. Drawing on Homeric and Spenserian resources for his seductive appeal, Comus constructs a peculiarly modern version of this mode of self-dissolution, to tempt the Lady as a deliberative work in progress, a self-conscious, conscientious early modern autonomous subject. Inspired and challenged by the example and memory of his mother, he specializes not just in the eroticizing of objects of desire, but in the very manufacture of desire itself, the creation and multiplication of appetites, the lure of whose delusive gratification can only be an impetus to further futile desire. By presenting to the Lady distorted simulacra of her own emerging desire, Comus serves paradoxically as a demonic catechist who provides her an opportunity to make clear to herself what she believes about what she has been taught and about what her desire seeks, and, in the public ritual, to iterate her newly and personally claimed beliefs in the presence of her family and community.

In "Girl Power: The Profession of Virginity," the fifth chapter, I examine the performative means by which the Lady is able to transform her potential vulnerability as a physically undefended virgin into the source of her strength. In her confrontation with Comus, the Lady does not just defend her virgin state, she discovers *in* that state the strength she needs to defy and defuse Comus's temptation and threat. She thereby translates medieval notions of magical celibacy as a fugitive and cloistered virtue into a reformation exercise of chastity as virginity's being toward the world, an activist virtue engaged in critical argument, self-transcendence, and world transformation. Virginity's activist power lies in its concentration of physical poise with psychological and rhetorical force, which the Lady exercises triumphantly in her great encomium to "the sage / And serious doctrine of Virginity" (786–87). The Lady disarms Comus with an ingenious rhetorical invention: she threatens him with what she could say if she wants to, but chooses not to. The act of refusing to disclose the source of her power corresponds to the reserve of her virginal self-presence, associates her speech with God's own inaccessible voice, and generates the irrefutable strength of her outward verbal armor. Imagistically supplementing the Lady's verbal mastery, Elder Brother's exegesis of the iconography of "that snaky-headed *Gorgon* shield / That wise *Minerva* wore" as "rigid looks of Chaste austerity / And noble grace that dash't brute violence" (447–51) provides a key to the spectral source of the Lady's charisma. The image of Medusa's head, a dread and indeterminate icon of female sexuality, bears the same paralyzing relation to the look of Minerva's—and the Lady's—virgin beauty that the terrifying implied Word of virginity bears to the Lady's spoken words. The Lady's "look" claims the Medusa's head as her own emblem of paralyzing erotic power. The terror of her look, like the terror of her speech, depends upon its implication of a power not fully present and all the more powerful in its ghostly imminance. This redoubled authority, mastering both verbal and visual fields, paternal and maternal authorities, associates the Lady with mythologized powers which Comus, Circe's still dependent best boy, does not dare to challenge.

Chapter 6, "Milton's Lady and Lady Milton: Chastity, Gender, and Prophecy," refocuses the study of chastity in the *Maske* by freshly examining the significance of Milton's identification with the Lady. This identification makes chastity the gender crossroad where the poet discovers his prophetic voice. In developing this argument, I confront two mutually reinforcing critiques of Milton's identification with the Lady: the psychoanalytic argument that his investment of poetic aspiration in her amounts to a kind of imaginative disablement and self-restriction on his part; and the feminist argument that Milton's projection of a female speaker and eventual retraction of her capacity to speak evidence the male colonization of the female voice. On the contrary, I demonstrate how the scriptural cues provided in the related texts of the Latin Elegy 6 and the *Apology against a Pamphlet* articulate a Reformed theology of the body. In Milton's positioning of those scriptural texts, the discipline of chastity so interinvolves the identities of male and female subjects as to render them equivalent and interchangeable. The cross-gendered identification made possible by chastity also makes possible the disguised empowerment of both character and author. The Lady associates the eschatological power of her poetic reserves with the prophetic scriptural tradition in general, and more particularly with the climax of Jesus' prophetic and rabbinical career in the Passion narratives. By implication and extension, the lyric, argumentative, and prophetic voice of the Lady establishes a place and a model for women's voices and commitments in both the public and the literary spheres. For Milton, in turn, the sexual persona of the Lady enacts a desire for imaginative and bodily autonomy, for an imaginative projection of desire that cancels the binaries of conventional gender formation, and opens up the field of poetry as the expression of desire's mobile and radical freedom in the exercise of faith.

If, as I am claiming in this book, the Lady's initiation provides triumphant evidence of her attainment of prophetic and public power, a power and opportunity in turn exemplary for and accessible to other women, how are we to account for the *Maske*'s immobilizing and silencing of her in the final movements of the ritual drama? The final two chapters of this book revolve around these puzzling focal points of stasis and silence. Chapter 7, "Girl, Interrupted and the Changing Woman," examines how the Lady's temporary bondage in Comus's chair and her release from it by the river goddess Sabrina make sense as features typical of rituals of initiation consonant with the psychological development that Milton is staging. Consistent with his steady attention to his precursor Spenser, Milton patterns the Lady's dilemma on the captivity of Amoret to the enchanter Busyrane in *The Faerie Queene*. Whereas Busyrane is a dark figment of Elizabethan nostalgic fascination with medievalism, including its tortured idealization of courtly love, the media-friendly Comus brandishes the wit, patter, and debonair sexiness of Stuart libertinism. The Lady proves that she is not vulnerable to Comus's suasions and threats in the way that Amoret is to Busyrane's enchantments. Her temporary paralysis is a sign not of Comus's latent mastery or of her hysterical resistance to desire, but of an excess of strength, the self-armoring of an intact ego in formation. As Amoret must wait upon her rescue by another woman—the hero Britomart, rather than her betrothed Scudamore—so Milton deprives the Lady's brothers of the full rescue of their sister: the Lady needs a woman's touch to release her from her bondage and complete her initiation. The dea ex machina Sabrina, a willing Christlike and Iphigenia-like victim to sexual and political violence for the sake of redeeming female sexuality, is a Spenserian figure well suited to release Milton's Lady from her Spenserian dilemma. As Comus perversely catechizes the Lady in the first part of her trial, Sabrina presides over the second part of the trial as a tutelary godmother and benevolent female deity. She corresponds to the figure of Changing Woman in Cibecue Apache rites of passage, mediating the generative mysteries of womanhood to the Lady, and transforming her exercise of chastity from a necessary posture of self-protection into a dynamic, ardent, questing engagement with the world.

The final chapter, "Homecoming Queen," sets the concluding movements of the *Maske* within the framework of the "reaggregation" moment of traditional rites of passage. At the moment when she exchanges places with Sabrina, the Lady becomes like the Cibecue Apache girl who, at the completion of her rite of passage, is sanctified as a power figure whose fertile magic showers wealth and blessing on the gathered people. The Lady's silence in the homecoming movement of the *Maske* is a sign of this transformed condition. Her silence indicates, more powerfully than speech could, the Lady's new status. The *Maske*'s concluding revels and the gorgeous pastoral eschatology of the Attendant Spirit's Epilogue stage the Lady's transformed condition and project the very transformation of the mythic structures by which it can be understood. Evoking the feminized otherworldliness of the earthly paradise, the Attendant Spirit intimates that the Lady's body has become a this-worldly figure for a redeemed and redemptive sexuality and for the vitally reconfigured cosmos in which it flourishes. The newly grown woman Alice Egerton's recognition and embrace by her parents, her reentry as Lady into the household of her father, an incarnational type of the human Psyche's exaltation to the celestial courts of Jove (1003–11), marks the assumption of the redeemed feminine into the Symbolic order. That order is in turn transformed by its feminization, its structures renewed and refreshed by the spirit of festive community, of which the Lady has become the radiant harbinger. The final movements of the *Maske* suggest that it is not the Lady alone who is translated by her initiation, but the very order of things, on earth and in heaven.

4

My book concludes, then, with attention to the *Maske*'s compelling resolution at every level of its operation—ritual, psychological, aesthetic, and ethical—of a Renaissance dilemma posed and elegantly but more formulaically resolved by Milton's precursor Ben Jonson: the reconciliation of Pleasure and Virtue. The courtly performers of Jonson's *Pleasure Reconciled to Virtue* might have danced the night away in the splendidly intricate labyrinths of dance and beauty and love, to awaken unchanged in a world unchanged by their performance, with the privileges, customs, and social positions of a ruling and conspicuously consuming class intact and resacramentalized. The Lady of Milton's *Maske,* and those who participated in her coming of age, might have awakened to the sense of a world made new by their ritual experience and awakened with the courage and the desire to see to the provision and ongoing renovation of that world through the exercise of chastity and the pleasure that flows therefrom.

As a final living challenge to its modern readership—for who else remains to attend to it?—the *Maske* concludes with a celebration of virtue as the only form that true pleasure can take and as the very basis of human freedom as it is rightly understood:

> Mortals that would follow me,
> Love virtue, she alone is free,
> She can teach ye how to climb
> Higher than the Sphery chime;
> Or if Virtue feeble were,
> Heav'n itself would stoop to her.
>
> (1018–23)

The thematics of virtue in Milton's writing have been fruitfully treated in recent years. Victoria Kahn, in particular, studies how Comus's Machiavellian virtuosity requires the Lady to develop an exercise of virtue as a character-constituent and political force that does not trust itself to a priori claims of allegory, class, or monarchical affiliation. Gina Hausknecht's study of "the gender of civic virtue" primarily in Milton's prose shows how Milton subtly and crucially disengages virtue as a "masculine" public value from the inherent rights and capabilities of the male sex.[43] Both of these texts provide a basis for understanding Milton's innovative formation of "a teenage girl [with] the moral and intellectual stamina not only to resist temptation bodily but to reject it with 'seasonable and well grounded speaking' (*CPW* 2:585)."[44] The account of virtue developed in this book tries to supplement such rhetorically and historically intelligent readings by responding in part to what seems to me the categorical imperative of the *Maske*'s ongoing claims upon its readers. If Milton's *Maske* is formative in the way it envisions modern subjects and societies, does it provide evidence of what it means to live a virtuous life that can continue to engage and inspire people living out the conditions of postmodernity?[45]

We can study the *Maske*'s dramatization of the motive power of virtue as the self-delighting exercise of freedom, but as a living practice, the exercise of such virtue is bound to baffle many of Milton's modern readers, as it does Comus, our cynical proxy in the drama of virtue's self-discovery. Comus is among the earliest of early modern subjects to typify the accedia that opens within a selfhood frustrated by the unpredictabilities of a life given over to the practice of virtue and consequently given over instead to selling himself and others short, for the seemingly concrete and immediate gratification of what appears to be an unbounded pleasure principle. We tend to learn to live with less abandon than Comus, mindful of the self-destructiveness of his pleasure package, but not quite willing to believe in the lasting possibility of bliss, nor that it could come from the self-giving of loving imagination. Our primary models of identity, if we consider them at all in the postmodern labyrinth of originless and endless simulacra, tend to derive from the trauma theories of Freud, who creates a mythology of the agonistic emergence of the ego, a tension-structure fashioned as a border crossing between the libidinal ocean of inchoate drives and the punitive, socially determined conscience of the superego; or from the materialist accounts of Marx and Foucault and their successors, for whom society precedes and inscribes consciousness and determines social groups and their relations and for whom every discourse—and thus every subject interpellated by such discourse—proposes as an ethic a mystified naturalization of the interests of power.

Milton offers the poetic substance of an alternative to these powerful determinations of society and selfhood. He challenges us to consider virtue as essential to identity formation, and he makes this claim a matter of desire rather than a matter of duty. Virtue provides desire a teleological structure as the cause of personal and social transformation, in every logical sense of the term "cause": formal, material, instrumental, final: the condition, the substance, the agency, and the end.[46] From this point of view, modern paradigms of identity based on repression, ideological construction, or signifying indeterminacy are inadequate to account for the motive power of virtue in the selves and societies it constitutes. Virtue, as the Lady discovers it in her initiation, is dynamic and expansive, a transpersonal opening into a communally recognized and shared realm of value and pleasure not accessible through the all-too-familiar and seductive bling of commodification and immediate gratification of desire as it is marketed by Comus. In Milton's reckoning, virtue is the only way to do justice to the complex pleasures and challenges of human life: "Wherefore did God create passions within us, pleasures round about us, but that these rightly tempered are the very ingredients of virtue?" (*Areopagitica,* 733). Studying the pressures of passion within us, pleasures and prohibitions round about us, Freud made his life project the explication of the formula "Where it [id] is, there I [ego] shall be."[47] With no less respect than Freud for the appeal of pleasure and the pull of passion, but with greater optimism about the possible outcomes of our negotiations with them, Milton would inflect Freud's formula differently: "Where it [id] is, there virtue shall be." Milton's idea of virtue is not identical to Freud's idea of the ego, but it creates and fashions that ego in connection to the organizing, transpersonal ground of value that speaks and supports the self.

Thus the several cultural and psychological analysts upon whom we will draw in reading the *Maske* can take us a long way down the road with Milton's Lady, but to travel into the open horizon of ethical adventure, we have to leave them behind. The Lady's translated and charismatic status at the *Maske*'s conclusion, embodied in the dances of the revels and mythically explicated in the Attendant Spirit's Epilogue, dramatizes the possibility of an altogether new ordering of the relations between self and society, Imaginary and Symbolic, female and male, the life of desire and the life of language. Here is where the various determinisms that govern our criticism open up to translation by the optatives of the moral imagination, where Milton challenges us belatedly to read beyond the limits of the modern models that have allowed us to read him, and to envision human character and culture vested in what Blake would call "the lineaments of gratified desire."[48] Milton's projection of a redeemed and self-transcending conception of the human subject, as well as of a culture and a cosmos in which that self discovers and exercises its freedom, is a surprising and ever-renewable possibility that we cannot without some suspicion conceive or allow for, but one which our critical and speculative terminologies, riddled as they are with skepticism, nevertheless provide us a language to postulate.[49] This book, then, is offered hopefully as an exercise of such freedom.

1
"Growing a Girl": The Masque of Passage

1

AMONG THE BEMBA PEOPLE OF NORTHERN ZAMBIA, THERE IS A RITE of passage for girls called *chisungu*. The elder women of the tribe who supervise the ceremony account for it this way: "We do the rite to grow the girl."¹ Audrey Richards, the anthropologist who documented and interpreted the ceremony, describes it as "changing an alarming condition to a safe one, and securing the transition from a calm but unproductive girlhood to a potentially dangerous but fertile womanhood."² In *chisungu,* girls learn "the things of womanhood."³ They learn these things through symbolic actions and dance, through allegoric riddle singing, and through stylized ordeals and encounters involving ancestral figures and representatives of tribal myth and tradition. "The things of womanhood" include the tasks and social networks of mature women, "the secret language of marriage," the proper attitudes toward women's work and marital roles,⁴ and the true nature of the spiritual and cosmic order that endows the newly grown woman's social status with meaning and value.

Richards's description of the practices of *chisungu* provides a vivid particular instance of Mircea Eliade's more general—although masculine-gendered—account of the social purposes of initiation: "through initiation, the candidate passes beyond the natural mode—the mode of the child—and gains access to the cultural mode; that is, he is introduced to spiritual values . . . it is a fundamental existential experience because through it a man becomes able to assume his mode of being in its entirety."⁵ In *chisungu,* as in comparable rites of passage, the inevitable process of biological transformation—physical growth and sexual maturation—provides the occasion and opportunity for the cultural formation and placement of a self. The newly grown woman's sense of personhood and body image, the direction of her desire, and her sense of the world do not come naturally, through self-discovery. They are culturally translated and supervised through ritual drama.

"Growing a girl" into a woman is the central project of Milton's *A Maske Presented at Ludlow Castle*. Studying the *Maske* as a rite of passage analogous to *chisungu* provides an interpretive paradigm that clarifies the *Maske*'s cultural and political functions, its poetic structures, and their psychological and ethical implications. Like other Renaissance masques, Milton's *Maske* works in ways analogous to the rituals of premodern cultures. It creates a mythic stage for the intersection of person, culture, and cosmos. It humanizes the universe in intelligible symbolic forms and in turn "naturalizes" human behavior as a set of virtues and obligations that make sense in and of that world. But while Milton understood and adapted the generic protocols of the Stuart masque, he reinvented its function and effects. He revised its cultural purpose and dramatized a new kind of masque subject—"subject" as both the moral plot and content of the *Maske* and as the kind of person who emerges from its action.

The conventional court masque was no ritual of initiation, but a royalist extravaganza. A multimedia efflorescence of the Stuart aspiration toward absolute power, it displayed as its crucial trope the dazzling figure of the king as god of power. Leading its players and its audience in the motions and emotions of an idealized court, it rehearsed the lesson that all power and influence derive from the king. And so it provided a symbolic network to mystify the centralization of power in a monarchically governed society. Such an event was not likely to be to the taste of Milton, even in his ambitious and starstruck youth. In a startling swerve from tradition, especially in public view and by so young an author, Milton turned the idealizing mirror of a king into a ritual test that grows a girl into a woman.[6]

This was no private valentine or social debut. Alice Egerton's initiation into womanhood relocated the magic source of power in the masque and in so doing implied an analogous social change. In the court masque, the king was both the source of transformational power and the end which it sought. Milton's masque entrusts and invests that power in the chaste conscience of the freshly constituted Puritan self. Although we are right to recognize in that self some of the emerging features of modern subjectivity—inwardly directed ethical autonomy, privacy of conscience, integration of spiritual and worldly concern, inductive empiricism—we need also to recognize the features of the society and the world in which that subjectivity is implicated. For the formation of a new and powerful conception of subject implies a resettling of the kinship patterns and institutional relations in which that subject is confirmed and situated. Beyond these discernible social patterns, we can recognize in the *Maske* a different cosmic picture emerging, designed to support the emerging self and order its will and desire. For the initiation of Alice reconfigures and sublimates the mythological sources which we might call the unconscious of the masque. In that reconfiguration of myth, the order of the world re-presents itself, as it always does through the symbolization of ritual.

It might at first seem disproportionate to recognize structural and functional resemblances between the expensive, allegorically supercharged entertainments of the Jacobean and Caroline aristocracies and the oral ceremonies of a traditional and materially constrained African culture like the Bemba. Although some may find in these resemblances the evidence of mythological universalism, it seems to me more productive to think of these resemblances as a consequence of the common needs of peoples forming and maintaining societies and of the homologous solutions to those needs that they develop. In the course of this reading, I highlight these cross-cultural resemblances for several reasons. In reviewing documentary research into early modern social practices, I have found little recorded evidence of ceremonial performance of girls' passage into womanhood. I suspect that this lack can be explained by the ways in which a self-reinforcing patriarchy might suppress or overlook such performance and in part by the emergence of the culture of the book in the early modern period, in which texts like conduct books become powerful popular determinants and disseminators of prescriptive patterns of gendered social identity. In turning to anthropological accounts of initiatory practices in order to understand more deeply the pattern of the initiation that Alice Egerton undergoes, I have discovered structural parallels and a socializing logic to them that have pressed me into a deeper and more coherent reading of Milton's *Maske* than I expected to gain from such materials. As a consequence of this, I hope to demonstrate that the importation of culturally alien yet structurally and functionally comparable materials into European Renaissance studies can usefully challenge its readers to think outside the ethnocentric boxes that our studies construct and privilege, and in confronting the undiscovered riches of other cultures to think more creatively about the ones that we claim to have formed us.

The masque as a genre reveals its archaic ritual origins in several

1: "GROWING A GIRL": THE MASQUE OF PASSAGE

ways. Enid Welsford traced its origins to seasonal folk festivities of fertility and transformation. At the heart of the ritual prototypes of the masques is a trust in the efficacy of ritual as a mode of sympathetic magic. The primitive impersonation of supernatural powers in masked dance and ritual agon serves to assure agrarian communities of the ongoingness of vegetative and social life beyond the seasons of frost and fallow: "There is then method in the madness of the mummers. They come leaping and dancing that the crops may grow, they perform sword-dances and dramas of death and resurrection to help on by imitative magic the eternal struggle between summer and winter, darkness and light, life and death."[7] By the time Ben Jonson began creating masques at the behest of his queen, the political needs of the Tudor and Stuart courts and the cultural cross-fertilizations of the courts of Renaissance Europe had prepared the way for a hybrid, allegorically sophisticated entertainment for the aristocracy, which virtually concealed its peasant and agrarian origins, preserving them parodically in the carnival uproar of the antimasque. The masque still served the cultural function of a fertility ritual, although in a form dictated by the developing doctrine of divine right of kings, which required a figurative identification of the ruling monarch with the rising god of the vegetative mysteries:

>   Whence is it that the air so sudden clears,
>   And all things in a moment turn so mild,
>   Whose breath or beams have got proud Earth with child,
>   Of all the treasure that great Nature's worth,
>   And makes her every minute to bring forth? . . .
>   Behold a King
>   Whose presence maketh this perpetuall spring,
>   The glories of which spring grown in that Bower,
>   And are the marks and beauties of his power.
>   'Tis he, 'tis he, and no power else
>   That makes all this what Fant'sy tels;
>   The founts, the flowers, the birds, the bees,
>   The herds, the flocks, the grass, the trees,
>   Do all confess him. . . .[8]

In the hyperbolic imagination of the masque, the king becomes both a divine fecundator of all Nature and a male Proserpina figure, and it is not incidental that he seems to be feminized through such imagistic networks. The court masque libidinized monarchic authority in part by invoking traditional suggestions of feminine power associated with nature and fertility and then sublimating and investing them in the singular and transcendent male monarch. Through its proliferation of images, symbols, and gestures of fertility, the masque, like its seasonal folk prototypes, sustained and orchestrated the human longing to exercise generative magic and ritual control over nature and natural process. The scope of this mastery over nature included the ritual organization of human desire. The crisply delineated ethical and political drama of the Stuart masque unfolded a pattern of anarchic release, orderly repression, and visionary sublimation of desire. An intermission period of ritually sanctioned and contained anarchy in the antimasque yielded to the stately formal harmonies of the masque proper, even as the strategic permission and encouragement of social festivity and sportive activity on the wider social stage of Stuart England augmented monarchic authority and invested it with the aura of generosity.[9]

The masque, like its folk prototypes, staged this orchestration of energies through multimedia performance. Poetry, song, music, dance unfolded on the play space of a ritual stage. Whether realized in primitive form by peasants and artisans in a local pasture or fantastically designed and constructed for a banqueting hall by a master architect, this ritual stage was set off from ordinary space for the occasion of an event in time that enacts the eternal and recurrent. As with the mummeries, festivities, and licenses of folk rites, masques served to "retribalize" the elite community, to secure its solidarity through the ritual dramatization of its generative and organizing myths. The figures of myth that populate the poetry and the plots of masques may at first glance seem more decorative than existential or archetypal. But archaic elements, residues from classical literature, as well as distant and less self-regarding folk traditions, continually surface in them. Sometimes the implied myths pull away from the harmonizing narrative of the masque plot. In the resulting tensions between the narrative core of the myths and the symbolizing structures into which the masque wishes to fit them, myths prove to be eruptions of the archaic, and the "royal road to the unconscious" of the culture.[10]

Although its elaboration was far more costly and sophisticated than its folk prototypes, its festivities more self-regarding and carefully scripted, the Stuart masque generated what Victor Turner calls *communitas,* the levelling surge of fellow feeling that precedes, sustains, and periodically renews all forms of social structure without being altogether implicated in or constrained by them.[11] Periodic ritual suspension of the hierarchies and constraints that govern social structures releases and recirculates the bound-up energies that ultimately reinvigorate those structures. A good, well-planned party, Turner and other anthropologists show us, performs a serious social task. It reenergizes society by allowing us release time from conventional roles. Interrupting ordinary routine and upending ordinary structure, it creates a temporal, spatial, and psychological intermission in social activity that allows for and orchestrates personal experimentation, social fluidity, collective innovation. The *communitas* so generated enables us to return to what we tend to call, with unconscious pathos, the "real world," better prepared and motivated to live with it and in it, with a renewed sense of hope and commitment to its possibilities.[12]

William Kerrigan calls Milton's *Maske* itself "a ceremony of investiture,"[13] but this is not quite the case. The official ceremony of investiture by which John Egerton, the Earl of Bridgewater, assumed the office of Lord President of Wales was a judicially sponsored ritual, performed more or less according to ancient custom. It was an event required by English society for the successful ongoing execution of its administrative and judicial life. Institutionally sanctioned, the ritual was indifferent to persons: the same performative structure could just as well have authorized another man's exercise of administrative power over the English/Welsh border territory to which he had been appointed. Milton's *Maske,* on the other hand, prepared and performed in honor of that occasion, supplemented the official ceremony of investiture. It was not required by the culture, and the earl's social authority did not depend upon its performance, although his prestige was surely enhanced by it. It was written on commission, historically specific and occasional, inspired by and directed to the event. It suited its plot and fictive characters to those most intimately involved with and affected by the event.[14]

Inscribing its rite of passage for a single performance, written as entertainment to support the power-confirming ceremony of a prosperous, literate, complex, and rationalized society, Milton's *Maske* contrasts with the cyclically recurring ceremonial of *chisungu* in its modes of conception, production, and transmission. Because they are serviceable to very different cultures, the rites construct very different versions of mature selfhood. Behind *chisungu* is immemorial tradition, not a private author. *Chisungu* is transmitted through oral tradition and orchestrated collectively by elders who are the custodians and exemplars of that tradition. *Chisungu* stamps young Bemba women on the template of traditional tribal ideas about women, creating of each girl a coherent and conformable social *persona.* It shapes individuality through the collective will, and submerges the personal in the social. The young women who emerge from the rite have assumed the knowledge, attitudes, and behaviors necessary to be efficient and responsible wives, mothers, and laborers in the culture of scarcity that depends on their reliable performance in those roles.[15] Although Milton's *Maske* also ritually inculcates in its Lady the idealized wisdom appropriate to her status, class, and sex in pre-revolutionary England, it positions her in a considerably different relation to the social roles that she can henceforth be expected to assume. The *Maske* works, as we shall see, to highlight, strengthen, and confirm the principles and motives of ethical individualism. The *Maske* fashions and mobilizes its Lady as an independent subject and moral agent, the inviolably private, conscience-governed self of Reformation England's early modern culture. She can make choices about the social roles she is to play and how she is to play them. She gains through her initiatory ordeal the necessary critical wisdom about how to determine those choices and what to expect of their outcomes.

In other words, the *Maske* exercises the Lady in knowledge and grace about the social roles she can be expected to assume, but part of that exercise is to develop a critical, discriminating relation to those roles. Her sense of "self" is not identical with them. Nor is her appropriate relation to family and community to be obediently identified with the collective will or with the interests of her father, the one who claims to speak that will to the family. Although its performance generates *communitas* and ultimately engages the community gathered around the Egertons as a collective player, although it restores the Lady and her brothers to the protection and direction of their father in its celebratory conclusion, the *Maske* makes of her worldly homecoming a prefiguration of her heavenly one.[16] It reminds everyone in the celebratory assembly that because her strength is not of this world, neither is her final filial loyalty. The radical freedom and responsibility of Reformation faith in God takes precedence over familial and social obligation, which only make sense in relation to her faith. The chastity that becomes, through her initiatory ordeal, the Lady's signature virtue, is the social evidence and exercise of that faith. In the ordered, idealized society that masques pretend to represent, loyalties to family, king, and God, hierarchically harmonized, do not compete with one another, but mutually reinforce one another, and Milton's *Maske* decorously appears to concede this harmonic integration. But Milton's embodiment and authorization of the free Christian conscience in the person of the

Lady significantly reforms the order and circulation of power within this network of loyalties.[17] When the social contract is under stress, and the authority to determine the terms of that contract is contested, as was the developing situation in the England of 1634, when it was performed, and 1637 and 1645, the years of its first publications, chastity, as the Lady exercises it, becomes a potentially revolutionary virtue.[18]

2

Female self-fashioning of this sort was a unique achievement in the masque as a society-forming ritual. Masques were not rites of passage that grew girls into activist women of conscience, but, as we have observed, cyclical rituals that magically displayed and consolidated monarchic power. The masque was the mythic theater of the Jacobean and Caroline court. The early and incomparable musical drama team of Ben Jonson and Inigo Jones fought over the aesthetic shaping and intention of the masque. Whereas Jones sought to exploit its spectacular potential, its ability to create a visual space bright with the imaginary plenitude of dreams, Jonson worked to invest the form with lyric precision and ethical discipline and to ensure its lastingness in the carefully wrought clarity and integrity of his written texts. Their tense and embattled collaboration invented the Stuart masque as a sophisticated and compelling type of political liturgy, "secular acts of monarchic worship in an aura of learned mystery."[19] They dramatized the imperturbable harmony of a divinely ordered cosmos, a harmony that irradiated the hierarchies of monarchic society and the virtuous and generative stability of the aristocratic psyche. "As models of the universe, as science, as assertions of power, as demonstrations of the essential divinity of the human mind . . . [masques] are the supreme expressions of Renaissance kingship."[20]

In contrast to the initiatory function that Milton would develop in his *Maske,* the masques of Jonson and his contemporaries primarily performed rites of cultural exorcism and power consolidation for the Stuart courts. There were three parts in the structure of the masque, marked off from one another yet also linked by transitional dissolves: antimasque, masque, and revels. The rowdy antimasque yielded to the masque proper, either by the hinge of a spectacular transformation scene or by a "gradual process of refinement,"[21] and the masque in its turn opened into the revels, when the dramatic wall between masquers and spectators vanished, and the masque's fiction absorbed—and was absorbed into—the full festivities of the state occasion. The antimasque drew, perhaps unconsciously, on the genre's festive populist origins, staging what appear in some instances as the potentially threatening energies of the court's political unconscious. Burlesque figures of demonic energy—witches, satyrs, pygmies, animated bottles and tuns—played out rowdy schemes of anarchy, abandon, and usurpation. Ethnic, class, and gender tensions and anxieties took ludicrous and ultimately harmless form in these grotesques, monstrous comic projections of social forces and groups whose pressure on aristocratic attention the Stuart court aesthetic was in part designed to dispel. The carnivalesque figures of the antimasque, potential disrupters of cosmic and social order, took temporary possession of the stage, only to be routed or reformed without resistance. In masque after masque, they vanished like shadows at the advent of the luminous figures of virtue, silently personified by members of the court, whose own ethical and aesthetic energy stemmed from the king. The masque proper thus mastered the energies stirred up in the antimasque by countering and containing them with stately symbolic figures representing the stabilizing and regenerative powers of ethical and political authority. The dissolve into the wider evening's revelries began with a call to the dance, as the newly released and triumphant energies of revealed virtue provided the spirit of *communitas* for the gathered court.

This symbolic staging of the eruption, repression, and sublimation of unruly psychic and social forces provided a public spectacle of participatory wish fulfillment for the court. The antimasque set loose the libidinally charged, volatile, anarchic, specular images and instinctual pulsations of what Jacques Lacan calls the Imaginary register. In the cut or dissolve into the masque proper, these Imaginary flarings-forth seem to vanish not *from* but *into* the orderly living iconography of the Symbolic register, the register of the truth of the Law that guarantees the social order, of which the king is the master signifier. Finally, the festive energies of the revels recharge that social order with the vitality and color of the Imaginary sanctioned and released now in a play of energies constrained, orchestrated, and stylized by the formal and ideological requirements of the Symbolic.[22]

As public ritual, this wish fulfillment had both moral and political consequences. Masques provided an idealizing allegory of attempts by the Stuart regimes to regulate their own internal tensions, steer a course of pacifist accommodation with the Catholic states of Europe, and tighten their hold on an increasingly restive nation.[23] The masque's ritual mastery of the anarchic powers set loose in the antimasque obliquely gestured toward such historical anxieties and conflicts and provided a sublime comic resolution of them. Such imaginary mastery no doubt reassured the court, but self-gratifying fantasy trips of this sort dangerously aggravated the problems of, rather than entertained solutions for, the gathering conflict in England over governance, ecclesiology, and control of wealth. With its price tag often in the range of thousands of pounds, the masque was a kind of party that instanced Renaissance magnificence of an almost unimaginable sort.[24] But that, of course, is the point of the ideology of "magnificence": when the king revels, the universe revels with him. Masques mystified royal and aristocratic power in part by spectacle, in part by the sheer cost of spectacle. Money was no object in the production of the court masque. Masques make money less significant than the dream of a king for whom the material cost of staging cosmic joy is immaterial. For the more ethically rigorous and fiscally scrupulous Puritan classes of London merchants and progressive gentry, among whom resistance to Stuart policy was consolidating, such excesses were hardly self-justifying. They were regarded bitterly as symptoms of a decadent, self-indulgent, and arbitrary exercise of power that was destroying the economy, the polity, and the spirituality of Protestant England.[25]

By temperament, principle, and self-interest, Ben Jonson was no enemy of royal power and no friend of Puritan interests. His masque scripts provided the aesthetic and mythological rationale for the fantasy of absolutism.[26] But he was also a moralist and reformer, no less in his masques than in his lyrics and more savage satiric dramas. Jonson was a canny enough observer of human folly and corruption frequently to satirize the gap between the lives of the nobility and the virtues they professed and personified in art. But as a classicist convinced of the instructive power of art, he wanted to believe in and continually reasserted the morally instructive power of poetry and the formative effect of role-playing. In his masque scripts, he committed himself to the potentially formative effect of masquing, devoting his craft not just to the flattery but to the ethical self-disciplining of the ruling class, including, remarkably enough, its ruler: "Even praise, for Jonson, was theoretically a form of instruction—an encouragement for those mirrored in his art to emulate their own idealized image."[27]

This is why, in what would lead to his contention with the dramaturgical miracle worker Inigo Jones, Jonson tried to stress the enduring moral power of the poetic and textual soul of the masque over its spectacular but evanescent special effects:

> It is a noble and just advantage that the things subjected to understanding have of those which are objected to sense that the one sort are but momentary and merely taking, the other impressing and lasting. Else the glory of all these solemnities had perished like a blaze and gone out in the beholders' eyes. So short lived are the bodies of all things in comparison of their soules. . . . This it is hath made the most royal princes and greatest persons, who are commonly the personaters of these actions, not only studious of riches and magnificence in the outward celebration or show, which rightly becomes them, but curious after the most high and hearty inventions to furnish the inward parts, and those grounded upon antiquity and solid learnings; which, though their voice be taught to sound to present occasions, their sense or doth or should always lay hold of more removed mysteries.[28]

Jonson here describes the creative dynamic of the masque by posing a series of oppositions between spectacle and text. These oppositions delineate the struggle that the Lacanian Imaginary and Symbolic orders stage in the dreamworld of the masque: "sense"/"understanding," "bodies"/"soules," "outward celebration or show"/"inward parts," "riches and magnificence"/"antiquity and solid learnings," "voice"/"sense," "present occasions"/"more removed mysteries." Jonson defends the solid substance of his poetry against the flashy but evanescent effects of the scene maker. He volunteers himself as defender of the Symbolic, which is to say the political and moral order that both authorizes and derives its authority from the king, against the morally enervating attractions of the Imaginary, staged with such wealth, dizzying profusion, and spectacular but subversive energy by Jones. Yet Jonson's argument implicitly concedes its own impossibility or the impossibility of a decisive final triumph of the Symbolic. The circulatory reiteration and positional reversals between apparently opposing terms in Jonson's series has the effect of blurring distinctions and binding the terms together rather than reinforcing their polarity. This suggests by its reversibility and its potentially infinite copiousness the necessary dependency and the creative interchangeability between apparent oppositions.[29]

The concluding hortatory clause, which seems to reinforce the Symbolic lesson of the passage, participates in the destabilizing momentum of the Imaginary chain of associative impressions that it wants to claim that it can overcome. "Voice," which the polarizing system of the passage nominates as the instrument of linguistic, and thus of Symbolic, self-evidence, is put to the service of "present occasions" in all their illusory evanescence; while "sense," linked by the polarizing system with the faulty, partial, and fleeting evidences available to sense perception, becomes the medium for comprehension of "more removed mysteries." The evocative but evasive final phrase, "more removed mysteries," ends the passage on a note of uncertainty. Indexing itself as the suggestion of an absent rather than the declaration of a present truth, it seems no less specular and inaccessible a verbal formation of truth or meaning than any of the visual and dramatic images staged by Jones, the brilliant technician of sight. At the same time that Jonson asserts the necessity and the priority of the text, the word, the Symbolic, to the permanent meaning and moral value of the masque, he cannot avoid acknowledging the necessity, and thus the potential priority, or at least equivalency, of the feigned action, the visual image, the Imaginary, to the persuasive and ethical effect of the Symbolic word.[30]

The hesitating "or doth or should" in the final verb phrase marks Jonson's recognition of this problem, which is both epistemological and ethical, and therefore political. His final declaration of faith in art's formative power, then, is more tentative than it first appears. His affirmation can only be optative and ethical rather than indicative or declarative. He is hopeful rather than fully confident. This conclusion tentatively indicates his belief in the power of art to make a lasting moral impression on those who perform it, even those who are initially only charmed by the superficies of its sensory pleasures. Indeed, the passage acknowledges that the hope for a lasting and transforming moral impression depends upon the power of those sensory pleasures, which are not only visual and dramatic but verbal as well.[31]

The noble masquers personifying virtues and heroes were situated in the performance so as not to be contaminated either by drama or speech, which would be far beneath their stations. Antimasque parts and parts requiring speech were reserved to professional male actors, so that the masquers, male and female, could dwell in the pure air of spiritual allegory. Miming virtue in the ritual space created by the masque would thus subliminally inculcate virtue in the aristocratic performer. Masques "teach, they celebrate virtue, they persuade by example; they lead the court to its ideal self through wonder," as Stephen Orgel has explained.[32] The most profound and morally serious of masque writers before Milton, Jonson wanted the masque to make better people of its performers. For all its sophistication as entertainment, then, masquing as a moral enterprise recapitulates the performative implication at the heart of primary rites. In Stuart masques as in traditional masking rites, when dancers assume the power and the identity of the supernatural figure or the ancestor whom they personify, they provisionally step out of themselves to live as the undying virtue and power they personify. With the dance's eventual dissolve into ordinary social time, they are not divested of that power but carry it back with them into daily life, to revitalize and moralize its activities and obligations.[33]

Ethically optimistic, the conventional court masque was also politically conservative, powerfully elaborating and celebrating the mystique of royal authority. In structure, image, and performance, the masque announced and reiterated that aristocratic virtue owed its very being, force, and grace to the king. Jonathan Goldberg notices the coincidence between Jonson's textual and political purposes:

> Text and monarch stood in the same relationship to the performance onstage; at the masque, there was another silent text, the king himself. As much as Jonson's invention, he was the soul of the masque. Silent, uncostumed, offstage, no part of the visible design, yet there would be no design without him. All the words, all the spectacle aim at him. He embodies the mystery of the masque. His is the permanent form of the masque, its life beyond words, a living image, represented. . . . The invention of the masque is translated into the flesh of the king.[34]

Masque choreography reiterated this silent, almost mystic, centroversion, in occasion after glorious occasion. The closing of the masque's ritual drama was always an opening into the revels. In the concluding movements peculiar to its genre, the masque dissolved its illusory fourth wall and opened out in festive dance and song to include its audience in the harmonious vision.

Shakespeare's epilogues close his great romantic comedies with the poignant dissolve of their healing illusions and the more poignant dispersal of spectators who hunger for more delight and more consolation than the "real world" to which we return can provide. Masques reversed this pattern by dissolving the "illusion" of audience distance and empiricism. Instead of decorously and poignantly sending everyone home, masques absorbed their spectators into the mythic time of the higher and healing vision which they pretended to be more real than the world of conflict, intrigue, and labor. At this moment of dissolve between performers and spectators, the mythic hierarchy itself deferred to the king as its true head, the sovereign witness who was the source of its energies and the resolver of its dissonances: "The ruler gradually redefines himself through the illusionist's art, from a hero, the center of a court and a culture, to the god of power, the center of a universe."[35] Occupying the seat of honor which was literally the one spectatorial position where all of the masque's lines of perspective converge, the king, by implication, was divinely situated to coordinate and resolve the competing interests of society. A living totem of fertility, the king was displayed as the generative source of society's well-being and identified with the life-renewing principle of Nature itself. Imagistically linked with the sun, the king was the still point of the turning world, the human representative and representation of God, the living icon of that divine presence which secures all things in its vast design. As the masque unfolded into courtly song and dance, it opened out on a cosmos that danced to its music. A whole class rose to its feet and dynamically unfolded in its own motions the spiritual harmony charging all existence and consecrating the hierarchic authority of monarchic society.

3

Women of the court figured importantly as sponsors, producers, and performers of masques, but their roles in this most hierarchic and hermetic of entertainments ritually glamorized and mythologized their social subordination. The decorum of the court masque depended upon strict divisions drawn between professional players and aristocratic masquers. Professional players took the speaking and singing parts, particularly in the carnival uproar of the antimasque, while courtly masquers silently moved through a different aesthetic and mythic space, beyond the fury and the folly of social strife. With decorous, even mystic silence, they bodied forth selves simplified to essentials, living exemplars of the virtues that underwrote and motivated the world order. The dynamic interplay of the two great sexes which animate the world (*PL* 8.151) was no less subject to Jonson's mythmaking than it would be to Milton's. Jonson's early masques—the *Masques of Blackness,* of *Beauty,* and of *Queens*—written at the explicit behest of Queen Anne, elaborated ingenious female-centered plots, provided a dazzling stage setting for the greatest and most powerful women of the kingdom and elaborated a fascinating mythology of the feminine.[36] Masques created a feminine mystique in the idealized fusion of beauty, virtue, and power, yet ultimately revealed the contingent status of this mystique, dramatizing its emanation from the primary authorizing power of the king.[37]

The Masque of Queens, composed upon commission by Queen Anne for Candlemas festivities in 1609, provides an instructive example of this process of veiled and idealized subjection. It is Jonson's first complete exercise in the structuring of antimasque as thematic foil and inversion of the masque proper.[38] In this masque, Jonson contrasts types of female power. In the antimasque, twelve monstrous hags and their Dame act out a frantic and impotent opposition to the occasion itself, and to the authority of the king whom it celebrates. In the masque, a pageant of twelve virtuous queens of history and legend reaches its visual pinnacle and thematic climax in Bel-Anna, the mythic *persona* of Queen Anne, whose consummation of everything fruitful, valorous, and worthy of fame in female virtue derives, finally, from her self-subordination to James. Although Jonson's later *Pleasure Reconciled to Virtue,* with its introduction of a rollicking, triumphal Comus, "the god of cheer, or the belly" (5), and its concluding exhortation to seek heavenly Virtue (291–317), is frequently cited and studied as a precedent for Milton, the *Masque of Queens,* in its spectacular projection of activist female virtue and power, provides a more relevant anticipatory contrast to the Lady's discovery of virtue and exercise of power in the Ludlow *Maske.*

The witches who cyclone through Jonson's antimasque are frustrated social and metaphysical bomb throwers. They typify the carnivalesque figures who will succeed them in later masques. They spin about the stage in antic dances, cackling and ranting out threats and charms fit to delight their audience with mock terror and entertain a king who considered himself an authoritative demonologist. Their Dame tries to hatch the "blue drake" (245), the very devil or one of his hell-fiend lieutenants, whose rising would rain down ruin on the supposed tranquillity of the court culture, on James's pacifist efforts at European diplomacy,[39] and on the cosmic order itself:

> Ill lives not but in us.
> I hate to see these fruits of a soft peace,
> And curse the piety gives it such increase.
> Let us disturb it then, and blast the light,
> Mix hell with heaven, and make Nature fight
> Within herself; loose the whole hinge of things,
> And cause the ends run back into their springs.
>
> (131–37)

This threat recollects the catastrophic aftermath of Macbeth's murder of Duncan and anticipates the vengeful terrorism of Milton's Satan. But the universe of *The Masque of Queens* is not that of Shakespeare's Scottish play or of Milton's epic. The aesthetic framing of such intentions determines their seriousness. In the securely hermetic framework of Jonson's masque, danger can be laughed away. When the weird sisters' words suggestively and uncannily implicate themselves in the Macbeths' own will to power, a king dies, and nature turns to nightmare: fair and foul, conscious and unconscious, manliness and impotence, the familiar and the uncanny, the natural and the supernatural, all confuse themselves in one another, as the tragic drama unravels the demarcation lines that secure and stabilize political authority and succession.[40] But Jonson's ethical classicism articulates decisive rational boundaries between all the oppositions that are dissolved by Shakespeare's tragic imagination. The frenzied hags of the *Masque of Queens,* poor self-deluded mimics of Shakespeare's witches, pose only a parodic and ritual threat to the masque's confident orchestrations of power. They take manic temporary possession of the stage but disperse without resistance or complaint at the very moment when they anticipate the advent of their hellraiser.[41]

In the midst of their "magical dance full of preposterous change and gesticulation" (327–28), a loud blast of music sounds, "with which not only the hags themselves but their hell into which they ran, *quite vanished; and the whole face of the scene altered, scarce suffering the memory of any such thing.* But in the place of it appeared a glorious and magnificent building, figuring the House of Fame, in the upper part of which were discovered the twelve masquers sitting upon a throne triumphal, erected in form of a pyramid and circled with all store of light" (s.d. 335–40; italics mine). The hinge of the Jonsonian masque is a spectacular moment of revelation and simultaneous repression. No dramatic conflict unfolds here. The witches are not routed from the playing space; they "quite vanish," and leave not a trace behind, mysteriously dissolving like a bad dream into the abysm of forbidden wish and unconscious dread out of which it was bred.

In masque after masque, antimasquers vanished like this, ephemeral shadows cast by the advent of the luminous figures of virtue, silently personified by members of the court, whose ethical and aesthetic power in turn originated with the king, the unmoved mover who was center, source, and primary spectator of the event. In an Augustinian dialectic, masques staged evil as insubstantial, the shadow and the empty parody of the good. Figures of virtue in masques are substantial antitypes, radiant and proportionate doubles, of the antimasque freaks whom they dispel and replace. In the courtly allegory of the *Masque of Queens,* the witches, "sustaining the persons of Ignorance, Suspicion, Credulity, etc. [Falsehood, Murmur, Malice, Impudence, Slander, Execration, Bitterness, Rage, and Mischief], the opposites of good fame" (s.d. 15–16), pose the potential devastation to reputation, prestige, and sociability wrought by the intrigues, connivings, and plots of court life. Bred by and feeding on envy and ambition, the hags act out the shadow side of the noble life, the inevitable yet necessarily concealed paranoia of a socially circumscribed community for whom power, glamor, and wealth are the manifest signs of rank, yet whose attainment and retention of those signs depend in large part upon the unpredictabilities of royal favor.[42]

The epiphany of the House of Fame annihilates this threat and stabilizes the social anxiety expressed by it. The twelve queens who crown the House of Fame, impersonated by Queen Anne and her ladies, represent and enact the virtue of true nobility. Whereas the witches are all rant and no action, the queens are strong, silent types. They need say nothing or do nothing, for their very presence is an unassailable expression of the power invested in virtue. Both time and art render them unassailable by vice and suspicion. Jones's stagecraft majestically represents them as above it all. History has already exalted their virtue, and the transcendentalizing authority of "Men-making poets" (362), including Jonson, secures it beyond change or second-guessing. As the supreme and present instance in the masque of poetry's power to transform historical character into ethical icon, Queen Anne sits at the head and peak of the pyramid of female power as "Bel-Anna." The only contemporary figure in this regal constellation, she is a legend in the making, who sums up the virtues of all her legendary predecessors.

Barbara Lewalski has noticed that Jonson's selection of queens makes a formidable, even dangerous lineup. They are notable for "their militancy, gender inversion, and conquests of men."[43] Lewalski argues, therefore, that they "appropriate rather than destroy the power of the witches," and that consequently the masque explicitly preserves and glorifies an element of female independence from and resistance to the patriarchal absolutism invested in the king:

> these militant Queens whose force is directed against Kings and husbands need, and find, a female referent in Queen Anne, not in King James. The trajectory of power and compliment returns quite explicitly to the Queens in the final songs. It is their fame, and especially that of Queen Anne (who is the present repository of their virtues) that confers benefit on James's reign. . . . And the Queens' virtue and good fame

(including, presumably, Queen Anne's) will outlast empires (including, presumably, James's).[44]

All court masques are exercises in wishful thinking, and so is this interpretation. Although its optimistic feminism would have flattered Queen Anne, it overstates the idealization of female virtue in the masque to claim that the masque bears "the imprint of Queen Anne's 'authorship' in its subversion of the trajectory of power, and of James's own ideology of gender and male sovereignty."[45] If this masque covertly symbolizes the possibility of oppositional power for the queen and her countercourt, it is a virtual or imaginary power, invested in and bounded by the masque's game playing, rather than power with significant political or historical impact. After all, as Lewalski herself stresses, it was the king who footed the bill for the entertainment and thus determined not only the occasion of the performance but the diplomatic guest list.[46] James was content to let his wife play the Amazon at a court entertainment, as long as her personal preferences did not interfere with his diplomatic tightrope walk between France and Spain.

It is true that the warrior queens of Jonson's roster, whose careers he elaborates in his instructional notes about the masque for Prince Henry, include an impressive, and threatening, number of world beaters and man killers, among them Penthesilea, Tomyris, Artemisia, Zenobia, Valasca. Kathryn Schwarz forcefully evaluates these figures as evidences of oppositional power that ultimately cannot be contained by the masque's patriarchal discourse:

> The challenge is posed by images of female excess, bearing no resemblance to the king; the space between James and the stage becomes not conceit but ellipsis, and masquers' bodies, women's bodies, figure opposition rather than compliment. Jacobean queen's masques detach the display of women's power from the referent of the king. Instead power is articulated as martial, exotic, and historically inimical to men, the implications of violence progressing towards the literalism of an armed female body.[47]

Yet, despite the critics' vigorous claims, the masque does contain and domesticate the potential menace of such power in the several folds of its aesthetic envelope. First, it can't be maintained that the queens, as Lewalski asserts, "appropriate rather than destroy the power of the witches," because the witches of the masque display no power to be appropriated. All their ranting is harmless illusory froth, full of sound and fury, signifying nothing. In contrast to the impotent witches, the power embodied in the queens does not happen to coincide with their virtue; it is a function, a consequence, and an expression of their virtue. In the supplementary notes on the various exploits of the queens, Jonson tends to stress their ferocious commitment to nation-building and family-preserving values. He thus minimizes the anarchic and destructive implications of the legendary material, rendering the queens' power serviceable to the interests of legitimate monarch-husbands like James. Valasca the Bohemian, the exception to this exercise in mythic spin control, remains as a negative exemplum to courtly husbands to mind their manners: "To redeem her sex from the tyranny of men . . . [Valasca] led on the women to the slaughter of their barbarous husbands and lords."[48] The remarks about Hypsicratea, Mithridates' wife, are more typical: "She is solemnly registered by that grave author [Valerius Maximus] as a notable precedent of marriage-loyalty and love—virtues that might raise a mean person to the equality with a queen, but a queen to the state and honor of a deity."[49]

Notably absent from the all star cast of queens is its most recent yet no less legendary apotheosis, Elizabeth I: Belphoebe, the Virgin Queen, the Faerie Queene, Astraea, destroyer of the Armada. Bel-Anna conspicuously occupies the seat that English popular opinion, legend, and nostalgia reserved for the former queen. Indeed, the queens of the masque significantly ignore the recently living example of a queen whose militancy, courage, and cunning matched theirs. They invest their virtues instead in a queen whose power is symbolic and derivative:

> hourly hearing (as what there is old?)
> The glories of Bel-Anna so well told,
> *Queen of the ocean;* how that *she alone*
> Possessed all virtues, for which, one by one,
> They were so famed; and, wanting then a head
> To form that sweet and gracious pyramid
> Wherein they sit, it being the sovereign place
> Of all that palace, and *reserved to grace*
> *The worthiest queen:* these, without envy, on her
> In life desired that honor to confer
> Which with their death *no other should enjoy.*
> (390–400; italics mine)

The italicized phrases, with their stress on Bel-Anna's exclusive claim to virtuous sovereignty, mark the place where Bel-Anna's ascendancy coincides with the mythic erasure of Elizabeth. This tactical displacement signals the Stuart royal couple's concern to create for themselves a countermyth of exclusively male monarchy radiant enough to dispel their sense of living in the shadow of Elizabeth's lingering glamour and power.[50] Their countermyth depends, paradoxically, upon the heroic memory that the masque is staged to efface. Slavoj Žižek describes the operative principle of such effacement: "This foreclosed ('primordially repressed') myth that grounds the rule of *logos* is thus not simply a past event but a permanent spectral presence, an undead ghost that has to persist all the time if the present symbolic frame is to remain operative."[51] Elizabeth is the spectral presence, the Banquo's ghost, at Anne and James's banquet of female worthies.[52] Her impossible enthronement in the House of Fame—at the apex where Bel-Anna is seated—would signify the reality of an autonomous female power, beholding to no one other than the queen herself, rather than the masque's location of female power as an Imaginary signifier of masculine authority: that of the king and that of the poet.[53]

The Masque of Queens thus suggests a model of female sovereignty quite different from the cult of Elizabeth. Bel-Anna indeed cuts a different mythic figure from Elizabeth, and from the queens who honor her. Bel-Anna is no activist, and deeds of heroic valor and military conquest do not accrue to her. Her virtue, typifying the fugitive and cloistered virtues of masque personae, displays itself in the radiance of being rather than in the sweat and blood of doing. The queens confer upon her a common commitment to honor and virtue that has disarmed itself of the capacity for tenacious aggression. This disarmament is symbolized and explicated by their escort, the master of ceremonies Perseus, who represents "heroical and masculine virtue" (342). Perseus stakes his own reputation on the slaying of Medusa, a triumph that he explains tropologically: "When Virtue cut off Terror, he gat Fame" (351). Freud saw in the myth of the Medusa's head a psychoanalytic parable about the imaginary castration of the mother; the Medusa's head is for Freud a specter that haunts the oedipal formation of the subject.[54] Jonson explains the myth ethically rather than psychoanalytically, but his explanation is also psychologically and culturally suggestive. Anticipating Freud, he implies a depotentiating transformation of the feminine through a masculine act of aggressive excision. This condensed moralization of Ovid entails a striking set of gender reversals: "When [masculine] Virtue cut off [feminine] Terror, he begat [generated] [feminine] Fame." As Jonathan Goldberg notes, "Perseus acts as a kind of male mother. The full appropriation of generative powers to the father makes him father and mother at once."⁵⁵ In re-presenting the queens to the courtly audience, Perseus as Virtue in effect disarms them of the terrorism implicit in their reputations. He subjects their power, or rather directs them to subject their power, to the patriarchal authority of the sovereign.

What survives this mythological disarmament is a fame so dehistoricized and a female virtue so conventionalized and submissive as to render itself docile and serviceable to the complimentary intentions of Jonson the court poet and flattering to his royal patron James. Anne completes the pattern of self-subordination of female virtue in the masque. As her spectacular presence sums up all the virtues of the famous queens, she in turn "humbl[es] all her worth / To him that gave it . . . to that light, from whence her truth of spirit / Confesseth all the lustre of her merit" (402–7). Bel-Anna's fame, unlike that of her unacknowledged predecessor Elizabeth or of the more distant legendary predecessors who defer to her in the masque, strikes no terror, because her strength is not her own: "Bel-Anna's creativity and activity are continually subordinated to the poetic conceit and political situation."⁵⁶ Perhaps this explains why the verse celebrating her virtue, and tracing its source to the king, seems so laborious: it is hard, even for a master technician like Jonson, to crank up a convincing rhetoric of awe, when the secret task of the rhetoric is to demystify and displace the source of the awe. In Perseus, Jonson projects himself into the masque. Perseus accomplishes with his sword what Jonson achieves with his pen: the idealization of a female virtue that revels in the *curettage* of its own independent strength and gloriously mirrors the supreme monarchic power that claims to engender and order it.

The *Masque of Queens* was the high-water mark of Queen Anne's sponsorship of and participation in masques and remained the most striking example of seemingly activist female virtue in the masque before Milton's writing of his *Maske:* "In court masques after 1613 the Queen's ladies were relegated to the minor roles of dancing partners in the revels. The Queen could no longer find a way to register her own worth and claims in such performances, and looked to other venues."⁵⁷ During the personal rule of Charles I, after a seven year period in which no masques were performed, Henrietta Maria inherited and enlarged the Queen's roles, in patronizing and ideologically shaping the masques, as well as in performing in them. "The Queen frequently assumed much of the ordering power. . . . *Albion's Triumph, Tempe Restored,* and *Coelum Britannicum* all depict Henrietta Maria as the Queen of Love and Beauty who draws toward herself the heroic love of her regal spouse and the chaste and orderly desires of the entire Kingdom. She becomes the means for demonstrating the power of chaste love to effect inner and social peace."[58] Such highlighting suggests the enlarged and idealizing influence of Charles's consort, at least in the projection of her ideals into the spheres of courtly ethics and domestic arrangements. It is not surprising that the robust vitalist Jonson's aesthetic influence waned under the more fastidious reign of Charles, as the court turned in upon itself and orchestrated its self-image around a more continental, extravagant, and seemingly "feminine" idealism.[59] But the Neoplatonic courtly love cult of Henrietta Maria, and its efflorescences in the late Caroline masques, like the exotic woman warrior fantasies of Anne, advertised a prestige and eminence achieved through the king's sponsorship. The domain of its influence was primarily aesthetic, contained within the dream world of the masque.[60] Even within that dreamworld, it depended for its claim to authority and mystique upon the real as well as symbolic power held by the king. In the masques, in effect, Charles's consort serves as a type of Muse and a material emblem of his own benevolence and virtue. Women of the court, following Henrietta Maria's lead, thus enjoyed power in the late masques as philosophic play, as the bright effluence of the bright essence (*PL* 3.6) and presiding majesty of the king.

At the same time, as Suzanne Gossett documents, under Henrietta Maria's influence the strict aesthetic and ideological boundaries informing the masque and segregating its parts and performers began to dissolve. Aristocrats began to "perform" the acting and singing parts formerly reserved for the professional performers. Women themselves began to speak and sing and even to take on the vocal roles of women in the antimasque formerly reserved for male actors. These innovations upon dramatic convention were experiments with class and gender mixing of considerable social consequence. Aesthetic promiscuity of this sort proved to be an aesthetic and social scandal that provoked criticism and resistance, not only by Puritans like William Prynne in *Histriomastix,* but among traditionalists at court. The masque's performative reinforcement of royal sovereignty and courtly hierarchy foundered in part on the cultural confusion generated by the creation of speaking roles for women, and the restoration of stability required their silencing. After a high-water mark of role experimentation in Aurelian Townshend's *Tempe Restored* (1632) and Walter Montague's pastoral *The Shepherd's Paradise* (1633), male courtiers continued to breech generic categories and frolic in disguise among the actor professionals, but masque roles developed for women of the court were resegregated into the idealized silences of Neoplatonic allegory.[61] The unique and powerful voice of the Lady of Milton's *Maske* emerges out of this silence.

4

With this review of the Stuart masque's structure, political interests, and positioning of women in mind, it is hard to calculate the genre shock and gender shock of Milton's *Maske,* which breaks several of the primary rules of the game in its plot structure, its conception of masque characters, and its ideological intentions. Consistent with other Caroline experimenters, Milton lengthens out the conventional masque's symbolic action. But whereas late Caroline extravanzas like *Tempe Restored* and *Coelum Britannicum* stretch to the bursting point into loosely episodic occasions for spectacle and its consequent suspension of ideological skepticism,[62] Milton tightens his masque into a series of debates and decisions that articulate a coherent dramatic plot, unified by the deep structure of the temptation moment that will subsequently motivate all of Milton's mature poetic narratives. In a way analogous to Shakespeare's romantic comedies, Milton energizes the masque by focalizing it as an expression and study of youth, removing its young masquers from the decorative margins of traditional masque entertainments and placing them center stage to perform crucial speaking and singing parts and decisive, character-forming actions.[63] Moreover, the masquing parts assigned to the youths are comparatively transparent. In contrast to the role-playing fantasies of heroes, gods, and virtues created for the aristocratic performers of conventional masques, the children essentially represent themselves, articulating and testing ideas, anxieties, and aspirations consistent with their stages of life.

Most significant, Milton's *Maske* develops a protagonist's role and speaking part for a young woman and stages its moral drama around her initiation into womanhood. Milton spotlights the fifteen-year-old Lady, Alice Egerton, rather than her father, the king's proxy, as the exemplary agent and embodiment of virtue. Stella Revard notices that, remarkably, "despite the prestige of [the Earl of Bridgewater's] royal appointment, and Bridgewater's close connections with Charles I, Milton never mentions Charles directly or indirectly in the Masque."[64] The *Maske* revises the mythic code for the circulation of power in the nation by obscuring and possibly eliminating the king's position in the chain of command and magic influence. Leah Marcus observes that the "Neptune" of the Prologue (18) could be allegorically construed as Charles, but Milton subverts that expected association, by investing in his Neptune a more expansive imperial power than even the Stuarts claimed for themselves, and by withholding the topical and historical markers that customarily secured the absolutist allegory: "The image of unitary political authority which might be anticipated is dispersed to several figures and a gap appears where the audience might reasonably expect a strong image of monarchy."[65] This suppression of explicit reference to the king as the source and security of legitimate power in the nation burnishes the Attendant Spirit's explicit compliment to the Earl of Bridgewater as "a noble Peer of mickle trust and power" (31). Perhaps Milton hints here at his emerging republican hope for England, in the form of a reformed meritocracy guided by "noble Peers." This stress upon the God-given authority of the peers may in turn subliminally position the king, who had committed himself to rule alone when he dismissed Parliament in 1629, as a despotic type of the Satan who aspires, in *Paradise Lost,* "To set himself in Glory above his Peers" (*PL* 1.39).[66]

The *Maske* thus performs a double reverse on conventional expectations of the genre. It initiates a ritual discourse on virtue that is not founded in and dependent on royalist ideology, and indeed, is implicitly critical of it. Milton's association of the *Maske*'s Lord of Misrule, Comus, with the extravagances and libertinism of traditional aristocracy, and with the papist superstitions of Laudian liturgical reforms, subtly relocates the social center of anxiety represented in the antimasque from *outside* court culture to *inside* court culture, from the instabilities of the discontented classes to the corruptions of the court itself. Furthermore, by casting the Lady as the hero of the *Maske* and rendering her trial as its central action, Milton feminizes both the discourse on heroic virtue and the mythologized cosmos that legitimates and consecrates that virtue. In collaboration with court musician and Egerton family music tutor Henry Lawes, Milton concedes with all due respect to masque requirements for a program of aristocratic compliment celebrating the Earl of Bridgewater. But he organizes the program in such a way as to instruct both performers and spectators in the achievement and practice of a virtue that is not driven by the class interests of a self-regarding nobility, the absolutist myth of royalty, or the social privileges of complacent patriarchy. As Victoria Kahn puts it, "the question of political sovereignty is relocated to the self. . . . The question is no longer how to present (and justify) the magistrate's power as virtuous but how to present individual virtue itself as a source of power."[67] Virtue in the *Maske* proves to be the exercise of providential freedom, generated from the morally sufficient individual's transformative encounter with temptation, not from dependence on and proximity to the king.

The *Maske* thus symbolically resituates the center of moral and aesthetic energy in the Protestant nation, from the seat of monarchic power to the autonomous, actively virtuous soul:

> Virtue could see to do what virtue would
> By her own radiant light, though Sun and Moon
> Were in the flat Sea sunk. . . .
> He that has light within his own clear breast
> May sit i'th' center, and enjoy bright day . . .
> (373–75, 381–82)

Elder Brother here asserts his confidence in virtue's self-sufficency even in the face of a cosmic meltdown of the sort we saw demonically envisioned by the cackling hags of *The Masque of Queens* (131–37). This unobtrusive trope steals its light from the solar king who is the cynosure of conventional masquing and centers it instead in the upright hearts and pure (*PL* 1.18) of a potential thousand points of light, self-sufficient yet mutually cooperative peers in the contemplation and exercise of virtue.[68] Conventional masques, as we have seen, revolved around the figure of the king or his surrogate as a totemic idol, his body itself the true body politic, the seat of social harmony and productivity, moral energy, and generative magic. Since the Lady is the ritual examplar of virtue in his *Maske,* Milton's staging of Alice Egerton's passage into womanhood reconfigures the totemic magic of the masque by feminizing it, making the figure of this virtuous young woman the emblematic human center of the regenerative energies of the world. Milton subsumes the customary and conservative genre of celebratory monarchic liturgy into the novel and progressive task of initiation of the conscientious early modern self, and he personifies that self as a young woman.

Some of the structural particularities and supernatural characters of the Ludlow *Maske* can be understood as a response to this revised function. In constructing the *Maske* as a rite of passage like the Bemba *chisungu,* Milton fuses the antimasque/masque/revels pattern of the classic court masque with the initiatory paradigm. The *Maske*'s linear plot of moral challenge and progress has been noticed in passing by several critics, but not fully considered, as a "drama of initiation."⁶⁹ If the initiation of the Lady is the central plot of the *Maske,* then reading that plot by means of the initiatory paradigm as its structuring force provides a perspective from which to reconceptualize its actions and characters, and to measure the nature and degree of its aesthetic and ideological innovations.

Victor Turner distinguishes three stages in traditional rites of passage: separation, liminality, and reaggregation.⁷⁰ These stages, formulated from fieldwork observations of primary rites of passage by Turner and other anthropologists, offer a map for the dramatic stages of the ritual script of Milton's *Maske.* In the first stage, children are separated from families, removed to unfamiliar or dangerous territory, and isolated there in gender-segregated age-mate groups. This first stage temporarily severs the initiates from the kinship ties and positions that have previously secured their places as dependent children in the identity-defining structures of society. The second stage is the crucial "liminal" period of testing and instruction. "Liminality" is a threshold or transition space and time, identified with the uncharted and unchartered forest, bush, or wilderness where familiar social rules, regulations, and hierarchies have no power. In the liminal stage, initiates typically endure ritual humiliation, marked by binding, blinding, taunting, or sometimes, in the case of girls, aggressive courtship by "mock bridegrooms." They may abstain from ordinary food, but engage in ritual drinking.⁷¹ As they symbolically die to their former lives as children and prepare for entry into their new lives as adults, initiates may go through purifying baths.⁷² The guides, teachers, and symbolic adversaries of the liminal phase are masked elder figures, who stage the culture's wisdom and transmit its myths and traditions in the ritual gestures and expressions of initiation. As they make contact with these personifications of the ancestral and mythical powers in the no-man's-land of the liminal phase, initiates become charged with the supernal energy circulating therein, and when they are restored to their community, they carry that energy in its socially constructive valence with them. The third stage of the circle of initiation is a "reaggregation," where initiates, having completed the ritual ordeal, are welcomed back to family and society in an occasion of festive renewal: "The passage is consummated and the ritual subject . . . reenters the social structure."⁷³ This reaggregation, involving the "solemn exhibition" of the successful initiate,⁷⁴ provides an occasion of great festivity for the whole community, which recomposes itself around the newly mature members. The freshly formed characters of the youths, newly grown into adults, and energized for social roles and commitments that come with adulthood, provide the revitalizing *communitas* for the whole gathered community.

Milton's *Maske* directs the Lady through these three identifiable stages in its symbolic formation of her adult identity and character. Most of the action of the *Maske* occurs in the liminal stage, for the Lady and her brothers have already been separated from family and home by the time the *Maske* opens. The Attendant Spirit's Prologue (1–92), Comus's frenzied antimasque (93–169), and the Lady's initial solo stage appearance (170–243) announce and reiterate the phase of separation and mark out the performing space as the ambiguous and uncanny liminal zone. The Attendant Spirit and Comus introduce themselves as supernatural figures—ethereal *daemon* and forest spirit—to whom the initiate Lady and her brothers are to be exposed in their liminal ordeal. The Attendant Spirit, played by an appropriate and familiar tribal elder, the renowned court musician and Egerton family music tutor Henry Lawes, presents himself as master of ceremonies, establishes the mythic framework, sets the cosmic and terrestrial stage, and provides plot outlines in his expository prologue (1–92). When Comus bursts onto the liminal stage with his monstrous rout, choreographing the Dionysian rock and roll of the antimasque (93–144), he boisterously completes and signals the Lady's separation from familiar society and gives a local habitation and a name to the ambiguities and licenses of the liminal space.

The Lady finds herself in a forest domain, the liminal space where traditional rites of passage typically occur. No one went literally out into the forest on the night of the *Maske*'s first performance. The *Maske* creates its liminal space by turning the world inside out and outside in. The staging space of Ludlow Castle's Great Hall becomes Ludlow Forest, and the Castle becomes the distant and longed-for place of civil safety and enclosure beyond this Imaginary forest's labyrinthine nightworld. Victor Turner's account of the ambiguous challenges and threats of the liminal stage could serve as anthropological liner notes to the production of the *Maske:*

> [The liminal stage is] essentially ambiguous, unsettled, and unsettling, ... betwixt and between the categories of ordinary social life. Symbols and metaphors found in abundance in liminality represent various dangerous ambiguities of this ritual stage, since the classifications on which order normally depends are annulled or obscured—other symbols designate temporary antinomic liberation from behavioral norms and cognitive rules. This aspect of danger requiring control is reflected in the paradox that in liminality extreme authority of elders over juniors often

coexists with scenes and episodes indicative of the utmost behavioral freedom and speculative license.[75]

Moral and symbolic confusion, the controlling directive presence of elder figures, "episodes indicative of the utmost behavioral freedom and speculative license": what Turner describes here is the Lady's experience of the unsettling, dangerous, tempting no man's land of Comus's uroboric forest, spatially registered as "the perplex't paths of this drear Wood, / The nodding horror of whose shady brows / Threats the forlorn and wand'ring Passenger" (37–39). The *Maske*'s primary actions—the Lady's entrapment by and confrontation with Comus, the rescue operation mounted by the Attendant Spirit and her brothers, and the saving lustrations of Sabrina—occur in this liminal space. Each of these episodes entails contact, instruction, testing, and exchange between the children and the supernatural masquers, whose ritual task is to mediate, through narrative and dramatic tests, primary cultural wisdom to the children. Bound, taunted, courted by a "mock bridegroom," offered ritual drink, released into dance and song by the purifying bath of a supernatural godmother, the Lady's experience matches in its crucial components the initiatory experiences of girls undergoing primary rites of initiation in traditional cultures.

The rite of passage completes itself when the Lady reemerges into public, newly grown and newly instructed, from isolation, threat, and immobility. The *Maske*'s third stage, reaggregration, occurs when the children are restored to their parents, and the *Maske* reconsolidates the community in celebratory revels that dissolve, as all masques do, the fictional divide between masquers and audience:

> *Noble Lord, and Lady bright,*
> *I have brought ye new delight,*
> *Here behold so goodly grown*
> *Three fair branches of your own.*
> *Heav'n hath timely tri'd their youth,*
> *Their faith, their patience, and their truth,*
> *And sent them here through hard assays*
> *With a crown of deathless Praise,*
>   *To triumph in victorious dance*
> *O'er sensual Folly and Intemperance.*
>
>   (966–75)

The Attendant Spirit here testifies to the providential scripting and authorization of the Lady's formative ordeal. The youths, like the

Bemba daughters of *chisungu,* emerge from the forest "goodly grown." The *Maske*'s concluding songs and dances restore the Lady as a transformed initiate to her family and society as a freshly mature woman, knowing in "the things of womanhood," the mysteries of female being,[76] and capable of the social exercise of this newly integrated knowledge and the moral power it confers. The dances of the revels are in fact the social and aesthetic testimony to and fulfillment of this transformation. The celebration is not just *on account of* the children's return, but symbolically *made possible by* the children's return, for the Lady returns as the reason for the celebration, a blessing giver, the incarnation of the very spirit of festivity, Turner's *communitas,* that promises regeneration for the gathered community. The Attendant Spirit's restoration speech highlights the tropological and anagogical significance of this moment: with "a crown of deathless praise," the children are to "triumph in victorious dance / O'er sensual folly and intemperance."

It is hard to give due critical weight to the *Maske*'s revels themselves, enjoyed on Michaelmas night, 1634, because they are recorded as an already vanished trace between the lines of the surviving texts: *"The dances ended, the Spirit epiloguizes"* (s.d. after 975). The ritual confirmation of the Lady's homecoming and reintegration of her and her brothers into the community rejuvenated by her ordeal, the revels would have taken up more time, involved more people, and released and orchestrated more social energy on the *Maske*'s original performance night than the staging of the *Maske* itself. But now they are a blank space and timeless moment that is easy to overlook in the reading of the *Maske* text because they are not actually *in* the text.[77] This aporia seems paradoxically appropriate to the eschatological widening of the significance of the Lady's homecoming, which cannot be adequately represented in the spatiotemporal field of the *Maske*'s social drama. The worldly journey home signifies the heavenly one as well. As the Lady's liminal trial occupies the field of salvation history and promises the possibility of universal reformation, so her homecoming festivities evidence the celebratory joys of the community of the redeemed, like the "solemn troops, and sweet societies / That sing, and singing in their glory move," into which Lycidas is received ("Lycidas," 179–80), and the epithalamial "festal orgy" whose songs and dances climax Damon's welcome among the saints ("Epitaphium Damonis," 218–19). As the nuptial music of both these redeemed communities is "unexpressive" ("Lycidas," 176) to mortal ears, so the now unheard melodies of the long-ceased revels of September 29, 1634, are in an anagogical sense truer to the eschatological moment of homecoming they evoke than any restaging of their worldly performance could possibly be. The Attendant Spirit's Epilogue (976–1023), prepared by Milton for the printed texts of 1637 and 1645, brings the *Maske* to a visionary conclusion by expanding into the interpretive and verbal space left silent and seemingly empty by revels, dances, and music that could not be textualized. The Epilogue verbally and imagistically evokes and explicates the eschatological completion that the revels were staged to enact and widens the final vision from the redeemed community, incarnate in the Ludlow revellers, to the cosmic order, itself delighting in the spirit of *communitas* generated by the Lady's passage.

5

The Lady's ritual progress, as we have mapped it, and as we will examine it in greater detail, is not hers alone, but is "doctrinal and exemplary to a nation" (*Reason of Church Government,* 669), and, indeed, for humanity as Milton understands it. If initiation is a ritually staged crisis that distills the essential challenges and potential wisdom that a mature person will be expected to encounter and embrace in her particular cultural setting, then the ordeal of initiation is not self-contained and left behind, but a symbolically orchestrated anticipation of the rigors of experience to which the initiate will henceforth be exposed. This means that the Lady's rite of passage is "typical," both in the common sense of being characteristic of a wider range of human experience and in the typological sense specific to Milton's cultural and intellectual milieu. Reformation typological reading entailed not only the study of correspondences between Hebrew and Christian testaments, but between scripture itself and the already-written and still-unfolding text of history. To make sense of the typicality of the Lady's ordeal, then, we need to conclude this chapter by biblicizing and historicizing its account of the Lady's ritual adventure and the implied historical consequences of her triumph. We can widen the frame of consideration of the *Maske* from the Lady's particular experience to the open field of human encounter by observing how Victor Turner's account of the "dangerous ambiguities," risks, and challenges of the liminal stage, cited above, corresponds in several ways to Milton's explanation, in *Areopagitica,* of what people must be subjected to "in the field of this world" in order to learn what matters:

> Good and evil we know in the field of this world grow up together almost inseparably; and the knowledge of good is so involved and interwoven with the knowledge of evil, and in so many cunning resemblances hardly to be discerned, that those confused seeds which were imposed on Psyche as an incessant labor to cull out and sort asunder, were not more intermixed. . . . Wherefore did [God] create passions within us, pleasures round about us, but that these rightly tempered are the very ingredients of virtue? . . . This justifies the high providence of God, who, though he command us temperance, justice, continence, yet pours out before us, even to a profuseness, all desirable things, and gives us minds that can wander beyond all limit and satiety. (*Areopagitica*, 728, 733)

The crucial reference here to the laborious test of Psyche, a test of discernment, faith, patience, and trust, thematically links with the *Maske*'s climactic reference to Psyche "entranc'd" in Celestial Cupid's embrace "after her wand'ring labors long" (1006) as a visionary validation of the exemplary and anagogical significance of the Lady's ordeal.

As Milton would profess it throughout his career, existential instruction of the sort that the Lady undergoes does not come in cloisters or libraries but in the bewildering liminal space into which worldly life itself continually opens. Liminality provides formative challenge, and in Milton's estimation, such challenge is always potentially problematic and ultimately providential. It makes possible the achievement not only of intellectual mastery, but of ethical integration, an inward structuring of the whole rational, sentient, social, and prayerful being of a person. The poet himself will pray for this when he invokes the Muse to inspire his great epic in a time of darkness and seeming defeat: "chiefly thou O Spirit, that dost prefer / Before all temples th' upright heart and pure, / Instruct me, for thou know'st . . . what in me is dark / Illumine, what is low raise and support" (*PL* 1.17–23). As the Lady prepares to enter the labyrinthine darkness with her tempter Comus, even though she does not yet consciously recognize him for who he is, her prayer is a briefer, more modest sounding of the same ardent reliance that will instruct *Paradise Lost:* "Eye me blest Providence, and square my trial / To my proportion'd strength" (329–30). On her way from girlhood to womanhood, without yet knowing that this passage will make her the first of Milton's heroes of Christian liberty, she does not ask, "lead me not into temptation," but "make my strength sufficient to it."[78]

The Lady carries not only the prospect of her own well-being into the liminal challenge of Comus. Comus undisguises himself and gets back to basics in his hasty and aggressive final pitch to the Lady, the climax of his ritual threat to her: "But this will cure all straight. . . . Be wise and taste.—" (811–13). The Lady's ordeal restages the temptation of the biblical Eve in the original liminal ordeal, alone in the suddenly unpredictable paradise turned wilderness, where a serpent speaks and seems to turn authoritative wisdom topsy-turvy with his appeal to the specious wisdom that comes with experience. Genealogically and textually, the Lady is a typological descendant of the biblical Eve, but her successful resistance to the lure of her tempter positions her as an antitype to Eve by the same logic that understands Christ, in his perfect obedience, as the second Adam, the typological fulfillment of the human identity and destiny as image of God that Adam abandoned in his moment of choice.[79] Mary the mother of Jesus will be mentioned as the "second Eve" in *Paradise Lost* (*PL* 10.183), where Milton follows exegetical tradition in honoring her for her perfect obedience through direct affirmation and acceptance of the Creator and Redeemer's will. As the "second Eve" of the *Maske*, the Lady finds herself positioned to make a choice that closely parallels that presented to Eve. Saying "no" to her tempter, the Lady participates in Milton's restaging of the Fall in order to undo its consequences. In the poetry and pamphlet wars about gender in the seventeenth century, there are defenses of Eve and apologies for Eve.[80] Where else but in Milton's *Maske* are we given the extraordinary typological revision of the narrative of the Fall, in which the postlapsarian woman cast as a second Eve refutes and rebuffs her tempter, holding fast until she can be delivered from the bondage that flesh is heir to?

The Lady's undoing of the sin of Eve is a promising inauguration of her career of moral and erotic choice, but its typological framing widens the event horizon of both her initiatory ordeal and her career to come, setting them in the narrative field of biblical salvation history. The timing of the *Maske*'s performance on September 29, coinciding with Michaelmas Day, provides liturgical support for her achievement, as it subliminally refers to and rehearses the great archangel's vanquishing of Satan and the gathered powers of darkness.[81] The Lady's creative rehearsal and correction of the primal crime and trauma of the Fall releases the human will, exemplified now by the Lady, from its love affair with sin and death, so that it can exercise the gift of its freedom without the apprehensive certainty that its acts will sooner or later necessarily betray themselves and destroy themselves from within. That this founding gesture of a redeemed and redeeming human freedom clears the way for the reformation of the human society to which the Lady returns makes it seem almost incidental to observe that this reformation would include the redemption of women from the place of sorrow and submission enjoined upon Eve in the postlapsarian scene of judgment (*PL* 10.193–96; Genesis 3:16) and perpetually invoked in the long tradition of exegetical and homiletic misogyny. I describe this historically exciting consequence as "almost incidental" because of its relative importance in the primary narrative of human freedom that Milton, here as elsewhere, is determined to invoke. The Lady serves here, quite remarkably, as an Every(wo)man figure whose trial is exemplary and efficacious for the fate of humanity, which includes both male and female. Though her ordeal is specific to her sex, and her achievement is consistent with Milton's program of dignification of women and enlargement of their moral and intellectual prospects, neither she nor her author is a special advocate or representative of women's interests and prospects in and of themselves.

Maryann Cale McGuire characterizes *Comus* as a "dissident masque." It is "the work of a Protestant radical who rejected absolute institutional authority, emphasized the primacy of the individual pursuit of enlightenment, and posited that stasis is impossible in the fallen world, that individual and collective organisms must either grow spiritually or die."[82] Ben Jonson noted of his 1618 masque *Pleasure Reconciled to Virtue,* which introduced an earlier model of Comus as a rollicking bon vivant figure of misrule, "the god of cheer, or the belly" (5), that "this pleased the king so well, as he would see it again, when it was presented with these additions" (321–22).[83] Milton's reconciliation of pleasure with virtue in his *Maske* would not have been so dainty a dish to set before the king, and not only for the conspicuous absence of royalist cheerleading in it. Like Jonson, Milton exposes the conventional opposition of pleasure and virtue as a misconstrual of their true natures, an imposition of what Blake would call "negations" upon what should rightly be understood as mutually challenging and creative contraries.[84] But for Milton, looking ahead in this regard to his antinomian disciple Blake rather than back to the classicist Jonson, virtue is fashioned and earned through imaginative challenge and discernment, not bestowed by the fiat of royal magnanimity, the necessary lesson of the Jonsonian masque.

Milton masks the private person Alice Egerton in the ritual persona of the Lady in order to test, instruct, and energize her as a responsible citizen and visionary moral agent in the republican Puritan culture that his texts would do their part to try to fashion. In terms appropriate to Milton's sense of her place and moment in history, Alice Egerton, the newly grown woman, enters the bonds of kinship, law, and ethos in which she will realize her social identity and status and through which she will henceforth exercise her freedom: a radiant branch of her parents' virtue (968); a respectful yet independent-minded daughter; a chaste and charismatic bride-to-be; member of an ethically responsible, charitable, and temperate ruling class; an exemplary wayfaring, internally alert and consistent, and activist Puritan conscience.[85] The Lady emerges from her ritual agon as an imaginative activist for whom true pleasure takes form in the exercise of the virtue of chastity. Chastity, in turn, as the *Maske* reforms and amplifies our understanding of it, proves to be not a fugitive and cloistered virtue (*Areopagitica,* 728), but a public, political, and dynamic one, that lives out the possibilities of Christian liberty in such a way as to reform the common wealth for the mutual good of all.

The *Maske* is thus a far cry from the extravagant fantasies commissioned by and staged for Queens Anne and Henrietta Maria, by title the most powerful women in their kingdoms, but duly subjecting themselves to their royal husbands in the very rites that they sponsored to mythologize their power. In Lacanian terms, the elaborate textual and dramaturgical sleights of hand of these rites evoke the repressed Imaginary of female power in order to resubject it to and absorb it in the Symbolic projection of an absolutist monarchy.[86] This aesthetic project sought to soften, even feminize, the face of the ideology of power by means of a benign Imaginary infusion and inclusion. Ironically, this co-optation and investment of the Imaginary proved ultimately to subvert the Symbolic design. Isolated and insulated from the public opinions of the streets and many landed gentry, Charles and his supporters in court came to believe too literally in the myths they projected about themselves and the fantasies they played out in masque performances:

> [T]he Caroline masque ought to have been able to function in a more productive, creative, or enabling way. The spectacle of king and subjects dancing together in a loving accord and graciously acknowledging their mutual dependence should have been a forum in which symbolic exchanges could be made, a relationship of trust established, and bridges built between the crown and those with reservations about Charles's government, yet who had no desire to plunge England into crisis.[87]

Narcissistically captive to a mythworld projected in and glorified by the masques, the king and court recognized too late and too superficially the political Real of national discontent and gathering resistance and consequently failed to orchestrate an ideological and institutional engagement sufficient to mediate and contain such forces short of the extreme clarification of power staged in the contest of civil war.

Milton dramatizes the activation of a different set of political and spiritual hopes in a rite that stages, comparatively modestly, a fifteen-year-old girl's coming of age. Compared to the great court masques, the Lady's ritual drama is more down to earth, more modest in scale and plot, and more authentic, in its enactment of the nature and the prospects of power, including women's power, in this world rather than in the world of monarchic make-believe.[88] The *Maske* scripts Alice Egerton's coming of age, but its political subscript projects the coming of age of Protestant England as well. Milton's ritual project schematizes a different system of relations between the psychoideological registers of Real, Imaginary, and Symbolic. His reformatory *Maske* enacts the possibility of a redeemed, innocent Imaginary infusing, feminizing, eroticizing, and terrestrializing the Symbolic. In her response to her demonic catechist Comus, the Lady lays down the law. She knowingly and confidently speaks for the divine Father, in all his judgmental power, and thus legitimates the Symbolic even as she takes on its power by means of her speech. But this does not make her indifferent to or contemptuous of the claims of the female Imaginary; her refutation of Comus is not the compromised achievement of a disguised "phallogocentrism." For the Lady remains a Lady, released and translated by Sabrina's lustrations into a luminous apotheosis of the Imaginary, redeemed from the enervating and self-dissolving spell of Comus. That translation in turn affects both the Real—in this aspect, the conditions of women's domestic and political life possibilities—and the Symbolic—the structural projection of the cosmic totality that endorses and consecrates this translation, even as it depends on it.

The staging of the Lady's growth from girl to woman, then, is not just a challenge to the conventions of masquing and to the interests and expectations of the courtly class it entertained and instructed. One of the revolutionary surprises of the *Maske* is its representation of the Lady's discovery of her own moral sufficiency and imaginative strength, and thus its implication that what Milton will later call with such excitement the "reforming of reformation itself" (*Areopagitica*, 743) is perhaps best represented by the activation of ethical and intellectual freedom by and for women. In the *Maske*'s revels, which publicly celebrate the Lady's coming of age in this life in Ludlow circa 1634, and in the Attendant Spirit's Epilogue, which in the 1637 text and thenceforth celebrates the Lady's terrestrial homecoming even as it projects her destiny beyond, Milton reconceives the very nature of the cosmos, the order of things, in order to recognize, accommodate, and consecrate that freedom.

2
Singing Master of the Soul: The Attendant Spirit

O Sages standing in God's holy fire
As in the gold mosaic of a wall,
Come from the holy fire, perne in a gyre,
And be the singing-masters of my soul.
   —W. B. Yeats, "Sailing to Byzantium"

1

IN TRADITIONAL RITES OF PASSAGE, THE INITIATE'S ENTRY INTO THE liminal realm exposes her to symbolic realities in personified forms that become more real to her than the familiar faces of the world from which she has been severed. In the sophisticated mythopoesis of Milton's *Maske,* the Attendant Spirit, Comus, and Sabrina occupy the positions of the supernatural figures who confront the initiates: "masked figures, representing gods, ancestors, or chthonic powers, may appear to the novices or neophytes in grotesque, monstrous, or beautiful forms. Often, but not always, myths are recited explaining the origin, attributes, and behavior of these strange and sacred habitants of liminality."[1] Each of these figures assumes an explicit set of functions in the Lady's rite of passage. Answering to the conventional masque specification of a presenter, the Attendant Spirit is the "glist'ring Guardian" (219), daemonic guide, reciter of myths, tribal elder and Medicine Man who both orchestrates and interprets the ritual proceedings. Comus is the Lady's ritual antagonist, "mock bridegroom," and demonic Other. Sabrina, whose own story makes her a tragic type of the Lady, is her female sponsor and ritual savior, analogous to the fairy godmother of European folktales and the guiding mentor of traditional rites of passage.

The Attendant Spirit's position as "impresario of the good"[2] is the most encompassing of the three masked figures, and his freedom of movement is virtually unlimited. But his relation to the Lady, the *Maske*'s central character, is surprisingly detached and indirect. Before we enter the labyrinthine forest of interpretive choice with his most advanced student, the Lady, we need to consider the multivalent significance of the Attendant Spirit whose visionary lyrics frame and inform her initiatory ordeal, and yet whose dramatic and ritual relation to her is oblique. Both Comus and Sabrina are *genii loci,* local terrestrial powers with particular histories and functions that are disclosed to us through the Attendant Spirit's narrative allegories. They are *genii loci* in the literary landscape as well, Comus sporting the bloodlines of a set of classical figures, Bacchus and Circe, and Sabrina materializing the legendary history of the Severn River and its associations with the tragic foundation myths of England. The ethereal Attendant Spirit cannot be pinned down to a particular textual locale, since he participates at once in the Bible's narratives of angelic emissaries, Plato's myth of the guiding *daemon,* and classical myths of divine emissaries, Hermes or Mercury in particular.[3] In his human form as Thyrsis, he assumes the multiple associations of the good shepherd in the pastoral traditions of both Scripture and classical poetry. He is also a moralized descendant of Shakespeare's tricksy spirits, Puck and Ariel, with their character fluidity, their creative energy, and their bemused curiosity about human nature as they intervene in human affairs.

Textually multiple and mobile, the Attendant Spirit moves freely up and down the vertical scale of spirit that joins heaven to earth and freely about the horizontal range of the terrestrial landscape. He is capable of shape-shifting like Homer's gods and Milton's archangels, while Comus, his dark double, is a master of disguise and visual special effects. The Attendant Spirit encompasses the several dimensions of the heavens and earth and the several philosophic and poetic modes of representing them, while Comus more or less confines himself, with his self-circling rhetoric and logic, to a single ultimately blank spot, "the navel of this hideous Wood, / Immur'd in cypress shades" (520–21). Like a timid gang leader, Comus keeps close to the turf he has staked out for himself, where he reconstructs for himself an Imaginary space in which he can replicate his enchantress mother's sensuous wizardry and recollect the omphalic darkness of his intimacy with her. Dancing to the music of time without being bound to it, the Attendant Spirit as guardian and mediator of the Symbolic widens the horizons of poetic invention, interpretive understanding, and moral choice, explicating the significance of things beyond the immediate experience of them.

As master of ceremonies, the Attendant Spirit frames and orchestrates the *Maske,* and within its plot he serves as tutelary guide to its wayfaring youths, their mentor in the arts and processes of *poesis* and interpretation.[4] Both the Attendant Spirit and Comus present themselves to the children in the guise of shepherds. Why should we trust the word of the Attendant Spirit over that of Comus? In large part, because he has the first and last word, and because he claims to speak oracularly, for "high *Jove*" (78). His position as "ritual expert" provides him a self-authenticating language equivalent to that of the elders in traditional initiation rites: "The authority of the elder, fresh from contact with the ancestors, infuses his words with power."[5] He has not only the first and last but the most words. He speaks and sings the greatest number of lines in the text (400 out of 1023, by my count, nearly as many as Comus [238] and the Lady [166] combined). Of the five song settings preserved in the composer Henry Lawes's hand—that is to say, since Lawes plays the Attendant Spirit, his own hand—he sings all but the Lady's Echo Song.[6] His various speeches and lyrics provide an encyclopedic compendium of Renaissance poetic types and modes: philosophic exposition, allegory, genealogical invention, pastoral, narration, description, exhortation, incantation, benediction, panegyric, song, ekphrasis. Verbally exemplifying his own energetic fluidity of character, these categorical poetic types are sometimes hard to isolate as specimens in the text because of the ways they variously echo and elide into one another. The Attendant Spirit maintains a stage presence in every scene except the Lady's crucial debate with Comus (659–813), and offers a comprehensive vision of the world in which the *Maske*'s action attains its true significance. He unfolds the map of the various zones of the *Maske*'s universe and evokes them, sometimes with the impressionistic strokes, sometimes with the painterly density, of a master verbal landscape painter: "the starry threshold of *Jove*'s Court" (1), the great oceans and the "Sea-girt Isles" (19–21), the "perplex't paths of [Comus's] drear wood" (37), the more hospitable pastoral precincts that surround and overlap with it (531–48), the familiar domain of Ludlow Castle, the children's "Father's residence" (947), and, finally, the visionary mythscape of the Gardens of Hesperus, to which he anticipates his own return (976–1011).

Like the elders in charge of initiates in traditional rites of passage, whose task is in part to communicate the "specialized knowledge" of social and metaphysical structures, sometimes by "direct exegesis,"[7] much of what the Attendant Spirit has to say involves the narration and explication of the uncanny world of myth. Providing both visionary and trustworthy information about the nature of the world and the outcome of the ritual, he provides the *Maske* its metaphysical security, its explicit interpretive coding, and its dramatic reassurance. He is the custodian of the mythic in the *Maske*. His presence gives security, coherence, and direction to the ordeals of its wandering youths and to the spectators whose cultural hopes the youths will carry into the future. Insofar as the redeemed moral imagination will be the vehicle of those cultural hopes, he also exemplifies to them the extraordinary range and power of *poesis,* of the moral imagination's power to make substantial, coherent, and compelling the more than mortal world it contemplates and in which it draws its life breath.

2

This glistering guardian angel who sets the stage and the tone of the *Maske* is thus no soft-focus archetypal messenger from an anthology of Jung, nor the glowing-haired Pre-Raphaelite beauty of a New Age self-help book, but an ardent Neoplatonist with a virtuoso's musical and poetic skill, formidable political tact and purpose, and a briskly superior attitude. He has unimpeachable literary bloodlines in Hermes-Mercury of Homer and Virgil, the divine messenger and psychopomp, the mediator between divine and human realms, and in the comparable angelic messengers of the Bible. Beyond these discernible prototypes, yet subliminally coordinated with them, his initial self-disclosure hints that he might just be a poetic demiurge, not just the mediator but perhaps the creative source of the truths he unveils:

> Before the starry threshold of *Jove's* court
> My mansion is, where those immortal shapes
> Of bright aerial spirits live inspher'd
> In regions mild of calm and serene air,
> Above the smoke and stir of this dim spot
> Which men call earth . . .
>
> (1–6)

The first word of the *Maske,* "Before" seems to secure its meaning as a residential location in the heavenly regions.[8] In this case the Attendant Spirit discloses that his "mansion" is enviable real estate, near to the center and source of power and authority in the universe, while dependent upon it and derivative from it. But where do those "bright aerial spirits live inspher'd"? In Jove's court, or in the Attendant Spirit's mansion? Syntax does not clarify the problem and indeed blurs the seeming clarity and distinctive properties of the celestial setting that it proposes to map out. The word "Before," especially when no verbal cue precedes it, momentarily suggests temporal and causal priority, as in "before the sun, / Before the Heavens thou wert" (*PL* 3.8–9), or "Before the Hills appear'd, or Fountain flow'd, / Thou with eternal Wisdom didst converse" (*PL* 7.8–9). These quiet invocations in *Paradise Lost* to Milton's "holy Light" (*PL* 3.1) and heavenly Muse mysteriously merge personified evidences of creativity with the self-delighting creative power of divine love itself, a manifestation of the divine, subordinate to God yet more intimately and originally bound to him than anything subsequently brought into being. The Attendant Spirit, evasive about his own origins and destination, yet the final source of all that is knowable about any of the realms envisioned in the *Maske,* may occupy a similarly intimate relationship to the Deity figured as "Jove" in the poem. He may not quite be the mysterious primordial demiurge of Plato, but perhaps that creative force assimilated to the charitable Christian *mythos* of the poem, and veiling itself, first as Attendant Spirit, and then as the shepherd Thyrsis, in the act of condescension to human understanding. Gale Carrithers nicely gestures toward this evocative and expansive sense of the character when he observes, "The Spirit's gifts of discernment are god-like in a way that makes him look like an attendant on the Holy Ghost, a way that makes his uncoercive comings and goings like inspiration in the mind."[9]

Whatever we can guess of his "true" nature and ontic or theological status, as a "Divine Interpreter, by favor sent / Down from the Empyrean" (*PL* 7.72–73), the Attendant Spirit takes his place in the *Maske* as Milton's working prototype for the archangelic instructors Raphael and Michael of *Paradise Lost.* Lauren Shohet gracefully and succinctly puts it that "The Spirit . . . figures *charity:* the illuminating edification that crosses the divide between heaven and earth."[10] Like Raphael, he trains the brothers in the *Maske* and its audience as well in the reading and making of poetry. From start to finish he does this by signalling the ways in which the objects, places, events, and characters we encounter in our worldly sojourning have depths, histories, and purposes that exceed our immediate apprehension or commonplace understanding of them, He also does this by gesturing to his own origins and destination in a Beyond that his mythopoeic power can evoke only by analogy and allegory, and that, ultimately, his own allegory cannot contain. The visionary panoramas of the heavenly court (1 ff.) and the Hesperian Gardens (976 ff.) with which he frames the action of the *Maske* are metaphoric simulacra, complementary to one another, that encourage a kind of visionary imagining released from the inertia of libidinal materialism cultivated by Comus. They speak to our knowledge and delight in sensory phenomena and to our intuitions that these phenomena, rightly apprehended, lead beyond themselves: they are not the closed outer limits but the spiritual thresholds of the real. In this sense, the Attendant Spirit, like Raphael, activates and makes self-conscious an analogic imagination that respects the truth telling of metaphor without requiring its fixation in formula. He establishes an implicit contract with the *Maske*'s spectators, and with his young charges in the *Maske,* that, as Raphael will assure Adam and Eve,

> for thy good
> This is dispens't, and what surmounts the reach
> Of human sense, I shall delineate so,
> By lik'ning spiritual to corporal forms,
> As may express them best, though what if Earth
> Be but the shadow of Heav'n, and things therein
> Each to other like, more than on Earth is thought?
> (*PL* 5.570–76)

The Attendant Spirit's narrative expositions and interpretive instructions thus determine, without delimiting, the structure of the *Maske* and meaning in the *Maske*. Through him Milton exercises the narrative and interpretive imagination necessary for the composition of epic. Indeed, in the range, mastery, and penetration of his utterances, the Attendant Spirit is the first fully realized instance of Milton's epic voice.[11] The transcendentalizing pressure of such narrating and explicating on the lightweight form of the conventional masque would be enough to explode it, were it not for Milton's ability to compose a plot with enough ethical substance to bear the weight of the emerging style.[12] The Attendant Spirit's narrative layering of backstories, the remarkable series of vistas evoked through his vivid verbal scene painting, the visionary panoramas that he projects in the Prologue and Epilogue, all *textualize* the *Maske*'s vision in such a way as to recover for the verbal text of the masque genre the poetic density and moral seriousness that Ben Jonson tried to defend as an endangered species against the special effects wizardry of Inigo Jones.[13] To estimate this verbal and ethical recovery, we need to recall the imperial visual extravagance of the court masques like *Coe-*

lum Britannicum which were more or less contemporary with the modestly staged Ludlow *Maske*. Such spectacles, even when composed by cavalier master lyricists like Thomas Carew, allowed for only a limited range of imaginative work or political or moral reflectiveness by their spectators and participants.[14] Indeed, to Jonson's dismay, their visual brilliance stunned and stupified the ethical and imaginative capacities of the court that staged and consumed them in ways that Comus would have commended, promoting philosophic allegory as self-absorbing and self-affirming light entertainment for the ruling class. Through the Attendant Spirit's speeches, Milton reverbalizes the domain of the visionary spectacular that Jones had created as a flattering mirror for the Stuart court. In doing so he refits the masque as a genre dedicated to moral instruction and enlargement of philosophic vision.[15]

In effect, even in its first public appearance as a performance, the *Maske* insists that it be read as text rather than viewed as spectacle. Its true performance is in reading, and the hermeneutic practice in which its readers are trained is an allegoric and comprehensive one. Every event, datum, decision requires both recognition of its immediate presence and consideration of the ultimate horizon of its meaning.[16] This is a process in which spectators and subsequent readers of the *Maske* as well as the children performing the *Maske* are challenged to participate. The Attendant Spirit explicitly addresses his auditors as readers and readers as auditors in both his Prologue and his Epilogue, creating a bridge between the dramatic fiction of the *Maske* and the interpretive framing of it built collaboratively between his explication and our comprehension. He highlights moments of special interpretive significance by signaling for the audience's awareness: "And listen why, for I will tell ye now / What never yet was heard in Tale or Song / From old or modern Bard, in Hall or Bow'r" (43–45); "List, mortals, if your ears be true" (997). These explicit rechargings of the audience contact at moments of heightened significance coincide with his assurance of the brothers, overheard by his audience, as he prepares them for the challenge of rescuing their sister:

> 'tis not vain or fabulous,
> (Though so esteem'd by shallow ignorance)
> What the sage Poets taught by th' heav'nly Muse
> Storied of old in high immortal verse
> Of dire *Chimeras* and enchanted Isles,
> And rifted Rocks whose entrance leads to hell,
> For such there be, but unbelief is blind.
>
> (513–19)

"Unbelief" is here designated a failure of poetic faith, and a risky one at that. The skeptic who is blind to the truth veiled and unveiled through poetic fiction is all the more vulnerable to the experiential dangers it projects, because he fails to take them seriously.[17] Interpretive clarity is a necessary prerequisite for the exercise of moral wisdom in a world of bewildering appearances. Much of what the Attendant Spirit has to teach, then, involves the narration and explication of the uncanny world of myth, inaccessible to the "shallow ignorance" and worldly skepticism of the badly educated, the willfully blind, or to the hyperkinetic epicureanism of Comus's pleasure addicts. Things invisible to mortal sight (*PL* 3.55) become apprehensible through the verbal apprehension of texts. Imaginative fictions, literary texts, mediate this uncanny world, and so communicate the true or ultimate meaning of things and provide thereby the basis for moral realism in the exercise of choice in this mortal life.

The various moments of heightened interpretive awareness for which the Attendant Spirit prepares us insist upon a truth that overcomes materialist skepticism, and the Spirit's stress is upon the *literary* mediation of that truth. He prepares the brothers for his account of the realm of Comus by telling them to believe the literally unbelievable. He prepares his wider audience for the climactic vision of the tragic but regenerative love of Venus and Adonis and the sacred marriage between Cupid and Psyche (996–1011) by challenging them to listen with "true" ears—ears tuned, that is, to ordinarily inapprehensible mysteries like the music of the spheres. The Attendant Spirit prefaces his remarkable accounts of Haemony (629–54) and of Sabrina (824–58) by detailed and explicit expression of literary indebtedness. The "Shepherd Lad" who discloses the mysterious "small unsightly root" (629) of Haemony, has been nominated as Milton's compliment to himself, Henry Lawes's collaborator in the *Maske*.[18] Commentators interpret "*Meliboeus* old," "The soothest Shepherd that ere pip't on plains" (822–23), as Spenser, whose *Faerie Queene* provides to Milton a recently available account of the tragic fate of Sabrina.[19] These various moments highlighted by the Spirit mark the interpenetration of the historical and the fictional, the natural and the supernatural, the ordinary and the fabulous, the literary and the providential, the questing spirit in its moment of self-discovery and self-origination and the resources for self-fashioning provided by literary tradition.

The healing and protective secrets emblematized in Haemony and personified in Sabrina, both supernatural resources available to and provided in timely fashion by the Spirit, are symmetrically positioned around the deliverance and release of the Lady. They are also structured in parallel and mutually reinforcing ways as poetic symbols. Haemony is offered the brothers as protection against the "hellish charms" (613) of Comus, "of sovran use / 'Gainst all enchantments, mildew blast, or damp, / Or ghastly furies' apparition" (639–41). Sabrina, invoked to release the Lady from her imprisonment in Comus's "marble venom'd seat" (916), exercises parallel powers, "Helping all urchin blasts, and ill-luck signs / That the shrewd meddling Elf delights to make" (845–46), and in particular "she can unlock / The clasping charm and thaw the numbing spell, / . . . To help ensnared chastity" (852–53, 909). Haemony's power is critical, prophylactic, and immunizing; Sabrina's is liberatory, curative, and restorative. Haemony is a gift to the brothers to protect them from capture, their ordeal implicitly paralleled to that of Odysseus as they prepare for the lures and snares of the son of the sexual enchantress Circe. Sabrina appears as a numinal presence to the Lady who releases her from capture, the physical bondage and residual trauma of her ordeal at the same son's hands.

Each of these symbols is quite simple—a magic plant, a fairy godmother—and yet overdetermined. Its associative effects and thus its symbolic value exceed any specific ideational content supplied to explain it; as Angus Fletcher neatly remarks, "Milton has the power of extreme concentration. He holds a whole tradition of exegesis suspended in the little speech on haemony."[20] The same could certainly be said of Sabrina. Thus, Haemony is variously figured by critics as temperance, chastity, right reason, "love of honestie and hatred of ill," grace, the blood of Christ, humility, conscience, and the power of poetry itself. Equally weighty and precise explanations of Sabrina as divine grace, mediated variously by nature and by human arts and institutions, have been supplied, such that Lauren Shohet observes, "Sabrina might be taken to figure figuration itself; not the 'analogical' firmness of premodernity, but something more like undecidable, self-contradictory, modern 'signification.'"[21] Plants with magic power and fairy godmothers are so deeply and primarily components of primary folk, fairy, and epic traditions that they necessarily precede and therefore exceed the rationalizations of them that sophisticated and philosophically designed developments of these traditions, such as the *Maske* and its expositors, encourage and invite. They do not close off meaning so much as open it up; they function as supercharged value clusters that associate several related meanings without eliminating any of them.[22] So rather than try to solve the provocative riddle of what these figures mean, which is ultimately undecideable, I want to consider how they gather significance and generate meaning through their function in the plot of the *Maske* and what Milton might be implying about the literary tradition from which the Attendant Spirit draws them.

Both Haemony and Sabrina are evidently providential powers, immanent in the natural world, serviceable in exposing and dispelling illusion, preventing or releasing the mind from its dependence on or bondage to the senses, and curative, regenerative. But to say that they represent salvific or providential power immanent in nature is to overlook that the nature in which they are immanent is always already a text representing nature. Poetry discloses itself as the mediator of this naturalized, this-worldly providence. Milton's Haemony is analogous to, and thus a literary derivative of, Homer's Moly, yet it is "more med'cinal" (636–37). Sabrina is the legendary spirit of the Severn, near to Ludlow Castle, whose melancholy history transmits itself to Milton through a series of writers, beginning with Geoffrey of Monmouth, but whose role was never before so amply creative and regenerative as it is in the *Maske*. Literary tradition, then, represents itself in the *Maske* as the natural "ground" in which providential resources are to be discovered. But Milton's suggestion, insofar as both Haemony and Sabrina transform and transcend their literary origins, is that these resources are only an immanent potential until actively, vigorously engaged, cultivated, and released by the dynamic free imagination. *Poesis,* the making of poetry, simultaneously a creative and an interpretive act, the making of imaginative constructs that discover the deep truth of reality, provides both a touchstone for the exposure of false and misleading simulacra, and a curative, regenerative principle in language itself.[23] Haemony is the emblem of this insight and, complementarily, Sabrina is its dynamic personification.

This is essentially what the Attendant Spirit's tutorial of the two brothers, and of the audience who witness and participate in their ordeal, is all about. In retelling the story of Comus and informing them of their sister's endangerment, in bestowing Haemony and guiding them in the attempt to capture Comus and release the Lady, he is guiding them from the naive iconics of their debate about the protective power of chastity to a more complex and operational recognition of poetry's power to instruct, protect, and heal. His process of instruction involves a redemptive reordering of his students' relation to their literary resources. In the case of Haemony, this reordering of knowledge establishes a "simple" critical grounding or rootedness (627–29) in the providential order of things, disclosed by poetry, that wards off mystification and seductive enchantment.[24] In the case of Sabrina, whom he recalls from the deep swift waters of English literary tradition in order to release the Lady, this reordering of knowledge involves the disclosure of providential paradox, also deeply instilled in the book of nature, that "can unlock / The clasping charm, and thaw the numbing spell" (852–53).[25] The paradox, unfolding narratively and explicitly in Sabrina's case and imagistically through implication in Haemony's case, is resonantly linked to redemptive sacrifice. Sabrina's sacrificial death is melodramatically spectacular, and its Christlike elements evident (824–42); Haemony's prickles, its unsightliness, trod on daily by the "clouted Shoon" of "dull swains" (629–35), associate it with the suffering servant of Isaiah (Isaiah 53), whose prophecy is fulfilled, for Christians, by the Man of Sorrows, with his prickly crown of thorns and his saving blood.[26]

The full significance of the two figures thus discloses itself only in an eschatological horizon, mediated by the *urtext* of Scripture. Part of the Attendant Spirit's tutorial involves this prophetic expansion of his students' perspective beyond the range of the sensible and experiential. The neglected Haemony, he explains to the brothers, "in another Country . . . / Bore a bright golden flow'r, but not in this soil" (632–33). His valedictory blessing of Sabrina (922–37) foreshadows the return of a Golden Age of temperate fruitfulness and peace, with biblical echoes, in its towers and terraces, its "Groves of myrrh and cinnamon" (937), of the Bride of the Song of Songs, and of the heavenly Jerusalem, and all the hymeneal blessings that attend on her. The Attendant Spirit will elaborate this eschatological promise of a renewed Heaven and Earth in his Epilogue (976–1024). Haemony and Sabrina signify, then, in distinctive yet complementary ways, the harmonic power of poetry and its symbols to "hold all Heav'n and Earth in happier union" (Nativity Ode, 107–8). Grounded in terrestrial elements—in Haemony's case, earth, in Sabrina's case, water—and taking on their true significance in the light of what is to come, poetry's saving metaphoric structures link the origin and the end of worldly pilgrimage. They do so by way of a crossing that is marked by sacrifice, and mediated by a Shepherd's voice, that is, a poet's pastoral voice: the Shepherd Lad (619), "*Meliboeus* old" (822), Thyrsis, "my father's shepherd sure" (493). Poetry thus instructs the human condition, in fact it *is* the human condition, if we would but realize it. The Attendant Spirit is there to help the brothers and the audience realize it, and to impress upon us the liberatory urgency of this realization. Haemony and Sabrina are salvific symbols of this realization.

Displaying the integrated, totalizing, and efficacious knowledge to be achieved through the discipline of studious and creative processing of poetic resources, the Attendant Spirit is an idealized projection of the very education he advocates and institutes. But insofar as he speaks only and always what Milton knows and believes in, he is in particular the product and projection of Milton's career of reading and of Milton's own aspirations toward an absolute and yet evermore about to be poetic knowledge:

> When the cycle of universal knowledge has been completed, still the spirit will be restless in our dark imprisonment here, and it will rove about until the bounds of creation itself no longer limit the divine magnificence of its quest. Then most happenings and events about us will become obvious so quickly that almost nothing can happen without warning or by accident to a man who is in possession of the stronghold of wisdom. Truly he will seem to have the stars under his control and dominion, land and sea at his command, and the winds and storms submissive to his will. Mother Nature herself has surrendered to him. It is as if some god had abdicated the government of the world and committed its justice, laws, and administration to him as ruler. (Prolusion 7, 625)

Although "Il Penseroso" expresses Milton's aspirations toward such power through knowledge ("Il Penseroso," 85–96), the Attendant Spirit is Milton's first fully developed projection of it. His identity as *daemon* in human guise makes him a celestial double of the scholar-poet celebrated in the Seventh Prolusion as potential demigod. Milton's ontology in the *Maske* stresses processive continuities rather than disruptive dichotomies in the spectrum of rational being and projects the spiritual evolution of the virtuous

> Till oft converse with heav'nly habitants
> Begin to cast a beam on th'outward shape,
> The unpolluted temple of the mind,
> And turns it by degrees to the soul's essence,
> Till all be made immortal.
>
> (459–63)

We might say that the Attendant Spirit represents a condition of fully realized and redemptive rational consciousness toward which his students are directing their own moral and imaginative energies.

The fantasy of power over nature that Milton projects in his Prolusion is a fantasy of the sort that the Jacobean masque was designed to cultivate and reinforce, but to reserve exclusively for a monarch. It is a fantasy also dramatized by Shakespeare in the masque-informed *The Tempest,* whose events Prospero the avenging ruler-scholar-poet, a virtual "god of power" in the play, supervises in ways less disinterested and more directly interventionist in human affairs than the activities of the Attendant Spirit. In comparison to these monarch figures endowed with virtually absolute power, or absolute virtual power, by the scripts of their performances, the Attendant Spirit is remarkably self-constrained in the exercise of his absolute knowledge in the form of power. Whereas the nervous Prospero, surrounded by former and present adversaries, is understandably something of a control freak, manipulating the several plots of potential usurpation with a nervous attention to detail, the Attendant Spirit's celestial origins provide him balance and stability and a certain generous detachment from the actions of others that allow him, in a way that foreshadows the all-mighty Father of *Paradise Lost,* to set limits to the exercise of his own freedom in order to enlarge the possibilities of it for others.[27] Although he is figured as royalty in neither his celestial nor his pastoral guises, the Attendant Spirit provides a model of the free sovereignty of knowledge as well as the responsibility that comes with such knowledge that counters the mystique of benign absolutism reiterated in celebrations of the king's wisdom throughout the reigns of James and Charles.

3

Whereas the brothers, and their audience of readers, can rely on the Attendant Spirit for their tutorial in the liberatory promise of reading, the Lady is sequestered from this seminar. In the *Maske*'s rite of passage, she has reached the stage in her education where she must work it out largely for herself. Comus steps into the space of instruction that the Attendant Spirit occupies for her brothers but seems to vacate in her case. Comus is a libidinally volatile demonic double claiming virtuosity in the same traditions of myth and poetry of which the Attendant Spirit is the true custodian, to attempt to seduce the Lady into a self-subverting idea of the pleasure and the promise of the text. Her virtue cannot henceforth be that of "a youngling in the contemplation of evil"; she has reached that stage where "that which purifies us is trial, and trial is by what is contrary" (*Areopagitica,* 728).

2: SINGING MASTER OF THE SOUL: THE ATTENDANT SPIRIT

Representing himself to the brothers as Thyrsis, "a Swain / That to the service of this house belongs" (84–85), the Attendant Spirit confesses his concern for their sister's vulnerability, but he also hints why it is that he has not actively intervened to protect her. He describes to them a series of contrasting musical performances, each of which displaces what proceeds it. First, he recreates the leisurely pastoral torpor of his day's end, when he "began, / Wrapt in a pleasing fit of melancholy, / To meditate my rural minstrelsy, / Till fancy had her fill" (545–48). Then he describes the abrupt cacophonic disruption of this mood of self-indulgent ease by the "barbarous dissonance" (550) of Comus's crew. Then this:

> an unusual stop of sudden silence
> Gave respite to the drowsy frighted steeds
> That draw the litter of close-curtain'd sleep;
> At last a soft and solemn-breathing sound
> Rose like a stream of rich distill'd Perfumes,
> And stole upon the Air, that even Silence
> Was took ere she was ware, and wish't she might
> Deny her nature, and be never more,
> Still to be so displac't. I was all ear,
> And took in strains that might create a soul
> Under the ribs of Death.
>
> (552–62)

This luscious passage answers to and counterpoints the Echo Song (230–43) it recollects and interprets. With its melodious vowel rhymes, its open syllables and floating rather than forced enjambments, its fuguelike variations of liquid and sibilant consonants, it creates a mesmerizing synesthesia of its own by breathing a texture of sound so rich that it seems fragrant, redolent as "a stream of rich distill'd Perfumes."[28] As he continues his narrative of the Lady's captivity, the Attendant Spirit breaks off this delectable testimony to the power of the Lady's Echo Song, but its implications linger as sensory and metaphorical evidence that she incarnates already the power over nature and death and the creative command of the literary resources in which that power is inherent, that the Attendant Spirit must mask in himself as he accommodates himself to the naive idealism, the sense of class privilege and superiority, and the more elementary poetic attainments of the boys.

As a matter of social and aesthetic decorum, this is a beautiful compliment to the richness, sweetness, delicacy, and grace of Alice Egerton's voice, but the way that it keys in to the thematic of music as power gives it a substance that outlasts any element of ephemeral flattery that it might be accused of. Thyrsis's speech registers not only a series of displacements, but a series of fillings: he himself sings "Till fancy had her fill" (548). The uproar of Comus's gang "fill'd the Air with barbarous dissonance" (551). But the Lady's song transcends both Thyrsis's fable of his meditative self-pleasuring and the actual noise pollution of the revellers. Silence itself is quickened to consciousness at the very moment of her displacement, ravishment, and possession, and even longs for her own extinction. The Attendant Spirit, becoming "all ear" (561), describes entering the ecstatic moment of pure musical apprehension, in which state he imagines Death itself fecundated, filled with a living soul. This is orphic capability passing beyond itself, indeed the moment when the orphic incants the Dionysian, as Nietzsche rhapsodizes about it in *The Birth of Tragedy.* Singing her Echo Song, the Lady becomes, in Thyrsis's account, an apotheosis of the very spirit of music that carries the deep power of universal life, displacing thus not only Silence, Thyrsis's self-consciousness, and Death, but Comus himself. Thyrsis here reveals the Lady as the true avatar of Dionysus's dissolving power over life and death.[29] Orpheus's moment of mortal apprehension—glancing back toward his half-regained Eurydice at the threshold of the daylight world—cancels his own heroic effort to revivify his bride with his song. There resides in the optative tentativeness of Thyrsis's "*might* create a soul / Under the ribs of Death" a sense of the tragically doomed wish-fulfilling nature of this moment in the archetypal poet's career.

As if in concession to the fragile brevity of this hope in a world of real danger, Thyrsis interrupts his imagination in midline in order to recall himself and the brothers to the peril in which he has left the Lady. That he has decided to leave her to face Comus on her own, after initially assuring the audience of his mission to provide "safe convoy" to "any favor'd of high *Jove*" who "Chances to pass through this advent'rous glade" (78–81) indicates that the Attendant Spirit has likely been moved and persuaded by the power of the Lady's achieved voice that she is sufficient to answer Comus's temptation and his threat on her own. Even as he highlights her vulnerability by comparing her plight to that of the savagely defiled Philomela—"'O poor hapless Nightingale,' thought I, / 'How sweet thou sing'st, how near the deadly snare!'" (566–67)—his testimony about her song proleptically anticipates another Nightingale, Keats's "immortal bird" which was not born for death, the richness of whose enraptured voice seems to stop time and stirs the anxious, tragically burdened self with the longing to be given over altogether into the sweet extinction of the pure presence of song.[30]

4

The Attendant Spirit serves, then, as a go-between in several senses. He mediates not only between celestial and terrestrial, grace and nature, textual tradition and present occasion, but also between the internal dynamic of the *Maske*'s fictional plot and the social reality of its spectators.[31] He faces into the ritual stage to direct and participate in the action there; he faces out to the audience as the ritual's interpreter and expositor, the figure who negotiates the poetic "truth" of the *Maske* and the political "reality" of its occasion. His manifold position in the ritual explains something of the ironic complexity of the mask he adopts and the expository authority he commands. The Attendant Spirit is, we would ordinarily say, "not really" a heavenly messenger and guardian. He is "really" Henry Lawes, eminent court musician and music tutor to the Bridgewater children, who is "playing" the Attendant Spirit. But "really" and "not really" are problematized, as we have seen, by the mythological idealism of the masque as a form. The essential selves of aristocratic masquers are supposed to be revealed in the characters of virtue that they personify. Although Lawes's status as a performing professional locates him in the category of actors typically distinguished from the silent noble members of conventional masques, his symbolic importance and the coincidence of his social and dramatic roles makes him, like his pupil the speaking and singing Lady Alice, a liminal figure who crosses the social, allegorical, and aesthetic oppositions that structure the conventional masque. It is fitting for the Egerton household's master of music to be the ritual drama's presiding tutelary figure, its orphic shepherd and mediator of "What the sage Poets taught by th'heav'nly Musc / Storied of old in high immortal verse" (515–16). The speech of the Attendant Spirit is in this respect doubly trustworthy. As Henry Lawes, he is familiar to all as a skillful and highly honored musician, already renowned at court, and as esteemed servant to the Egerton household, the master of ceremonies *for* the *Maske* who has probably recommended Milton to write the masque script and collaborated with him on it.[32] As the Attendant Spirit, descending from heaven, his testimony has divine sanction, and his role as master of ceremonies *within* the *Maske* is of higher origin. "The sole repository of virtue and inclusive skill in the piece," his "actual" social position and his ritual role in the *Maske*'s formative fiction create a circle of self-validation which is uncontestable.[33]

When he dons "the Weeds and likeness of a Swain / That to the service of this house belongs" (84–85), Lawes as Attendant Spirit takes on another mask that less obscurely reflects his actual social station. He seems to become more recognizably himself when he changes his heavenly costume of "sky robes spun out of Iris' Woof" (84) for a worldly one. In masking himself as Thyrsis, he folds both his social and metaphysical identity into the less lofty pastoral fiction of the *Maske*'s terrestrial action. Accommodating himself to the children's understanding of a world in which they find themselves suddenly at a loss, he provides them a familiar face, in whom and through whom they can be reassured of providential concern in their distress. "My father's Shepherd sure" (493): he reintroduces to them—or at least, initially, to the boys—the security and relief of recognizable friendship and stewardship and provides them confidence for the ordeal they face.

The profession of music as both a worldly and otherworldly vocation is perfectly suited, personally and thematically, to the role of Lawes/Attendant Spirit/Thyrsis in the *Maske*.[34] As a Miltonic shepherd, he is divinely charged with the pastoral care of souls and with the "rural minstrelsy" (547) of music. Music is always a possible stairway to heaven for Milton, variously keyed and set to epiphanic moments. Just as the Lady, Alice Egerton, will come to incarnate chastity for us, so Henry Lawes in his fictive roles and his social person incarnates the sublime possibilities and spiritually instructive capacities of music, or more expansively, through the pastoral *topos,* of poetry as verbal music. In his hands as Thyrsis, this music sounds gracefully yet understatedly orphic, well tuned to the mode of pastoral romance, "still[ing] the wild winds when they roar, / And hush[ing] the waving Woods" (86–88; 494–96). Yet in his Prologue and Epilogue, Lawes as the Attendant Spirit raises such transformational music to a higher key of sublimity, soaring toward the apocalyptic and visionary in its strains.

"In Caroline court circles Henry Lawes occupied a privileged status rather like that, in Venice, of Claudio Monteverdi."[35] Lawes had composed and would compose music for several other more conventional masques, and he had recently composed for and performed in the spectacular *Coelum Britannicum,* perhaps wearing, as the Attendant Spirit, the very stellar costume that he wore in Carew's extravaganza.[36] Milton provides and enlarges for him a role perfectly

2: SINGING MASTER OF THE SOUL: THE ATTENDANT SPIRIT 99

consonant with such activity. In Milton's *Maske* Lawes represents the true ethical Spirit of the masque genre, opposed to Comus's parodic and degenerate spirit. He mediates between the genre as authorized and developed in court circles and the radical experimentation in form and ethical formation that Milton inscribes for his production on the Welsh frontier. Lawes's commissioning, oversight, and performance provide legitimacy for the young poet Milton in his first significant public work outside the university. Indeed, to gain the patronage of the Dowager Countess of Derby would be no small accomplishment and no small career opportunity, in light of her previous support of poets Milton admired and emulated: "Milton's 'Entertainment' for the Countess of Derby allowed him to place himself in the long line of staunch Protestant writers she patronized, most notably Spenser."[37]

Milton rewards the opportunity provided and returns the compliment by giving Lawes the greatest single male role (outside the symbolic role of the king in the court masques) in the history of masquing, investing in him all the virtue and value of Milton's own aspirations to poetic knowledge and power. Lawes, as the sublime Attendant Spirit and the orphic and pastoral Thyrsis, represents the complete poet whom Milton aspires to be, even as the Lady represents the poet in his moment of emergence and public self-dedication. Lawes returns the favor again by sponsoring the first publication of the *Maske* in 1637, notably endorsing and praising it and linking his name and prestige to it, even as the author remains at least ostensibly anonymous. Dedicating the print edition to the young John Egerton, Lord Brackley, the Elder Brother in the *Maske*'s performance, Lawes remarks, "Although not openly acknowledg'd by the Author, yet it is a legitimate off-spring, so lovely, and so much desired, that the often copying of it hath tir'd my pen to give my severall friends satisfaction, and brought me to a necessitie of producing it to the publick view."[38]

In addition to his several actions as go-between in the performance of the *Maske,* Lawes performs a double mediation for Milton personally in his role. He mediates between verse and music as complementary and mutually enriching arts. In turn, in an idealized and symbolic sense, he mediates between Milton the aspiring poet and his father, the accomplished musician and practical man of business who, at least in Milton's testimony in "Ad Patrem," questions the viability of poetry as a vocation. The timing of the *Maske,* both in its 1634 performance and in its 1637 publication, is important for Milton. At both moments Lawes, with his investment of confidence in the young poet, is a crucial professional and personal catalyst of his aspiration and supporter of his achievement. Milton composes and revises the *Maske* in the period of his "studious retirement" in Hammersmith and Horton after formal completion of his Cambridge studies, that time of withdrawal, of intense and studious preparation for an as yet undetermined vocation. Noting Milton's tendency to procrastinate and the likely tensions between him and his supportive but perhaps impatient father in the close quarters of their sustained residence together, John Shawcross suggestively correlates the publication of the *Maske* in late 1637 or early 1638 with the composition and publication of "Lycidas" in the memorial collection for Edward King and the composition of Milton's personal *apologia pro vita sua poetica,* the epistolary Latin poem "Ad Patrem." Shawcross argues that the timely publication of the *Maske* and of "Lycidas" provide Milton the substantial public evidence as well as the emerging self-confidence to address his father's doubts about his investment in and dedication to poetry.[39]

In "Ad Patrem," the poet addresses his musical father's objections to his devotion to a poetic vocation. Without the revelatory sense provided by verse, Milton claims, music is empty and inane (50–55); with it, music is revelatory of divine mysteries and powerful in the mastery of nature and even the supernal (17–40). He admonishes his father that it makes no sense for him to denigrate the poetic calling, since his own musical avocation has recognized and amplified the value of poetry:

> Dismiss no more the holy Muses' gifts, I pray,
> Nor count them null or vain, who bless you with the skill
> To wed harmonious numbers with a thousand sounds,
> Through endless change to lead the melting voice,
> Which merits you a name as Arion's heir.
> Why wonder that I should be a poet born,
> If we, by precious blood itself so dearly joined,
> Should find ourselves by kindred arts and passions stirred?
> Phoebus, who wished to split himself between the two,
> To me gave certain gifts, and to my parent more;
> Progenitor and child, we share the riven God.
>   (56–66; my translation)

Milton justifies himself to his father by noting the mutually inspiring complementarity of their two artistic gifts, music and poetry, and by praising his father for the inspired responsiveness to verse and voice that he shows in his own musical compositions. Music and verse properly share in an intimate consanguinity, like that of an idealized father-son bond. Reciprocally, Milton suffuses his relation to his father with the exalted harmonics he praises in his father's own settings of verse.

Milton will later honor Henry Lawes in similar terms, in the sonnet that accompanies his presentation of the *Poems 1645* to his friend. Sonnet 13 praises Lawes's innovation of musical settings that support verse recitation rather than subject verse to the rhapsodic and harmonic imperatives of music: "Harry, whose tuneful and well measur'd Song / First taught our English Music how to span / Words with just note and accent, not to scan / With *Midas'* Ears, committing short and long / . . . Thou honor'st Verse, and Verse must lend her wing / To honor thee, the Priest of *Phoebus'* Choir . . ." (Sonnet 13.1–4, 9–10).[40] For Milton as for Lawes, poetry and music are not competing powers, but powers necessary to each other's fulfillment. The practical and aesthetic collaboration of the artists exemplifies this shared understanding in the production of the *Maske,* both as a staged event and as a lasting text.[41] In the *Maske,* they together realize the full possibility of verse and music's mutual consummation, Lawes by infusing Milton's lyrics with music and thereby exalting their sensory and metaphysical range, and Milton by scripting for Lawes the magisterial and eloquent role of poet as singing master, a vivid dramatic anticipation of Shelley's exalted vision of the poet as "the hierophant of an unapprehended inspiration."[42]

John Shawcross insightfully proposes that Milton's resolution to his oedipal anxieties comes by means of an "idealized identification" with his father. In the full mythic projection of this psychological theme in *Paradise Lost,* "The superego of the Father has become the ego of the Son."[43] The Attendant Spirit in the *Maske,* not incidentally played by Lawes, is the vehicle of this "idealized identification" at a decisive moment of maturation and emergence in Milton's career. A singing master who honors poetry, Henry Lawes both publicly and privately gives Milton the esteem and encouragement he seeks from his father. A dozen years Milton's elder, Henry Lawes perhaps is not quite old enough to be a father figure for the poet. But Lawes's acquaintance with John Milton the elder through their shared love of and attainments in music would make Milton's association of Lawes with his father inevitable. The very name "Lawes" might reinforce this association by its homonymic convergence with the Law, the Symbolic province of the oedipal Father. In this sense, the Attendant Spirit played by Lawes in the *Maske* serves as an idealized father imago, with whom the poet identifies through the investment in Lawes of his own vision of poetry, and to whom he can offer unqualified praise as music master. As Nietzsche longed for *"a Socrates who practices music,"* to heal the fatal dualisms of a mythologically impoverished, rationalizing, decaying, warring nineteenth-century Europe,[44] Milton honors Henry Lawes and mythologizes the Attendant Spirit as a musician who loves and practices poetry, and Milton endows him with the full power of a poet. In this composite figure, the "riven god" (66) of "Ad Patrem" is made one again, and, as Shawcross says, "the superego of the Father becomes the ego of the Son." In the internal dynamic of the *Maske,* we might modify Shawcross's suggestive formula to "the superego of the Attendant Spirit becomes the ego of the Lady."

5

Henry Lawes had become a Gentleman of the Chapel Royal in 1626, and a member of the King's Musick in 1631. As a distinguished and favored court musician and veteran masquer, Lawes would be assumed to represent, in his collaboration with Milton, the conservative practices and ideology of the masques staged at court. Milton appears to accept and reinforce this position by identifying the Attendant Spirit as a distinctly patriarchal custodian and lieutenant of both the heavenly and terrestrial orders, dispatched by "Sovran *Jove*" at the outset of the entertainment (41) and safely restoring the children to their parents, *"Noble Lord, and Lady bright"* (966) at the conclusion of the masque action. This is not the sort of figure through whom we might expect the young Milton to offer his critique of the masque genre, or to express directly his more radical ethical and political purposes. But the role Milton scripts for his friend Lawes and the position that Lawes occupies in the *Maske*'s action, addressing and focusing audience expectations, allow for the poet to interrogate and transform masque practice in ways that may have been only subliminally noticeable to that first audience at Ludlow Castle. I think this is a deliberate dramatic strategy. Milton spotlights Lawes as spokesman and supervisor of the entertainment in such a way as to give the performance itself automatic legitimacy and a more or less conventional appearance: "As Lawes's music for *Comus* could be taken as an extension of the art he practiced at court, so his very appearance at remote Ludlow Castle could be taken as a reflection of the royal power at Whitehall."[45] With Henry Lawes as the Attendant Spirit securing his audience's attention and consent, the *Maske*'s more radical and surprising reformations can accomplish themselves without setting off alarm signals.

There is nothing noticeably subversive about the Attendant Spirit's majestic Prologue, with its affirmation of essential forms and hierarchies and its apparent support for monarchies as divinely sanctioned. With the calm and measured assurance of his stately iambics, the Attendant Spirit places the world of the *Maske*—both the liminal night world of Comus and the orderly social world of Ludlow Castle—in an imperturbable, vertically ascending cosmic scale. The cosmic myth that organizes the ritual of the *Maske* is an allegorized Christian version of Platonic dualism, a hierarchical, patriarchal ordering of power that supports the possibility of vertical ascent by means of virtue from the world of the flesh to the world of the spirit. The Attendant Spirit describes in considerable detail the orderly distribution of power throughout the universe: first among the three sovereign Olympians, *Jove* (1), *Neptune* (18), and "nether *Jove*" (20); then, in Neptune's domain of the waters, among the various "tributary gods" (24) who reign over various lands, including the "blue-hair'd deities" (29) of Britain; and finally, in particular,

> all this tract that fronts the falling Sun
> A noble Peer of mickle trust and power
> Has in his charge, with temper'd awe to guide
> An old and haughty Nation proud in Arms;
> Where his fair offspring nurs't in Princely lore,
> Are coming to attend their Father's state
> And new-entrusted Scepter.
>
> (30–36)

Notice the swift and decisive distribution and legitimation of political authority by means of myth, a socially shared poetic fiction. Allegorizing Renaissance Christian hierarchies through classical frames of reference, the Attendant Spirit deftly downloads a humanist cosmic and mythical program into the immediate political circumstance and particular occasion for which the *Maske* is performed. The Prologue honors the Earl of Bridgewater with the proclamation that the whole universe, divinely ordered, stands behind his appointment. At the same time that he pays this appropriate political compliment, in keeping with the occasion and the event of the *Maske,* the Attendant Spirit lays the groundwork for the *Maske*'s plot: the sojourn of the children through the tangled forest domain of Comus to their Father's inaugural celebration (36–42).

For all the appearance of aristocratic cheerleading, Milton quietly qualifies both the authorization of worldly power and the nature of the children's journey in this Prologue. He indicates that all the power of worldly rulers, God given, is also God permitted and God limited. We have noticed already the apparent marginalization, if not exclusion, of royal authority from this distribution of power. The Earl of Bridgewater, "A noble Peer of mickle trust and power" (31), seems to have received his commission directly from Neptune. Rapid shifts of perspective, setting the immediate, world-bound close-ups of terrestrial authority in contrast to the cosmic long shots of the Attendant Spirit's omniscient vision, serve to distance and diminish human claims to political self-importance. As symbols of power, the Lilliputian imperial toys of "Sapphire crowns" and "little tridents" (26–27) are of lesser account in heaven's view than the iconic "Crown that Virtue gives" (10) and the "Golden Key" of Virtue that opens the way to its attainment (13). The children's journey to their Father's house in honor of his investiture proves to be a more important event, in the ethical and theological scheme of things, than the political occasion itself: the children's journey is an allegorical prefiguration and an actual stage of their virtuous wayfaring toward Heaven.

The Attendant Spirit's actions in the role of Thyrsis within the plot of the *Maske* seem to extend and reinforce the position his Prologue establishes for him as omniscient spokesman and omnipotent custodian of patriarchal orthodoxy, but they also complicate his authority and his agency in equivalent subtle ways. Thyrsis remains curiously removed from the Lady, the central character of the plot. He approaches her only by indirection and through the agency of others: her Brothers and Sabrina. In the plot of the *Maske,* he hardly provides the Lady the "safe convoy" (81) initially promised. In the first stage of the *Maske* plot, he renders himself "viewless" (93), while passively observing Comus's revelries and subsequent deception and abduction of her. In the second stage, he presents himself to the Lady's brothers and prepares them for her rescue (490–658), thus turning his attention away from the Lady in her danger to the initial stages of the passage for her brothers. This ultimately works to her release, but at the moment of her greatest need this leaves the Lady curiously bereft of a benevolent supernatural sponsor for her ritual ordeal. He offers no intervening assistance or preparatory tutorial for her of the sort that Telemachus and Odysseus receive from Hermes and Athena in the *Odyssey,* or Aeneas from Mercury in the *Aeneid,* or that Adam and Eve will receive from Raphael in the middle books of *Paradise Lost*.[46]

This dissonance between announced intention and unfolding plot and between the claims to power and knowledge invested in the Attendant Spirit and his seemingly inconsistent exercise of them exemplifies what Victoria Silver describes as the hermeneutic tension between the masque's mimesis and its allegory, between the messy and recalcitrant worldliness of what we actually see happening and the Neoplatonic decoding that would seem to explain it all neatly away. Silver keeps our attention on the inexplicably bodily dilemma of the Lady, stuck in Comus's "marble venomed seat / Smeared with gums of glutinous heat" and "redolent with connotations of sexuality" (48).[47] The seeming neglect of the Lady in the hour of her need and the rescue mission that the Attendant Spirit orchestrates are similarly disconcerting. The brothers botch their rescue, as they arrive too late and act too clumsily to bring about Comus's capture or the Lady's release, and the Attendant Spirit reprimands them for it (814–19). For all the succeeding delicacy and splendor of Sabrina's epiphany and her magical translation of the Lady from a captive girl into a dynamic and gracious woman, the Attendant Spirit's cobbling together of an alternative rescue plan after the boys' abortive mission suggests either that plot has reached a crisis over which he discovers he is not in control, or else that he has foreseen this failure and the plot at this moment requires that he *appear* not to be in control.[48] In either case, the airtight symbolic assurances of typical masque fiction are temporarily and explicitly crossed by dramatic tension and uncertainty. This sudden uncertainty makes the reassertion of the logic of masquing in the figure of Sabrina and the symbolic resolution she accomplishes all the more stunning, but it seems to destabilize the Symbolic authority that the Attendant Spirit has established for himself in his Prologue and his coaching of the Egerton brothers.

Some critics have remarked that the plot of the *Maske* is confused, lacking in unity and taut narrative drive.[49] Much of such criticism has been dispelled by studies of the *Maske*'s relation to masque and dramatic conventions and to Milton's disposition to press his literary structures toward what Angus Fletcher has called "transcendental form."[50] But if the *Maske* is to be read as a rite of passage for the Lady, a similar case might be made about its ritual confusion, both as a masque and as an initiation ritual. Nearly a third of the *Maske*—indeed, its central third (331–658)—is taken up with the brothers' debate over the power of chastity and the vulnerability of their sister and with the Attendant Spirit's appearance and preparation of them for the ordeal ahead. This seems to be a curious displacement of and distraction from what I take to be the ritual core of the *Maske,* the Lady's ordeal. Then the ritual rescue proves unsuccessful. Masques typically require the immediate failure and dissolution of the conspiracy plots hatched by the rabble of the antimasque, when the sublime idea of order that orchestrates the masque proper discloses itself in luminous, brilliant form. Is there another instance in the history of the masque genre in which the turn from antimasque to masque is so curiously bumbled, and the presenter figure himself seems so temporarily discomfited in his orchestration of the turn? Rescue is complete, spiritual restitution accomplished, and reaggregation begun, only when the Attendant Spirit pulls a final trick out of his literary hat, the wonderful dea ex machina, Sabrina.[51]

There are several ways to think about these structural curiosities. The most obvious one is the necessity of the occasion. In honor of the Egerton household, the younger brothers must be included in the entertainment, and the plot wittily does so. Even though it occupies the structural center of the *Maske,* the plot involving the brothers provides a secondary restaging of the initiatory ordeal of the Lady in a comic-heroic, masculine, minor key. Drawing on the logic of both fairy tale and family romance, the *Maske*'s plot insures that they, like Prince Charmings, will be involved in the rescue of their captive sister. Although the brothers are younger than Alice, and the biological and social pressures that motivate her plot are less immediate to them, they too, scholars in virtue, must move from the innocence of the schoolroom into experience and begin their sojourn toward ethical autonomy. The parallelism of their ordeals is evident when Attendant Spirit presents the three children together to their parents as champions of virtue and praises the brothers as they share in their sister's triumph (966–75). Maryann Cale McGuire describes a *common* experience of growth through testing for *all* the children: "Theirs is a youngling virtue that is converted through trial by what is contrary into a force more active, more informed, and more capable of defending itself in a threatening world."[52] The brothers' debate, preparation, and action in the center of the *Maske* is thus positioned as political and cultural business as serious as that which is staged in her rite of passage. After all, it is Elder Brother, John Egerton, who stands to inherit the property, the titles, and the prerogatives of the Egerton family. Collectively, the children's emergence from their liminal ordeal signals the potential emergence of the new generation of a reformed aristocracy, the hope of Protestant England. But the Attendant Spirit's particular tutorial engagement with the two boys seems to reinforce his importance as the ritual supervisor preserving stability and continuity in the transmission of patriarchal authority and privilege.[53]

As we noted before in studying the Attendant Spirit's response to the Lady's Echo Song, it is also consistent with Milton's ethical concern for the formation of character that at a crucial point his heroes be left alone with only what they have learned of virtue and what they believe in providence to sustain them through threat and temptation: "The Attendant Spirit must allow [the Lady's] encounter with Comus and devise the brothers', so that they all gain the knowledge and choice that makes virtue not a metaphysical cipher but an ethic."[54] Her Echo Song has provided the Attendant Spirit evidence of her imaginative and ethical capability, so it makes sense that the Attendant Spirit refuses to intervene when Comus leads the Lady off to his palace of delusory enchantment. Adam and Eve will be declared by the Father himself in *Paradise Lost* as "Sufficient to have stood" (*PL* 3.99). The Attendant Spirit's detachment indicates similarly that the Lady is sufficient to stand on her own, and it is time for her to prove it. As she treads off with Comus, believing only (and wrongly) that she cannot be putting herself in a less secure place than the desolate forest, the Lady seems to accept the trial ahead with not just sobriety and bravery, but courageous expectation: "Eye me blest Providence, and square my trial / To my proportion'd strength" (329–30). It makes dramatic and ethical sense that the Attendant Spirit provides the more immature brothers, falling all over themselves to prove their manhood, the moral armament and the critical perception they require in order to storm Comus's dream chamber, even though they do not quite live up to their own heroic expectations. In the interests of ethical realism, Milton defers the intervention of a dea ex machina until the youths have had the chance to act in their own interests, in order to articulate and temper their strength through trial, until they reach, and acknowledge, the limits of their own ethical resources.

Finally, though, the Attendant Spirit can only approach the Lady indirectly and obliquely because of Milton's sense of ritual decorum. Milton has assigned himself the complicated ritual task of inscribing a female rite of passage within the given framework of a state occasion celebrating patriarchal authority and succession, by means of a performative genre that is conventionally serviceable to such occasions. The complication of the *Maske*'s plot lets its readers realize that a female rite of passage excludes the possibility of male control and manipulation of its central mysteries.[55] The primary rites of traditional societies "form part of a complex of cosmological and social order, in which the opposition between male and female is linked to other dualisms in mutual reinforcement."[56] Initiation is the prerogative and the domain of groups of elders and previous initiates who guard the central mysteries with a sense of sacred proprietary interest. In some cultures, initiation into sexually segregated secret societies coincides with the passage from childhood to maturity, but in most, the sex of the initiate determines which sex will be participants and which spectators of the drama of passage.[57] According to such customs, Alice Egerton should not be ritually directed or touched by a male figure in the official position occupied by her music master in the *Maske*.

So Milton assigns the Attendant Spirit a masque presenter's customary task of expressing and speaking to the official concerns and expectations of the *Maske*'s audience and its celebratory occasion. He leaves the hands-on work of the initiation of the Lady to other supernatural representatives. Henry Lawes as the well-known, dignified, and visionary master of ceremonies creates a tactical diversion from the more radical transformations accomplished by the *Maske*. In keeping with the protocols of administrative legitimation and dynastic succession, Milton scripts for Lawes, the court insider, the mythologized patriarchal proclamation of his Prologue and sets the instruction of the Egerton boys at the structural center of the *Maske*. As the Attendant Spirit, Lawes can instruct the boys directly and oversee these initial and crucial stages of formation of the boys' characters. In keeping with his poetic ambition to explicate the metaphysical framework and the poetic structures and processes that secure the rite of passage, Milton honors his friend Lawes with a double role as archetypal poet and music master. Lawes as the Attendant Spirit is the public face of their collaboration and their shared vision of the healing and liberating power of art. As the Attendant Spirit, he plays the revelatory and mystagogic role of Hermes-Mercury, visionary explicator of the Beyond. As Thyrsis, he assumes a shepherd's pastoral role and the guise and the burden of Orpheus, making a revivified nature responsive to the power of human song and explicating the providential resources inherent in both nature and in song for the protection and the nourishment of human virtue. Meanwhile, he tactfully leaves the Lady to a formative ordeal in which a custodial male, even one of such extraordinary attributes and charitable intentions as he, has no ritual business. If he were make himself known to her prematurely or to intervene in her test, it would amount to ritual contamination and compromise the possibilities of her erotic, imaginative, ethical, and political maturation and emancipation. It would dispel the ritual magic that grows a girl into a woman.

3
Tragedy in Translation

1

IT IS VERY DARK IN COMUS'S FOREST, AND THE LADY HAS LOST HER way. She has no idea where she is and has only the sharp and all the more frightening apprehension that she is not alone. The fading light turns solid form to shadow and no longer provides guidance toward the path she has left behind. With the disappearance of her brothers, the "kind hospitable Woods" (187) have become a brooding labyrinth whose darkness closes in around her, and the forest echoes with the half-wild, half-human cries of Comus's riotous crew. There is nowhere other than toward these haunting and threatening voices that she can go without becoming more lost: "O where else / Shall I inform my unacquainted feet / In the blind mazes of this tangl'd Wood?" (179–81). There are other forests and wild, lonely places like this in literature, Dante's savage forest above all, Spenser's "wandring wood" (*FQ* 1.1.13.6), but also the New England forest of Hawthorne's Hester Prynne and Goodman Brown, the brooding moors of the Brontës, and the wild indifferent bleaknesses of Hardy's unforgiving terrains, and the Evil Forest that hedges in Chinua Achebe's Umuofia. The forest of the *Maske* concedes nothing to these forbidding sites in terms of the risk, the threat, the potential for panic, the experience of absolute aloneness, that is the Lady's initial and necessary condition for her passage from childhood to adulthood.

The Lady's aloneness in the *Maske,* of course, is staged, as it is in every initiatory ritual, but the ritual staging of separation makes the moral and emotional experience no less real and no less risky. Although the Lady has rehearsed this rite of passage and so foreknows the experience she will undergo with greater certainty than most neophytes in traditional rites of passage, she is, like them, virtually and symbolically torn away from everything and everyone familiar to her in order to leave childhood and childish ways behind. There is a brutal impersonal element in rites of passage, no matter how stylized they are. For the initiates, it is always the first and often the only time for such an experience of abandonment, disorientation, aloneness, dread, threat, and pain. Knowledge of what happens in the rite is kept secret, the precious bond between those who have previously gone through it. Initiates are not told what to expect, although some may have the modest security of solidarity and of competition with other initiates in their age group going through the rite with them, a bond that the Lady is denied. Initiates will meet in their ordeal persons whom they ordinarily and formerly know, perhaps even of their own family, but these persons will be strangely masked, alien in voice and action, and unpredictably threatening in their ritual behavior, and so the uncanny doubling of familiar and unfamiliar will make these confrontations all the more soul shaking. Induced by such isolation and disorientation, panic—that terror inspired by the forest god Pan—is the psychic centrifuge that can split the immature self apart, so that it can be fashioned anew in resilient adult form.

In this chapter, I want to begin to study in greater detail how the circuit of the Lady's ritual experience of isolation, testing, and restoration to her family corresponds to the circuit traced by traditional rites of passage: separation, liminality, and reaggregation. The Lady and her brothers have already been separated from family and home by the time the *Maske* opens. The Attendant Spirit's Prologue (1–92), Comus's frenzied antimasque (93–169), and the Lady's initial solo stage appearance (170–243) dramatically announce and reiterate the phase of separation and mark out the performing space as the ambiguous and uncanny liminal zone. By dislocating the dramatic world of the *Maske* from the social world in which and for which it is performed, the Attendant Spirit and Comus sequester the Lady and her brothers, as ritual characters, from the familiar "real-world" setting of Ludlow's Great Hall and from the family and friends who are present to share in the entertainments and celebrations. By the time she takes the stage (170 ff.), the Lady has already been triply separated from familiar social supports: separated *in* the plot, first from the protection of her father's household; second, from its zealous youthful proxies, her plucky but untested younger brothers; and third, separated *by* the ritual fiction of the plot and the ritual contract from the ordinary space and time of her former social life. By the tacit contract established between the masque performance and its spectators, spectators respect the boundaries of the performance stage as circumscribing a ritually inviolable space and thus establish the Lady's initiatory separation as virtually absolute. The spectators tacitly understand that insofar as her ordeal is "real," she must undergo that ordeal for her good, and perhaps for their good as well.

The liminal stage, set in unfamiliar and uncanny border zones, forest, bush, or waste, outside society's law and order, is the crucial space and period for ritual testing and instruction. It is not surprising that the scholarly resourceful, socially engaged, and psychologically penetrating young Milton would create for his Lady's initiatory ordeal a zone of testing that is multiply resonant and overdetermined in its symbolism, but also feels real, not just imaginary. The liminal zone of the *Maske* is simultaneously a geographic, social, psychological, and textual space where transformation occurs. Milton combines the characteristics typical of the liminal zones of anthropological description with the imagined landscapes of Europe's and England's literary traditions and with the particular this-worldly setting of the border terrain where Ludlow Castle, the *Maske*'s performance site, is situated. The Lady's rite of passage, likewise, answers several ritual, cultural, and dramatic requirements. As all initiations must do, it turns a biological moment into a cultural event. It socializes and acculturates the Lady's transformation from childhood into adulthood. Yet different cultures produce different kinds of character by means of their initiations. The particular form of the Lady's socialization will prove consonant with Milton's sense of the kind of adult character adequate to the challenges of his period: an independent subject and moral agent, the inviolably private, conscience-governed self of Puritan culture in formation. In dramatically enacting the formation of that socially capable, inwardly directed character, the *Maske* cultivates and deploys the stylistic and psychological resources developed in the drama and poetry of the early Stuart period for the representation and investigation of subjectivity.

Ludlow Castle itself occupied a geographically liminal space as a fortress of civilization and civility in the scarcely tamed wild west of Britain. Situated on the frontier between English civilization and Welsh wilderness, the castle was something like a cavalry fort in Apache country, an important symbol of the English colonial control of its own island territory, and Lord Brackley was its newly arrived civilizing agent.[1] Young women were raped in the woods around, and their pleas for justice miscarried. The Lady symbolically embodies that real-world risk to young women's innocence, and her father Lord Brackley represented for the powerless and voiceless the possibility of greater judicial equity in a lawless region.[2] Michaelmas Eve, on which *Comus* was performed, was a traditional occasion for lawless revelry in the area.[3] The anacreontic song and whirlwind dance of Comus's mad crew, with its dark swerve toward necromantic danger (128–42), capture the orgiastic festivity and the abandonment of such sport. This identification of the *Maske*'s fictional danger zone with the real-world setting of its performance gives a local habitation and a name to the mysteries and dangers faced by the Lady. It grounds her ordeal in her historical moment, reminding us that the character formed in the *Maske* will be no vapid archetype, but a particular identity fashioned to address, with her newly formed moral freedom and energy, both the immediate dangers and the larger social problems of prerevolutionary England in a period of colonial expansion and internal political and religious conflict.

At the same time that his *mise-en-scène* references geographical and political realities whose immediacy and topicality are atypical of the fantasy worlds of Stuart masques, Milton situates the Lady's liminal ordeal in a thickly overgrown literary forest, whose symbolic implications are at once so obvious and so elusive as to make any explicit explanation of it seem simplistic. It is the "selva oscura . . . selvaggia e aspra e forte" where Dante found himself lost (*Inferno* 1.2, 5), the green world of Shakespeare's pastoral comedies, and the forest of Spenser's enchantment, where prototypes of the Lady, young, ardent, and innocent, have wandered through the dangerous labyrinths of desire, delusion, and desolation. It also prefigures the wilderness of temptation, "the bordering Desert wild, / And with dark shades and rocks environ'd round" into which Milton imagines Jesus wandering, as he recasts the temptation narrative of Luke's gospel (Luke 4:1–14) into his brief epic, *Paradise Regained* (*PR* 1.193–94). This wood in the *Maske* is both familiar and uncanny, a symbolic condensation of the world of fallen nature itself, isolating, tangled, baffling, threatening, teeming with false appearances and unforeseen possibilities. It is a place where the protecting and constraining capacities of culture, its law and order, do not extend, where reason must come to terms with all that it is not, where the human discovers itself as an indeterminate question rather than a complacent assumption. It is the place where, lost to the world, one meets oneself, although, perhaps, in forms one is not prepared to recognize.[4]

In his Prologue, the Attendant Spirit has already foreshadowed the forest's environing character of moral abandonment, passionate excess, physical danger, and spiritual disintegration (36–77). In the anything goes choreography of his antimasque, Comus has already exuberantly displayed both its charms and its dangers (93–144). The Attendant Spirit calls the wood "drear" (37) and "ominous" (61), a "thick shelter of black shades" (63), "The nodding horror of whose shady brows / Threats the forlorn and wand'ring Passenger" (38–39). He renders its imbowering (63) and immuring (521) densities virtually tactile, by his thick alliterative interweaving of fricatives, sibilants, and murmuring nasals in these descriptive passages. Later describing to the two brothers Comus's seat of operations "Within the navel of this hideous Wood, / Immur'd in cypress shades" (520–21), the Attendant Spirit, presenting himself as the familiar shepherd Thyrsis, establishes the labyrinthine and claustrophobic closeness of the place as an enveloping, indeed suffocating, maternal space appropriate to Comus's efforts to "Excel his Mother [Circe] at her mighty art" (63).

Anthropologists remind us that such a setting is not nature in the raw, but nature typified and organized by the cultural imagination to serve particular ritual purposes. Victor Turner's general remarks concerning liminality suitably characterize this unmappable, unpredictable magic space: "*cunicular,* 'being in a tunnel,' would better describe the quality of this phase in many cases, its hidden nature, its sometimes mysterious darkness."[5] Mircea Eliade's account of the symbolism of the forest in traditional initiations suggestively explains both the infernal and the maternal associations of Milton's wilderness: "The bush symbolizes both hell and cosmic night, hence death and virtualities; the cabin [where initiates are secluded and tested, as the Lady is in Comus's "stately Palace"] is the maw of the devouring monster, in which the neophyte is eaten and digested, but it is also a nourishing womb, in which [s]he is engendered anew."[6] So it is that in her removal from the protective moral supports and constraints of family, the familiarities of place and norm which secure identity, the Lady herself becomes a liminal being, ambiguous in her own status, disposition, and potential, and open to the presence of unfamiliar and supernal powers. Victor Turner would call her a "liminar."[7] But "liminar" sounds rather like a diet supplement or a slightly dated model of Chevrolet, so maybe we can think of her as a borderer or wayfarer, a temporary boundary being. As the *Maske* creates its liminal setting by turning the inside of the castle's Great Hall into the outside of the forest, so it blurs the distinction between external and internal nature. The liminal wilderness in which the Lady wanders is as much the undiscovered country of her emerging interior life as it is the perplexed paths of the wood. Left to herself, she is temporarily lost inside herself as she is lost in the forest.

2

Not surprisingly, she is near to panic. It is a panic that she is able so far to keep under control. Comus alerts himself to "the different pace / Of some chaste footing" (145–46) as she approaches, and the iambic steadiness of her entry monologue gives evidence of that "chaste footing" and reflective poise. But the shifting imagery of her self-reflection signals uncertainty. Bereft of the paternally sanctioned escort and familial security supposedly provided by her bodyguard brothers—just kids, we will learn, less capable of handling the forest's labyrinthine mysteries and obscure threats than she proves to be—the Lady projects both bewilderment and hope onto the dark, ambiguous surround of the natural world. What had been "kind hospitable Woods" (187) in her brothers' company have become "the blind mazes of this tangl'd Wood" (181) in their absence. "Grayhooded Ev'n / Like a sad Votarist in Palmer's weed" (188–89) has yielded to "thievish Night" and "single darkness" (195, 204). Interior and exterior merge through sound and visual blackout as she reaches the dancing ground of the antimasque:

> This is the place, as well as I may guess,
> Whence ev'n now the tumult of loud Mirth
> Was rife and perfect in my list'ning ear,
> Yet nought but single darkness do I find.
> What might this be?
>
> (201–5)

The Lady's description of her listening indicates an ambivalent response. "Rife and perfect in my list'ning ear" carries just a hint of curious pleasure in a sound which is as much inside as outside her. "Rife and perfect" are not pejorative adjectives, and "rife" is just a single phoneme, a close of the lips, away from "ripe," one of Comus's signature terms and themes (59, 296, 668–71, 743–44).

This bewildered passage provides a bridge into a rather startling confessional moment, as the Lady shifts into a Shakespearean register to testify to stirrings of hidden voices that seem to well up from her unconscious:

> A thousand fantasies
> Begin to throng into my memory
> Of calling shapes and beck'ning shadows dire,
> And airy tongues that syllable men's names
> On Sands and Shores and desert Wildernesses.
>
> (205–9)

Although the swarming specters to which she alludes here seem to linger in the air as the aural aftereffect of Comus's revels,[8] "fantasies" and "memory" mark them as psychic rather than external in origin. In this moment of panicky disorientation, the "single darkness" seems as much an interior as an external state, for she registers as fantasies, memory, and thoughts a plenitude of spectral images and evocative sounds that resist definition and efface their origins even as they call and beckon, hypnotically and erotically, toward an encounter with the unknown. The strangely mesmerizing intensity of these insistent fantasies registers in the multiplication of nominative plurals, and in reiterative adjective-noun variations that link vague alluring sound with uncertain shape—"calling shapes," "beck'ning shadows," "airy tongues." The brief materialization of "men's names" out of the swarming indefinites of these spectral voices hints at the sort of veiled sexual content that intrigues and terrifies early adolescence.[9] It is as if the Lady is temporarily lost in the labyrinths of a maturing body suddenly alert to newly insistent rumors of desire. We might compare the disoriented Lady's forest experience, faced with a temptation that is also a threat by an uncanny power, to Macbeth's encounter with the "weird sisters" at the outset of the Scottish play. Comus will materialize out of and silhouette the Lady's erotic bewilderment, just as the "weird sisters" both plant and dramatically objectify the thoughts of regicide and usurpation that come to possess Macbeth.

The Lady has been drawn, strangely, to what she fears. She seeks out the bacchanalian scene which her own chaste footing has just interrupted and dispelled:

> This way the noise was, if mine ear be true,
> My best guide now; methought it was the sound
> Of Riot and ill-manag'd Merriment,
> Such as the jocund Flute or gamesome Pipe
> Stirs up among the loose unletter'd Hinds,
> When for their teeming Flocks and granges full
> In wanton dance they praise the bounteous *Pan*,
> And thank the gods amiss. I should be loath

> To meet the rudeness and swill'd insolence
> Of such late Wassailers; yet O where else
> Shall I inform my unacquainted feet
> In the blind mazes of this tangl'd Wood?
>
> (170–81)

The Lady's motivation may be more complex here than it first appears. She is a good girl in a bad spot. She has taken a reluctant decision that involves some calculation of risk as well as some fascination in the risk. It makes some sense to seek out human protection when lost and alone in a forest dense with terrors real and imagined. Yet the signs of human activity that she describes are fraught with potential danger, suspended between the crudely civilized and the savage, between harvest thanksgiving and riotous indulgence, Michaelmas revelries running out of hand. She "*should* be loath" to seek out such a party, but is she? An orgy in progress doesn't seem to be the most promising setting in which to look for protective companionship and guidance. The Lady seems to understand this risk. Although she expresses well-bred contempt for "the rudeness and swill'd insolence / Of such late Wassailers" (178–79), it does not altogether muffle a guarded fascination about the kinds of unlettered and unfettered pleasures they might be enjoying, the kinds of pleasures from which her privileged household has so far sheltered her. "Jocund Flute" and "gamesome Pipe" seem to stir in her a certain kind of pleasurable curiosity, and in imagining the overflowing fecundity of the harvest, the implicit easy sexuality of "loose unletter'd Hinds," she momentarily savors a this-worldly richness more closely attuned to the erotic freedom, festive dynamism, and natural bounty of Comus's world view than to the Orphic severity of the Attendant Spirit's.

I am not trying to indulge in a nudge and a wink at the Lady's straight-faced struggle to sustain moral seriousness in the face of erotic self-discovery. That would modernize—and cheapen—the complex peril, the delicacy, the psychological realism, and the ritual logic of her situation.[10] To notice the obscure, disorienting erotic elements in her initial self-presentation is not to diminish the Lady's integrity, but to recognize that her initiation participates, like other puberty rites, in what Eliade describes as "the revelation of sexuality."[11] The cultural deployment, sublimation, and domestication of the "natural" mystery of sexuality is one of the central functions of such rites. The task can only be accomplished by the ritual exposure of the initiate to the compelling and polymorphous power of sexuality. Such exposure requires provisional and temporary suspension of the culturally determined constraints which protect and direct us as sexual and social beings. The liminal space which paradoxically allows for a ritually ordered suspension of such restraints is, as Turner typifies it,

> essentially ambiguous, unsettled, and unsettling, . . . betwixt and between the categories of ordinary social life. Symbols and metaphors found in abundance in liminality represent various dangerous ambiguities of this ritual stage, since the classifications on which order normally depends are annulled or obscured—other symbols designate temporary antinomic liberation from behavioral norms and cognitive rules. This aspect of danger requiring control is reflected in the paradox that in liminality extreme authority of elders over juniors often coexists with scenes and episodes indicative of the utmost behavioral freedom and speculative license.[12]

Comus's midnight playground is certainly one of "antinomic liberation from behavioral norms and cognitive rules," and it at least aspires to "utmost behavioral freedom and speculative license." In this instance, the liminal space of the *Maske* requires that the Lady step forward from the fugitive and cloistered virtue, unexercised and unbreathed (*Areopagitica,* 728), of her childhood. Her virtue must be tested in order to be proved, to be refined, to be strengthened, to be claimed as her own.

Milton tells us in *Areopagitica* that trial of the sort which purifies us is "by what is contrary" (*Areopagitica,* 728). He indicates that the "contrary" materializes not only in threats and temptations from the world without us, but in the inward motions of heart, will, and mind, with which external threats and temptations often correspond. Vice and virtue are twins to one another, fashioned of the same libidinal stuff: "Wherefore did [God] create passions within us, pleasures round about us, but that these rightly tempered are the very ingredients of virtue?" (*Areopagitica,* 733). An early index of the Lady's virtue in formation appears in the very midst of her confused attraction to and revulsion from the unseen revelry of the antimasque. She gives the revellers the benefit of her doubts, attributing their "ill-manag'd Merriment" to misguided devotion—"thanking the Gods amiss" (177)—rather than to depraved self-indulgence. This, it turns out, is wishful thinking on her part. It reveals the naive and essentially optimistic character of her as yet unchallenged chastity. But it also hints that her chastity is already at work, shaping both the uncertain occasion and her ambivalent response to it as an obscure opportunity for divine service and praise. Even in the midst of discovering feelings she did not know that she had, she is tempering them into optimistic and ethically serviceable shape.

In an act of intellectual discipline that provides a brief prologue to the larger temptation plot of the masque, the Lady demonstrates how to temper potential passions and pleasures into the substance of virtue. Compared to the tragic soliloquies of Shakespeare, in which the unthinkable compels its own relentless exploratory self-expression, Milton provides his initiate a meditative self-control that resists and halts the disturbing momentum of her thronging fantasies:

> These thoughts may startle well, but not astound
> The virtuous mind, that ever walks attended
> By a strong siding champion Conscience.
> O welcome pure-ey'd Faith, white-handed Hope,
> Thou hov'ring Angel girt with golden wings,
> And thou unblemish'd form of Chastity,
> I see ye visibly, and now believe
> That he, the Supreme good, t' whom all things ill
> Are but as slavish officers of vengeance,
> Would send a glist'ring Guardian, if need were,
> To keep my life and honor unassail'd.
>
> (210–19)

What appears initially to be the conventional piety of this private, moral pep talk makes it seem flat and repressed in comparison to the tormented wanderings, uncertainties, and desperate commitments of the isolated heroes of Shakespeare and other Jacobean playwrights. We might say that her turn here seems dramatically weak, because she falls back on a set of dogmatic abstractions that she has been instructed to believe.[13] But we might on the contrary say that her turn here is dramatically exciting, because she discovers at a moment when it actually matters that what she has been instructed to believe is true and capable of creative adaptation to critical moments of self-recognition. Compare the self-correction of the Lady's speech to the syntax-warping lure of the transgressive in Macbeth's fantasies of regicide (1.7.1–28, 2.1.33–61), or the self-bewildering momentum of despair for its own sake in Hamlet's brilliant ramblings (1.2.129–59, 3.1.56–87). Imagine Hamlet or Macbeth or Othello halting a train of association midcourse by saying, "no, I'm not going to follow that line of thinking; there are better ways to look at this."

Milton does not typically allow for the irresistible momentum of the unconscious, as Shakespeare does. He primarily trusts the soliloquy when, in *Comus* as in *Paradise Regained* (*PR* 1.196–292, 2.66–104), it can serve his character as a reason-directed instrument for ethical reflection and principled self-analysis.[14] The Lady here, as the first of his great characters, subjects the momentum of the stricken self-conscious Shakespearean subject to the deliberative poise of rational conscience and the imaginative resources that form it and upon which it depends. The strength of the Lady's resolve, which will fortify her and defend her in the encounter with Comus, gathers itself out of the recognition of and resistance to her own potentially tragic ambivalences and insecurities. Her strength, in fact, sublimates itself out of its own potential vulnerability. The energies that ultimately subvert and dissolve the coherence of the Shakespearean tragic subject become the constructive source of Miltonic self-fashioning.

It is not that Milton, in his staging of the Lady's emerging subjectivity, provides a regressive holding action or resistance against the impetus of character formation dramatized so forcefully by Shakespeare. Rather, he scripts a different mode of character formation that acknowledges interiority and the complex pressures on the emerging self, while maintaining that rational and ethical self-determination are distinct authorizing prospects and projects rather than discursive illusions. The Lady is not a throwback to an earlier mode of characterization than Macbeth or Hamlet, Othello or the Duchess of Malfi. She faces dilemmas similar to theirs, which arise from the prospect of decision making in a world where certainty is acutely problematic. She is just ethically stronger and more self-consistent than Shakespeare's tragic heroes and other heroes of the Jacobean stage, and her strength comes from her conviction, what we might call her certainty principle, which authorizes itself through speaking itself. She powerfully and paradoxically discovers her chastity and constitutes herself on its basis in the moment of crisis and vulnerability, even as Macbeth's self-consuming ambition and Hamlet's self-doubt discover and constitute and reiterate themselves in crisis.

Looking more closely at the surprising turn in the Lady's thought, we can see how a rigorous meditative discipline reorients the Lady in the first stage of her liminal ordeal. Conscience, Faith, Hope, and Chastity are simply rendered in clear moral and pictorial outline, as if the Lady were actually calling to mind images from emblem books and allegorical paintings she has studied, as a way to fortify her "virtuous mind" (211) against the threatening sounds and tempting thoughts that have startled her. This constellation of personified Christian virtues powerfully counterpoints and shields the Lady against the dark pagan trinity of goddesses whom Comus has invoked in his orgiastic rite: the Venus of profane love, Cottyto, and Hecate (124, 129, 135). The commonplaces of the Lady's moral education take on existential importance for her as a way of ordering her thought and action in a newly unstable and far more complicated world than she had known in the safe confines of her father's house. As she reiterates these newly necessary and newly understood topics, she not only internalizes them as objects of meditation, she visualizes them—"I see ye visibly"—as characters in the moral landscape of the liminal.[15]

As the climax of the Lady's moral epiphany, Chastity is mysteriously and suggestively indeterminate, pure "unblemish'd form," the one cardinal virtue which the Lady beholds without an emblematic attribute. This visionary detail, or absence of detail, is suggestive in several ways. It demonstrates the Platonic intensity with which Milton links chastity to the heroic and visionary profession of poetry.[16] Chastity's "unblemish'd form" strikes the first note of a distinctly supersensual poetic by which the Lady will eventually defend herself and decisively repudiate her ritual adversary Comus (779–806).[17] An invariable theme in Milton's own self-assessments, chastity displays reverence and gratitude to God for the gift of the body, as well as the deepest form of self-respect. It sets men and women in just and equitable relation to one another and prepares the soul for the apprehension and discernment of intelligible forms and religious mysteries. A pure outline in the Lady's apprehension of it, Chastity awaits its sensible manifestation in the *Maske,* but of course the definition of chastity and the revelation of its power are to be the central theme of the *Maske.* The Lady's signature virtue, its more removed mysteries are already ineffably intelligible to her alone. But its form will be finally and fully manifest to the *Maske*'s spectators in her own embodiment of it at the time of her homecoming. An incarnational poet committed to ethical realism, Milton would not have us idolize virtues abstracted from the human achievement and practice of them. By the end of the *Maske,* we need look in no emblem book for a rudimentary symbol of chastity; the Lady has become its living avatar.

Her announcement of this epiphany in a site which only a dozen lines before she had characterized as "single darkness" (204) marks her own access to a prophetic mode of vision. The *Maske*'s field of vision becomes enormously complicated at this point. Spectators are obliged to acknowledge the baffling coincidence of several kinds of seeing, including one in which they can only participate by a faith and intuition responsive to and directed by the Lady's. Comus had projected, with his "Magic dust," his carnivalesque mastery of the realm of spectacle: "Thus I hurl / My dazzling Spells into the spongy air, / Of power to cheat the eye with blear illusion, / And give it false presentments" (153–56). But in bragging in public of the tricks of his trade, he permits the *Maske*'s audience to see through them. Although he exercises a trickster's manipulation of the sights of the phenomenal world, which is, in the *Maske,* the theatrical world, the *Maske*'s informed spectators control a perspective outside that world and so can see through his tricks, at least the visual ones. But for the Lady, Comus's tricks are, at least initially, her sensory facts.[18] As a character confined to the *Maske*'s liminal zone, the Lady has to go it on her own, taking its appearances at least initially for her realities, using her eyes to get around, although, as a true Protestant, subjecting their sensible evidences to her ear, "My best guide now" (171).

But when she announces that she can see her tutelary virtues "visibly," she sees more than the staging of the *Maske* can reveal to the audience and thus more than the senses by themselves can register. Conscience, Faith, Hope, and Chastity process before her in a pure masque of a higher order of intelligibility. This invisible masque within the *Maske,* to which she testifies, requires no aristocratic personifiers. It occurs in a theater of moral imagination that spectators have already been prepared to take on faith, because of the reliable testimony they received about it in the Prologue by its messenger, the Attendant Spirit. The Lady, newly secured in a moral and intelligible order that transcends and contradicts the evidence of her senses, now confidently intuits what the audience has already been assured of: that a heaven-sent "glist'ring Guardian" will assist her "if need were / To keep my life and honor unassail'd" (219–20). The *Maske*'s staging provides immediate and startling confirmation of her intuition:

> Was I deceiv'd, or did a sable cloud
> Turn forth her silver lining on the night?
> I did not err, there does a sable cloud
> Turn forth her silver lining on the night,
> And casts a gleam over this tufted Grove.
>
> (221–25)

This moment coordinates the Lady's internalized supersensible perception with the visual field of the playing space, the viewless theater of her moral imagination with the theatrical world of representation over which Comus has claimed dominion. Light: voice: light: voice: doublings are doubled here. In a call and response between providentially ordered nature and providentially awakened imagination, a light is unmuffled and flashes twice from the wings or from overhead, and the Lady reiterates her sense of its salvific promise, first as a startled question (221–22) and then as an affirmation (223–25). That this theatrical moment advertises itself as pure special effect, the most elementary of stage tricks, does not diminish or ironize its magic: the Lady discovers that the structure of the represented world answers to her vision of faith. That this light is visible to the audience of her ordeal serves to realign its field of vision with hers or at least to convince it of the invisible realities to which she testifies. Her "new enliv'n'd spirits" (228) are new enlightened spirits, prepared to turn hopefully from the inward self-confrontation and discovery of her now completed soliloquy, toward the world without, confident now in the prospect of renewed fellowship. The fellowship of perception between Lady and audience sealed by the stage light's epiphany is the first evidence of that moral and imaginative solidarity: along with the Lady, her spectators are prepared for more wonders than may meet the eye.

The soliloquy's dramatization of the swift emergence of forceful creative character, improvising her sense of who she is and what she stands for from a situation of sudden distress, seems to be a far cry from the dislocations and dispossessions of traditional rites of passage, which typically work to conform the initiate's character to social norms rather than to individuate her. The separation and early sequences of the liminal phase in such rites are composed so as to render the initiates passive and "structurally invisible," to empty them of social status and attributes, so that their emergent adult characters can be fashioned in socially appropriate and time-honored patterns of knowledge, attitude, and behavior: "The passivity of neophytes to their instructors, their malleability, which is increased by submission to ordeal, their reduction to a uniform condition, are signs of the process whereby they are ground down to be fashioned anew and endowed with additional powers to cope with their new station in life."[19] A related observation could be made of this soliloquy's distance from the static speeches of Stuart court masques, which provide the generic surface form for Milton even as the logic of initiation provides its deep cultural structure. The ideological and allegorical imperatives of conventional court masque, even in the hands of its lyric and didactic master, Ben Jonson, rule out the deployment of writing codes which fashion credible character psychology.

Milton, however, sensing the elasticity and the progressive possibilities of the masque as form, not only transforms its cultural function but its modes of representation. He does so by developing his central character in the *Maske,* in her introductory self-presentation, by means of the writing strategies developed to index subjectivity in the earlier Stuart drama. Insofar as the Lady registers for the *Maske*'s public the shifting texture of her private thoughts—her perceptions, her anxieties, her hesitations, her confusions, her aspirations, her intuitions, her longing, her resolve—she is the literary godchild of the tragic Hamlet, Ophelia, Macbeth, the Duchess of Malfi. If the Lady's ethical rigor differentiates her from such tragic characters trapped in the undertow of their own desires, her self-conscious inwardness marks her kinship with them.

In turn, we could say that the psychological complexity and independent decision-making capability displayed by the Lady are entirely suited to the demands of the culture for which Milton has scripted her initiation. That is to say, ethically motivated individuation is the appropriate socializing process for Milton's *Maske.* Although the *Maske,* like traditional rites of passage, ritually inculcates in its Lady the wisdom appropriate to her status, class, and sex, the wisdom she acquires is different from that of traditional societies; it is the energizing wisdom of dynamic and iconoclastic Puritanism. If she is to be an authentic practitioner of this wisdom, she cannot be a passive receiver of it. She must decide for herself what to do about the crisis of the moment. Even in this, her first verbal self-representation, she positions herself in a critical and reflective relation to urgings and uncertainties within and to threats from without, to the demands of the social roles which she can henceforth be expected to play, and to the values out of which she will fashion her sense of civic selfhood. If the kind of adult person which this unique but exemplary rite of passage is determined to fashion is the independent, reflective, resourceful, constant, and conscientious moral agent of ethical Puritanism, the Lady's soliloquy wastes no time in beginning the task of character formation.

3

The Lady's creative response to the tragic potential of her own soliloquy prefigures the larger patterns of resolution of the *Maske* itself. As a formative rite, the *Maske* concerns itself with spiritual instruction and cultural formation more than with the extreme psychological explorations, no matter how destructive and terrifying, of

Jacobean tragedy. But the larger pattern of the *Maske,* like the Lady's soliloquy, shapes itself out of a resistance to and reformation of the spirit of tragedy. Since tragedy is not raw experience, but experience distilled and mediated by literary and dramatic texts, the liminal space in which the Lady confronts the challenge and the future of her desire is a textual space as much as it is a ritual space. Indeed, in the Renaissance, reading itself becomes a type of ritual. So the Lady's confrontation with Comus in the *Maske* occurs not only at a cultural and psychosexual threshold, but at a textual threshold as well. Her liminal agon is, like Jesus' contention with Satan in *Paradise Regained,* a battle of the books. The Lady discovers herself at the threshold where classical narratives of mythological violence against women and ensuing pathos are newly enacted and recouped into moral energy and order. In fact she *is* the threshold. She becomes the liminal figure through whom that recuperation freshly takes place. Both critic and poet, she rewrites tragic catastrophe into the *Maske*'s cosmos-transforming harmonics. In her ritual ordeal, she opens the dark text of Ovid's *Metamorphoses* in particular and relives its stories of pity and fear, especially of feminine anguish, in order to reinterpret and translate them into a higher order of poetic and ethical possibility than the tradition of tragic melodrama and conventional moral recuperations of it allowed for.[20]

To observe how the Lady opens the text of tragedy and opens herself to that text in order to translate it into a new key, we need to trace her passage from the disciplined self-reckoning of her soliloquy to the radiant sublimation of the lyric song to Echo that issues from it. Alone in the dark wood, deprived of the protections as well as the constraints of her father's household, the Lady discovers not only forest fear but also the pressure and anxiety of a newly awakened, obscurely felt desire. Her soliloquy sublimates this desire into the radiant form of chastity, beheld visibly by the Lady and confirmed by the poetic faith of her audience. It is in the spirit of imaginatively enlivened hope for fellowship, the social form of chastity, that she offers up her song to Echo. Giving voice to this hope, and given voice by this hope, she makes of it a song that consummates the moral recovery and poetic aspirations already set in motion by the visionary intimations of the soliloquy:

> *Sweet Echo, sweetest Nymph that liv'st unseen*
> *Within thy airy shell*
> *By slow Meander's margent green,*
> *And in the violet-embroider'd vale*

> *Where the love-lorn Nightingale*
> *Nightly to thee her sad Song mourneth well.*
>
> *Canst thou not tell me of a gentle Pair*
> *That likest thy Narcissus are?*
> *O if thou have*
> *Hid them in some flow'ry Cave,*
> *Tell me but where,*
> *Sweet Queen of Parley, Daughter of the Sphere,*
> *So mayst thou be translated to the skies,*
> *And give resounding grace to all Heav'n's Harmonies.*
>
> (230–43)

The associative circuits opened by this invocation resonate with the muffled dangers of Comus's night world. The beautiful, wistful, fragile song is an echo chamber of sexual confusion, tragedy, and transgression that oddly reiterates the Lady's isolated condition and her longing to be restored to the presence of her brothers. It is, in effect, the Lady's lyric farewell to childhood, a tender parting from the luxurious intimacies and enclosures of a protective family romance, and a preparation for more solitary, uncertain, and arduous, yet more sublime adventures of the spirit. "In its aspiration, elocution, awareness of cosmic resonances, appeal for spiritual ratification and rewarded vision, the Lady's song to Echo is a paradigm of the poet's creative act."[21] More specifically, it exemplifies the poet's active reception and "translation" of literary types and figures for the sake of chaste and heroic self-fashioning.

Themselves victims of submersion in self-absorbing mirages, Echo and Narcissus seem at first glance hardly the appropriate figures to appeal to for assistance in escaping from the Imaginary night world of Comus. In the *Metamorphoses,* Echo is the nymph whose garrulous distraction of Juno from Jove's philanderings leads Juno to curse her with the loss of voice. All that is left to Echo is the repetition of the tail end of what she hears. In love with Narcissus, Echo's incapacity to respond to him with anything but a reflection of his own words renders her imperceptible to him, which seals the doom of both. Deep in the Echo myth is a jealous, dangerous goddess akin to Hecate, Cotytto, and Circe herself, who fill Comus's pantheon (128–37, 252–60). Cursed by the goddess, dispossessed of an originating, self-generating voice, wasted by a love that she cannot express, at a loss for a substantial body image, Echo dies in effect of anorexia nervosa, withering into the ghostly voice of pure reflectivity.[22] Narcissus, subsequently absorbed in his own reflection, is locked into a self-mirroring dynamic of desire that feeds on itself. Narcissus ultimately withers away in his hermetic isolation from the sustenance of otherness.

The fates of Echo and Narcissus are uncannily interinanimated and incomplete without each other. In his commentary on the episodes, Milton's contemporary, the mythographer and poet George Sandys, notices the twinned *contrapasso* of their fates, both in the allegory of moral consequence and in figurative representation: "Well therefore was vaine-glory fained to affect selfe-love; who rejected, converts into a sound; that is, into nothing. . . . The image of the voice so often rendred, is as that of the face reflected from one glasse to another; melting by degrees, and every reflection more weake and shady then the former."[23] Echoism appears to be an inverted, feminized narcissism. For Echo there is no self left; for Narcissus there is nothing but the self. For Echo there is disappearance into the invisible, insubstantial world of sound; for Narcissus there is captivity in the evanescent seeming-fullness of image. Both lovers are ironic victims of the problems implicit in the Imaginary register which, in the *Maske,* Comus stakes out as his territory. Lost in the mirror play of phantom desire, they are consumed by that desire, whose tantalizing objects are both ungraspable and inescapable and whose terminus can only be death.[24]

For all its beauty, then, the Lady's invocation gestures toward a myth of self-discovery that appears fatally regressive.[25] The Lady expresses an understandable longing for the familiar, for what Blake would call the unorganized innocence of childhood. Blake would expand the secret gardens of the Lady's song into the precious looking-glass world of the "Vales of Har," the timid Thel's retreat from the ardors and terrors of experience into a perpetual childhood where she must languish and die, perhaps without pain but also without fulfillment.[26] Milton's Lady tries to redesign the "blind mazes of this tangl'd Wood" (181) into a shimmering sanctuary like the Vales of Har, a series of protective enclosures: Echo's "airy shell," the Nightingale's "violet-embroider'd vale," the "flow'ry Cave" where she hopes her brothers might be kept safe. Comforting as they are, these *loci amoeni,* as containing spaces of sensual overfulness, evoke the narcotic womb-world of Comus's mother Circe. The "flow'ry Cave" is a cradle space for the Lady's brothers, who are imagined as innocents no more different from one another than Narcissus is from his reflection. The Lady merges invisibly into this identity-diffusing fantasy as well, for she is imagining for her brothers a protection that she would like for herself. Identifying with Echo, the Lady herself would be content with the protection of invisibility. Invisibility means passively dwelling as a vocal confirmation of the substantial existence and careers of others. This is a longing for the safety of a typical girl's role: a self-effacing sponsorship of the identities and careers of the significant male others.

Yet the act of singing paradoxically accomplishes the Lady's differentiation from and "translation" of Echo. In singing to Echo, the Lady addresses and transcends her own nascent and potentially tragic self-recognition. She "translates" her potential lovelorn alienation, vulnerability, and longing for the securities of a now lost protected childhood into a maturing imaginative resource. Although her lyric does not immediately solve her crisis or locate her brothers, it transcends that crisis. The Echo whom she apotheosizes in the final lines of the poem is not the lost, lovelorn invisible girl of Ovid, nor is the Lady herself the human incarnation and instance of Echo's fragile pathos. Like the trinity of feminized virtues—Faith, Hope, and Chastity—whom the Lady has just announced she can "see visibly" (216), Echo personifies a newly discovered imaginative and moral resource that gains its strength from its consonance with the natural law of a providentially ordered world.

How does an Echo work? As a physical phenomenon, it depends upon an active voice, a solid world beyond the self to reflect that voice, and an ear attuned to its reception. To call out for Echo is to trust in the stability and responsiveness of the sonic structure of the world where the Lady finds herself, like Ovid's Echo herself, shut off from sight. She hopes that her song will "awake the courteous Echo / To give me answer from her mossy Couch" (275–76). The sonic reverberation of her song announces her position and sounds out her bearings in a world where navigation by sight is perilous. She hopes both to locate herself and to awake a sympathetic answer from the world. The immediate effect appears ironic. Her voice does not echo back to her. Comus materializes out of the "single darkness" (204) to answer her distress cry, and she is unable to penetrate his disguise as he leads her into greater danger and isolation. Yet the irony is providential, for Comus gives a local habitation and a name, a determinate shape, and ultimately a voice to the "thousand fantasies" (205) that have besieged the Lady. In this sense he provides a dramatic echo to her fears as well as, through the trial to come, a challenging confirmation of her independent position in the world.[27] The Echo she awakes reverberates that confirmation through successive rings of apprehension, beyond the listening ears of Comus, to the Attendant Spirit, who communicates it to the brothers, who in turn, like Narcissus, are so close to their sister that they are not capable of apprehending her otherness, to Sabrina, and of course to the *Maske*'s audience. As C. L. Barber puts it, "The act of singing is an exercise of the Lady's integrity; she is internally related, beyond the darkness, to what she looks to and realizes in the song."[28]

How does an Echo work? As a literary device, it operates through selective repetition of a previous statement. The Echo who dies to herself survives only in the faint repetition of another voice, yet what survives as original and distinctive other in her reveals itself through the way in which the echoing statement ironically draws out and highlights a secret or latent message in the already spoken. In various seventeenth-century plays upon the literary convention of echoing, this principle of Echo can be deployed in several emphatic ways to intensify pathos, fatality, or unforeseen providential possibility.[29] Since no audible echo issues from the labyrinth of darkness in response to the Lady's song, Milton seems to refrain from the literal artfulness of the conventional echo song in order to deploy Echo as a dramatic and metaphysical principle in the *Maske*. Yet the Lady's song, with its flexible double stanza and rich internal resonances, provides an echo of itself. John Hollander notes that "the song is in some measure a hymn in praise of music itself": "It addresses itself to its own resonating effects (its echoes, here personified as the nymph Echo herself, not only a favorite pastoral figure but a favorite metaphor for the relationship of actual human music to the heavenly harmony)."[30] In this respect, the song does reiterate its classical precedents, yet in the act of selective reiteration it evokes and inscribes saving possibilities buried in the original tale of pathos. Within the lyric itself, the Lady calls this act of transforming reiteration "translation."

A key word for the whole *Maske,* "translate" is a loaded word. Among the meanings of "translate" available to Milton in the composition of the *Maske,* the primary one is religious, specifically biblical: "To carry or convey to heaven without death" (*OED* I.1.b), as the Old Testament figure Enoch was carried up in a cloud "to walk with God / High in Salvation and the Climes of bliss, / Exempt from Death" (*PL* 11.708–10; Genesis 5.21–24). The other important meaning of "translate" upon which the Lady plays is familiar enough to us to obscure its now obsolete religious significance: "To turn from one language into another" (II.2). Also available, and operative in the Lady's lyric deployment of the term: "II.2.c. To use in a metaphor or transferred sense. . . . 3. To interpret, explain; also, to express one thing in terms of another. . . . III.4. To change in form, appearance, or substance; to transmute; to transform, alter. . . . 6. To transport with the strength of some feeling; to enrapture, entrance." "Translate" is a verbal complex whose multiple associations enrich rather than restrict one another. Derived from the past participle of the Latin verb "transferre," "to carry across," its crucial transference is between ontological and verbal change. "Translation" is a type of death-defying metamorphosis that Comus and Circe cannot practice. It is simultaneously a religious mystery and a poetic invention, a change from mortal to immortal substance without the natural intervention of death, intimated and enacted through poetic change.[31]

Angus Fletcher remarks of *Comus* in general, "Its verbal echoing is a radical process, a going to the bottom of language. By recollecting so many poets dead and gone, Milton revives their voices and their ghostly persons."[32] The Lady personalizes and particularizes this revivifying activity. What the Lady discovers in the act of singing is the salvific power of singing itself. Poetic "translation" prefigures and embodies spiritual "translation" by its denial of death. Metaphor itself and the changes of substance it accomplishes are a providential and rapture-giving sign of our hope for immortality, for an enduring and glorious life "after this mortal change" (11).

Courteously, and with spiritual humility, the Lady offers "translation" to Echo in the optative bestowal of blessing, not ultimately hers but Heaven's to give: "So mayst thou be translated to the skies, / And give resounding grace to all Heav'n's Harmonies" (242–43). The grace note of the passage, as Milton revised it in the published version of the text, combined with the specific biblical application of "translated," makes this lyric moment as explicitly Christian in its implications as the *Maske* will get. Yet the playing version of the lyric, which Alice Egerton actually sang in the 1634 performance, is not a weaker line, or a diminished form of the lyric's conclusion, only an alternative version of the Miltonic sublime: "So mayst thou be translated to the skies, / And hold a counterpoint to all Heav'n's Harmonies." Both "counterpoint" and "grace" operate as musical notations with spiritual implications. "Counterpoint" adds one melody to another by way of accompaniment; "grace" carries the musical meaning of resonant ornamentation or embellishment.[33]

In each case Echo's "translation" enriches both terrestrial and celestial harmonies. If we consider John Hollander's observation, noted above, that Echo is "not only a favorite pastoral figure but a favorite metaphor for the relation of actual human music to the heavenly harmony," we might say that Echo's counterpointing or her provision of a grace note to the heavenly music makes it sensible and audible. She mediates the otherwise "unexpressive notes" of heaven to our human ears.[34] In turn, she fulfills and completes, humanizes, and feminizes the heavenly consort. We could imagine that the harmonies of that austere patriarchal assembly envisioned by the Attendant Spirit in the Prologue of the *Maske* (1–5) would be severe and solemn. The resounding grace of Echo's accompaniment, if it carries a vocal and musical sensibility like the Lady's, would brighten, sweeten, vary, and modulate that "unexpressive" music.

The song's delicate lyric sweetness and elegant courtesies tend to veil its imaginative, even prophetic, implications. The Lady "translates" Echo in this moment of prophetic generosity, as the "uncouth swain" of "Lycidas" will "translate" his missing shepherd-friend:

> So *Lycidas,* sunk low, but mounted high
> Through the dear might of him that walk'd the waves,
> Where other groves, and other streams along,
> With *Nectar* pure his oozy Locks he laves,
> And hears the unexpressive nuptial Song,
> In the blest Kingdoms meek of joy and love. . . .
> Now *Lycidas,* the Shepherds weep no more;
> Henceforth thou art the Genius of the shore,
> In thy large recompense, and shalt be good
> To all that wander in that perilous flood.
>
> (172–77, 182–85)

In the Lady's magnanimous imagination of her, Echo becomes a tutelary and protective spirit for all that wander in the perilous wood. "Sweet Queen of Parley," she becomes the Lady's muse, a translated personification of the Lady's own "new enliv'n'd" (228) lyric and oracular power, an ego ideal who inspires imaginative and moral confidence for the newly energized poet-wayfarer. Echo is "translated" from the tragic melodrama of Ovid's tale to the spiritual sublimity of Enoch and other enraptured biblical heroes, from pathetic isolation to vibrant participation in cosmic harmonies, from classical mythology to Christian salvation history. As a supernatural guardian like Lycidas, she secures passage for steadfast wayfarers through the impenetrable forests of this pendant world, a figure of providential imagination in whom all the resources of literary and mythological tradition are put to the service of the redemption of experience. The redeemed fate of Echo itself will be echoed in turn in the miraculous "translation" of Sabrina, another maiden made deathless by poets' "translation" of her tale (824–47), and it prefigures the adventure of the Lady herself, whose ultimate destination will be remythologized in the triumphant figure of Psyche "sweet entranc't," embraced by "Celestial Cupid . . . After her wand'ring labors long" (1004–6).[35] For what is a rite of passage such as Milton's *Maske,* if not a "translation" of a girl into a woman? And what is the final joy of human desiring in biblically formed culture if not the mystical embrace of God?

4

The "translation" of Echo rather than the discovery of the Lady's brothers constitutes the central event of the lyric, but the lyric supplements and enriches this event by other echoings of precursor texts, each of which contains a pivotal moment of "translation." The Lady's reference to the lovelorn nightingale evokes an Ovidian narrative of sexual danger and revenge that prefigures her own vulnerability and captivity.[36] Like Ovid's Philomela, the Lady will find her virginity threatened by a false escort who gains her trust by promising safe swift passage to a family reunion. Reviewing the violent episode from the *Metamorphoses* will provide a stronger sense of the tragic pressure on the Lady's allusion, and on the Attendant Spirit's later evocation of it when he laments for the Lady as "poor hapless Nightingale. . . . How sweet thou sing'st, how near the deadly snare!" (566–67). In Ovid's rendering, the Thracian King Tereus gains as his bride Procne, the daughter of Pandion, for relieving a hostile siege of Athens. It is a marriage of ill omen:

> This, nor *Juno* blest;
> Nor *Hymen,* nor the Graces grac't that feast.
> The snake-haird furies held the sputtering light
> From funeralls snatcht, and made the bed that Night.
> (OME, 277)

A boy child, Itys, is conceived under these fatal signs. Several years pass. With Procne clamoring for a visit from her sister, Tereus goes as emissary to promise Philomela safe escort from her father's palace to Procne. Inflamed with lust, Tereus detours into a forest, where he sequesters Philomela in a lodge and rapes her. Philomela refuses passive victimization, and cries out,

> Thou shalt not scape due vengeance. Sense of shame
> I will abandon; and thy crime proclaime:

> To men, if free; if not, my voice shall breake
> Through these thick walls, and teach the woods to speake:
> Hard rockes resolve to ruth. Let heaven this heare;
> And Heaven-thron'd Gods: if there be any there!
>
> (*OME*, 280)

And so Tereus cuts her tongue out to prevent her from broadcasting her violation. Not to be silenced, Philomela weaves the tragic story into a tapestry that she smuggles to Procne. In a bacchic rage and under the veil of bacchanalian revels, Procne releases her sister and plots a revenge in kind. In "cruell joy" the two women murder the child Itys, and Procne serves him as a dinner feast to Tereus. When the king calls for his son, Philomela rushes from the wings and hurls the head of Itys in the face of his father. Tereus in his fury chases the sisters until they are all transformed into birds: Philomela into the nightingale, Procne into the swallow, Tereus into the lapwing.

This is a horror story of obscene intensities, "the darkest side of Ovid's poem, that realm where metamorphosis is fused with the perversions of love and family relations as well as with abominations that range from exogamy to cannibalism."[37] Philomela's story forcefully counterpoints that of Echo. Philomela, like Echo, loses the power to speak for herself. Unlike Echo, who continues to speak but only as a vocal reflection of others, Philomela is forced into silence, doubly removed from a world that could answer to her woe. Unlike Echo, Philomela resists passivity. Her tongue severed, she discovers other, more horrifying modes of symbolic communication: the gruesome tapestry, the head of Itys.[38] In both tales desire dangerously blurs the boundaries between self and other, but whereas one tale dies out into haunted pastoral stillness, the other erupts into a nightmare of violence. Echo and Narcissus both become absorbed *in* the love object, so immersed in the unattainable image of desire as to die out into insubstantial shadows. Philomela, Procne, and Tereus become tangled in a terrifying scenario of explosively contagious violence *against* the love object. The logic of this scenario requires a sacrifice, and so at its climax a mother murders her own child and a father devours him. Whereas Echo and Narcissus are figuratively consumed by desire, Tereus literally feeds on what he loves.

George Sandys diagnoses the cycle of erotic contagion as a psychic disorder driven by passionate excess, characteristic of Tereus's race, the Thracians, "a furious and barbarous people" devoted to a deadly combination of celestial influences, Venus and Mars:

> For over-violent love is little lesse then madnesse: which imboldens the frantick lover to rush on whatsoever is forbidden and horrid: one wicked

deed begetting another; who violates first his faith and her honour; and then cuts out her tongue to conceale his offence, with as great an impiety. But flagitious crimes cannot long ly hid. All knowne to *Progne,* shee bends her thoughts on a strange revenge; and through her owne bowells strikes at her husband. So cruell is the rage of an injured woman. (*OME,* 301–2)

"To rush on whatsoever is forbidden and horrid": the prohibited becomes the most desirable. As with Echo and Narcissus, Tereus, Philomela, and Procne become lost in the erotic doublings and repetitions of an Imaginary process ungoverned by, even exacerbated by, Symbolic constraints. The tale unfolds as an accelerating series of Imaginary identifications and mergers that precipitate violent transgression. Generated and inhibited by intense family ties, the Imaginary identifications proliferate, in their turn disintegrating those ties and the discrete identities they confer and secure.

Tereus fantasizes himself in Pandion's place when he watches Philomela's seductive pleading with her father. Thoughts of a doubly incestuous transgression, violating the sister of his wife and replacing the father as the object of the daughter's devotions, stir up his "wilde desire": "Her kisses and imbraces [of her father] heat his blood: / And all afford his fire and fury food" (*OME,* 278). After her rape, Philomela laments the catastrophe produced by Tereus's brutality in terms of the breakdown of familial roles and identities:

> O what a wild confusion hast thou bred!
> I, an adultresse to my sisters bed;
> Thou, husband to us both; my only hate;
> And to expect a miserable fate.
>
> (*OME,* 280)

As Tereus had identified his own desire in Philomela's embraces of her father, Procne, reading the tapestry smuggled from her sister's captivity, discovers her own sorrow in the emblem of her sister's violation: "in a wofull verse her state beholds. / She held her peace: 'twas strange! griefe struck her mute. / No language could with such a passion sute" (*OME,* 281). Philomela's speechlessness twins itself in Procne's mute shock. Could a language be found to suit such passion and express such woe and rage, perhaps the fatal script they then compose might not have been written in a child's blood. Twinned by their shared outrage, the sisters merge into a composite nemesis as single-minded in the plotting of revenge as the malevolent furies who presided over Tereus and Procne's nuptials. The final, fatally displaced Imaginary merger involves Procne's identification of the guilty Tereus with her guiltless son Itys. The brutal dismemberment of Itys doubles and amplifies the original violation and mutilation of Philomela, exhausting a cycle of self-generating, self-destroying desire that devours the very possibility of generativity. To Tereus's inquiry about their son, Procne ruthlessly yet uncannily quips, "Thou hast . . . within thee thy desire" (*OME,* 283). But the cost of mimetic revenge is no less to her, as Sandys notices: "Through her owne bowells [she] strikes at her husband" (*OME,* 302).

This gothic melodrama might seem like too much tragic freight to load on the vehicle of a couplet's reference to a reclusive yet melodious bird. We could avoid laborious digressions and more dangerous implications by writing the Lady's nightingale reference off as a decorative allusion, a schoolgirl flourish of innocent classical ornamentation. But exegetical shortcuts are risky with Milton, especially in a formative poem like the *Maske,* where he is consistently invoking, interrogating, and pressurizing his classical resources in order to make them serviceable to his emerging heroic and aesthetic designs. As Angus Fletcher puts it,

> Somehow Milton courts exegetical overrefinement in *Comus*. Its verbal echoing is a radical process, a going to the bottom of language. . . . Verbal and literary echoes here achieve a baroque extension of the etymological domain, so that it covers, not merely linguistic roots in the classical language (with puns from Latin and Greek), but closer, denser literary roots within the linguistic area of English poetry. *Comus* seems to have been written to prove the coherence of this root structure.[39]

It is difficult, in short, to read too much into a poem "Where more is meant than meets the ear" ("Il Penseroso," 120). The "principle of echo," as Fletcher refers to it, is a going to the bottom of mythology as well as of language.

In this particular instance the Attendant Spirit, as Thyrsis, confirms the seriousness of the Lady's nightingale reference when he parallels her situation with the fate of Philomela: "'O poor hapless Nightingale,' thought I, / 'How sweet thou sing'st, how near the deadly snare!'" (566–67). Despite his spiritual confidence in the self-sufficiency of virtue, the Attendant Spirit has no more foreknowledge of the outcome of the Lady's trial or opportunity to intervene at its crucial moment than the angels or Adam will have in Eve's temptation scene of *Paradise Lost.* So we have to assume that, although the Spirit's account to the two brothers of his discovery of the Lady's capture by Comus is a pastoral fiction (540–79), the anxiety it conveys is genuine. The danger to the Lady, and by extension, to the ties that bind her to her family, is genuine, as genuine as Philomela's, as real as Eve's will be when she finds herself "though fairest unsupported Flow'r, / From her best prop so far, and storm so nigh" (*PL* 9.433–34).[40] That the Lady is, like Philomela, someone else's daughter, someone else's sister, deepens her desirability to the plunderer.

The transformation of the daughters of Pandion into birds was allegorized in the Renaissance in such a way as to transmute the savage violence that precedes and precipitates it. Sandys, whose translation and commentary on the *Metamorphoses* is nearly contemporary with Milton's *Maske*, typifies the strategy of disjunctive allegorization:

> Such also [Nightingalls are] fained for their mournfull songs and seeming lamentations. The Nightingall chanting in the solitary woods; deservedly called *Philomela,* or a lover of musicke, in that no bird hath so sweet a voice among all the silvan musitians: singing fifteene dayes and nights together, when the leaves begin to afford her a shelter, with little or no intermission. So shrill a voice in so little a body, and a breath so long extended, is worthy admiration; shee alone in her songs expressing the exact art of Musicke in infinite variety. Neither have all the same tunes and divisions, which shewes their skill to be more then naturall. . . . The Nightingall & Swallow are alluded to Poetry & Oratory: called sisters, because there is in both a similitude of Harmony: the one affecting solitary places; sequestered from the converse of men, but frequented by Gods & Muses; differing in argument, as in affection, from the other: who delights in citties, exercising her eloquence before tribunals, in Senates, and assemblies. Yet as the Nightingall excells the Swallow in sweetnesse, skill, and variety; so doth Poesy Oratory. (*OME,* 300, 302–3)

This is very pretty and suggestive allegory, clearly applicable to the musical figure of the Lady's song. But it bears a somewhat problematic relation to the tale that it interprets. Sandys perhaps signals this problem with the introductory words "fained" and "seeming": he acknowledges that the interpretation of Ovid's fiction is itself a fiction, especially in its application of aesthetic typologies to the order of nature. There are gaps between the emotional chaos of the myth, the natural phenomenon to which it is tied, and the aesthetic security and orderliness of the allegory. Disjunctures of this sort seem inevitable because Ovid cultivates and encourages them with his own constant juxtapositions of and reversals between savagery and sublimity, grotesque violence and beauty. Indeed, Ovid's aesthetic, like that of his subversive weaver hero Arachne, is founded on the paradoxical and miraculous "translation" of sensationalistic elements of tragic violence and pathos into cool yet stinging elaborations of lasting beauty.

The medieval and Renaissance practice of allegorical reading exploited this contrast. Sandys's eclectic management of the Philomela tale is typical. Compartmentalization of the literal tale from its figurative and tropological significations diminished the impact of the literal. The general disposition to deploy allegory as a way to correct, efface, or conceal the troubling features and details of classical texts was a habit that Renaissance thinkers inherited from medieval exegetes. The typical Renaissance strategy of interpretation and application was an expansive moralization, an unfolding of the myth according to the tropological coordinates of morally ritualized conduct. Elaborate interpretive mechanisms, whether euhemerisitic, naturalistic, Christian, Neoplatonic, or some improvised combination of them all, ingeniously sanitized, baptized, and domesticated Ovidian terror.[41] Moralized explications of Ovidian narrative filter out the violent and the tragic element for the sake of ethical intelligibility and philosophical schematization. Such practices translated Ovid's narratives into tropological exempla and spiritual mysteries that the Roman author himself would have found amusingly incoherent and unrecognizable.[42] Modern interpretation of Renaissance literature has in turn been influenced by such tropological patterning, taking the word of Renaissance exegetes as the way into the allegories of Milton, Spenser, and others.

As a mythographer, Milton was as independent as he was in other dimensions of poetic invention. In mythography as in theology, he was never content with received meanings or "implicit faith," but vigorously active in the transformative engagement with his great sources.[43] Richard DuRocher explains "the crucial question of [his] study" of Milton and Ovid as "how one fiercely independent poet, overtly skeptical of glosses and commentaries, incorporated and adapted the *Metamorphoses* within his epic."[44] Milton forces the same question upon us in *Comus*. He wants to rediscover and confront the danger and the risk of Ovidian romance in order to "translate" it into the transcendental possibilities discerned in the *Maske*, not to dissolve it into conventional platitudes. There is no disputing that in his school studies and his rustication Milton deeply familiarized himself with scholarly commentaries and mythological dictionaries.[45] The kind of spin that Sandys gives to the Philomela tale would have struck a deep chord in him. But in the *Maske* he wants not to reproduce that meaning as a received truth, but to simulate the emergence of that meaning, its enactment in the ritual ordeal of the Lady and in her own active "translation" of the very tales in Ovid which speak to and of her condition.

T. S. Eliot captured this paradox in the ekphrasis of the mantel painting in the claustrophobic interior of *The Waste Land:*

> Above the antique mantel was displayed
> As though a window gave upon the sylvan scene
> The change of Philomel, by the barbarous king
> So rudely forced; yet there the nightingale
> Filled all the desert with inviolable voice
> And still she cried, and still the world pursues,
> "Jug Jug" to dirty ears.[46]

Bodily violation: inviolable voice. Eliot neatly condenses the Ovidian paradox amplified in Sandys's commentary without explaining it away. Like Milton, Eliot strews his text with ravaged and abandoned maidens as a way of contemporizing the Ovidian archetype and restoring the danger and degradation of Ovidian truth telling as the challenging source of strong and tragic poetic imagination. Eliot forces us to see that there is no reassuring passage across the gap between body's rude forcing and inviolable voice. They are oppositional figures, yet deeply implicated in one another. There is no adequate mediating term to explain their relation, other than the poetic tradition's steadfast assertion of it.

This is what makes it a vital paradox. The traditional humanist account of their relation draws on the classical topos of *pathe mathos.* Suffering leads to wisdom, and wisdom, or the truth it claims, is beauty. This account depends on the logic of cause and effect, and yet because the terms stand in synchronic relation to one another, their causal and temporal relations are potentially reversible. In this case, we might consider it to be the case that beauty causes suffering, certainly true for a large range of characters in Ovid. More starkly put, we might say that poetic beauty, inviolable voice, requires suffering. The logic of the dyad *bodily violation: inviolable voice* is a logic requiring sacrifice. Bodily sacrifice is the precondition of vocal sanctification; rude forcing is the nature of metaphoric change. Yet the voice's sanctification is itself posited upon the desubstantiation of its source. A voice's inviolability depends upon its immateriality, or insubstantiality; as Sandys remarks of Echo's fate, she "converts into a sound; that is, into nothing" (*OME,* 156). A voice that is inviolable is both sacred and untouchable; sacred, it is overfull and prophetic; untouchable, it is empty, "unsubstantiall" (*OME,* 156). As

Jonathan Goldberg cryptically renders it in his treatment of the Lady's Echo Song, "to be the voice of nature, the tongue must be sacrificed."[47]

This paradox, modernized for us by Eliot, is central to Milton's poetic. Michael Lieb argues that Milton's orphic ambitions are shadowed as well as generated by anxiety over the body's fate: "underlying Milton's sensibility is an anxiety about the body faced with the horrifying possibilities of mutilation and dismemberment. . . . This is an anxiety deeply rooted in the Miltonic psyche, one intimately tied to Milton's sense of his own sexuality, his notion of gendered self, and the culture out of which his selfhood emerges."[48] Sandys's nightingale, "expressing the exact art of Musicke in infinite variety" (*OME,* 300), is a figure for the poet, but Sandys's allegory tends to divorce the art of music from the sacrificial cost for such beauty. By evoking the myth of Philomela as a subtext for her own ritual ordeal, the Lady reopens the myth in order symbolically to reenact it. She recovers the necessarily tragic source of the poetic voice. She reminds us of the gap between myth and allegoresis in order to rehearse the passage across that gap, in her bodily ordeal and in the song to which it gives rise. She reopens the myth in order to regenerate the allegoresis.

Because the sexual horror of the tale of Philomela cannot be fully recuperated by the moral and metaphysical fullness of Renaissance allegorization, it keeps the poetry of the nightingale's compensatory voice rooted in the tragic, in the prospect of ravishment and mutilation, in tonguelessness and silence. The story deepens the nightingale's resonance as a figure for poetic creativity. It deepens the tragic undersong implicit in its sensory beauty, "mourning well" in the way that Beethoven's brooding late quartets mourn well. "Affecting solitary places; sequestered from the converse of men, but frequented by Gods & Muses" (Sandys, *OME,* 303): how near we are already, in the Lady's evocation of the nightingale singing, to Echo's secret habitation, and to those moments of threatened inspiration when Milton will utter his most intimate prayers to the Heavenly Muse:

> Then feed on thoughts, that voluntary move
> Harmonious numbers; as the wakeful Bird
> Sings darkling, and in shadiest Covert hid
> Tunes her nocturnal Note. . . .
>
> Standing on Earth, not rapt above the Pole,
> More safe I Sing with mortal voice, unchang'd

> To hoarse or mute, though fall'n on evil days,
> On evil days though fall'n, and evil tongues;
> In darkness, and with dangers compast round,
> And solitude; yet not alone, while thou
> Visit'st my slumbers Nightly, or when Morn
> Purples the East. . . .
>
> (*PL* 3.37–40; 7.23–30)

The Lady's mourning nightingale, with Echo as her responsive Muse, already prefigures the solitary tragic poet of *Paradise Lost*. Like the Lady discovering and projecting the sources of her own strength in her moment of greatest isolation and danger, like the nightingale whose sublime mourning is large recompense for a career of unspeakable suffering, Milton in his epic discovers his intimate and saving relation to the Muse in the dark solitude and vulnerability of his unpremeditated nightsongs.

5

A further legendary resonance, no less hauntingly tragic, to the Lady's song is more remote, less determinate and verifiable, like an echo so faint in its dying that the trace to its source in suffering has to be imagined in order to be heard. The vales made melodious by nightingales, where the clustering narcissi die into life, the haunts of the powerful Dionysos and his devotees, recall the sacred groves of Colonus evoked in Sophocles' great ode in *Oedipus at Colonus*:

> In the god's untrodden vale
> Where leaves and berries throng,
> And wine-dark ivy climbs the bough,
> The sweet, sojourning nightingale
> Murmurs all night long.
>
> No sun nor wind may enter there
> Nor the winter's rain;
> But ever through the shadow goes
> Dionysus reveler,
> Immortal maenads in his train.
>
> Here with drops of heaven's dews
> At daybreak all the year,
> The clusters of narcissus bloom,
> Time-hallowed garlands for the brows
> Of those great ladies whom we fear.

> The crocus like a little sun
> Blooms with its yellow ray;
> The river's fountains are awake,
> And his nomadic streams that run
> Unthinned forever, and never stay.
>
> (118–19)[49]

The various details of this lush, secluded, numinous, and protective *locus amoenus* recur in brief in the Lady's evocation of the "violet-embroider'd vale": the narcissi, the murmuring nightingale, the nomadic stream like "slow Meander," the shadowy figure of Dionysos as *genius loci,* attended by his devotees. We might even collate the resident protective spirits of the Eumenides, "those great ladies whom we fear," with Sabrina, for all are sanctifying female guardians of fertility and justice.[50]

On this hallowed secret threshold of Colonus, Oedipus in his death is miraculously "translated," not unlike the biblical Enoch:

> But in what manner
> Oedipus perished, no one of mortal men
> Could tell but Theseus. It was not lightning,
> Bearing its fire from Zeus, that took him off;
> No hurricane was blowing.
> But some attendant from the train of Heaven
> Came for him; or else the underworld
> Opened in love the unlit door of earth.
> For he was taken without lamentation,
> Illness or suffering; indeed his end
> Was wonderful if mortal's ever was.
>
> (163)

Oedipus becomes godlike at the end of Sophocles' cycle. His life of wandering penance for primal crimes against family, against community, against the human ordering of sexual generativity itself, receives its divine recompense. The wasted old body condemned to exile from all human community becomes the awesome totem of an enduring public blessing for the city of Athens and a token of the harsh sublimity of Sophocles' late poetry.

The withered, arrogant, suspicious, irascible old sinner Oedipus might seem a tenuous precursor for a girl as yet unscarred and uncorrupted by experience, and so the allusion is faint, subliminal. But the Oedipus legend appears in her ode, along with Philomela, Echo, and Narcissus, to suggest that the Lady begins to figure out who she is by reading her own situation in relation to classical stories. They are, significantly, tragic tales, of selves in the crises of desire, suffering the disintegration of identity boundaries and familial relations, sexual transgression, and consequent physical and psychological metamorphosis. The Lady finds herself at that threshold between the Imaginary and Symbolic orders where the imagination, if it anchors itself patiently in chastity, discovers its power to transfigure violence against the person into inviolable voice. We see in the Lady's iteration and translation of the Echo myth, counterpointed by skillful allusions to Philomela and Oedipus, an instance of that transfiguration. Her song works through her deepest longings and anxieties at this threshold of crisis. By her sequence of allusions, the Lady transforms the possibilities of incestuous self-duplication and self-absorption, of the self's vanishing in the perilous domain of the Imaginary, and of sexual transgression and redounding violence, into a focused and reassured request for aid that ends in a generous bestowal of blessing. Through translation of her archaic sources the Lady makes of this incantation of the mirroring realm of the Imaginary the opportunity for confirmation and communication of her maturing place in the world. Provisionally regressing into contemplative identification with violated and silenced selves, she awakens her own inviolable voice and discovers in that voice a power to protect the vulnerable body. Invoking Echo, she translates potential lovelornness into a principle of self-transcendence. She translates her own potential condition of lostness, isolation, vulnerability, victimhood, longing, perpetual self-effacement, into the ground of communicability, opening out beyond immediate threat and disorientation into a larger network of identification and relationship than the senses provide firsthand evidence for.

4
Double Trouble: Comus and His Bloodlines

1

COMUS MATERIALIZES OUT OF THE TWISTED UNDERGROWTH OF THE liminal forest as his father Dionysus's surrogate, the dark double to both the Attendant Spirit and Sabrina, and the Lady's antithetical initiator. He is the master of the nocturnal revels that parody and seek to pervert the framing entertainment of Milton's *Maske*. Of the "masked figures, representing gods, ancestors, or chthonic powers [who] may appear to the novices or neophytes in grotesque, monstrous, or beautiful forms"[1] in rites of passage, he is the first to appear to the Lady, and the only one to whom she ever directly speaks. He pretends to give a local habitation and a name, and a direction, to the Lady's emerging desire, to the "thousand fantasies / [That] Begin to throng into [her] memory / Of calling shapes and beck'ning shadows dire, / And airy tongues that syllable men's names / On Sands and Shores and desert Wildernesses" (205–9). He wants her to give those mysterious beckonings his name, and to satisfy her curiosity and her fear in him. Her parents' worst nightmare, Comus is not a safe blind date for any girl. But because he is sexual danger personified, he is all the more crucial to the Lady's growth. The *Maske* scripts for Comus the ritual position of a "mock bridegroom" figure to threaten and tempt the Lady. In the *chisungu* rite practiced by the Bemba people of Zambia, the mock bridegroom's role involves sexual teasing and threats to the initiate—in effect, a licensed ritual form of sexual harassment. These actions provide adversarial instruction to the girl in the dangers of aggressive male sexual potency and in the management of her proper response to it.[2]

Milton makes this ritual archetype culturally specific. Since this initiation performs itself in the specific social setting of Caroline England, by means of the masque, the genre of social drama favored by its ruling class, Comus's ritual aggression against the

4: DOUBLE TROUBLE: COMUS AND HIS BLOODLINES   143

Lady dramatizes the aristocratic spirit of self-destruction that Milton intends to critique and reform. The namesake of the belly-god of Puteanus's *Comus* and of Jonson's masque *Pleasure Reconciled to Virtue,* Comus is a suppler and subtler avatar than they for moral anarchy and spiritual gluttony.³ Although Milton follows Jonson in consigning his Lord of Misrule to the antimasque, he expands Comus's role beyond the conventional containing structure of the antimasque, assigns a significant set of culturally recognizable arguments to him, and endows him with the mesmerizing eloquence to elaborate them. Sleek and sexy as a rock star, he is no slothful Silenus or fat jolly clown. So it is impossible to dispell Comus's charms, like those of Jonson's gargantuan reveller, through laughter. In his luscious extravagance, debonair cynicism, rhetorical ease, and moral triviality, he represents the decadent spirit lurking beneath the apparent idealism of the Stuart masque itself.⁴

In the cultural coding of Jacobean and Caroline poetics, Comus expresses the predatory allure of libertine sexuality. In his initial formulaic pass at the Lady, he comes on to her in terms typical of masque flatteries and vanities:

> Hail foreign wonder,
> Whom certain these rough shades did never breed,
> Unless the Goddess that in rural shrine
> Dwell'st here with *Pan* or *Silvan,* by blest Song
> Forbidding every bleak unkindly Fog
> To touch the prosperous growth of this tall Wood.
>
> (265–70)

This flattery positions itself suggestively in the canon of Milton's work. It virtually reiterates the praises of the Countess Dowager of Derby, stepmother of John Egerton, for whom Milton had collaborated with Henry Lawes to compose *Arcades* two years prior to *Comus:* "Such a Rural Queen / All Arcadia hath not seen" (94–95). Within the *Maske,* it forecasts, by an irony unknowable to Comus himself, the countervailing, healing powers of Sabrina (842–47), the authentic *genius loci* invoked by Attendant Spirit to "listen and save" (866, 889) at the epiphanic climax of the plot. And it anticipates the hyperbolic Petrarchan flatteries with which Satan will initiate his courtship of Eve in *Paradise Lost* (9.532–48). By translating his former praises of the Countess of Derby into the easy, glozing pick-up lines of Comus that menacingly anticipate Satan's erotic bravado, Milton establishes in his own script a critical distance from the conventions of masque rhetoric and highlights them as potentially seductive idolatries.

Although Comus intimates an aristocratic palate of refinement, his appetite discloses itself as crudely binary: either the Lady is to be part of his "well stock't . . . fair . . . herd" (152)—good breeding stock for his harem—or "she shall be my Queen" (265)—set apart from cruder pleasures of the flesh for delights reserved for the most cultivated tastes.[5] These two images of women exist in complementary rather than oppositional relation to one another, endlessly succeeding one another as libertine desire circulates forever between aspiration and possession, idolatry and degradation, absolute singularity and monotonous anonymity. To imagine that the Lady would be his queen is, ironically, for Comus to imagine for her a more or less conventional place in the masque of cupidity that he proceeds to orchestrate around her. The queen, like James I's Anne and Charles I's Henrietta Maria, can be both patron and star of the masque. The masque, we have seen, is a privileged form for the staging of queenship. Yet even in the apparently feminized court extravaganzas of the Jacobean and high Caroline periods, masques stage the power of women of the court as self-containing fantasies that ritually disguise, libidinize, and renew their dependence on and subjection to the king.

A perverse logic links Comus's fantasy about the Lady as his queen to his enthronement of her in the enchanted chair of her captivity. Schooled in the libertine idea that women both need and desire subjection, Comus creates in his palace of worldly delights a setting for what he expects to be the Lady's ready submission of her will:

> *The Scene changes to a stately Palace set out with all manner of deliciousness; soft Music, Tables spread with all dainties. Comus appears with his rabble, and the Lady set in an enchanted Chair, to whom he offers his Glass, which she puts by, and goes about to rise.*
>
>   *Comus.* Nay Lady, sit; if I but wave this wand,
>   Your nerves are all chain'd up in Alabaster,
>   And you a statue; or as *Daphne* was,
>   Root-bound, that fled *Apollo*.
>
> (s.d.; 659–62)

This mise-en-scène recurs in literary bondage fantasies from Amoret's masochistic suffering in Spenser's House of Busyrane (*FQ* 3.11–12) to O's adventures at Roissy and Stanley Kubrick's stylized adaptation of them in the ponderous orgy scene of *Eyes Wide Shut*.[6]

The Lady finds herself perversely enthroned by Comus's fantasy of her, simultaneously idolized and held captive. The seat of her prestige is the site of her bondage. It might be read as a mirroring parody of the seat of power occupied by her father as a witness to Milton's *Maske*.[7] Milton's structuring of the seduction episode implies that the Lady's plight is a cultural position inevitably assigned to women by the erotic imagination of the conventional masque and of the culture that sustains and is sustained by it.

2

Milton's archetypal libertine Comus is the bastard son of the transformative sex goddess Circe and the Greco-Roman god of ecstatic release, Bacchus, or Dionysus. In the previous chapter, we studied how the *Maske* opens the prospects of tragedy for its Lady to contend with. With his genealogical invention, Milton focuses, deepens, and enriches the interpretive link between his *Maske* and tragedy by identifying Comus with two mythic figures of considerable psychological power and complexity:

> *Bacchus* that first from out the purple Grape
> Crusht the sweet poison of misused Wine,
> After the *Tuscan* Mariners transform'd,
> Coasting the *Tyrrhene* shore, as the winds listed,
> On *Circe's* Island fell. . . .
> This Nymph that gaz'd upon his clust'ring locks,
> With ivy berries wreath'd, and his blithe youth,
> Had by him, ere he parted thence, a Son
> Much like his Father, but his Mother more,
> Whom therefore she brought up, and *Comus* nam'd. . . .
>
> (46–58)

This means double trouble for those who encounter Comus, and it means trouble more subtle and powerful than the mix of sex, drugs, and rock and roll that are the outward signs of the pleasure package that Comus is marketing. To calibrate the complex nature of the challenge that the Lady faces in Comus, we turn now to this inheritance.

First, the Dionysian heritage. That Comus is Dionysus's bastard son may be an implicit comment on Milton's part about the hybrid nature of the masque as a genre. Although Jonson provided theoretical legitimation of the masque as a genre by aligning it with neoclassical accounts of Aristotle's *Poetics,* Stuart masques do not typically yield pleasure of the sort that we associate with tragedy.[8] But Milton summons the ghost of tragedy that subliminally haunts the masque as genre, and gives it the name of Comus. He invests Comus with enough of the light-footed, shapeshifting, hallucinogenic, seductive, and mind-obliterating energy of his absentee father Bromios the Thunderer to imply that the Ludlow *Maske* is a distilled and sublimated version of tragic experience. Michael Lieb demonstrates that the story of Orpheus dismembered by the maenad horde of Bacchus had the status of a formative personal myth for Milton. Comus's threat to the Lady is the poet's first full imaginative treatment of it.[9] Milton's invention of Bacchus's paternity for Comus weaves into the *Maske*'s fabric the rich collection of tales in Ovid's *Metamorphoses* that occur under the influence of and in relation to the devastating power of Bacchus, as well as older versions of tragic drama which are linked more explicitly to the legends and rites of the ecstasy god, particularly Euripides' *The Bacchae*. To make more sense of the contribution of Dionysus to the *Maske,* we need not only to look backward toward these dynamic myth clusters, but to look forward. Milton anticipates Nietzsche's *The Birth of Tragedy* in recognizing the liberating and obliterating potential of Dionysus and in positioning Comus in the role of tragic challenger to the Lady's emerging sense of self.[10] Reciprocally, Nietzsche's meditation on Dionysus clarifies some key tragic elements of the *Maske* and sharpens the contrast between Milton's risk-taking engagement with mythic sources and the more conventional allegoresis of his contemporaries.

Nietzsche argues that tragedy's aesthetic poise and the pleasure that issues paradoxically from its representations of destruction depend upon the presence of Dionysus, the ecstasy god, the music god, the god who presides at revelatory rites of disintegration. Dionysus is a double god of mobile, volatile energy, a bestower of the blessings of peace and a destroyer. As Milton's contemporary George Sandys describes him, Dionysus is "in himselfe made up of all contrarieties; valiant and effeminate, industrious and riotous, a seducer to vice, and an example of vertue" (*OME,* 161). Richard Halpern describes him as "a liminal god who either mediates or collapses or overthrows the structural oppositions on which Attic culture was based, oppositions that include male and female, citizen and slave, culture and nature, Greek and barbarian."[11] Dionysus represents the great amoral power and ground of life, Schopenhauer's world-will, which precedes and sustains every distinct entity and presses toward individual self-forgetfulness and annihilation in the energetic flux of existence in itself (*BT,* 36–38, 44–45). Dionysus promises release from the tense fiction of individual identity, ecstatic disintegration of what Nietzsche takes to be the necessary illusion of selfhood.

Tragic heroes, carrying their cultures' investments in the myth of individuation, resist Dionysus at their peril. The deeper their resistance, the more powerful their assertion of autonomy, the more suddenly and blindingly comes the reversal and recognition of their resemblance to him and subjection to his power. Euripides' rigidly self-confident young rationalist Pentheus in *The Bacchae* provides the starkest and least disguised instance of this resisting hero who fatally discovers his own kinship to the mystery god.[12] Pentheus ominously prefigures the Lady as a youth staking claim to autonomy. Comus's challenge to the Lady parallels Dionysus's temptation of Pentheus. At the critical moment of the Lady's potential emergence as activist, conscientious self, representative of Puritan culture, the figure representing the god appears as her androgynous double to offer sweet release from the burdens of selfhood. The moment of her potential self-definition becomes a ritual ordeal, with a Dionysus figure as divine antagonist: a moment of potential tragedy. It seems that the Lady has only herself to protect, but in fact, like Pentheus, the young king of Thebes, she carries in her profession of chastity the burden of an emerging culture's defense.

Nietzsche traces tragedy's origins to nature ritual. Tragedy originates with music of ecstatic abandonment, in the songs of a chorus of satyrs, who are companions and primitive devotees of Dionysus (*BT*, 61). Comus's glistering forest crew, completely given over to the rapturous self-forgetfulness promised by their god-priest and bestialized by their absorption in his ecstasies (66–77), represent Milton's adaptation and ethical positioning of the satyr chorus in his moralization of the tragic. As Comus himself is double natured, Comus's "rout of Monsters" are both the Circean feral sports and the bacchic troupe of Milton's *Maske*. So lost to self and abandoned to the god as to become his hunting dogs, the Bacchae are a constant specter haunting Milton's aspirations toward the Orphic mastery of poetry.[13] If the "orient liquor" (65) distilled from his mother's charms by Comus promises self-forgetful degeneration of human form into sensual folly and spiritual lassitude, the restless circling of his horde intimates a disastrous potential outcome to the Lady's resistance to Comus: like Pentheus, like Orpheus, her denial of the power of the god could lead to her suffering as the sacrificial victim of Dionysian *sparagmos* and *omophagia,* the tearing apart and devouring of the victim's flesh by which the bacchic devotees in manic possession merge with their god.[14]

The career of Dionysus that the satyr chorus beholds and incants is itself a career of mutilation and dismemberment at the hands of envious Titans, and of miraculous reanimation and reintegration. Every tragic hero, in Nietzsche's reckoning, reenacts this primordial fate:

> The one truly real Dionysus appears in a variety of forms, in the mask of a fighting hero, and entangled, as it were, in the net of the individual will. The god who appears talks and acts so as to resemble an erring, striving, suffering individual . . . the hero is the suffering Dionysus of the Mysteries, the god experiencing in himself the agonies of individuation. . . . Thus it is intimated that this dismemberment, the properly Dionysian suffering, is like a transformation into air, water, earth, and fire, that we are therefore to regard the state of individuation as the origin and primal cause of all suffering, as something objectionable in itself. . . . the hope of the epopts looked toward a rebirth of Dionysus, which we must now dimly conceive as the end of individuation. (*BT*, 73)

Nietzsche's reading of the central myth of Dionysus as a parable of individuation has the character of a Renaissance allegorical reading: the great god of omnipotent, indivisible nature torn into the discrete elements and forms which constitute our world.[15] But in Nietzsche's account of the strong Greek sensibility, an ontology based on those elemental constituents and discrete entities is an illusion, a necessary illusion perhaps, but one that tragedy rapturously challenges. Dionysus intact represents primordial unity of being and of cosmic will; Dionysus dismembered stands for that unity shattered into the apparitional world of individuation and multiplicity. Paradoxically, tragedy effects a metaphysical double cross. The tragic hero stands for the suffering Dionysus, yet the death of the hero is also the triumph of Dionysus. The rebirth of Dionysus coincides with the end of individuation. As tragic plot literally represents the painful destruction of an "erring, striving, suffering individual," it enacts the return, agonized yet joyous, of being to itself, released from the illusory net of individual will. Through the apparitions of tragedy, the Greeks glimpsed into the dynamic and indestructible abyss from which all phenomenal forms issue, and discovered the metaphysical comfort "that life is at the bottom of things, despite all the changes of appearance, indestructibly powerful and pleasurable" (*BT*, 59).

Apollo, Dionysus's great antagonist and collaborator in Nietzsche's tragic paradigm, is bound to him and necessary to his representation in tragedy. Greek myth and cult recognized their kinship.

Apollo and Dionysus enjoyed a time-sharing arrangement in the prophetic shrine at Delphi, and they were joined as stepbrothers in Greek mythic genealogy.[16] Nietzsche schematizes them as oppositional powers, yet he treats their opposition, as Blake would have put it, as true friendship. Nietzsche delineates their opposition at the outset of his argument, because tragedy emerges from their dialectic. Through music and intoxication, Dionysus induces the rapturous and self-forgetting call of pure existence in itself, unencumbered and unlimited by discrete form, dissolving the apparitional boundaries of selfhood. Apollo, the god of sculpture and of "the soothsaying faculty" of poetry (*BT,* 35), embodies the illusory and luminous power of dream and sponsors the luminous emergence of form, and the appeal of visual beauty. Hence he authorizes and represents the sublime fiction of individual existence, the illusion of selfhood: "We might call Apollo himself the glorious divine image of the *principium individuationis,* through whose gestures and eyes all the joy and wisdom of 'illusion,' together with its beauty, speak to us" (*BT,* 36).

Although tragedy contemplates Dionysian disintegration, it does so through the eyes of Apollo. Human kind cannot bear very much reality:[17] Dionysus cannot be known to us without the saving mediation of Apollo. "Of this foundation of all existence—the Dionysian basic ground of the world—not one whit more may enter the consciousness of the human individual than can be overcome again by this Apollinian power of transfiguration" (*BT,* 143). "Dionysus," indeed, individuated and numinous as a deity, is always already known to us in Apollinian form and by Apollinian name, a fictive personification of the nameless, formless world-will that precedes, transcends, and ultimately destroys all contingent beings. Tragedy is thus "a symbolization of Dionysian wisdom through Apollinian artifices" (*BT,* 131). Apollinian artifice recuperates for cultural service the Dionysian energy that erupts in tragedy. We might say that in tragedy Dionysus instigates a centrifugal momentum across the dramatic sequence, pressing its central character toward obliteration, whereas Apollo introduces a stabilizing, ordering counterforce that endows the plot with mythic coherence and significance.

As we return to Milton's *Maske* by way of this excursus into Nietzsche's account of tragedy, we need to clarify and qualify certain features of Nietzsche's argument, in order not to invent or exaggerate correspondences between the two texts. Although Nietzsche wishes to polarize the vocations of his tutelary spirits, Apollo, closely considered, participates in several of the activities that Nietzsche reserves for Dionysus, and the Dionysus of tragedy is in turn no less involved in the Apollinian vocation. Nietzsche identifies Apollo as the author of visual "illusion," but we know of Dionysus's destabilizing mastery of the visual field through acquaintance with the several trompes l'oeil in the *Bacchae,* as well as with the various narratives of confused, blurred, and hallucinatory vision associated with Bacchus and his frenzies in the *Metamorphoses.* Comus thus claims a mastery of visual illusion inherited from his father: "Thus I hurl / My dazzling Spells into the spongy air, / Of power to cheat the eye with blear illusion, / And give it false presentments . . ." (153–56). Apollo, in his turn, is traditionally associated with primordial music; indeed, the Greeks themselves recognized Apollo as "the *only* god of music."[18] In interpreting Apollo's boastful pursuit of Daphne—his first erotic misadventure in Ovid's *Metamorphoses*— George Sandys notes, "Because the sunne is placed in the midst as Lord of the rest, whose motions (according to *Pythagoras*) doe make an incredible harmony, he therefore is said to have invented Musicke" (*OME,* 73). Milton consistently alludes to Apollo's skill with the lyre as the ideal of a resonant polyphonic music.[19] An instance of this in the *Maske* is Younger Brother's admiration of Elder Brother's confident celebration of chastity: "how charming is divine Philosophy! / Not harsh and crabbed as dull fools suppose, / But musical as is Apollo's lute" (476–78). Milton's *Maske* participates in one of the musical duels of the Renaissance, representing Apollinian music as of a different register and a higher order than the "barbarous dissonance" (550; *PL* 7.32) of Dionysus, contemplative rather than ecstatic, conceptual rather than intoxicating. So the *Maske* prefigures the Nietzschean opposition, though *within* the respective domains of music and vision, rather than *between* them.

Furthermore, the creative contraries of Dionysus and Apollo in Nietzsche's account *do not* play themselves out as an opposition between passion and reason. Nietzsche wants to get beyond, or before, that opposition. He diagnoses the opposition of passion to reason as the triumph of Socratic rationalism, which destroyed the culture of tragedy and generated the weakened postmythological societies and selves of modern Europe: "Wherever Socratism turns its searching eyes it sees lack of insight and the power of illusion; and from this lack it infers the essential perversity and reprehensibility of what exists. Basing himself on this point, Socrates conceives it to be his duty to correct existence" (*BT,* 87). One could turn this element of Nietzschean sarcasm upon Milton, of whom it might also be remarked that he "conceives it to be his duty to correct existence." In any case, to read the dialectic between Dionysus and Apollo as the strife of passion and reason is to subject the tragic myth to a Socratic analysis of it. Nietzsche attempts to recover a conceptual state prior to the Socratic intervention, to invoke a psychological and metaphysical dialectic that exposes and overwhelms the insufficiencies of Socratic analysis.

Milton, a Protestant humanist deeply instructed by the dualisms of monotheist ethics and of Neoplatonic mysteries, cannot really think outside the Socratic paradigm that Nietzsche criticizes. It would be difficult to discriminate the Apollinian from the Socratic in Milton's *poesis,* and it would be a significant misrepresentation of it to try to do so. In his *Maske,* Milton vigorously moralizes the Dionysian myth to which his Lady is subject; his interests are both Apollinian and Socratic. As Comus stands for Dionysus, the Attendant Spirit stands for Nietzsche's Apollo, yet he is a platonized Apollo figure.[20] The first and last figure to appear in the *Maske,* the Attendant Spirit securely frames the ritual as an Apollinian triumph. The epiphanic Prologue opening (1–11) conjures majestic images of celestial order and the luminaries of an Olympian hierarchy, the fullness, formal clarity, and radiance of which is, in Nietzsche's account, the province of Apollinian imagination. Symmetrically framing the *Maske,* Prologue (1–92) and Epilogue (976–1023) securely explicate the dramatic situation in ways typical of the tragic frames of Euripides, Milton's favorite tragic poet.[21] In Nietzsche's estimation, Euripides is the Socratic betrayer of tragedy at whose hands the genre "died by suicide" (*BT,* 76):

> [Euripides] put the prologue even before the exposition, and placed it in the mouth of a person who could be trusted: often some deity had to guarantee the plot of the tragedy to the public, to remove every doubt as to the reality of the myth. . . . Euripides makes use of this same divine truthfulness once more at the close of his drama, in order to reassure the public as to the future of his heroes; this is the task of the notorious *deus ex machina.* (*BT,* 85)

For Nietzsche, whose critique of Euripides as the rationalizing destroyer of the tragic spirit is a perverse sign of his anxious respect, such dramatic self-explication represents an early and fatal stage in the Socratic demythologization of tragedy. Unsure of the power of the myth to compel the spectators' poetic faith, such divine speeches rely on the authoritative mystique of oracles, and so, according to Nietzsche, give too much away to rationalized authority.

Yet for Milton, such framing speeches are tutelary, not reductively rationalizing, but exemplary exercises in holy imagining.[22] They demonstrate how rightly to imagine the world beyond "the smoke and stir of this dim spot, / Which men call Earth" (5–6). The Attendant Spirit is the Apollinian custodian of the mythic in the *Maske*. His presence gives coherence and direction to the ordeals of its wandering youths, and to the spectators whose cultural hopes the youths will carry into the future. Nietzsche writes, "The images of the myth have to be the unnoticed omnipresent demonic guardians, under whose care the young soul grows to maturity and whose signs help the man to interpret his life and struggles" (*BT,* 135). This sentence from *The Birth of Tragedy* could hardly describe more vividly and precisely the role of the Attendant Spirit, the "unnoticed omnipresent demonic guardian" of the ritual drama. If Henry Lawes's position as music tutor to the Egerton children adapts the Socratic model to their ritual ordeal, his higher calling and more expansive role as Apollinian messenger and mediator of supersensible form prophetically enlarges the Socratic model. He presents a wider prospect of virtue's imaginative place within the horizon of myth than the experientially bounded hedonist Comus is capable of offering. He thus exalts reason from its potentially self-limiting position as the critical, analytic, and regulatory faculty denounced by Nietzsche—and, incidentally, mocked by Comus (706–9)—to serve in its expanded Renaissance sense as Right Reason, the mind awakening to knowledge of its providentially ordained role as viceroy of the divine, the shepherd and steward of the created order.[23]

The Lady, in turn, apparently sequestered from the resources and evidences that might support her exercise of virtue, dramatically instantiates the Attendant Spirit's Apollinian wisdom. During the separation stage of her ordeal, her only communication with the Attendant Spirit is through the echo chamber of the ritual text. Yet she discovers and exemplifies, in response to the antithetical challenge of Comus, what the Attendant Spirit enunciates and stands for. She dramatizes and incarnates this awakening of Right Reason to its own revelatory potential. Milton thus anticipates and resolves a crippling dualism in Nietzsche's text by absorbing the Socratic in the Apollinian, the rational and critical in the imaginative and visionary. The Lady, in her turn and as a figure for Milton the poet, emerges as an Apollinian lyric artist, translating the Dionysian impulse of Comus's music of self-abandonment into the harmonic, resonant strains of music "that might create a soul / Under the ribs of Death" (561–62). "This is the phenomenon of the lyrist: as Apollinian genius he interprets music through the image of the will, while he himself, completely released from the greed of the will, is the pure undimmed

4: DOUBLE TROUBLE: COMUS AND HIS BLOODLINES 153

eye of the sun" (*BT*, 55). The release from "the greed of the will" and the solar image link Nietzsche's account of the lyrist's genius to what Milton means by chastity as a source of lyric and ethical power and takes us close to the secret of the *Maske*'s translation of the tragic into the visionary sublime. The lyric purity and creative freedom of the Lady's inviolable voice, "completely released from the greed of the will," is the auditory sign of the "Sun-clad power of Chastity" (782) that both protects and inspires the Lady in her wayfaring through the Dionysian forest. This is her saving difference from her tragic prototype, Euripides' Pentheus, who blindly and ruthlessly trusts the greed of his individual will to secure his assault on and defense against Dionysus. A ruthless psychoanalyst, Euripides' Dionysus rightly calculates Pentheus's resistance as prurient prudery rather than chastity and consequently destroys him by soliciting his fascination and identification with that which he most fervently denies.[24]

As we have seen in the instance of the Lady's Echo Song, the broad array of tragic stories invoked and echoed in Milton's text reveal a subtext of Dionysian reference that seems to resist allegorical closure and threatens to disrupt the conventionality of the *Maske*'s moralized ritual. Milton intentionally creates a sort of mythological dissonance, in the interests of disrupting the complacent self-assurances of the masque genre and freshly translating tragedy's potential into the *Maske*'s providentiality. There is no question of outcome in Stuart masques, in part because of the autocratic myopia of the court that staged them, and in part because they arrayed themselves as allegories with triumphalist outcomes already determined by Renaissance habits of reading myth. Allegorical engagements of this sort, ingenious as they are, evidence the critical, rationalizing spirit, the legacy of Socrates, which Nietzsche accuses of diminishing our openness to existence. Milton resituates his selected myths in a stage prior to the allegorical tradition's optimistic rationalization of them, to provide the textual unconscious of his ritual drama. He intends for these tragic evocations to invest, sometimes subliminally, sometimes explicitly, elements of serious danger and risk in the Lady's situation. He thus releases tragic myth from standardized and moralized interpretations of it, in order to try, and thus to purify and energize, the Apollinian imaginative translations of his *Maske*. If Dionysus is to be confronted and mastered, and his energies made serviceable to the higher calling of Reformation character and culture, he must be confronted and transformed by Apollinian imagination rather than explained away by Socratic analysis.

And so Milton in effect deprives the Lady of the consolations and securities of allegorical solutions to her crisis. He keeps opening the wound of the tragic, by echoing what has been repressed or neglected in poetic and exegetical adaptations of Ovid's tales and the tragic dilemmas of dramatic characters like Oedipus and Pentheus. He places the Lady in the liminal space where the wound occurs, between the moment of victimization and the moment of recuperation, the crisis moment where Dionysus dangerously discloses himself, in suffering and in triumph, prior to the various forms of interpretive recuperation that express themselves as metamorphoses or allegorical explications.[25] If we recover Nietzsche's insight that the hero of tragedy is not only the *victim* of Dionysus but also a masked *type* of Dionysus as victim, we discover that the Lady as Apollinian hero and poet paradoxically triumphs over her mythic antagonist through identification with him. By occupying the position reserved for Dionysus and enduring subjection to his surrogate Comus in the tragic plot, she channels his potentially obliterating energies into the creative project of Apollinian self- and culture formation.[26]

Her rite of passage thus requires the Lady to cultivate a discipline of vulnerability. By restoring the danger and terror of myth to the Lady's ritual experience, and exposing her to it in the person of Comus, Milton puts the potentially devastating energies of tragedy to the service and support of a sublime, resilient, and integrated conception of ethical selfhood. The Lady endures exposure to the threat, temptation, and terror suffered by her mythological types—Echo and Narcissus, Philomela, Pentheus, Daphne, Hyacinth, Proserpina, and Sabrina among them—in order to recoup, in the very moment of vulnerability, the potential for translation, for the refiguration of tragic energies into the imaginative activism of the Puritan conscience. Nietzsche's Dionysus does not have the last word in the *Maske,* nor indeed does Apollo. Christ does, but only in the veiled form of the redemptive allegory which is, for Milton in his emerging maturity, the only kind worth writing. For Christ, the "Celestial Cupid" of the *Maske*'s epilogue (1004), contains the antinomies of Dionysus and Apollo, at once the victim of a redemptive violence and the ground and harmonic ordering power of existence, its Apollinian *principium individuationis.* Thus Milton invokes the tragic, in order first to confront and recuperate its metaphysical and existential potency and then to direct this potency into the *Maske*'s harmonic ritual ordering. The echoing, restless pressure of tragic *mythos* on the ordering, ritualizing patterns of the poetic and dramatic surface of the poem ultimately contribute to its aesthetic splendor and its ethical strength.

The threat of Dionysus antithetically inspires the Lady's poetics. It deepens, strengthens, and gives resilience to the creative moral character that expresses itself in her inviolable lyric and prophetic voice.

3

The unmediated call of Dionysus, as Pentheus discovered horribly, threatens all civilizing impulses and claims, and all social ties, even, or in particular, the most intimate one that bonds mother to child. Dionysus's own birth trauma—lightning severed from the smoking womb of his mother Semele—chiasmically repeats itself in Pentheus's dismemberment at the hands of his mother and her sisters. This suggests that tragedy's gravitation toward intrafamilial violence perhaps has its source and center not in the Oedipal rivalry stressed by Freud, but in the tense and consuming bond between mother and child.[27] This Dionysian potential gives an extra and volatile twist to Comus's mythic inheritance from his mother Circe. "Much like his Father, but his Mother more" (57), Comus shares in the filial bond to the mother that breeds tragedy. Having studied the Dionysian pressure toward the tragic that shapes the Lady's ritual ordeal, we turn now to the all-consuming bond of potentially violent affection that makes Comus a particularly dangerous mother's boy and the threat that this bond represents to the Lady.

Circe is a witch goddess whose metamorphic power was read in the English Renaissance primarily in terms of the enervating and dehumanizing lure of "sensual Folly and Intemperance" (975).[28] In his notes on his artistic collaborator Aurelian Townshend's allegory of *Tempe Restored,* an extravagant recent masque precedent for Milton, Inigo Jones explains Circe's double nature thus: "Circe here signifies desire in general, the which hath power on all living creatures, and being mixed of the divine and sensible, hath diverse effects, leading some to virtue and others to vice. She is described as a queen, having in her service and subjection the nymphs, which participate of divinity, figuring the virtues, and the brute beasts, denoting the vices."[29] In the plot of *Tempe Restored,* Townshend's Circe, potentially disposed toward spiritual beauty, virtue and reason, and capable of motivating men to seek and achieve them, signifies her willing submission to these higher orders of value by yielding her rod of enchantment to Minerva. Milton eschews mythic bipolarity of this sort. He will allow no such disposition toward the good nor change of heart to his tempter figure. He is less sanguine about the easy idealization of vagrant desire, or its ready submission to the claims of virtue, and so he revises the happy ending of *Tempe Restored,* as he revises the allegoric formulae of his other masque precedents.[30] Although Comus will paradoxically serve the ritual purposes of Milton's *Maske* by leading the Lady to virtue through trial, it is not because of his own countervailing potential for virtue, an uncultivated good side to his character. Like other Miltonic tempters, Comus appears to be unreformable, thus unredeemable: he who tempts and runs away lives to tempt another day. Comus manages to escape with his rod in hand (s.d., 815 ff.), a sign of Milton's ethical realism regarding the recalcitrance of self-willed desire to domestication by virtuous intentions in a still fallen world.

The Attendant Spirit diagnoses the operations of Comus's strange brew, in imagery suited to the mythological networks of signification in the *Maske:*

> Soon as the Potion works, their human count'nance,
> Th' express resemblance of the gods, is chang'd
> Into some brutish form of Wolf, or Bear,
> Or ounce, or Tiger, Hog, or bearded Goat,
> All other parts remaining as they were.
> And they, so perfect is their misery,
> Not once perceive their foul disfigurement,
> But boast themselves more comely than before,
> And all their friends and native home forget,
> To roll with pleasure in a sensual sty.
>
> (68–77)

Following the commonplace Renaissance allegorization of the Circe episode in the *Odyssey,* Milton treats the transformation of Comus's victims as a demoralizing submission of sovereign Reason, the image of God in man, to the life of the senses.[31]

In keeping with the anthropology of humanism, it is fitting for human beings, "the breath and similitude of God,"[32] to have human form, unique and comprehensive: our mortal bodies are already the specific form that our animal nature takes in the natural world, as well as the sign of our spiritual privilege. The warping of the human countenance into the form of other creatures evidences both the plasticity of human nature and the tragic possibility of its being reduced and distorted from its specific providential design.

Those enchanted by Homer's Circe experience the horror of entrapment in bestial form, for they retain their human consciousness, their memory, their longing for home. They do not want to be swine.

The essentially and indomitably human in them painfully resists their metamorphosis. But Comus's victims, like those of Spenser's Acrasia (*FQ* 2.12.85–87), undergo a spiritual transformation that signifies itself in their disfigurement and anonymity. They have lost their minds, as Spenser's Palmer explains: "these seeming beasts are men indeed, / Whom this Enchauntresse hath transformed thus, / Whylome her louers, which her lusts did feed, / Now turned into figures hideous, / According to their mindes like monstruous" (*FQ* 2.12.85.1–5). Their situation is less tragic but more pathetic than that of Odysseus's crew, for they have abandoned self-consciousness, with its accompanying human burdens and gifts of shame, memory, longing, and hope. Their metamorphosis, less complete physiologically than that of the poor souls of the *Odyssey*, is more complete where it matters. In this respect, it seems, Comus has improved upon his mother's techniques and "Excels his Mother at her mighty Art" (63).

As the Attendant Spirit explains to the brothers, Comus has inherited the dark sanctuary of liminal testing, "the navel of this hideous Wood" (520), as well as his metamorphic powers, from Circe. Mircea Eliade describes the liminal forest space in which traditional rites of passage occur as a maternal space of spiritual disintegration and gestation, analogous to Comus's "thick shelter of black shades" (62): "The bush symbolizes both hell and cosmic night, hence death and virtualities; the cabin [where initiates are secluded and tested, as the Lady is in Comus's "stately Palace"] is the maw of the devouring monster, in which the neophyte is eaten and digested, but it is also a nourishing womb, in which [s]he is engendered anew."[33] Comus's power center, the imbowered and labyrinthine shades of the uroboric forest, "the perplex't paths of this drear Wood" (37), materializes the self-entangling and regressive cycle of the pleasures he profers. He only comes out at night, and he chants and speaks, as he dances, in circles:

> We that are of purer fire
> Imitate the Starry Choir,
> Who in their nightly watchful Sphere,
> Lead in swift round the Months and Years,
> The Sounds and Seas with all their finny drove
> Now to the Moon in wavering Morris move,
> And on the Tawny Sands and Shelves
> Trip the pert Fairies and the dapper Elves;
> By dimpled Brook and Fountain brim,
> The Wood-Nymphs deckt with Daisies trim,

> Their merry wakes and pastimes keep;
> What hath night to do with sleep?
> Night hath better sweets to prove,
> *Venus* now wakes, and wak'ns Love.
> Come let us our rites begin,
> 'Tis only daylight that makes Sin,
> Which these dun shades will ne'er report.
>
> (111–27)

Pert, dapper, dimpled, trim, and merry: Comus casts himself as carnival barker for the festal games and morris dances of Merrie Olde Englande at their most wholesome, natural, and innocent.[34] At first glance, who could fault him for this, or resist his invitation, with its promise of tireless pleasure and life renewal? To sublunary spirits it sure must sound like more fun than the frosty solemnities and sober patriarchal hierarchies of those "Regions mild of calm and serene Air" (4) from which the Attendant Spirit has just so reluctantly descended. Still, the dramatic evidence of the antimasque contradicts his self-promotion: he is not surrounded by delicate and weightless folk sprites like Peaseblossom, Cobweb, Moth, and Mustardseed, but by monsters. Comus's merry-go-round of pleasure traces the cycle of club-drug addiction: this endless spinning in circles driven by the wheels of stars and seasons would become dizzying, then frantic, then deadeningly monotonous.[35]

If we set the first stanza of Yeats's "Sailing to Byzantium" next to Comus's opening cadences, we can recognize the melancholy undertow of Comus's sprightly carousel of natural pleasure:

> That is no country for old men. The young
> In one another's arms, birds in the trees
> —Those dying generations—at their song,
> The salmon-falls, the mackerel-crowded seas,
> Fish, flesh, or fowl, commend all summer long
> Whatever is begotten, born, and dies.
> Caught in that sensual music all neglect
> Monuments of unageing intellect.[36]

Comus would no doubt respond, if he could, that Yeats's speaker against "that sensual music" is one of the aging spoilsports, spokesmen of "sour Severity" (109), against whom he rails. And he would be in part right. But that would be a way of distracting from the question of what it is that Comus offers when he conjures up his promises of terrestrial delight. Cyclical repetition, bound to the reiteration of natural process, is one component of his lifestyle. Another is the either/or habit of compartmentalizing experience that belies the fluidity and energy he claims to speak for. He associates the night world with revelry, youth, abandonment, joy, and pleasure. He associates the daylight with effort, age, law, duty, and repression. This polarization is as inadequate to comprehend the complexities of experience as the severe, repressive, and voyeuristic society of elders he imagines peeping in on him from the other end of the diurnal pole. Comus cannot imagine the possibilities of *daylit* joys and pleasures, as his genuinely innocent prototype, the speaker of "L'Allegro," can.[37]

This is no doubt because Comus seems to have no direct experience of daylight activity. The containment of his experience to the night world links Comus to folk spirits of the night and the forest more ambiguous and less innocent than the Fairies, Elves, and Nymphs of his imagined train. He joins the "flocking shadows pale" and "fetter'd Ghosts" who flee the daylight in Milton's Nativity Ode (232, 234), as they are also said to do in *A Midsummer Night's Dream* (3.2.378–87) and *Hamlet* (1.1.148–56).[38] It is not so surprising that when he invokes supernatural sponsorship of his revels, Comus turns to the dark goddesses Cotytto and Hecate, as his own cadences momentarily lengthen and gather weight, turning from light tetrameters into somber pentameters, loaded with harsh glottals and plosives, and melancholic nasals:

> Hail Goddess of Nocturnal sport,
> Dark veil'd *Cotytto,* t'whom the secret flame
> Of midnight Torches burns; mysterious Dame,
> That ne'er art call'd but when the Dragon womb
> Of Stygian darkness spits her thickest gloom,
> And makes one blot of all the air,
> Stay thy cloudy Ebon chair
> Wherein thou rid'st with *Hecat',* and befriend
> Us thy vow'd Priests, till utmost end
> Of all thy dues be done, and none left out.
>
> (128–37)

The tone darkens, and the dancing measure falters here.[39] Midsummer and Michaelmas festivities, permitted and encouraged by the Crown and by the church of Archbishop Laud, yield to darker pagan solemnities that Milton leaves largely to the imagination.[40]

But an audience imagination informed by Ovid's treatment of Medea's witchcraft (*Metamorphoses* 7.192–301) would not likely shrug off the reference to Hecate as preparation for some good clean fun.⁴¹ Comus's *carpe diem* appeal is rather a *carpe noctem* appeal, warping desire toward the darkness and stagnancy of an eternal round of "barbarous dissonance" (550, cf. *PL* 7.32) over which these goddesses preside, far from the light of day. His invocation, with its specification of dues owed to the Goddess in her form as the Teeth Mother, implies ritual sacrifice, and sacrifice requires a victim, a pure one if possible.⁴² The Lady's arrival is timely for the rite that Comus wishes to stage in blasphemic contradiction to the framing rite composed for the Egerton festivities. Comus's invocation here provides an additional ritual framework in which to read his capture of the Lady and the malevolent catechism he will subject her to. If she is at risk, on one hand, from the circling of Comus's pack of would-be bacchantes, his enchanted chair serves as a potential altar of blood sacrifice to the dark mother-goddesses to whom he devotes himself.

As a second-generation energy god driven by the rhythms of seasons and tides, Comus stakes out a position for himself as Nature's advocate. Yet for all his discussion of Nature's bounty in his appeal to the Lady, he expresses a curiously utilitarian notion of the uses of Nature. He understands divinely ordained plenitude primarily in terms of supply and demand. Although he condemns the temperate use of natural gifts as living "like Nature's bastards not her sons" (727), he is in fact Nature's bastard, and glamorizes the bastardization of nature, the self-gratifying libertine exploitation of its secret resources. The specious magnificence of his paean to natural fertility conceals a raging hunger:

> Wherefore did Nature pour her bounties forth
> With such a full and unwithdrawing hand,
> Covering the earth with odors, fruits, and flocks,
> Thronging the Seas with spawn innumerable,
> But all to please and sate the curious taste?
>
> (710–14)

In *Paradise Lost,* Milton will lift the glamorous mask of Comus and disclose that it is Death who wears it:

> To mee, who with eternal Famine pine,
> Alike is Hell, or Paradise, or Heaven,
> There best, where most with ravin I may meet;
> Which here, though plenteous, all too little seems
> To stuff this Maw, this vast unhide-bound Corpse.
>
> (*PL* 9.597–601)

Comus's palate appears to be more sophisticated, and his manners a bit neater, than Death's, yet he is driven by the same immense hunger. What fills him ultimately does not seem to matter, for the overbundance he assigns to Nature leads to a breakdown of qualitative distinctions between "odors, fruits, and flocks," the natural goods of the earth as objects of insatiable desire and consumption.[43]

4

What makes Comus so voracious? Angus Fletcher notes that "in *Comus* the most important instance of subsurface implication is the use of the myth of Circe. . . . Milton is withholding much of the direct narrative content of the myth of Circe, and it is this withheld context that fills the interior spaces of the myth of Comus, Thyrsis, the Lady, her brothers, and Sabrina."[44] Circe's latent influence, in other words, permeates the *Maske*. Fletcher implies that Circe serves as what Freud would call the repressed unconscious material of both Comus the character and *Comus* the ritual drama of initiation. We can begin to explicate this "withheld context" if we raise the question, provoked by the text of the *Maske,* of Comus's relation to his mother: what would maturation be like for a Dionysian man-child who has Bacchus as an absentee father, and Circe, sensual desire personified, as his mother?

We have already noticed the Attendant Spirit's observation that Comus is "Much like his Father, but his Mother more" (57). A strange elision creates a telling ambiguity in this observation. The primary meaning of the line seems to be "Much like his Father, but [like] his Mother more." The absence of the second "like," which would establish a likeness between Comus and his Mother analogous to that between him and his Father, suspends and oddly intensifies the nature of the maternal bond. Syntactic compression for the sake of scansion creates the effect of linguistic deterioration into a more archaic, imprecise, less clearly differentiated mode of articulation. With its lulling, suckling alliterations and its suspension of contextual anchors, "his Mother more" is orally evocative of the primal romance of nursing, where subject and object and act dissolve in one another. More like his Mother, Comus likes his Mother more. Comus never had it so good as when he was Circe's baby boy. Bereft of her, he tries to recapitulate the luscious sensual fullness of his infancy. He can never get enough of what he imagines Nature, in Circe's place, has to offer. Comus populates his imaginative world with maternal figures who appear irresistible, virtually omnipotent and potentially all-consuming, yet who invite aggression and possession. This suggests that his desire is regressive and infantile and that it involves reproducing such desire in the objects of his desire. His ambition at maturity is both to "Excel his Mother at her mighty Art" (63), and to recreate, in the "thick shelter of black shades imbow'r'd" (62), "the navel of this hideous Wood" (520), the womblike maternal surround of his upbringing. His impossible longing to excel his mother is also a longing to restage the scenario of his mother's ego-dissolving tendernesses. So he parodies the perverse and promiscuous fertility of Circe by using her cup of pleasure to give birth to monsters.

As we have noticed, Comus serves as "vow'd Priest" (136) to the spectral mother figure Cotytto and her crony Hecate, dark surrogates and analogues for Circe, in the hallucinatory night world of his "conceal'd Solemnity" (142). Wicked female grotesques, as we can see in Jonson's *The Masque of Queens,* or the masque scene in Beaumont and Fletcher's *The Maid's Tragedy,* are no strangers to the anarchic uproar of antimasques, but Comus's goddesses derive added sinister force by the very invisibility of their sponsorship of his revels. The infernal orgiast Cotytto, consorting with Hecate, usurps the patriarchal domain of the stars (1–5) and blurs its celestial mapping with a stratospheric, all-contaminating menstrual discharge: "mysterious Dame, / That ne'er art call'd but when the Dragon womb / Of Stygian darkness spits her thickest gloom, / And makes one blot of all the air" (130–34). Comus also reminisces more bucolicly about

> My mother *Circe* with the Sirens three,
> Amidst the flow'ry kirl'd *Naiades,*
> Culling their Potent herbs and baleful drugs,
> Who as they sung, would take the prison'd soul,
> And lap it in *Elysium; Scylla* wept,
> And chid her barking waves into attention,
> And fell *Charybdis* murmur'd soft applause.
>
> (253–59)

This narcotic lullaby, Comus testifies, "in pleasing slumber lull'd the sense, / And in sweet madness robb'd it of itself" (260–61). In this concentrated allusion to the sites of greatest danger to the resourceful and steadfast will of Odysseus—Circe, Sirens, Scylla and Charybdis—Comus discloses his nostalgia for a menacing yet cradling sensuality where he found himself most cozily at home.

Surprisingly, then, Comus's ritual function in the *Maske* as a male sexual aggressor entails a complementary and more subtle psychological threat, the lure of regressive absorption in the mythic Mother Goddess. William Kerrigan notices this linkage between phallic assertiveness and longing for the maternal surround, although he misdiagnoses it as Milton's problem rather than Comus's: "Perhaps this fusion of oedipal with preoedipal wholeness shows us why the phallic magic of Comus should reside in the navel of the woods, filling the scar that marks our original dismemberment."[45] Circe, Venus, Nature, Cotytto, Hecate: by whatever name he evokes her, Comus's mythic Mother keeps her children mesmerized with the lure of "th'all-worshpt ore and precious gems" hutched "in her own loins" (719, 718). Comus conjures up a Mother Nature who longs to be violated. If her riches were to go unplundered by her ungrateful children, she

> would be quite surcharg'd with her own weight,
> And strangl'd with her waste fertility;
> Th'earth cumber'd, and the wing'd air dark't with plumes,
> The herds would over-multitude their Lords,
> The Sea o'erfraught would swell, and th'unsought diamonds
> Would so emblaze the forehead of the Deep,
> And so bestud with Stars, that they below
> Would grow inur'd to light, and come at last
> To gaze upon the Sun with shameless brows.
> (728–36)

When we have analogous cataclysms in Shakespeare, they are produced by violations of, or dissensions within, natural order: the murder of a king (*Macbeth* 2.4.1–20), the "dissension" over a foundling child (*MND* 2.1.81–117). Comus perversely conjures the prospect of an apocalypse produced by the *refusal* to violate Nature.

This bizarre suggestion of an apocalypse of undevoured excess has psychological, ecological, and political ramifications. It is a dark and extravagant parody of the ecological reciprocities that will obtain in Milton's Eden, where Nature, requiring a gentler kind of human culling and cultivation, "Wanton'd as in her prime, and play'd at will / Her Virgin Fancies, pouring forth more sweet, / Wild above Rule or Art, enormous bliss" (*PL* 5.294–97). The Nature over which Adam and Eve are called to exercise their creative stewardship is prolific yet innocent.[46] Her fancies are virginal, and her abundance invites and responds to the delicate touch of human husbandry. By contrast, Comus imagines that his Mother Nature is neither virginal nor fanciful, but a kind of queen bee or termite. Her indiscriminate and ultimately self-smothering fecundity erases difference of species in the world order, disturbs class boundaries in the social order, and dissolves ego structure in the order of the psyche, until the very logic of generational distinction and progression collapses. Exploiting her riches will keep things in balance, Comus argues. More accurately, it will preserve the social order that supports and supplies aristocratic tastes and privileges. The ecological catastrophe resulting from Nature's unchecked fecundity would produce the political catastrophe of a world turned upside down, where "herds would over-multitude their Lords" (731) and "they below / Would grow inur'd to light, and come at last / To gaze upon the Sun with shameless brows" (734–36). The economic and ecological implications of Comus's position, with its legitimization of the rarefied tastes and extravagances of an aristocratic leisure class and its complementary suppression of the underclasses, are particular to the cavalier fancies of the Stuart era, yet the supply-side logic of unrestricted wish fulfillment makes his pitch anticipate the thematics and the consequences of the political economy of postmodern consumer capitalism.[47]

Comus's personal investment in and reproduction of his mother's arts accounts for the power of his appeal. He participates in and presides over a mythological representation of Lacan's Imaginary order.[48] In Lacan's account, the Imaginary order distills itself from the child's mirroring primary relation to the mother. Lacan observes, "Man's desire finds its meaning in the desire of the other, not so much because the other holds the key to the object desired, as because the first object of desire is to be recognized by the other."[49] The child desires the mother as his primary object choice, and the child's desire mimics the mother's desire for the child. The Imaginary, where the child's desire continually reflects and is reflected in the desire of the mother, produces a plenary field of erotically charged, intense yet briefly lived images: the Imaginary is "a 'dual relationship,' an ambiguous redoubling, a 'mirror' reflection, an immediate relationship between the subject and its other in which each term passes immediately into the other and is lost in a never-ending play of reflections."[50] In Lacan's psychoanalytic paradigm, the father eventually interrupts this charmed circle, alienating the child's desire from the all-absorbing desire of the mother and redesignating it according to the order of culture, where we are henceforth fated to mature our divided identities and destinies. The Symbolic is a culturally and linguistically patterned template for the social formation of a desire that is already, and always will be, charged with phantasmal objects and intentions that resist the threats, entitlements, and enticements of culture. Outbursts from the circuitry of the Imaginary register continually flare up to startle, disrupt, and redirect the Symbolic orchestrations of conscious intention.

In effect, Comus enacts such an outburst in the Symbolic psychodrama of Milton's *Maske*. The Attendant Spirit, a mediator of the Symbolic, speaking in the Name of the Father, intends to orchestrate the initiation of the Lady Alice Egerton and her brothers into the securities and opportunities of a patriarchally stabilized culture. His parodic counterpart, at once projection and captive and master of the Imaginary, Comus plays out the archaic and presocial claims of the Mother of desire, whose regressive call and mesmerizing image float through the liminal spaces of psyche and culture, resistant to and uncolonized by more complex, stressful, and morally charged forms of cultural knowledge. The inevitable rupture of the charmed circle of his own infantile enchantment with Circe leads Comus in the furious circling dance of endlessly generated, endlessly displaced, endlessly unsatisfied desire. The "light fantastic round" (144) of his dance is a figure for his longing and his lostness, his slippage through the labyrinthine self-entangled womb-world of unstable spectacle. The "light fantastic round" is a figure too for the Imaginary desire that drives his rhetoric. That he is a fast talker, a rhetorical whirligig whose delectably elusive images have the momentary and affective brilliance of an extraordinarily brief half-life, is a sign of his attempt to subject language—the signifying materialization of the Symbolic register—to the destabilizing momentum of the Imaginary.[51] He himself cannot slow down because his rapid-fire free-associative bravado is a way of veiling the anxious suspicion that he is tap-dancing across metaphysical quicksand.

Strangely but inevitably, Comus himself discloses, in his initial gambits of seduction, the spiritual exhaustion of the Imaginary roller coaster he is riding. Trying to soften the Lady up, he offers her the sprightly cordial in his magic glass:

> Not that *Nepenthes* which the wife of *Thone*
> In *Egypt* gave to Jove-born *Helena*
> Is of such power to stir up joy as this,
> To life so friendly, or so cool to thirst.
>
> (675–78)

"You must be tired; have a refreshing drink." This sounds like an inviting gesture of conventional hospitality until we consider the context of Comus's Homeric allusion. In the palace of Menelaos,

Helen offers the drug to her husband and to their melancholic young guest Telemachos, as an anodyne and sedative to quiet the youth's grieving for the lost father he seeks and to ease the sorrow it stirs in Menelaos as guilty survivor of the war over his marriage. Nepenthes: No Pain. The drug's effect is not to stir up joy, but to douse pain and memory in oblivion:

> Into the wine of which they were drinking she cast a medicine
> of heartsease, free of gall, to make one forget all sorrows,
> and whoever had drunk it down once it had been mixed in the
>   wine bowl,
> for the day that he drank it would have no tear roll down his face,
> not if his mother died and his father died, not if men
> murdered a brother or a beloved son in his presence
> with the bronze, and he with his own eyes saw it.
>
> (4.220–26)[52]

In the *Odyssey*, Helen is quick to offer this anodyne. In the haunted splendor of their shining palace, unblessed by male children of their own and surrounded by the memories of all who have died and all that has been destroyed for their sake, Helen and Menelaos might be presumed to depend on Nepenthes as the drug of choice to make their lives bearable.[53] Comus offers his potion to another wandering child on the threshold of maturity. Bereft of family and searching for home, the Lady is both Telemachos the searcher and Odysseus the lost wanderer. In Comus's hands, Helen's narcotic cup is also Circe's potion of sensual self-abandonment. It is not surprising that Comus resorts to a pharmacopœia of narcotics, distilled by skilled enchantresses, if his project is the dissolution of selfhood in the interests of primordial motherhood. But it is surprising that he would hint this so explicitly, so early in his seduction effort, to a well-educated and self-aware Lady who is already on her guard, and hardly subject to the spiritual enervation to which he appeals.[54]

Comus continues to ply his offer of solace and refreshment by teasing the Lady for

> Scorning the unexempt condition
> By which all mortal frailty must subsist,
> Refreshment after toil, ease after pain,
> That have been tir'd all day without repast,
> And timely rest have wanted; but, fair Virgin,
> This will restore all soon.
>
> (685–90)

Comus slows his pacing to intensify his appeal here, through the hypnotic tempo of slow-breathed lines, phrases spaced by languorous pauses, and the alternation of consonant rhymes that quietly seal off each line. This is a hypnotic incantation that seeks to produce the spiritual condition of exhaustion and relaxation by the act of description. Comus models this appeal on the virtuoso performance of one of Spenser's great rhetorical enchanters. Despayre offers death to the Redcrosse Knight as the final solution, as solace and refreshment for a wayfaring, warfaring, conscience-stricken life:

> Is not short paine well borne, that brings long ease,
> And layes the soule to sleepe in quiet graue?
> Sleepe after toyle, port after stormie seas,
> Ease after warre, death after life does greatly please.
>   (*FQ* 1.9.40.6–9)

Comus more or less successfully effaces his master source here, and gives a more upbeat twist to the outcome of his offering. But the voice, the very word, of Despayre surfaces in the phrases "Refreshment after toil, ease after pain," and in the promise of "timely rest."[55] This tells us more about Comus, at this stage of the ritual, than it does about the Lady. He attempts to project on her his own spiritual condition, as Despayre seeks to make men feel what he always and already is. It is strange to discover from this slight but emphatic Spenserian echo that Comus's libertine vitalism is a disguised version of the voice of despair, and despair is what he hopes to provoke in his test of the Lady's chastity. Still young in the career of chastity, the Lady has hardly reached the stage of afflicted conscience and battle fatigue that renders the Redcrosse Knight so vulnerable to Despayre's seduction. But Comus's cup of refreshment is no less deadly in its consequences than the dagger that Despayre offers to Spenser's hero. His rhetoric is a suicide bomb with a slow fuse.

5

We have seen how Comus's desire is to prevent the ritual of the *Maske* from growing a girl into a woman. There is double trouble, with both a masculine threat and a feminine allure, in his temptation and his threat to her. As the mock bridegroom of the rite of passage, he provokes and tests her curiosity and fear about male desire, seeking her subjection to libertine versions of sexuality and social order. As Circe's best boy, advance man for the claims of an ego-dissolving maternity, he spins out regressive notions of womanhood as models for self-fashioning. Cunningly, Comus offers the Lady both positions in the dialectic that drives his hunger for life. He reasons that the Lady's natural beauty, analogous to and dependent on the Earth Mother as a prolific generator, requires a gathering hand to keep it fresh:

> Why should you be so cruel to yourself,
> And to those dainty limbs which nature lent
> For gentle usage and soft delicacy?
> But you invert the cov'nants of her trust,
> And harshly deal like an ill borrower
> With that which you receiv'd on other terms.
> . . . .
> Beauty is nature's coin, must not be hoarded,
> But must be current, and the good thereof
> Consists in mutual and partak'n bliss,
> Unsavory in th'enjoyment of itself.
> . . . .
> Beauty is nature's brag, and must be shown
> In courts, at feasts and high solemnities
> Where most may wonder at the workmanship.
> (679–84, 739–42, 745–47)

Comus is a shrewd erotic economist. He employs two economic models of accounting for the Lady's beauty. In terms of the developing economy of mercantile capitalism, he represents her beauty as on loan from nature's capital. In this configuration, the Lady can take her place as a commodities trader in the sex exchange. Her prized commodity is her body—synecdochically, "those dainty limbs," a lovely but perishable portion of nature's overabundant stores. If she is to honor her covenant with nature and profit from it, she must put it into circulation, the sooner the better. In representing beauty as "nature's coin" (739) and "nature's brag" (745), Comus invokes a more traditional and class-specific mode of exchange, appropriate to the extravagant traditions of masquing. Noblesse oblige dictates the uses of beauty in this version of libidinal economics. If you've got it, flaunt it: the Lady is obligated by the protocols of aristocratic generosity and magnificence both to show and to share her inherited wealth. The two models converge in their appraisals of the economic value of the Lady's beauty. But her essential value, in Comus's scheme, is in being and acting beautiful. Comus's persuasion develops Petrarchan flattery beyond the idealizing objectification of female beauty into the modern commodification of it.

At the same time, in his carpe diem appeal—"If you let slip time, like a neglected rose / It withers on the stalk with languish't head" (743–44)—Comus appears to profer a kind of exploitative agency to the Lady. As the languishing rose head warns her of phallic disappointment, Comus suggests that the rifling of Nature's stores need not be the employment only of her sons. There is a certain degree of *trompe l'esprit* in this line of argument, for the Lady is invited to enjoy Nature's wealth at the same time that the invitation reduces her options, making her an emblem of Nature's potentially "waste fertility" and an object of enjoyment. This is a bait and switch operation that Satan will perfect in his seduction of Eve. The fast patter and specious logic tries to seal off objections or questions before they can be raised, even as Comus hopes for the subliminal prurience of his suggestions to linger and take effect. The trick is to convince the Lady that putting her beauty and her desire into circulation will enhance her own pleasure "in mutual and partak'n bliss" (741). Her beauty "*must not be* hoarded, / But *must be* current" (739–40) and "*must be shown* / In courts, at feasts, and high solemnities" (745–46; emphasis mine). Her beauty, he intimates, is not just ripe for the plucking, but a passport to aristocratic bliss. As agent and center of an endless suite of pleasure-giving sensations, she can participate in the creative ransacking of the earth. But the strange constructions of passive hortatory verb forms—the repeated "must be"—depersonalize the action and diminish the Lady's implied agency. The Lady is nowhere to be found as a subject in the syntax of these appeals. Their promises of mastery and of pleasure are Imaginary. His rhetoric thus gives away Comus's game just as he wishes the Lady to give away her beauty. The only modes of activity for which the Lady would be licensed in the libertine gaieties of Comus's circles would be the coquettries, submissions, seductions, and self-displays by which women played out the illusions of power in Renaissance courts like those of the Stuarts.

Cedric Brown observes of Comus's speech, "We are being shown the mind of a refined dissolute, and image of 'effeminate' aristocracy, seen through the glass of a precise Protestant."[56] But this is not only an appeal to the conventionally understood class interests and privileges of the Stuart court, it is good modern advertising strategy. Comus tries to cultivate of the Lady's emerging desire a selfhood whose primary obligation is to saturate itself in pleasures. To make her his queen or part of his herd is to restrict her social maturation, simultaneously subjecting her to the pressures of aggressive male desire and captivating her in the regressive fantasy world of the Imaginary, thus preventing her emergence as Milton's exemplar of the autonomous ethical self of progressive Reformation culture. Even as Milton's *Maske* stages the ritual formation of the Lady as self-conscious, reflective moral agent and experiential center of the world, it represents in the figure of Comus a canny dream manufacturer who reifies a parody of that self: a perpetual consumer who would be in turn consumed by the artificial projection and cultivation of appetite.

But in the moral dialectic typical of Milton, Comus ironically performs a cultural service he seeks to subvert, proposing and dramatizing for the Lady a demonstrably false set of solutions to the challenge of desire and parodic representations of the cultural paradigms that the Lady proceeds to integrate and internalize. As a type of demonic catechist, Comus prefigures the Satan of *Paradise Regained* and, more obliquely, the antagonists of *Samson Agonistes*. The Lady in turn becomes the first of Milton's great protagonists to be subjected to a purifying trial of knowledge by what seeks to disguise itself as cultural wisdom. Victor Turner describes the intellectual and symbolic challenge of the liminal stage in a way that makes ritual sense of the Lady's contention with Comus:

> During the liminal period, neophytes are alternately forced and encouraged to think about their society, their cosmos, and the powers that generate and sustain them. Liminality may be partly described as a stage of reflection. In it those ideas, sentiments, and facts that had been hitherto for the neophytes bound up in configurations and accepted unthinkingly are, as it were, resolved into their constituents. These constituents are isolated and made into objects of reflection for the neophytes by such processes as componental exaggeration and dissociation by varying concomitants . . . [and finally recombined] in ways that make sense with regard to the new state and status that the neophytes will enter.[57]

Comus serves this purpose of conceptual disruption in the *Maske* by presenting to the Lady perversions, created by "componental exaggeration and dissociation by varying concomitants," of the knowledge that she will proceed to reintegrate and articulate in her refutation of his appeal. The articulation of that truth both clarifies it and makes it her own, no longer the cultural wisdom she has taken in trust from her parents and tutors, but the existential wisdom she will henceforth need in her "new state and status."

The extraordinary range of the debate between Comus and the

4: DOUBLE TROUBLE: COMUS AND HIS BLOODLINES   171

Lady results from Comus's scrambled and distorted deployment of a series of Renaissance commonplaces, in what Turner calls "fantastic or monstrous patterns and shapes."[58] Eager to dissolve the Lady's emerging sense of self in the flux of interminable longing, his "gay Rhetoric" (790) dissolves discrete terms and figures in a verbal whirlpool where everything becomes a rib-nudging vehicle for the omnipresent and omnivorous tenor of desire. Yet every one of his claims proves to be a test of what the Lady thinks about God, Nature, desire, economy, labor, beauty, philosophy, selfhood, language, and the body. His attempt at seduction provides the opportunity for her to make clear to herself what she believes about what she has been taught, and, in the public ritual, to iterate her newly and personally claimed beliefs in the presence of her family and community. A rigorist of the imagination with a higher irony of her own, the Lady refutes Comus point by point by rescuing the elements of his discourse from the metaphysical and rhetorical whirlpool, patiently yet critically sorting them out and reconfiguring them as elements in a just social economy consonant with a productive natural ecology:

> Imposter, do not charge most innocent Nature
> As if she would her children should be riotous
> With her abundance; she, good cateress,
> Means her provision only to the good
> That live according to her sober laws
> And holy dictate of spare Temperance:
> If every just man that now pines with want
> Had but a moderate and beseeming share
> Of that which lewdly-pamper'd Luxury
> Now heaps upon some few with vast excess,
> Nature's full blessing would be well dispens't
> In unsuperfluous even proportion,
> And she no whit encumber'd with her store,
> And then the giver would be better thank't,
> His praise due paid, for swinish gluttony
> Ne'er looks to Heav'n amidst his gorgeous feast,
> But with besotted base ingratitude
> Crams, and blasphemes his feeder.
>
> (762–78)

This cold douche of a reply is a splendid, poised, critical, decorous, and startling response to Comus's pitch. Because it is a refutation so unexpected, we tend to overlook its dramatic, poetic, and political implications. It is, first of all, a remarkable challenge to the courtly witnesses of the *Maske,* since it questions the very principle of magnificence that motivates and underwrites such lavish entertainments. "No masque ever examined the moral bases of its own rituals more directly than this," observes Cedric Brown; it "prompts the audience to hold the seductions of the habitually rich spirit of festivity up to the proper standards of pious simplicity."[59]

It challenges the gender typologies of courtly poetics as well. That the Lady speaks at all is, as we have seen, a startling challenge to the conventions of the masque genre. More remarkably, the Lady sounds a female voice virtually unwritten and unheard in literary discourse outside the pamphlet wars of the period. Of the countless libertine seduction poems that populate anthologies of seventeenth-century lyric, then and now, how often is the woman under pressure given a voice to respond? The Lady's is a rare voice issuing from the tantalizing zone of female silence circumscribed by the traditions of masculine lyric love discourse: how coy is the coy mistress, how cruel the various tyrannesses and murderesses who occasion libertine longing and lament?[60] By refusing to engage Comus in his own terms and thus to sustain the tantalization, the Lady refuses to walk the walk and talk the talk of conventional masques and lyrics. She critiques and rejects the discourse of erotic wit for the sake of the higher moral and political decorum that orders Milton's transcendental masque. There is no love talk or sex talk in the Lady's response. This is not because she is a prude in the making, as Comus jokes and various critics of the *Maske* have long complained, but because she is already more grown up than Comus. With more serious things to consider than the erotic tenor of his boy banter, she refuses to provoke or encourage him. There is no self-defensiveness in the speech, only the sober certainty (263) of vital principles. We do not expect such disinterested poise, ethical maturity, and political insight of a fifteen-year-old girl, especially one in forced bondage whose virginity is at risk.

Like Comus, readers are startled by the Lady's high-mindedness; with her tough, frank talk, she does not behave enough like a Lady. The first true Miltonist, for whom poetry is the highest form of prophetic social action, she changes the primary subject of the conversation from sex to economic justice and its relation to authentic piety. Erotic self-abandonment, the subtext of Comus's appeal, yields to the Lady's discourse about conscientious and other-directed husbandry of resources: personal, social, natural, and rhetorical resources. Articulating natural law by analogy to the principles that govern the Puritan version of the early modern household and the wider social order in which the household is situated, the Lady projects an ecology and an economy that reconfigure desire into a commonwealth of social and political goods beyond the reach of immediate self-gratification.

In comparison to Comus's projection of mother Nature as a blind abyss of promiscuous fecundity, the Lady's image of Nature is intentional, just, and temperate. The Lady's chaste temperament discovers its foundation and authorization in Nature's own orderly, self-regulating processes.[61] The Lady recasts Comus's overwhelmingly prolific Mother Nature in the more sober garb of a principled, frugal, yet generous Puritan housewife: charity rather than extravagance, chastity rather than promiscuity, are the ordering principles of her fruitfulness and beauty. The Lady personifies Nature as the kind of matron she aspires to become. This figure has no place in Comus's dichotomizing typology of the feminine, corresponding neither to the beauty queen nor to the household drone, the caricatures by which he delimits women's destiny in the world. By so humanizing and domesticating her, the Lady demythologizes Comus's Nature and the destructive Imaginary feminine she represents and reconstructs her as a maternal imago answerable to the needs of an emerging autonomous and temperate subject and of the more equitable social world that supports her.[62] If Echo becomes for the Lady a muse, the translated form of her own chastity as it manifests itself in poetic and prophetic utterance (230–43), the hospitable Nature of her correction of Comus becomes a manifestation of the social form by which her chastity will reveal itself in and to the world.

The Lady's journey, then, entails a ritual regression into the Dionysian realm of the tragic and the Circean domain of the Imaginary over which Comus presides. The Lady's contention with Comus becomes a trial wherein she dramatically confronts the very spirit of tragedy in order to recoup its energies for the formation of a radiant, optative, and self-transcending poetics of identity. In the defense and formation of that identity, the Lady's resistance to Comus releases desire from the threat of tragic obliteration, from subjection to predatory male appetite, and from the hall of mirrors where the emerging self melts into the fleeting specular image of the lost but all-powerful Mother. Milton's ritual drama seeks to chasten from its Lady's emerging and maturing desire all that threatens it with self-destruction and to direct this chastened form of desire to the prophetic life of poetry and the charitable and just sociability that issues from such poetry. Renewed mastery of myth, as it is projected in the double trouble of Comus's parents, provides poetic energy for the Lady's self-fashioning and for the luminous harmonies of the text that scripts her initiation. In response to Comus laying the Imaginary snare of a world of equivocal and fleeting pleasure at her feet, the Lady masters and integrates the primary lessons of natural and social wisdom that will order her mature life in the world and consolidates a poetic that honors this world while holding out for the world to come.

5
Girl Power: The Profession of Virginity

1

AT THE END OF THE PREVIOUS CHAPTER, WE STUDIED THE LADY'S refutation of Comus and her reconstruction of his pretenses to knowledge, within what A. S. P. Woodhouse called "the order of Nature,"[1] which is, of course, Comus's ultimate although self-circumscribed and skewed horizon of knowing and desiring. It would have been enough for her to leave off here, in keeping with the aristocratic social decorum of the conventional masque and with the range of social virtues it sustains. So it is that in the Bridgewater Manuscript, which is as close as we are likely to get to a performance text of the *Maske,* Alice Egerton's last words are those that praise Nature's self-regulating "sober laws" (766) and argue for a just distribution of her abundance (762–79). But Milton frequently reaches a rhetorical plateau as the climax of an argument or image that proves to be the threshold of a new level of proclamation. There is yet more. The Lady completes her mastery of Comus and transfiguration of his offerings with the profession of virginity that Milton adds to the text of the *Maske* for its publication in 1637 (779–99). Milton adds this passage to the Lady's speech so that the Lady can reveal how it is that virginity, her seeming point of greatest desirability and vulnerability to her antagonist, is the very source of her strength, which is to say, of her poetry. If the first part of her repudiation of Comus exposes and responds to his offense against Nature, this visionary addendum exposes and responds to his offense against herself. Even though Lady Alice did not speak these words, they seal her initiation by disclosing and explicating the poetics of chastity embodied in her performance.[2]

Comus and the Lady are not arguing about abstractions. Because her body and its place in the world are the very subject of her rite of passage, her body is also the site where arguments about Nature, economy, justice, morality, energy, and poetics are staged. The

Lady's virgin state becomes the flash point in the ritual crisis of the *Maske*.³ Comus acknowledges it as the testing point of her virtue: "List Lady, be not coy, and be not cozen'd / With that same vaunted name Virginity" (737–38). Rising to iconoclastic eloquence, the Lady articulates in response an ethical and aesthetic self-recognition that signals not only her invulnerability to Comus, but also her prophetic arrival at moral and sexual maturity. William Kerrigan stresses Milton's spiritual materialism, or what we might describe as his incarnational literalism, when he observes, "The argument of *Comus* is trying to include the body, not just what the body means, in the order of grace."⁴ The argument of the *Maske*, that is, is not just *about* the body, it is *of* the body. As Comus bespeaks the condition of sensual dissolution, the Lady learns to bespeak the condition of virgin chastity. "Virginity is a force contingent solely on the innocent condition of the human body":⁵ the Lady's virginity, as she exercises it and represents it in poetry, song, and dance, discloses itself as the point where the temporal realities of corporal existence intersect with the spiritual possibilities of the eternal. If the mythic subtexts of her ordeal threaten her with dismemberment and dispersal, her virgin body is the outward and visible sign of continuity, integration, and unity.

The Lady and her brothers think of virginity and chastity as virtually synonymous. Given their youth and their unmarried state, this perspective is sensible and appropriate, although the *Maske*'s dramatic and thematic development complicates their naive identification somewhat, by representing virginity and chastity as distinct yet continuous and mutually identifying terms. Virginity, a physical condition and "natural" state of a body unmarked by sexual intercourse, is a cultural and biological universal, but its meaning and value are differently coded by different cultures according to their construction of sexuality. Because it is as yet unmarked by sexual contact, an ineradicable form of social encounter, it is both a mystery that precedes and resists cultural explanation, "an absolute physical and metaphysical fact,"⁶ and a blank slate on which cultures and subcultures project their fantasies and ideologies of sexuality. In its physical sense, virginity is a condition of complete simplicity,⁷ a state of physical intactness that represents biographical continuity with and continuation of the hopefully protected enclosures of childhood. Chastity is a more socially complex condition, signaling a potential openness to experience and to otherness, in contrast to the self-enclosure of virginity. Chastity marks a transference of values of steadfastness and nurturing affection for others from the closed system of the family to the larger arena of social relationship: "The question posed by chastity as an occupation of personhood—whose mastery does it signify?—extends beyond the virginal body to implicate the social roles played by women both outside and within marriage. As a willed assumption of sexual identity, chastity claims responsibility not only for the body but also for the social negotiations it inhabits."[8] Because it is a condition determined by social relations, it seems paradoxically a condition less enigmatic than virginity. Perhaps this is why Milton's interpreters have been more concurrent in their appraisals of the role of chastity than of the role of virginity in the *Maske*.

Married women and men may be chaste although they are no longer virgins. It is also possible, on the other hand, that a coquette or coy mistress could be a virgin yet not truly chaste. This assumption, a favorite of libertinism, informs many of the cynical nominalist poems that tease out the innuendoes of Comus's smirking, "List Lady, be not coy, and be not cozen'd / With that same vaunted name Virginity" (737–38). Virginity, then, marks a bodily condition that may either index or conceal a spiritual disposition, whereas chastity informs an ethical and spiritual disposition, publicly organized and socially conscious, toward the body. Both chastity and virginity are positions which situate people not only in relation to themselves but in relation to others.[9]

We can tentatively glean the difference between them in Milton's work by applying retroactively the controversial formula blueprinting Adam and Eve's relationship in *Paradise Lost:* "Hee for God only, Shee for God in him" (*PL* 4.299). I assume that if Milton were living at this hour, he would disarm our objections to this passage's apparent subordination of women by making explicit to us the notion that the epic proceeds to dramatize: the hierarchical element in this formulation, which apparently privileges Adam, is not rigid, but fluid and reversible, on account of the dynamic mutuality endlessly unfolding between Adam and Eve and transforming them in both prelapsarian and postlapsarian experience.[10] Each character stands naked in every respect before God and owes God primary loyalty, each discovers and honors something of God that would remain unknown but for the virtue and the love of the other. Even as we acknowledge the sweet fullness of their sexual experience, we might nevertheless propose, on the basis of Milton's ostensibly hierarchical formula, that Adam, "for God only," typifies the spiritual disposition of virginity, and Eve, "for God in him," typifies the spiritual disposition of chastity. Each condition stands in primary relation to God, but the virgin stands for and with God as God discloses himself in an unmediated way to the self. In the state of marital chastity, the chaste person stands for and with God in and through the other, the beloved.

In early modern England, the two terms do not form an opposition but a complementarity. Given that God alone knows the inward disposition of virginity and that chastity adapts and expresses itself interpersonally and situationally, their relationship must be fluid and indeterminate. Yet their relationship and their comparative worth came to be differently valued under the dispensation of religious reform during the sixteenth and seventeenth centuries. Ecclesial mythologization of virginity and extreme idealization of celibacy, characteristic of patristic and medieval thinking, were grounded in theological suspicion of expressive sexuality and in a feudal organization of marriage in terms of dynastic alliances and property settlements: what's love got to do with it? Reformation thinking, in reaction, sponsored companionate marriage as a sociable sexual ethic more consonant with scripture, correspondent with the interests of the classes benefiting from emerging capitalist enterprise and encouraged by the promise of spiritual freedom to the reformed believer. "For Anglicans no less than Puritans, we are told, marriage and conjugal affection became increasingly idealized and encouraged, while the sustained life of celibacy was devalued and dismissed as sinful popery."[11] Sanctified by God in the unfallen garden (Genesis 1:26–28, 2:21–25), typologized by Paul as a figure for Christ's relationship to the Church (Ephesians 5:22–33), and by John's vision of the eschatological marriage of the Lamb in Revelation (19:5–9, 21:1–4), marital chastity was advocated as the providentially authorized and privileged basis of social and personal good in this world.[12]

2

Yet Milton's Puritan *Maske* seems on its face to contradict or at least complicate the Protestant ethos, when the Lady extols virginity with visionary ardency and prophetic seriousness. It is time now to look at the speech:

> Shall I go on?
> Or have I said enough? to him that dares
> Arm his profane tongue with contemptuous words

5: GIRL POWER: THE PROFESSION OF VIRGINITY

> Against the Sun-clad power of Chastity
> Fain would I something say, yet to what end?
> Thou hast nor Ear nor Soul to apprehend
> The sublime notion and high mystery
> That must be utter'd to unfold the sage
> And serious doctrine of Virginity,
> And thou art worthy that thou shouldst not know
> More happiness than this thy present lot.
> Enjoy your dear Wit and gay Rhetoric
> That hath so well been taught her dazzling fence,
> Thou art not fit to hear thyself convinc't;
> Yet should I try, the uncontrolled worth
> Of this pure cause would kindle my rapt spirits
> To such a flame of sacred vehemence,
> That dumb things would be mov'd to sympathize,
> And the brute Earth would lend her nerves, and shake,
> Till all thy magic structures rear'd so high,
> Were shatter'd into heaps o'er thy false head.
>
> (779–99)

Georgia Christopher observes that "in *Comus* the mystic powers that folklore had associated with virginity suggest the mystery of such a union with Christ."[13] But this same observation can equally refer to pre-Reformation and Counter-Reformation imaginings of virginity as spiritual vocation. Virgin magic is a major theme in discourse about sexuality in the patristic and medieval period, the stuff of the golden legends of saints and of mystical theology. In the archaic image layers of Milton's *Maske* are residues of just such fantasies. Yet the *Maske,* composed in the secularizing dispensation of Reformation England, projects the Lady's virginity as the source of an activist, expressive, reformatory magic rather than as a fugitive and cloistered virtue (*Areopagitica,* 728). The Lady's body state expresses itself in a profession of virginity as its poet and prophet; her virginity makes her rhetorically and politically stronger, rather than more vulnerable.[14] So her high-minded, austere rebuke to Comus is not a recycling of medieval notions of celibacy. It advocates virginity as a preemptive defense of and preparation for a life of "redeemed sexuality."[15] Virginity's vocation is the enrichment of the body's life in the world and in the world to which it is properly destined, rather than a stigmatization and renunciation of that life.

Because Alice Egerton, as the Lady in question, never actually uttered these words in the *Maske*'s performance on Michaelmas Eve, 1634, it has been argued that this literary addendum complicates the performance script in such a way as to to open up a tension or even a contradiction between the complementary terms of temperance (767), chastity (782), and virginity (787). Arthur Barker noted this seeming inconsistency and still speaks for a number of critics in his observation that "what remains when these lines [779–99] are omitted is a perfectly consistent debate in which Comus derides abstinence as the absurd alternative to his sensuality and the Lady neatly counters with her description of temperance."[16] In other words, the Lady's sudden raising of her pitch and amplification of her argument at a moment when performance script turns into printed text seems to disrupt a decorous resolution to the developmental crisis she has already neatly resolved in favor of "the normative affirmation of temperate conjugal sexual behavior, the doctrine of 'married chastity.'"[17]

As if anticipating such complaints, the Lady's own prefatory remarks deliberately draw attention to the rhetorical and thematic shift in her argument: "Shall I go on? Or have I said enough?" (779–80). These questions are odd rhetorical markers. To whom are they addressed? Clearly she is not asking Comus, her dramatic adversary, for permission or assessment. She seems, rather, to be pausing to check in with herself, to be taking a deep breath to muster her energies for the vehement outburst to follow. She is also traversing the implicit boundary of the fictional and textual space to make verbal contact with us rather than her immediate adversary, with the reading audience looking in upon her ordeal, who may intuit from her speech what she refuses to disclose to Comus. In fact, she does not say what she would like to say. She refers in the subjunctive to the speech that Comus does not deserve to hear: "Fain *would I something say,* yet to what end? . . . Yet *should I try,* the uncontrolled worth / Of this pure cause *would kindle* my rapt spirits" (783, 793–94; emphasis mine). Her hesitations and her subjunctives highlight the crucial and problematic nature of the passage. Is it a literary afterthought that steers the *Maske* into ideological commitments inappropriate to its original performance occasion, or is it a kind of self-explicating completion of the performance?

One way to resolve these questions is to argue that the defense of temperance and chastity (755–78) was scripted for Alice Egerton's debut in such a way as to observe the decorum of the social occasion, of her family's expectations, and of her emerging status as marriageable young aristocrat, while the profession of virginity added in the published text of the *Maske* (778–98) is Milton's public articulation of his own poetic cult of virginity.[18] While this claim may seem sensible, it resolves the questions prematurely. Segregating the playing version from the published version of the *Maske* begs the critical question of whether the addition is indeed a Miltonic excess that spoils the *Maske*'s delicate interplay of the sensuous and the ethical, the erotic and the sublime. I think the extra passage is a necessary enlargement of the performed *Maske*'s field of vision and of rhetoric. It is consistent with the Lady's defiant declaration to Comus, "Thou canst not touch the freedom of my mind / With all thy charms, although this corporal rind / Thou hast immanacl'd, while Heav'n sees good" (663–65). It is consistent with the cosmic vision provided by the Attendant Spirit in his Prologue (1–17) and with the heroic iconography of the Elder Brother's idealism, which blurs the distinction between "saintly chastity" and "true virginity" (418–74). The Lady's visionary addendum announces and explicates the poetics and ethics implicit in the playing version of the *Maske,* and it alludes to more removed mysteries which the live performance of the *Maske* could only intimate indirectly. It elaborates the conditions of the mind's freedom and indicates the kerygmatic power of words spoken from the place of that freedom.[19]

For the unmarried Lady, of course, the textual coordination of chastity and virginity which vexes Milton's critics is not a disjuncture but a continuity. She cannot defend her virginity as a physical condition without defining and depending on chastity as an ethical condition. The strength of her chastity grows out of the value she assigns to her virginity and the fervency of her idealization of it. The *Maske* functions as a rite of passage that marks the point in Alice Egerton's life when her virginity passes from a familially endowed and patriarchally defended legacy to an active personal choice. Insofar as the *Maske* prepares her for productive and socially engaged womanhood, it invests in her virginal condition and fortifies it by an ethical possibility unavailable to her in childhood: chastity. Sniffing her emergent fertility, Comus backs her into a corner and forces her to defend her choice of virginity. In doing so, she defines chastity and discovers why it matters to her.

In the Lady's amplified speech, "the sage / And serious doctrine of Virginity" (787) appears as the third term in the doctrinal register of virtues that includes the "holy dictate of spare Temperance" (767) and "the Sun-clad power of Chastity" (782). Syntactic parallelism and continuity create a bridge from the performance text into the new material of the published text and create ambiguity about the relation of terms. Looked at one way, "the Sun-clad power of Chastity" seems virtually equivalent to and interchangeable with the "sage / And serious doctrine of Virginity": the Lady is using different yet parallel phrases to talk about the same condition. Yet the sequencing of the virtues also seems to position "Chastity" as a significant prior term in an ethical and spiritual series that climaxes in "Virginity." In this sense, chastity is a necessary prolegomenon to a unique and untranslatable order of being, virginity. This doctrinal trinity echoes and translates the Lady's previous fortifying vision of "pure-ey'd Faith, white-handed Hope," and "unblemish't form of Chastity" (213–15). In the earlier passage, finding herself alone "in single darkness" (204), the Lady invented iconographical markers for Faith, Hope, and Chastity, which invested them with the attributes—pure eyes, white hands, unblemished form—of her own virginity. In her defensive rebuttal of Comus, she now dogmatizes them as a way of stiffening their conceptual resistance to the corrosively equivocating "dazzling fence" (791) of Comus's rhetoric. Chastity, as she articulates it, is the dispositional armor of virginity. It is virginity made conscious of itself by the trial of passions within and pleasures round about (*Areopagitica*, 733) and made articulate in its self-defense.

Angus Fletcher suggests that the mystique of virginity is greatest when a young woman like Alice Egerton enters sexual maturity: "One can go on being chaste as long as one likes, but virginity (in its ideal essence, which is not to be confused with its merely physical aspect) suffers from entropy. Virginity at fifteen is more perfect than virginity at fifty."[20] This provocative insight strikes one of Fletcher's rare false notes. How could virginity "in its ideal essence" suffer from entropy, when it is the virginal body that grows old and withers, as libertine poets like Comus always like to remind their virgin prey? One could argue that under the Protestant dispensation, "virginity at fifteen is more perfect than virginity at fifty," since the sexual destiny preferred and proferred by the All-Giver of the Reformation is chaste companionate marriage. Yet Fletcher does not seem to intend this political point so much as to betray inadvertently that he shares with Comus a common male fantasy about the superior desirability of young and undefiled women. His misprision is valuable for its cultural implication: the symbolic and social value of virginity comes into focus during the period when the young woman discovers herself to be both erotically alive to herself and desirable to others. As a social value, to be virginal, attractive, and potentially fertile "guarantees to the female her value within the social system of reciprocity."[21] Construed this way, virginity is a marketable value that tends not to empower the girl for herself, but simultaneously renders her newly vulnerable to masculine interest and courtship and redefines her subjection to the patriarchal determination of family interests. At the same time that the girl debuts in the general social estimation as potential erotic object, conjugal partner, and bearer of children, her sexual purity becomes the dangerous focal point of male fantasy, desire, and competition.

This renders her, as Second Brother intuits, more threatened because more prized in male erotic estimation:

> You may as well spread out the unsunn'd heaps
> Of Miser's treasure by an outlaw's den,
> And tell me it is safe, as bid me hope
> Danger will wink on Opportunity,
> And let a single helpless maiden pass
> Uninjured in this wild surrounding waste.
>
> (398–403)

Elder Brother may be more optimistic and idealistic about virginity's ability to take care of itself, yet Second Brother proves to be a more shrewd observer of the way it perilously triggers male sexual response. Even his own response is uncannily suggestive in its naive conflation of erotic associations. "Unsunn'd heaps / Of Miser's treasure" might be the sort of telling phrase Comus would resort to in his complaints about the Lady's hoarded beauty.

Second Brother is no calculating libertine, but his projection of analogous imagery may give us a deeper glimpse into the constellation of Comus's desires. Linking female beauty with abundant wealth, boundless and secretive, kept in hidden places and suddenly displayed, "spread out" in a kind of erotic loosening before the forbidding entry of an "outlaw's den," Second Brother seems to mingle fantasies of genital and anal curiosity. "Unsunn'd heaps" of jewels would have obvious genital associations, while "unsunn'd heaps" of gold, according to Freud, have imagistic affiliations with childhood fantasies about feces.[22] Several critical episodes from *The Faerie Queene* briefly and suggestively surface and mingle in Second Brother's anxious outburst: Guyon's perilous detour through Mammon's den (2.7–8) combines with the desperate wanderings of Amoret and Florimell, the treasure of whose beauties seem always about to be plundered (3.1, 3.4–5, 3.7–8, 3.11–12, 4.4–5, 4.7, 4.11–12, 5.3), and with the horrific captivity of Pastorella (6.10–11) in the brigands' den, as traumatic a melodrama of bondage, violence, and threatened sexual degradation as English Renaissance poetry could imagine. Second Brother's anxieties reveal that unprotected virginity provokes a complex of aggressive desires: beauty provokes greed, sexual maturation provokes lust, gentleness provokes brutality, purity provokes hunger for defilement and degradation. These drives assume a more elegant veneer in Comus's courtly temptations, but the Spenserian allusions of Second Brother hint at the dangers of the "wild surrounding waste" in which his sister as a single maiden must discover both her vulnerability and her strength.

Yet the *Maske*'s plot dramatizes how the social vulnerability of young womanhood, which can render the young woman subject to the disposition of the father in her household and subject to the predatory fantasies of strangers outside the household, can be countered by the potential strength that virginity discovers in its exercise of self-mastery. The way to social and psychological strength proves to be through seeming weakness. The heroic exploits of Britomart and Belphoebe in Spenser's epic romance notwithstanding, virginity is a virtue that cannot typically defend itself by physical might; its strength rests in its concentration of physical poise with psychological and rhetorical force. Crossing through puberty to womanhood, the virgin discovers herself to be not just an object of desire but an active center and agent of desire. Her ethical recognition and orchestration of her own desire, rather than its repudiation, becomes the key to her charisma. Spenser's Britomart is the great model of this mobilizing transformation of desire. The strength of the virgin's resistance to sexual demand is increased by the strength with which she feels touched by the demand. Her virginity, that is, paradoxically discovers its strength in relation to the strength of the desire that it calls into being. Desire makes virginity consciously shape itself in the form of an idealized and hope-directed form of self-knowledge.

Reviewing the careers of Spenser's "dazzling Apollonian androgynes," Belphoebe and Britomart, Camille Paglia describes chastity as "a self-armouring of personality": "Every detail and edge is deeply incised, because Spenserian personality must be forcibly carved out of obdurate nature and defended against the erosion and lassitude of fatigue and hedonism."[23] The same can be said of their literary godchild, Milton's Lady, whose own charismatic desire defines itself in resistance to Comus's enervating appeal. This desire can be called charismatic for several reasons. It is a spiritual gift; it is uniquely striking and attractive; and it in turn is powerful not only in resisting but in reforming the desire it stimulates. If, as Lacan claims, "desire finds its meaning in the desire of the other,"[24] influenced by and reflective of a prior, more powerful and inclusive desire, the impenetrable and radiant self-certainty of chaste desire establishes its originary priority in the circulation of desire around it. It orders according to its own design the desire that discovers it.

Vividly recalling Spenser's militant heroines, Elder Brother projects an idealized vision of his sister's impenetrable virtue and heroic prospects:

> She that has that [Chastity] is clad in complete steel,
> And like a quiver'd Nymph with Arrows keen
> May trace huge Forests and unharbor'd Heaths,
> Infamous Hills and sandy perilous wilds,
> Where through the sacred rays of Chastity,
> No savage fierce, Bandit or mountaineer
> Will dare to soil her Virgin purity.
>
> (421–27)

No fruitless pining in a cloister for this virginal adventure hero. Elder Brother envisions for his sister a career of swashbuckling adventure and of romantic activism. The "Arrows keen" of the acolytes of Diana, "Fair silver-shafted Queen for ever chaste" (442), are the "sacred rays of Chastity" sublimated and emblematized as weapons in the wilderness of desire's errantry. In contrast to the "frivolous bolt of Cupid" (445), these arrow-rays signify the piercing single-pointedness of a desire cultivated both to protect and to express the integrity of virginal selfhood.

3

A desire both activated and disciplined by virginal self-recognition is the source of an uncanny power that the various characters of the *Maske* testify to as magical. The sources of this virgin magic disclose themselves if we consider the magic discovered by the Lady, in the course of her ordeal, in relation to the magic exercised by Prospero in *The Tempest*, from which Milton drew poetic resources for his *Maske*.[25] *The Tempest* is a drama about magic that circles around the crisis of female maturation in a world of male struggles for power. Miranda in *The Tempest* prefigures Milton's Lady as a girl entering sexual maturity and being tested and prepared for chaste marriage. Unlike the Lady, Miranda experiences no stage of familial separation or liminal self-examination in her drama. She has been Daddy's girl, and remains a good one, with little opportunity to show the spunk and improvisatory genius of Shakespeare's comparable romantic heroines, Rosalind, Viola, and Perdita. Miranda's emerging charisma and value as virgin remain at the disposal of and under the tutelary control of her father.

Prospero is the virtual god of power in Shakespeare's romance, yet his magic does not come from nowhere. Its intellectual sources are in his books, but its energy source is suggestively associated with his relationship with his daughter. Prospero's magic can be interpreted psychologically as the creative resolution of the conflict he feels in regard to his daughter's sexual maturation. Miranda, like the Lady, is passing through puberty to womanhood, and the question of her sexuality, first raised in the attempted rape by Caliban, takes on immediacy and urgency in light of the shipwrecked crew of Prospero's enemies. Miranda is the only woman on the island, and her relation to her father, who has nurtured, protected, and tutored her, is necessarily intimate and intense. Her virgin sexuality, fully at Prospero's disposal, yet respected and protected by him, and thus a sign also of her otherness from him, becomes the energy source of his magic.

His sustained renunciation of desire for her, figured forth in the tense master-slave relation to Caliban, returns to him in the sublimated form of Ariel, his eager and dynamic spiritual intimate. Caliban images forth to Prospero the specter of his own sexual anxieties, and Prospero's persecutory harshness toward Caliban is the projection of an uneasy self-mastery whose success receives its compensation in the aerial omnipotence of his magic, a sign of desire perfectly sublimated and serviceable. Prospero's testing of Ferdinand by setting him in Caliban's place as log man, by instructing him in the mastery of lust, completes the civilizing task that he had abandoned with Caliban. In effect, he so chastens and structures Ferdinand's desire as to teach Ferdinand to master the Caliban in himself, a project about which Prospero is constantly vigilant in his own life. Prospero's preparation of his daughter for chaste marriage must break the charmed circle of their relationship. He is necessarily preparing himself to abandon his magic and depart from the fantasy island where he has exercised it.[26]

The story of desire in *The Tempest,* then, is the story of Prospero's desire, yet his magic cannot be interpreted without noticing its synchronicity with his daughter's virginity. Despite a couple of anxious outbursts, Prospero's protective custodianship of Miranda is nearly flawless under the dramatic circumstances, infinitely more tender and generous than his tense yet affectionate control of Ariel or his ruthless domination of Caliban. Yet Miranda is curiously straitened as a Shakespearean romantic ingenue. C. L. Barber observes in

Shakespeare's late romances "symbolic action that, instead of freeing sexuality from the ties of family, works to restore family ties by disassociating them from the threat of degradation of incest."[27] In Miranda's case, the preservation of family ties insures that as long as she can trust in the protective assurances of patriarchy, she will be overshadowed and largely silent, however ardent, chaste, and honorable. She cannot speak for herself, nor will the potential magic of her condition be at her own disposal.

We might say that Milton constructs his dramatic experiment out of the question of what would have happened to Miranda if her father were not around to protect and direct her. The problem of desire is principally the Lady's to struggle with, not her father's, and so, consequently, the promise of desire will be hers to enjoy. She is triply isolated from his protection as well as from his intervention: by the scrim of the *Maske* fiction, which temporarily sets her in a different existential, social, and representational space than her father; by the liminal forest of the *Maske,* which redoubles her separation from the family interests, introduced in the playing space by her brothers; and by the mask of character, in which the historical character Alice Egerton assumes the symbolic ritual identity of the Lady. This triple sequestration, which we have seen corresponds to the "isolation" stage of traditional rites of passage, manages to disassociate Egerton family ties from "the threat of degradation of incest," so that the problem of a daughter's relation to her father, crucial to the plot dynamic of *The Tempest,* is preemptively resolved by dramatic structure.[28] Ritual release from paternal oversight in turn frees the Lady up for the liminal ordeal that will give her access to the power implicit in her virginity and centralize it in her own body, rather than mystify and defer it in the service of her father. The *Maske* thus dramatizes the transformation of Lady Alice's virginity from an unblemished physical condition, patriarchally sheltered, to an autonomous structure of ethical self-defense and ultimately to a source of visionary poetic energy. The Lady's exercise of erotic self-discipline allows her to participate in the magical power of translation whereby eventually even the sanctified body itself, the object and origin of desire, will be turned all to spirit (453–63), as desire purifies and perfects itself beyond the boundaries of the mortal senses, its destination the hymeneal *richesse* evoked by the Attendant Spirit in his Epilogue (976–1011).

The Lady prepares to become in effect a mage for herself, a dramatic development that strikingly marginalizes the Earl of Bridgewater, both as Lady Alice's father and as the king's representative, and thereby changes the absolutist nature of magic in the masque genre. "Surely Milton," Christopher Kendrick observes, "is denying the king's power its just representational weight."[29] Moral value and poetic energy disclose their epicenter and agency not in the father figure who represents the king, but in the virgin integrity of Alice the initiate. At the conclusion of the *Maske,* the Lady ultimately will be restored to paternal recognition and protection, yet only provisionally to the patriarchal disposition, for she has freshly discovered that her strength as virgin depends on a self-presence that entrusts itself to providence before any worldly ties. Perhaps we can take it as a biographical sign of this cultivated self-sufficiency that Lady Alice was not to marry until 1652, eighteen years after her performance in Milton's *Maske* and considerably later than conventionally expected of aristocratic maidens.[30]

4

By extending her self-defense with the profession of virginity, the Lady sharpens the focus of her differences with Comus by making them explicitly sexual. One might think that this is playing into his hands by talking about the one thing about which he keeps beating around the bush. Oddly enough, this in fact inverts the terms of their difference: her idealistic sexual frankness exposes him, with his grandiloquent indirection, as the coy one. But of course she introduces a mode of erotic self-determination that is, she announces, beyond his comprehension. At the same time, she makes explicit a coordinate theme that is fundamental both to her differences with him and to her self-determination: language. She triply reiterates the point that she will not walk the walk or talk the talk of Comus: "Thou hast nor Ear nor Soul to Apprehend . . . thou art worthy that thou shouldst not know . . . Thou art not fit to hear thyself convinc't" (784, 788, 793). Her speech is, indeed, less an account of the physical condition of virginity or an exposition of its "sage / and serious doctrine" (786–87) than a demonstration of the rhetorical power and poetic authority it authorizes and inspires.[31] Her primary subject becomes the conditions of communicability and the terms of communication by which her doctrine of virginity would be utterable and comprehensible.

In praising virginity, the Lady deploys a strategy which is similar to the traditional topos of inexpressibility, yet structured and nuanced differently. The topos of inexpressibility we know most famously from the *Divine Comedy:* what the poet or his character experiences is beyond the poor powers of even the most inspired human speech.[32] Perhaps because of his prophetic confidence in the providentially inspired word, Milton resorts to the topos rarely and briefly, particularly in the ambiguous epithet "unexpressive" (Nativity Ode, 115; "Lycidas," 176). Even in the most sublime passages of *Paradise Lost,* the angelic messenger Raphael expresses confidence in the powers of analogy and "process of speech" to accommodate divine and spiritual activity to human understanding (5.563–75; 7.176–79). The Lady also implies the compatibility of her concept and experience to language. It is not that what she has in mind could not be said. It is just that she will not say it, for certain good reasons, under the conditions where she finds herself. If she were to say it, Comus and everything about him would be blown away:

> Thou art not fit to hear thyself convinc't;
> Yet should I try, the uncontrolled worth
> Of this pure cause would kindle my rapt spirits
> To such a flame of sacred vehemence,
> That dumb things would be mov'd to sympathize,
> And the brute Earth would lend her nerves, and shake,
> Till all thy magic structures rear'd so high,
> Were shatter'd into heaps o'er thy false head.
>
> (792–99)

You go, girl! William Kerrigan notices the coordination of her rhetorical stance with her ethical position: "Her doctrine of virginity remains undivulged, itself virginal, as if speech this intimate would be equivalent to the sexuality her virtue forbids: the exhibition of the self to the other."[33] But Kerrigan implies an outcome to the possible divulging of the doctrine that is at odds with the Lady's own claim. The Lady does not imply that her doctrine or her sexuality would be defiled by her revelation of it to Comus. She implies that it would destroy him.

Perhaps we can call the Lady's rhetorical strategy the topos of reserved expressibility: in a highly charged dramatic situation, the indefinite figure of what *might* be said authorizes and creates the performative force of what *is* said.[34] Paradoxically, the actual words spoken invest in those yet to be spoken a power that most auditors will prefer not to question. We can recognize it in a pragmatic common ploy of parental discipline. Who among us has not quavered under the threat, "Just wait until I tell your father"? Could the telling itself ever measure up to the threat of telling in terms of its production of anxiety and guilt and remorse?

Donne deploys the figure of reserved expressibility to very different effect from the Lady in his cruelly brilliant amorous lyric "The Apparition."[35] Here the poetic speaker anticipates his own death from the scorn of his "murd'ress" mistress. He relishes his opportunity to provoke a guilt trip, not to generate her repentance, but to take pleasure in her guilty terror. He threatens revenge by promising a spectral reappearance to discover her betrayal of him and his memory in the arms of another. Musing on the moment of her terrified recognition of his ghost, he draws a curtain across the anticipated scene:

> What I will say I will not tell thee now,
> Lest that preserve thee; and since my love is spent,
> I'd rather thou shouldst painfully repent
> Than by my threat'nings rest still innocent.
>
> (14–17)[36]

The figures of this dark melodrama are already trapped in the toils and coils of the self-consuming love process that Comus is urging the Lady to join. Donne's speaker wants to be sure that he has the final word, which, he promises, will have power over life and death, innocence and repentance. The Lady makes use of the topos of reserved expressibility for the purpose of resistance to the vicious circle of predatory desire, yet she claims for the word not spoken a reformatory, iconoclastic power analogous to the dread-provoking force of the wounded plotter of "The Apparition."

As Kerrigan implies, the Lady's rhetoric functions in regard to the language it deploys like her virginity functions in regard to her sexuality: it gathers its power from what it withholds. Like virginity itself, a condition of self-presence that gains its authority from what it reserves to itself and God, this rhetoric reserves a pure "doctrine" from ears that are not fit to hear it. The power of the Lady's actual, audible speech comes from its implication and deferral of a higher order of speech which is never heard because in some sense it can only be fully present to itself. The power of this reserved word depends upon its not being spoken. Kathleen Wall refers appropriately to "the armor of Logos" as the source of the Lady's strength.[37] Yet it is the word *not* spoken, a transcendental yet internalized Logos that corresponds to her virginal self-presence, which generates the strength of her outward verbal armor. This internalized Logos is a "full Word" that can be represented only as a force that is both imminent and yet always already deferred. The "full Word" makes itself felt as a phantom presence authorizing and empowering the "empty word" of actual speech, which acknowledges its own comparatively limited expressive and performative power.[38] Yet if the "full Word" is an implication of actual speech, is it also really an effect of actual speech, a mystification of the power of language by a language that seems to confess its own apparent insufficiency? Must Father really come home in order for the threat to have already accomplished what it intends?

This deconstructive conundrum does not present itself to the Lady, who fully believes in what she implies, so she does not have to say it explicitly. "It is proper to the Word to cause to be understood what it does not say:"[39] her powerful deployment of the figure of reserved expressibility makes Comus a believer too. And so she gains the upper hand, in effect rhetorically disarming and unmanning him. Comus flinches:

> She fables not, I feel that I do fear
> Her words set off by some superior power;
> And though not mortal, yet a cold shudd'ring dew
> Dips me all o'er, as when the wrath of *Jove*
> Speaks thunder and the chains of *Erebus*
> To some of Saturn's crew.
>
> (800–805)

Comus gets the cold sweats here, a contrast to those seminal "gums of glutinous heat" (918) from which the Lady will have to be purified and released. The cold sweats are a symptom of dread before the epiphany of "superior power." The analogy associates this power with the punitive judgment of a wrathful divine patriarch. Not by what she *does* say, but by the power of what she claims she *could* say, the Lady has convinced Comus that divine justice stands for her and behind her. Yet Comus's analogy also blurs the difference between its comparative terms: the Lady has spoken thunder as Jove speaks thunder. The full Word of divine Logos coincides with the implied Word of virginity's self-announcement, and "sets off" her spoken words as instruments of reserved power. The Lady has turned the conditions of her vulnerability here—her femininity, her captivity, her constrained speech—into the sources of divinely authorized verbal power, by the rhetorical gesture of reserved expressibility.

Circe's best boy, the devotee of Venus and "vow'd Priest" of Cotytto and Hecate (124–38), Comus speaks for the mythic Mother

Goddess in her most copious, alluring, smothering, and sinister forms. Here he acknowledges that the Lady speaks for the Father, and the Father speaks—or would speak—for and through the Lady. This is, interestingly enough, not a claim that the Lady makes, but Comus's own testimony. If there is a phallic contest in this fencing match between an innocent girl and Comus, whose progenitor Bacchus is the god referred to by the mythographer George Sandys as "the father of generation" (*OME*, 196), Comus himself acknowledges that the Lady has won. As Lacan interprets the phallus of Freudian theory, the phallus is a signifier of power and of a desire which is synonymous with power. In the binary narrative of psychoanalytic tradition, only the father is the custodian of the phallus: the mother appears always already to have lost hers. Beholding the mother, the oedipal child and the adult who grows out of that child have reason to fear its loss and organize desire accordingly. With this concession and adaptation to the phallic authority of the father, the postoedipal child's desire socializes itself to the self-disciplinary requirements as well as the potential opportunities for partial satisfaction and mastery afforded by the Symbolic order, the order of language and of law, of which the father remains representative and custodian.[40]

Psychoanalytic fundamentalism would oblige us to interpret the Lady, a newly mature, self-conscious female, as already castrated, deprived of the phallus. We would say that she constructs her identity on this experience of lack; we might even say that her virginity is a compensatory idealization of this lack. Yet Milton challenges orthodoxies of all sorts, and so do his heroes. We can read his initiatory drama against the grain of the orthodoxy of psychoanalysis, a discourse not yet articulated out of the same textual and psychological ground in which Milton's own work is planted. The Lady herself demonstrates that the power of the phallus is not the exclusive biological or the cultural property of men. The power of the phallus, as of the Logos, lies in its spectral displacement from the moment and site of speaking and identification with an authority both incontestable and remote. She gains power over Comus by mastering the differential logic of the Symbolic order, the order of language that underwrites and oversees the order of culture. The authorizing term of the Symbolic order has been designated by Lacan "le nom du Père":

> The attribution of procreation to the father can only be the effect of a pure signifier, of a recognition, not of a real father, but of what religion

has taught us to refer to as the Name-of-the-Father. . . . the necessity of [Freud's] reflection led him to link the appearance of the signifier of the Father, as the author of the Law, with death, even to the murder of the Father—thus showing that if this murder is the fruitful moment of debt through which the subject binds himself for life to the Law, the symbolic Father is, in so far as he signifies this Law, the dead Father.[41]

The English translation, "The name of the Father," obscures the crucial French pun, "le *nom/non* du Père," "the *name/no* of the Father," but it is a pun which the Lady understands, even though she herself has fortunately never read Lacan. She speaks the paternal "no" to Comus's desire in such a way as to convince Comus that he imagines hearing the Father himself speak it.

5

Comus's fear and trembling fulfill the Elder Brother's confident prediction of virgin chastity's power over her adversaries:

> What was that snaky-headed *Gorgon* shield
> That wise *Minerva* wore, unconquer'd Virgin,
> Wherewith she freez'd her foes to congeal'd stone,
> But rigid looks of Chaste austerity
> And noble grace that dash't brute violence
> With sudden adoration and blank awe?
>
> (447–52)

Whereas the Lady speaks from the very condition of female chastity, articulating it as an ethical and rhetorical position, Elder Brother offers a complementary portrait from the outside looking in, a position of idealizing male respect, which is specular and iconographic. Elder Brother's iconographic formation of chastity, prior to the Lady's debate with Comus, anticipates the Lady's articulation and achievement of chastity; it also contrasts and completes it. Like the Lady, the brothers are works in progress, so Elder Brother's exercise in mythopoesis needs to be evaluated in terms of its inflections of his age, his experience, and his situational needs. He discloses his confidence that his sister's "hidden strength," chastity (418–20), will defend her "Virgin purity" (427) against any assault. Yet he interchanges the invulnerability of chastity with the spell-breaking power of "true virginity" (437). He marshals all his learning to demonstrate the mythical strength of the virtue, flourishing allegorical exempla with the sort of naive confidence in their referential security that the *Maske* elsewhere subjects to critical scrutiny.

Second Brother, more of the experiential pragmatist, especially because he can identify with his sister's vulnerability, stresses her experiential weakness as "hapless virgin" (350). As we have seen, he understands her virginity as a physical condition of fragile treasure that invites "the rash hand of bold incontinence" (397). Elder Brother's composite portrait fittingly expresses the respect, even awe, a younger sibling might have for the virtue of his older and more mature sister. Her profession of chastity provides a model for his adaptation of the virtue to his own eventual practice of it as a gentleman and eventual respect for it in women of his class and age. The fine distinction between chastity and virginity that the Lady introduces, to the great but productive vexation of Milton critics, is a nonissue for Elder Brother, perhaps because the hormonal surprises of puberty have not challenged him yet with the complexities of sexual maturation and articulation. His sense of gender differentiation seems similarly undeveloped, as his female figurations of chastity are decidedly masculine in their activity and attributes. There is very little of the passive feminine in his portraiture, although there is a certain amount of androgynous sex appeal: "She that has that [chastity] is clad in complete steel, / And like a quiver'd Nymph with Arrows keen / May trace huge Forests and unharbor'd Heaths, / Infamous Hills and sandy perilous wilds . . ." (421–24). Elder Brother would no doubt like the superheroines of DC and Marvel comics, chaste and ferocious, flying and jousting about in their metal swimsuits.

Elder Brother has read and mastered his Spenser. He enthusiastically if somewhat awkwardly sketches a composite figure of Chastity who is like Britomart, the warrior princess and champion of Chastity in books 3 through 5 of *The Faerie Queene,* and Belphoebe, the glittering and unapproachable huntress who makes her show-stopping entrance in book 2 (2.3.21–31). There is something cartoonlike in the bold clean outlines and the heroic postures of these figures. There is also a little bit of the iron man Talus of book 5, Artegall's squire and brutal justicer, in the figure "clad in complete steel." It is difficult to imagine someone so cumbered by armor, even of a metaphoric sort, moving lightly as a "quiver'd Nymph" through the underbrush of desire. Britomart draws upon Minerva/Athena for her archetypal mystique, and Belphoebe upon the virgin huntress Diana/Artemis. The mythic identity of both goddesses "is predicated on militant chastity. This chastity is a metaphor for power, freedom, and audacity."⁴² There are several other figures of female chastity in *The Faerie Queene* who trace the Spenserian wilderness without such self-protective resources, most notably Florimell and Amoret. Ignoring those more vulnerable heroines, Elder Brother's portrait is decidedly one-sided and incomplete. He defeminizes and militarizes chastity in a way that expresses the hero-worshipping disposition of a boy his age and provides vigorous reassurance to the anxieties of Second Brother, who imagines in his sister's plight a correspondence to his own sense of beleaguered vulnerability.

Yet Elder Brother's comparatively naive reproduction of conventional icons of militant chastity exposes certain kinds of mythological and psychological complexity in its formation and expression that a more sophisticated account of the virtue might knowingly obscure or refine.⁴³ Elder Brother marks off his presentation of Greek exempla with a brief pause and a rhetorical gesture that prefigures the Lady's challenging prologue to her own encomium to virginity: "Do ye believe me yet, or shall I call / Antiquity from the Old Schools of *Greece* / To testify the arms of Chastity?" (438–40). As he thus trumpets a cultural authority more impressive even than the sage and serious Spenser (*Areopagitica,* 728), he elevates the intellectual seriousness of his claims and, perhaps without being conscious of it, resorts to more archaic materials. Although his representation of the "silver-shafted Queen" Diana elaborates in a conventional enough way the previous Belphoebean image of "quiver'd Nymph with Arrows keen," the complex image of Minerva with the Gorgon shield flashes up out of the Ovidian repository that forms the troubling tragic subtext of the Lady's ordeal.

"Rigid looks of Chaste austerity" indicate the double power of chastity over the predatory eye.⁴⁴ The archetypal virgin, Minerva, goddess of wisdom and militant chastity, petrifies her foes both with her looking and with how she looks. She arrests and intimidates the gaze of the potential voyeur with an impenetrably rigid and keen gaze of her own, as well as with an armored body-image resistant to violence of thought or action. Her petrifying power results from her appropriation of and merger with her opposite. In Elder Brother's iconography, Minerva wears rather than carries the Gorgon shield, suggesting in the figure a coincidence of female opposites, the inspiring virgin and the young witch in Erich Neumann's archetypal schema.⁴⁵ The blood-freezing image of the beheaded Gorgon is accessorized to the armored body-image of Minerva and of the virgins she sponsors.

In his folkloric survey, George Sandys notes this strange coincidence in his observation that Minerva was "called *Gorgon* by the Cyrenians; a name agreeing with her war-like disposition" (*OME*, 47). Sandys's extended commentary on Perseus's slaying of Medusa reads it as an allegory that neatly parallels the Circean temptation posed by Comus to the Lady:

> *Perseus* is also taken for the reasonable soule; the *Graeae* [two sisters whose shared single eye provides Perseus direction toward the sleeping Medusa], for that knowledge and wisdome which is acquired by experience; without whose eye or conduction, *Medusa,* lust and the inchantments of bodily beauty, which stupifies our senses, make us altogether unusefull, and convert us as it were into marble, cannot be subdued. . . . Thus provided, *Perseus* kills *Medusa,* reason corporall pleasure: yet lookes not on her, but only sees her deformity in the shield of *Pallas* (as we view without prejudice to our sight the eclyps of the sun in the water) since it is not safe to behold what our hearts are so prone to consent too. (*OME,* 220)

Paradoxically, the icon of Minerva wearing "that snaky-headed Gorgon shield" suggests that the virginal and chaste are dominant over "lust and the inchantments of bodily beauty," but also that the virginal and chaste depend on the spectral image of vanquished "lust and the inchantments of bodily beauty" to exercise power over others. John Rumrich observes, "The theodicy-minded Elder Brother, quite in concert with the classical Greeks, perceives in the mythological sign of a rape and subsequent murder—the Medusa's head in Athena's aegis—the power of virginity to protect itself."[46]

This makes good ethical and psychological sense, although there are several ways to interpret it. We could begin with a rather straightforward feminist observation, that the virgin "wears" the sign of a "monstrous" female sexuality, threateningly opposed to males. But this account would not fully explain the virgin's power. For if she has suppressed her own sexuality, what is there about her that would render her frightening to men? We could develop this notion by considering that Minerva, the apotheosis and sponsor of chaste character, carries a sign of her overmastery of desire, not only the desire of others, but of the desire that potentially motivates her. Or we could say that the chaste virgin is empowered by the specter of what she has objectified, resisted, and sublimated in herself: the seductive or predatory feminine, familiar in figures like Spenser's Duessa and Acrasia, which is a potential that a young woman discovers at the moment she becomes conscious of her own sexuality. The strength that the chaste woman obtains from the mastery of desire in herself

5: GIRL POWER: THE PROFESSION OF VIRGINITY

becomes available to her as a defensive shield against the potential aggression she excites. Elder Brother's iconography seems to support these explanations. If we compare his deployment of the Medusa myth to those of Sandys, and of Ben Jonson in *The Masque of Queens*—"When Virtue cut off Terror, he gat Fame"[47]—we notice that in Elder Brother's elaboration, Minerva has reclaimed her shield from Perseus, in effect recovering its cephalic trophy as a sign of female, rather than male, mastery over whatever is symbolized in Medusa's stonifying power.

Chastity's power thus comes as a triumph of sublimation. With its Renaissance spiritual and alchemical resonances, "sublimation" is also the psychoanalytic term for the psychical process whereby erotic energies are released from their primary sexual motivations and objects and committed toward socially sanctioned and supported forms of self-satisfaction and engagements with the world. Interestingly, in psychoanalytic theory, sublimation "desexualizes" libidinal energies by way of a provisional narcissism:

> The transformation of a sexual activity into a sublimated one (assuming both are directed towards external, independent objects) is now said to require an intermediate period during which the libido is withdrawn on to the ego so that desexualisation may become possible. . . . "If this displaceable energy is desexualised libido, it may also be described as *sublimated* energy; for it would still retain the main purpose of Eros— that of uniting and binding—in so far as it helps towards establishing the unity, or tendency to unity, which is particularly characteristic of the ego."[48]

The Lady's ritual isolation in the forest of desire haunted by Comus, her response to the call of the "airy shapes that syllable men's names" (208), her defensive consolidation of her own awakened desire as the idealized form of a self resistant to erotic subjection: these stages trace the course of her desire through an episode of solipsistic self-reckoning, and prepare her for a reawakened and other-directed encounter with the world beyond herself.

The virginal self exemplified by the Lady thus emerges as the first achievement and initiatory act of a career of mature sublimation. When virginity becomes conscious of itself and chooses itself in this way, it becomes a positive translation of the echoism or narcissism evoked in the Lady's sublime lyric, her song to Echo (230–43). An idealized and coherent image of self becomes the project of desire and the commanding image to be displayed to the world.[49] Maturing ego and virginal body image coincide: the body becomes the perfect form and expression of the self in its nascent self-consciousness. St. Augustine wistfully, tormentedly longs for the gift of continence to restore such a condition of integrity: "Truly it is by continence that we are made as one and regain that unity of self which we lost by falling apart in the search for a variety of pleasures."[50] Yet although the body-self is cathected in this critical moment of the recognition of desire, it is not cathected as an object to be captivated by desire, but as an idea to be preserved, nourished, defended by desire. It emerges as a state of self-presence and self-dignification, without lapsing into the self-absorption or self-consumption that determine the fates of Echo and Narcissus, whose negative destinies the Lady has "translated" in her song.

But the figure of the Medusa's head, decapitated, fixed, framed, displayed on Minerva's shield, as the primary feature of her petrifying look, unsettles more than a little the neatness of this psychoanalytic alchemy. In a suggestive little essay, Freud links the terror of the Medusa to the child's dread sight of the mother's genitals, and the fear of castration that it engenders: "This symbol of horror is worn upon her dress by the virgin goddess Athena. And rightly so, for thus she becomes a woman who is unapproachable and repels all sexual desires—since she displays the terrifying genitals of the Mother. Since the Greeks were in the main strongly homosexual, it was inevitable that we should find among them a representation of woman as a being who frightens and repels because she is castrated."[51] Freud's analysis is compatible with Sandys's Renaissance explanation insofar as both understand the Medusa figure as an objectification of the fear and the threat associated with woman. In Sandys's account, Medusa stands for "lust and the inchantments of bodily beauty" (220); in Freud's account, she represents the fate of castration that waits upon the child who does not renounce the mother as primary sexual object. Yet although Freud detects the theme of female sexuality and links it to the practice of virginity, he composes a male-directed narrative of the Medusa's head as a monitory parable of castration. His sketchy account represses certain narrative elements and tries to finesse several contradictions. Freud draws our attention to the deep sexual character of the Medusa tale, but the elements of that tale can be reconstrued to yield a psychoanalytic reading more serviceable to our consideration of the poetics of chastity in Milton's *Maske*.

Several problems crop up in Freud's explanation of the Medusa's terror. If the Medusa figure is the particular crystallization of female dread and phallic loss produced by a "strongly homosexual" culture, why should it maintain the same horrific power in the normative heterosexual culture of Augustan Rome, the cultural setting of Ovid, or late Renaissance England, the scene of Sandys's mythography and of Milton's *Maske*?[52] The ambiguity of the Medusa's head as sexual signifier remains implicit yet unaccounted for in Freud's account: does he read it as a phallic symbol or as a symbol of the lack of the phallus? Freud suggests that the power of the image lies in what it does not show, the phallus which has been stricken from the Mother, "the absence of which is the cause of the horror."[53] Yet Athena paradoxically deploys it as a phallic emblem, a fetish implement of paralyzing power, not only in the accessorizing of the image by the snaky hair, which Freud interprets literally as the mother's genital hair, but symbolically as "a multiplication of penis symbols."[54]

Freud interprets the image as a terrifying sign of female lack. But the figure is deployed in such a way as to suggest a recovery: either what Freud might call the return of the repressed, the missing phallus of the mother, or something perhaps even more dreadful to patriarchally fashioned consciousness: what Julia Kristeva calls the *chora,* the maternal nest, the black hole of generation wreathed with phallic serpents, sign of all natural origin and end.[55] Finally, Freud overlooks certain elements of the Medusa tale which ambiguate his explanation of "woman as a being who frightens and repels because she is castrated." It is Medusa's beauty, rather than her horror, which turns her beholders to stone. If she were only repulsive to look upon, why would men be drawn to search her out and risk their lives for a glance? So Freud understands the virgin as "a woman who is unapproachable and repels all sexual desires," without accounting for the ambivalence she inspires by awaking the very desires she is able to repel, transforming the violence of lust, in Elder Brother's formulation, to "sudden adoration and blank awe" (452).

In *The Metamorphoses,* Medusa's beauty inflames Neptune to rape her in the shrine of Minerva. The offended goddess, in typical Ovidian fashion, blames the victim and transforms her hair to serpents. An excavation of the story's legendary layers might reveal that Medusa was originally a virgin devotee of Minerva, punished, like Callisto was by Diana, for sexual pollution of her shrine and her virginal rites. Yet in an irony typical of Ovid, Medusa's makeover is not only punitive but preservative. Henceforth Medusa will be protected by her serpentine corona from the threat of violation. Beware, beware, her flashing eyes, her floating hair: a beauty powerful enough to solicit the desire of a god is set off as taboo, a thing of dread and awe, not to be gazed upon directly.[56] From object of desire to image of dread to sacrificial icon: Medusa undergoes a sacrificial transformation that reverses the terms of her suffering. Ritually violated, identified, marked, shunned, decapitated, preserved as monitory emblem, she is a scapegoat of desire whose negative image is a charm against the desire she provokes and paralyzes.

Perseus is able to decapitate her, but only with the periscopic device of the shield supplied by Minerva. Sandys, we recall, stresses the importance of the shield, implying that it figures as the power of undistorted Reason in his allegory. The method of indirect and abstracted perception is crucial to his insight. Perhaps we could consider it as a mode of reflective consciousness, the gift of Minerva, apotheosis and muse of cunning intelligence. Since Perseus holds it as a mirror up to the nature of Medusa, we might furthermore associate it with the abstracting and framing nature of art. The shield as mirror is a blade that severs subject from object; the blade is a shutter that severs object from image; the shield that fixes the image is a frame that preserves it, uncannily lifelike, eternally and indifferently cold, chilling to behold. The shield of Pallas is a prophylaxis against the exposure to the Medusa that it represents, in the same way that the framing devices of tragedy are prophylactic against the powers of Dionysus that they invoke and represent.[57] Medusa, looking within the frame, sees herself first, and fatally: freeze-framed by her own terrifying beauty, she suffers the fate of Narcissus, only drastically, instantaneously foreshortened. Perseus, looking at her by means of the mirror-shield's indirect representation, can behold her beauty without perishing, as, Sandys notes, "we view without prejudice to our sight the eclyps of the sun in the water" (*OME*, 220).

Medusa's story, then, is another of the *Maske*'s several parables of translation, reverberating with other tragic tales through the echo chamber of Milton's allusive text. Medusa is ravished by a god, a common fate for the nymphs and women of Ovid's desire-driven myth, a virtual fate in which Milton's Lady subliminally participates through her confrontation with Comus. In a single metamorphic stroke, Medusa's beauty is transformed to horror: a counterpoint to the tale of Philomela's ravishing, also evoked in the *Maske* (234, 566), which transforms the horror of her mutilation and revenge into beauty. Medusa suffers an abbreviation of the fate of Narcissus, yet she does not reenter, as he does, the vegetative cycle of nature. She is removed from the life cycle to serve as an instance of a particularly powerful mode of representation. Her image is fixed on the mirroring shield that has destroyed her, translating it from a reflective frame to a representational icon, a performative work of totemic art that defends chastity. Although Perseus continues to use the shield as his ultimate weapon in his Ovidian adventures, it is on loan and in trust from Minerva. In Milton's tale, Elder Brother restores it to the goddess, in order to associate his sister with the attributes and resources of unconquerable virginity.

As the series of tales of threatened virgins provide the tragic subtext for the Lady's ritual sublimation of beauty into strength, the figure of Medusa beheaded becomes the iconographic key to the paradox of that sublimation. Medusa's head: a seal on the maidenhead and its uncanny double; a DO NOT ENTER sign on the virgin portal. Like the proliferation of snakes that wreathe it, the figure is multiple, ambiguous, and indeterminate in its significations, which only amplify its power. Freud suggests that it is the impossible, lost maternal phallus which, in Elder Brother's deployment of it, returns to haunt those who would defile daughters and devotees of chastity. It is at the same time the sign of that loss, a warning of castration to befall the violator of the paternal taboo. Exceeding both positions in the phallic system of psychic representation, it is an uncanny figure for the mystique of female sexuality, an enigma ultimately unaccountable by the economics of patriarchal symbolization. It is the iconic transformation of the collective fate of ravished women, displayed as visual horror and put to the retrospective task of paralyzing any assaults on chastity. It is an uncanny coincidence of female opposites: archaic, chthonian fetish brandished by transcendent, serene virginity.[58] In effect, the Lady's looks imply to the predatory Comus, "This uncanny emblem, this sexual fetish with its multiple and ambiguous associations, is in my possession and at my disposal, not yours. I invoke it and I wield it at your peril."

The image of Medusa's head thus bears the same mutually constitutive relation to the look of Minerva's—and by transference, the Lady's—virgin beauty that the implied Word of the "sage / And serious doctrine of Virginity" (785–86) bears to the Lady's spoken words. If her speech indicates her access to the symbolizing power associated with the phallic authority of the Father, her look evidences her association with the incalculable genital mysteries of the Mother. The terror of her look, like the terror of her speech, depends upon its implication, its deferral, its indexing of a power not fully present and all the more powerful in its ghostly imminence. Deploying the phallic verbal authority of the Father and the spectral, genital dread of the Mother, the Lady effectively rebuffs and overmasters Comus in both the verbal and the visual, the Symbolic and the Imaginary fields of their confrontation. Doubly phallic, the Lady seems invulnerable. One might be led to wonder, "This is quite a girl. Can she play tennis, too?" The point, though, of her concentration of invoked yet withheld and sublimated energies, is that the phallus, as we have been considering it, is itself a metaphor, a figuration of desire and of power. The virginal body, intact, untraversed and unwounded by sexual intrusion, impenetrably protecting interior mysteries, is itself an energy-charged outward and visible sign of this desire and this power.[59] Professing virginity as a spiritual discipline, the Lady expresses her imaginative freedom in a severe lyricism that gestures toward eschatology. Her intimation of virginity's iconoclastic and world-transforming power translates virginity into a trope for an unsullied and uncompromised Word of activism and independence, a figure for the freedom in Christ that ignites and sustains the regenerate subject's and redeemed community's liberatory engagement with the fallen world. No wonder that Comus gets the cold sweats.[60]

6
Milton's Lady and Lady Milton: Chastity, Gender, and Prophecy

1

AS WE HAVE SEEN, AT THE CLIMAX OF HER REFUTATION OF COMUS'S libertine blandishments, the Lady makes it clear that she will not walk his walk or talk his talk (779–99). With her oracular, even prophetic rhetoric, the Lady establishes herself in this moment as Milton's first fully developed hero of faith. Her profession of virginity is a declaration of independence, an early proclamation of the source of the Christian liberty that Milton committed his life to defining and defending. Milton's addition of this passage for the 1637 publication of the *Maske* makes explicit the dramatization of his own calling in the words and acts of the Lady. A rite of passage from childhood into womanhood for the Lady, the *Maske* becomes as well Milton's initiation of himself into maturity as a prophetic poet.[1] Flaubert reputedly declared, "Madame Bovary, c'est moi."[2] No less remarkably, Milton implies, "I and the Lady are one." We ought to be continually startled and unsettled that the reputed patriarchal bogeyman of English Literature made his first sustained dramatization of poetic, ethical, and political commitment in the persona of a young woman.[3] Before we proceed to examine the concluding movements of the *Maske,* the Lady's release from bondage and her homecoming, we need to consider more closely the imaginative gender crossing between the rising poet and the heroic character he creates. The chastity that the Lady defends and that defends the Lady is also Milton's chastity. Chastity in the *Maske* proves to be the gender crossroad where Milton discovers and exercises his own prophetic voice, and this voice, as articulated by the Lady, in turn activates and exemplifies the social prospects for deliberative and emancipatory female speech.[4]

Critics have noticed that the Lady's profession of virginity is one of Milton's most fervent expressions of his personal "chastity cult."[5] Although this phrase vividly indexes the particular and central place of chastity in Milton's ethics and poetics, the term "cult," connoting eccentric and extremist variations on religious doctrine or practice or the obsession-compulsion of neurotic private ritual, quietly implicates Milton in aesthetic pathology. Christopher Kendrick notes how the *Maske* powerfully centralizes a series of correlative virtues into the singular sexual virtue of chastity, which "makes the stuff of chastity into the very form of virtue. From being one of many, chastity becomes the thing itself."[6] William Kerrigan diagnoses a kind of erotic and imaginative paralysis issuing from the impact of Milton's peculiar convictions on the shaping of the *Maske:* "At the center of the entertainment chastity narrows to virgin chastity, a state of the soul evolving from, and unable to detach itself from, a precondition of the body."[7] Chastity, in these diagnoses, is the self-disciplinary secret to the unique centripetal force of Milton's imagination, but it is purchased at the cost of a wider range of humanizing virtues.

Milton's own claim, exemplified by the Lady in the *Maske* and made explicit in other key documents that articulate the doctrine, is that virginal chastity is the source of visionary power, lively in the making of heroic character, heroic poems, and heroic cultures. If we now revisit some of these other moments of self-disclosure, we can consider the logic of his position and its implications for Milton's projective identification with the Lady. Most crucial to the interpretation of the doctrine in the *Maske* are the Latin Sixth Elegy, which precedes the *Maske* by several years, and a key autobiographical passage from *An Apology for Smectymnuus,* which revisits the plot of the *Maske* several years after its initial publication.

In the 1629 Sixth Elegy, the Latin companion piece to the Nativity Ode, Milton discloses to his friend Charles Diodati the austere regimen of temperance, chastity, and blameless conduct required of the vatic poet whose "secret heart and very lips breathe Jove" (78) in poems of epic scope and divine aspiration:

> But he who wars would tell, and heaven under Jove mature,
> And pious heroes, leaders half-divine,
> And now the sacred consults of high gods would sing,
> And now the howling regions deep of the fierce dog,
> Let him the sparse rule of the Samian sage
> Observe; let herbs supply his harmless fare;
> Let brilliant water in his beech-wood bowl stand near;

> And let him draw his sober cups from the pure font.
> To this is joined a chaste youth, free from sin,
> Manners austere, and blameless hands unstained,
> As when you, augur, in holy vestments bright,
> From lustral waters rise to face the offended gods.
>
> (55–67; my translation)

Milton then cites a series of legendary poets and prophets whose visionary insight was the divine reward for such chaste asceticism: Tiresias, Linus, Calchas, Orpheus, Homer. As the implied climax of this series of sacred bards, Milton concludes his verse letter by announcing his own recent poetic breakthrough in the celebratory Ode:

> But if you would know what I do now, at least
> If you think it fit to know if I do anything,
> We sing the king who bears our peace, the seed of heaven,
> The blessed ages promised in the sacred books,
> God's wailing, and his stabling beneath a humble roof,
> Who with his Father dwells in heaven supreme;
> The star-bearing sky, hosts warbling in the ethereal sphere,
> And gods expelled at once from their own fanes.
> These gifts have we raised up for Christ's nativity,
> Gifts which the dawn's first light on me bestowed.
> These strains await you as well, on native pipes composed,
> And of their worth, when I recite them, you will judge.
>
> (79–90; my translation)

This birth announcement demonstrates the providential efficacy of Milton's regimen of chastity and temperance. His account of the history-transforming event of the Word made flesh coincides with Milton's declaration of his own incarnation as a poet and prophet, who can, like Isaiah, "join [his] voice unto the Angel Choir, / From out his secret Altar touched with hallow'd fire" (Nativity Ode, 27–28; cf. Isaiah 6:6).[8] Diodati, Milton's soul mate, is a trustworthy correspondent, and so the poet reveals to him what his prophetic persona the Lady will withhold from Comus, her untrustworthy and unworthy adversary in the *Maske:* the "sage / And serious doctrine of Virginity" (785–86) and the "sublime notion and high mystery" (784) of religious truth which it makes apprehensible.

During the heat and strife of the English revolution's pamphlet wars, the beleaguered poet includes in his autobiographical self-defense of 1642 an account of the earlier maturing of his convictions. In this section of *An Apology for Smectymnuus,* Milton's account of chastity's role in cultivating a poetic character committed to ethical and political reformation explicitly recalls the plot and the "abstracted sublimities" of his *Maske:*

> If I should tell ye what I learnt of chastity and love (I mean that which is truly so, whose charming cup is only virtue, which she bears in her hand to those who are worthy—the rest are cheated with a thick intoxicating potion which a certain sorceress, the abuser of love's name, carries about) and how the first and chiefest office of love begins and ends in the soul, producing those happy twins of her divine generation, knowledge and virtue—with such abstracted sublimities as these, it might be worth your listening, readers, as I may one day hope to have ye in a still time, when there shall be no chiding; . . . But having had the doctrine of holy scripture unfolding those chaste and high mysteries with timeliest care infused, that "the body is for the Lord, and the Lord for the body," thus also I argued to myself: that if unchastity in a woman, whom St. Paul terms the glory of man, be such a scandal and dishonor, then certainly in a man, who is both the image and glory of God, it must, though commonly not so thought, be much more deflowering and dishonorable; in that he sins both against his own body, which is the perfecter sex, and his own glory, which is in the woman, and that which is worst, against the image and glory of God, which is in himself. Nor did I slumber over that place expressing such high rewards of ever accompanying the Lamb with those celestial songs to others inapprehensible, but not to those who were not defiled with women, which doubtless means fornication; for marriage must not be called a defilement. (*An Apology,* 694–95)

Eight years after the performance of the *Maske* at Ludlow and five years after its publication with the peroration on virginity added to the Lady's speech, Milton reads the drama of his own maturing convictions through the ordeal he has inscribed for the Lady. Having provided the rising poet the mythological screen for the projection and ritual testing of his ideals, the *Maske* now provides the embattled polemicist a template for autobiography. The allegorical first sentence retraces both the ordeal and the outcome of the Lady's temptation as a protype of the poet's own life of strenuous trial: the cup of sensual pleasure proferred by the Circe figure, a parody and perversion of true love; and the promise of the "divine generation" of twins by the virtuous soul in love with God above all: "knowledge and virtue" in the pamphlet, "Youth and Joy" (1010) in the *Maske.*

An Apology further explicates what the discreet Lady has withheld from Comus about the "chaste and high mysteries" of a bodily life dedicated to God's service. Milton indexes several scriptural reference points in which such mysteries can be contemplated:

> *Now the body is not for sexual immorality but for the Lord, and the Lord for the body.* And God both raised up the Lord and will also raise us up by His power. Do you not know that your bodies are members of Christ? Shall I then take the members of Christ and make them members of a harlot? Certainly not! . . . But he who is joined to the Lord is one spirit with Him. (1 Corinthians 6:13–17; emphasis mine)

> But I want you to know that the head of every man is Christ, the head of woman is man, and the head of Christ is God. . . . For a man indeed ought not to cover his head, since *he is the image and glory of God;* but woman is the glory of man. (1 Corinthians 11:3, 7; emphasis mine)

> Then I looked, and behold, a Lamb standing on Mount Zion, and with Him one hundred and forty-four thousand, having His Father's name written on their foreheads. And I heard a voice from heaven, like the voice of many waters, and like the voice of loud thunder. And I heard the sound of harpists playing their harps. *And they sang as it were a new song before the throne, before the four living creatures, and the elders; and no one could hear that song except the hundred and forty-four thousand who were redeemed from the earth. These are the ones who were not defiled with women, for they are virgins.* These are the ones who follow the Lamb wherever He goes. These were redeemed from among men, being firstfruits to God and to the Lamb. And in their mouth was found no guile, for they are without fault before the throne of God. (Revelation 14:1–5; emphasis mine)

These citations indicate that Milton's "chastity cult" is not a personal private obsession but an effort at biblical exegesis whose aim is a Reformed theology of the body. This emerging theology of the body provides the foundation for a social theology as well, in that chastity is an exercise in relationship, with both God and others.

Milton's citation of scripture in *An Apology* problematizes the conceptualization of chastity as a "female" virtue, by suggesting that it is a harder but all the more necessary discipline for a man. Yet in personifying chaste love as feminine, he also problematizes the traditional gender hierarchy of male superiority. Paradoxically, in order to honor "the image and glory of God, which is in himself" through the exercise of chastity, a man needs to model himself upon the feminine: "a chaste man is feminine, or identifies with the feminine in so far as he is chaste."[9] This identification complicates the apparently incontrovertible statement of male superiority in Milton's claim that the man's body "is the perfecter sex." The parsing and distribution of glory in the passage invest identity and integrity in mutual relationship rather than in masculine autonomy. If the man must look to the woman to recognize his own glory and look in himself for evidence of the image and glory of God, his identity discovers itself intersubjectively, in triangulation and mutuality. Identification with the woman reveals his own glory to him. His bodily "perfection" is thus complete not in the gaze of narcissistic self-regard, but in the body's chaste participation in marital partnership. This dissolve between genders in *An Apology* looks back to the personal paradox that activates the *Maske*. In representing his own commitment to chastity and to the poetry that it authorizes, Milton has chosen—or we might say the dynamic of chastity requires him—to represent himself as a Lady. In turn, it endows the Lady with a rhetorical strength and systematically principled ethic conventionally associated with virtuous manhood.[10]

The passage from *An Apology* also blurs the differentiation between virginity and chastity in a way that revisits the *Maske*'s dramatic interinanimation of the terms. Like the two genders, chastity and virginity are distinct and yet indissoluble, defining and completing one another as virtues. The organizing term that motivates the whole passage, indeed the whole self-defense of *An Apology*, is *chastity*. The allusion to the fit audience though few who hear the unexpressive nuptial song of the Lamb invokes the order of self-dedicated virgins of John's Apocalypse, who alone would have ears to hear the divine music. Yet Milton insists on a more generalized reading that would include the chastely married among the celestial audience, "for marriage must not be called a defilement." In a revision of the literal word of scripture that anticipates the hermeneutic strategies of his soon-to-be-written divorce pamphlets of the early 1640s, Milton claims that John surely envisioned the chastely married among his company of virgins. Milton thus plays here a logical trump that reverses the conventional relation between categories: instead of virgins being accounted a subset of the larger set of the chaste, the chaste are included as a subset of John's eschatological set of virgins. Chastity is accounted a kind of virginity, although perhaps only from the anagogical perspective of the end time. Chastity translates not just the spirit but the bodily integrity of virginity into marital relations.[11]

Finally, in the context of *An Apology*'s larger purpose of public self-defense, Milton's explication of the centrality of chastity in his personal life indicates its centrality to his political efforts and convictions: "He who would not be frustrate of his hope to write well hereafter in laudable things, ought himself to be a true poem, that is, a composition and pattern of the best and honorablest things—not pretending to sing high praises of heroic men or famous cities, unless he have in himself the experience and the practice of all that which is praiseworthy" (*An Apology,* 694). The personal and the poetic are inevitably ethical and political for Milton. "Chastity is the alternative trope, borrowed from Spenser, by which Milton wishes to represent the essence of the poetical character, his own psychological constitution substituting in his prose for a description of poetic structure."[12] Chastity is not a fugitive and cloistered virtue of elevated self-regard, but the ethical structure of public and poetic character, the beginning of action on behalf of justice and the interests of love. As John Rumrich nicely formulates it, "Chastity is charity directed toward the self, though it expresses social responsibility; alms-giving is charity directed toward neighbors, though it expresses personal abundance."[13]

2

As Milton's persona, the Lady thus promises and prefigures the political commitments to the cause of true Reformation that he was to make more explicit in "Lycidas" and the prose pamphlets of the 1640s, and to which he would offer up his life service in the revolutionary and interregnum period. Some recent studies of the mystique of virginity in Milton and in this text in particular have released the concept from the various negatives that either endorsed Comus's opinion that the Lady is an insufferable prude or else determined that virginity is a patriarchal device to reinforce female subjection to the economics of patriarchal kinship systems.[14] In particular, John Rogers situates the Lady's encomium to virginity in the political and theological symbolism of emerging revolutionary discourse. In Rogers's account,

> Female virginity provided a symbolic model for the specifically seventeenth century image of the autonomous liberal self: she contained a physical guarantee of her privacy in the very existence of her hymen. . . . [The maintenance of virginity] could also be imagined, far more radically, as an actual historical precipitant for a spiritual, even political revolution. The new affirmation of the value of celibacy came to participate . . . in the millenarian optimism charging the revolutionary aspirations of the midcentury radicals.[15]

Rogers's documentation of the midcentury politicization of the figure of virginity makes of the Lady's speech a kind of revolutionary clarion call. Rogers's reading is consistent with the prophetic force and latent biblical sources of the Lady's images. The Lady speaks ominously in subjunctives of the power that *would* be released by her disclosure of a mystery too sublime for Comus to hear and apprehend:

> Yet *should* I try, the uncontrolled worth
> Of this pure cause *would* kindle my rapt spirits
> To such a flame of sacred vehemence,
> That dumb things *would* be mov'd to sympathize,
> And the brute Earth *would* lend her nerves, and shake,
> Till all thy magic structures rear'd so high,
> Were shatter'd into heaps o'er thy false head.
>   (793–99; emphasis mine)

Insofar as Comus represents the predatory self-indulgences and fantasies of the Stuart court aristocracy and the authoritarian mystifications of Laudian high churchmanship, the Lady's threat here anticipates rather than precipitates a social revolution.

The Lady seems constrained by neither gender anxiety nor the anxiety of influence, for she confidently and implicitly claims as her imaginative and political precursors archetypal male figures from the classical, and more important, the biblical, traditions. In her access to a "sacred vehemence" to which the very earth and its creatures would be responsive, she seems to allude to Orpheus here, as several critics have noticed: "The Lady represents herself, under the aspect of her virginity, as a new Orpheus."[16] The Lady's association with Orpheus, like her association with the endangered Pentheus of Euripides' *The Bacchae,* deepens the condition of her vulnerability, as it renders her doubly subject to the volatile energies and sparagmatic disposition of Comus's bacchic horde of revellers. Yet the natural sympathies awakened by Orpheus were pastoral and elegiac in tone. By awakening trees and rocks to sympathetic responsiveness to human loss, he invents the poetry of earth and the pathetic fallacy as a major key of that poetics. He is associated with the building of cultures rather than with the shattering of them. The Lady shows her mastery of Orphic pastoralism in her exquisite and powerful Echo Song (230–43), to which the singing master Attendant Spirit testifies (755–62), but the higher mood of her discourse with Comus, its thinning out of sensuous imagery in pronouncing the pure poetry of abstract doctrine, and its zealous promise of iconoclastic leveling, seem more attuned to the hard-edged, uncompromising outbursts of biblical prophecy that Milton studied and adapted to his calling, as liberatory evidences and examples of the world-transforming power of inspired poetry. Biblical prophecy was, like the Lady's withheld cause, a poetry of fire and and storm and earthquake, "a flame of sacred vehemence" (795), the Word of God active in and upon history, challenging, uprooting, and remaking the arrangements of worldly power.[17] It nourished Puritan sermonizing and sustained the millenial activism of the revolutionary period in England.

The Lady's turn to a prophetic strain suggests that her poetic disposition may be more thoroughly and specifically Christological than it is vaguely orphic in its authority and its promises. At the height of his power, Orpheus may have half-regained his bride Eurydice from the realm of the dead ("L'Allegro," 150), but he did not claim to utter "strains that might create a soul / Under the ribs of Death" (561–62), as the Attendant Spirit testifies to the power of the Lady's song. This is the sort of feat accomplished by Jesus in the healing of Jairus's daughter (Luke 8:40–56) and the summoning of Lazarus from his tomb (John 11:17–44). Orpheus is, of course, in his earth-summoning and death-challenging lyrics and in his sacrificial death, a pagan type of Christ, but ultimately, as Michael Lieb has argued, an insufficient and ungenerative one.[18] The virginal Jesus, who comes in the name of the Father, and speaks in the name of the Father, seems a more suitable sponsor and model for the virginal poetics of the Lady than the tragically married, subsequently misogynist Orpheus. As expressive Word, wisdom, and effectual might of the Father (*PL* 3.170), Christ is the incarnate manifestation of the Father's power. His life exemplifies without blemish the Pauline principle that "the body is for the Lord and the Lord for the body" (1 Corinthians 6:13). He is the figure with whom the Lady implicitly identifies, on the occasion of her own chaste self-recognition and self-disclosure as prophetic poet, who comes in the name of the Father and speaks for him.

Several motifs in the Lady's prophecy offer veiled parallels to gospel narratives of the acts and words of Jesus in his anticipation of and preparation for the *eschaton*. First, she reserves her word for those who have ears to hear. Comus, with neither "Ear nor Soul to apprehend" (784), is like those hearers of Jesus whose lack of faith prevents their comprehension of his parables:

And when he was alone, they that were about him with the twelve asked of him the parable. And he said unto them, Unto you it is given to know the mystery of the kingdom of God: but unto them that are without, all these things are done in parables: That seeing they may see and not perceive; and hearing they may hear, and not understand; lest at any time they should be converted, and their sins should be forgiven them. (Mark 4:9–12)

The Lady's declaration that "Dumb things would be mov'd to sympathize" (796) by her sacred vehemence may allude to Orpheus's stirring the ears of "Woods and Rocks / . . . To rapture" (*PL* 7.35–36), but it also evokes Jesus' response to the Pharisees upon his entrance into Jerusalem, that if his disciples were to hold their peace, "the stones would immediately cry out" (Luke 19:40). The anticipated destruction of Comus's "magic structures" (798) prefigures a key iconoclastic moment in Milton's poetry, Samson's mighty destruction of the temple of Dagon (*SA*, 1605–59). This cataclysm typologically prefigures, in its turn, Jesus' prophecy of the destruction of the temple in Jerusalem: "And as some spake of the temple, how it was adorned with goodly stones and gifts, he said, 'As for these things which ye behold, the days will come, in the which there shall not be left one stone upon another, that shall not be thrown down'" (Luke 21:5–6). If, in the religious and political context of the *Maske*, Comus with his glass of sensual enchantment is a type of Laudian or Catholic high priest offering a blasphemic eucharist,[19] the Lady's scriptural allusions set the ruin of his palace in a typological framework with other doomed sanctuaries of heresy, superstition, corruption, and idolatry. The Lady's image of the brute earth shaking continues to develop a parallel with Jesus' prophetic utterance, in this case the prophecy of earthquakes that Jesus anticipates as part of the turmoil of the last days (Luke 21:11). It also suggests the seismic aftermath of Jesus' own death as rendered in Matthew's gospel: "Jesus, when he had cried again with a loud voice, yielded up the ghost. And, behold, the veil of the temple was rent in twain from the top to the bottom; and the earth did quake, and the rocks rent; and the graves were opened; and many bodies of the saints which slept arose" (Matthew 27:50–53).

With this set of allusions, the Lady associates the eschatological power of her poetic reserves, invested in her declaration of virginity, not just with the prophetic scriptural tradition in general, nor with the broad career of Jesus as the fulfillment of that prophecy, but in particular with the climax of his own prophetic and rabbinical career in the Passion narratives. The medieval discipline of the imitation of Christ was traditionally private, devotional, and self-emptying, an exercise in the cultivation of passional quietism. But Reformation piety of the sort exercised by the Lady is public and activist in its orientation, and it cultivates an image of Christ who exemplifies and sanctions the practice of an ethically disciplined this-worldliness. The Lady's implicit rhetorical associations are with Jesus the prophetic preacher and exemplar of virtue, a figure whose heroic social engagement appealed more to Milton's Christian ethical activism than did the sacramental atonement of the God-man of sorrows on the Cross. Nevertheless, the Lady's dramatic agon and prophetic allusions align her with the narrative of Jesus' confrontations with established authority, his arrest, interrogation, persecution, and death.

The narrative of the Passion is the gospel sequence in which Jesus paradoxically reveals himself to be the Son of God through quiet endurance, exemplifying "the better fortitude / Of Patience and Heroic Martyrdom" (*PL* 9.31–32). Milton will prefigure this ultimate triumph of discipline and submission in the temptation sequence of *Paradise Regained,* a typological anticipation of the Passion. John Shawcross notes the parallelism between the Lady's ordeal and the gospel ordeal that is the subject of Milton's brief epic: "The masque is an elaboration of the temptation in the wilderness (see Matthew 4:1–11 and Luke 4:1–13) in mortal terms."[20] In *Paradise Regained,* Jesus endures Satan's endless and ultimately tedious harassment with a moral rigor and prophetic contempt that sounds a note of severity very like the Lady's:

> I never lik'd thy talk, thy offers less,
> Now both abhor, since thou hast dar'd to utter
> The abominable terms, impious condition;
> But I endure the time, till which expir'd,
> Thou hast permission on me.
>
> (*PR* 4.171–75)

These character parallels work reciprocally in the Milton canon. They reveal the Lady herself as a prototype of the heroic Son of God of the epics. They retrospectively authorize the Lady's profession of prophetic authority and provide a specifically biblical typological framework in which to consider the Lady's ritual ordeal.

As Jesus was bound, tormented, and relentlessly questioned, responding to his inquisitors only with enigmatic riddles and silence, the Lady raises a defense beyond Comus's capacity to comprehend, even though she is captive and subject to analogous harassment:

> Thou canst not touch the freedom of my mind
> With all thy charms, although this corporal rind
> Thou has immanacl'd, while Heav'n sees good.
>
> (663–65)

"While Heav'n sees good" matches the Lady's recognition of divine oversight to Jesus' "I endure the time, till which expir'd, / Thou hast permission on me" (*PR* 4.174–75). As Milton's Jesus understands that his Passion, and the wilderness training for it, are divinely ordained, so Milton's Lady acknowledges and trusts that her ordeal is ultimately staged by a providential author rather than by Comus and performed for a higher audience even than the Ludlow celebrants, a heavenly spectator and task-Master (Sonnet 7, v. 14) who sees, even in advance of its temporal fulfilling, the goodness immense brought forth from the challenge of evil.

3

This liberatory political and spiritual reading of the Lady's position challenges treatments of Milton's identification with the Lady that construe the principle of virginity in the *Maske* as a symptom rather than a strength. In such accounts, the Lady's expression of the courage of Milton's convictions is ultimately self-contradictory and disabling. William Kerrigan reads Milton's identification with the Lady and his commitment to the cult and the poetics of chastity as a kind of oedipal compromise. Kerrigan reasons that Milton symbolically unmans himself in the hope that his gesture will extract a paternal concession to his wish to write poetry. In effect, he concedes to the father the possession and control of the mother and identifies with the mother: "The doctrine proclaimed in *Comus* repeats as a choice the trauma of oedipal submission, prolonging his latency well into manhood. . . . Reenacting the genesis of the superego, the virtue of maternal love disappears from the text of *Comus,* replaced by the form of its sterile and unblemished opposite. Virginity is the response to a mother's love that, suspending his maleness, makes a lady of a son."[21] Furthermore, according to Kerrigan, Milton's oedipal paralysis immobilizes his persona, the Lady, in a self-limiting reflex of anal fixation: an acknowledgment of the incompleteness and impossibility of the declaration of independence uttered by the Lady. Katharine Eisaman Maus situates Milton's identification with the Lady in her broader treatment of male Renaissance poets' fascination with the female body's unreadable interiority as a powerful metaphor for "the particular privileges and paradoxes of Renaissance subjectivity."[22] In Maus's subtle reading, the *Maske* reaches paralysis when it exposes its inability to resolve the problem of the body's relation to the soul. Milton's disposition toward monism contradicts his identification with the Lady, "for if mind and body are inseparable, then it is a sheer impossibility for a male poet imaginatively to occupy a position physically designated as female, even while retaining the intellectual qualities associated with masculinity." It follows that, although "[Milton] wants to preserve virginity—the unpenetrated body—as emblematic of uncorruptible poetic creativity and the wellspring of virtue, . . . he is, realistically, aware that real bodies are indeed penetrable, suffering not only rape but disease, death, and decay."[23] Michael Lieb similarly finds the Lady's stance of impassioned chastity ultimately an illusory and insufficient fantasy, a naive idealization of chastity's strength that the mature tragic poet of *Paradise Lost* would lament as insufficient to the deadly challenge of a fallen world.[24]

Provocative as they are, such readings at once take Milton too seriously and not seriously enough. Their sophisticated analytic skepticism fails fully to account for an imaginative mobility on Milton's part that knowingly plays games with notions of stable gender identity. Yet it also fails to acknowledge Milton's Puritan commitment to the world-reforming prospects created by the exercise of a chastity that transcends and transforms gender. In chastity, if we can adapt a line from St. Paul, there is neither male nor female, for all are one in chastity (Galatians 3:28). Chastity is a crossroad for gender transformation and for the empowerment that can follow from it, because chastity cancels conventional binaries of gender in social expression. In chastity's nonmarital stage, the celibate condition forecloses genital self-expression, explicit or implicit, in ordinary social relations. Chaste men and chaste women do not identify themselves with the typical marks and practices of standard gender identification; they have more in common with one another than in difference from one another. In chastity's other stage, companionate marriage, the two become one flesh (Genesis 2:24): in the self-giving of marital love, chastity cancels gender difference in the act of erotic union. The necessarily chaste transaction between historical author and textual character is also a potential imaginative moment of binding and bonding that cancels gender difference. We would do better to read Milton's gender crossing by the way of chastity not as the disclosure of a symptom but as the discovery of a strength. In a ritual drama whose central theme is translation, this is in certain respects the most remarkable and most crucial.

Milton's identification with his Lady is a transcendental trump on the joke of his college nickname, "the Lady of Christ's." John Shawcross suggests that the teasing title marked several "feminine" features of the young Milton's public personality: his delicacy in appearance, his fastidious avoidance of and objection to sexual activity, his commitment to study, and his aversion to carousing and other conventional forms of male romantic and athletic self-assertion.[25] Milton himself jokes about the nickname in his Sixth Prolusion, but sexually reverses its implications in the metaphysical comedy he sketches, by declaring himself *Ens,* Substance itself, progenitor of all the accidents in the Aristotelian ontology:

> But how is it that I have so suddenly been made a Father? May the gods protect me! What is the wonder that beats anything in Pliny's books? Have I done violence to some snake and suffered the fate of Tiresias? Or has some Thessalian witch anointed me with magic salve? Or like old Caenius, have I been violated by some god and bought my male sex as the price of my dishonor, so that in this sudden way I have been changed from a woman to a man? For from some of you I have recently been getting the title of Lady. And why do I seem to them to be so little of a man? Is there no respect for Priscian? Do these grammaticasters attribute the marks of the masculine to the feminine gender? It is because I have never been able to swallow mighty potations like the all-round athletes; or doubtless because my hand has not been hardened by holding the plough; or because I never sprawled on my back in the midday sun like a seven-year ox-driver; or perhaps because I have never showed myself to be a man in the way that those debauchees do. How I wish that their asininity could be shed as easily as my femininity! . . . And now in my role as a father, I turn to my sons, of whom I see a respectable number, and see that the clever rogues acknowledge me as their father by a sly nod. Do you ask for their names. . . . I should like my sons to bear the names of the predicaments to show in this way that they are nobly born and live like free men; and I shall see to it that all of them are advanced to some degree before I die. (Prolusion 6, 620–21)

This mythopoetic tour de force displays Milton's comic ease with gender bending. He correlates sexual identity not with biological endowment or cultural construction, but with the accidental and fluid nature of grammatical gender: "Do these grammaticasters attribute the marks of the masculine to the feminine gender?" He contrasts his own gendered shape-shifting, associated with chastity, "culture, urbanity, or refinement" (Prolusion 6, 620), to the typecast virile masculinity of his undergraduate taunters, rigidly entrenched in crude and mindless displays of lower-class debauchery: "How I wish that their asininity could be shed as easily as my femininity!" Finally, he implies that his own imaginative transcendence of the accidentals of gender category gives him creative priority and potency, as *Ens,* Substance, father of the "predicaments." With undergraduate bravado, Milton thus claims "masculine" potency by a witty embrace and inversion of the taunting nickname "Lady."

The *Maske* makes no such inversion explicit, because it is ever present: Milton's own mask in the *Maske* is the Lady, who, in speaking fully for herself, speaks fully for him as well. The tone of the *Maske* and the Lady's central position in it indicate a more serious and more subtle kind of gender play, which associates the virtues appropriate to Ladyship with power. It is not that Milton finds himself impossibly and self-revealingly trapped in a female position; nor that the Lady finds her potential female subjectivity colonized by a male voice. If this female identification is, as Kerrigan claims, a gesture of submission or self-limitation on Milton's part, it seems strange that it should yield Christological and eschatological claims of poetic power. If this female identification is, as some feminist critics imply, an instance of male ventriloquism that characteristically dispossesses women of the power to speak for themselves, it seems strange that it should yield a female hero who uses the fictional space of the *Maske* to articulate her selfhood and to resist a masculinist determination of her destiny with a liberatory power of speech all her own.[26]

If we read against the grain of Freudian and feminist accounts of this identification and follow through on its mythic and rhetorical associations, we can see that this cross-gendered identification made possible by chastity is a moment of disguised double empowerment. As we have seen in the previous chapter, the Lady discovers and exercises for herself, in the course of her ritual ordeal, the full prophetic Word of the Father. The brilliant paradox of her prophetic gesture is that she convinces Comus that the potential force of what she *could* say is more powerful than anything she actually says. At the same time, she flourishes a stunning erotic charisma in her chaste bearing, which Elder Brother admiringly and suggestively invokes and explicates in the mythographic icon of Minerva wearing the Gorgon shield (447–52). Minerva-Athena's petrifying power results from her appropriation of and merger with her opposite, the ghastly figure of Medusa, an overdetermined figuration of the dread associated with female sexuality. "Rigid looks of Chaste austerity" (450) are doubly powerful: they present a seemingly impermeable body image, focused in a gaze of frightening self-sufficiency, and so they stop the potential aggressor cold, immobilized in thought or action. The force of virginity tested, strengthened, and vindicated in the Lady's ritual ordeal thus instantiates the theological premise of the present chapter: that chastity is, for Milton, the gender crossroad where prophetic authority discloses its access to doubly valenced power: paternal and maternal, Symbolic and Imaginary, verbal and spectral. The Lady's speech endows her with the authority of the Father, and her "look" links her to the female mysteries of the imagined Mother, sublimated and serviceable to the interests of chastity.

Would not Milton, by whom and for whom the Lady speaks, claim the same accession to a doubly engendered power? Indeed, to make a girl the prophetic spokesperson in a court masque is a gesture so unconventional, so against the grain of both genre and gender, as to disarm suspicion.[27] Chaste, silent, and obedient, the youthful female aristocratic subject of Stuart England is one position from which a serious oedipal or revolutionary challenge appears most unlikely to be waged. For Milton, the sexual persona of the Lady proffers a kind of imaginative mobility analogous to that of Shakespeare's cross-dressing romantic heroines, Rosalind and Viola. As they gain freedom and mobility by means of male costuming and the verbal and dramatic improvisation it supports, so does Milton from the adoption of a female persona. The mask of the Lady relieves him from the crisis of patriarchal indebtedness and expectations incumbent upon a son, anxieties of the sort that surface in his efforts to persuade his father of the value of his dedication to poetry in "Ad Patrem":

> However pleased you are, best Father, by this song,
> Its thinking may seem slight, for I have not yet learned
> How best to recompense you for your gifts unearned,
> For which my best would not be recompense in kind:
> Your charities excel the reverence I own
> In the fruitless gratitude of words alone.
>
> (6–11; my translation)[28]

The mask of the Lady also distances him from the contaminations of masculine conventionality parodied in the Sixth Prolusion and from positions of erotic aggression typically played out by male figures in the Ovidian substructure of the *Maske*.

The Lady's virginal affiliation with Minerva-Athena seems further to circumvent suspicion of the *Maske*'s subversions of gender hierarchies. Athena seems literally and completely a daddy's girl, a brainchild bursting from the forehead of Zeus. In *The Eumenides*, Athena claims to speak for the Father in all things:

> No mother gave me birth.
> I honor the male, in all things but marriage.
> Yes, with all my heart I am my father's child.[29]

If we read Perseus's decapitation of Medusa as an allegory of mastery over feminine sexuality or, following Freud, a mythological figuration of the moment of castration of the Mother,[30] Athena's supervision of the project seems to reinforce her independence from and antagonism to the feminine. Yet as an intellectual androgyne who professes militant chastity, Athena in action asserts a kind of autogenetic freedom, dependent upon and derived from neither mother nor father. She honors the male in all things, except the one thing that reinforces male control over the female in traditional patriarchal societies, marriage. In the Renaissance humanist allegorization of the virgin goddess, the condition she sponsors, virginal and rational self-presence, becomes a being for God only and for God in the self. In the Protestant dispensation, virginity is a figure for the soul's independence of all worldly claims: "Milton is attempting to preserve the virginity of the concept of faith against any contamination from works, even loving ones. . . . [C]hastity is a pervasive metaphor for faith among the Reformers."[31] Milton's virgin persona, the Lady, opens up poetry for him as the expression of faith's mobile and radical freedom.

Hélène Cixous, in a different type of liberatory polemic, calls gender crossing of the sort Milton practices in the *Maske* "vatic bisexuality . . . which doesn't annul differences but stirs them up, pursues them, increases their number": "this is, each one's location in self (repérage en soi) of the presence—variously manifest and insistent according to each person, male or female—of both sexes, nonexclusion either of the difference or of one sex, and, from this 'self-permission,' multiplication of the effects of the inscription of desire, over all parts of my body and the other body."[32] With her boundary-blurring advocacy of an erotic scripture that subverts the binary oppositions and hierarchies of patriarchy and offers a multiplication of sites of bodily pleasure, Cixous might be expected to find her prophet in Comus rather than in "the Lady of Christ's" or the Lady whom he projects in the *Maske*. But Comus, for all his gorgeous imagery and all his nudging and winking, is a conventional masculinist when it comes right down to it. His gaudy offertories, as the Lady discerns, are designed not to expand but to exploit female desire and to restrict and materialize the horizons of the body's pleasure. Sabrina will enter the poem to release the Lady from the threat of those constraining exploitations into the open field of erotic delight invoked by the very different rhetoric of Cixous. Releasing, awakening, and sanctifying her physically and emotionally, Sabrina relibidinizes and sanctifies the Lady's erogenous zones for an active life of chaste desire, "multiply[ing] the effects of the inscription of desire, over all parts of [the Lady's] body." At the same time, her ritual gesture is a symbolic transmission of power, a mythologized and feminized analogue to the moment of Isaiah's calling to prophecy, when the seraphim touches his lips with a burning coal and declares that his guilt is taken away (Isaiah 6:1–6). The Lady's regenerate body, we shall see, becomes the true form of Milton's *Maske,* its incarnate emblem of an ordered and sanctified erotic plenitude, and the implicit center and source of its moral and creative energies.

The Lady's triumphant intuition of desire's promise and destination and Milton's uncanny identification with her interests suggest that chastity, rightly construed as a condition of erotic concentration and enlarged anticipation is, remarkably enough, a Puritan way of intimating Cixous's "vatic bisexuality." Milton's imaginative identification with his Lady enacts a wish like Cixous's for imaginative and bodily autonomy, and for what Blake called "the lineaments of Gratified Desire."[33] Milton shares this wish through and with the imagined Lady who is, like Zeus's Athena, his brainchild. The retrospective glow of this visionary gender crossing illumines in its turn the passage of Alice Egerton, whose ritual actions and expressions in the *Maske* performance of 1634 only come to make full sense in light of the declaration of independence composed by Milton for her character after the event of her impersonation of him.

4

If my treatment of Milton's identification with his Lady to this point is plausible, it seems that Milton is breaking all the rules of gender in early modern subject formation even as he sets them into play. He himself identifies with and disappears into the persona of a young girl coming of age, discovers rhetorical and prophetic power in this gender crossing, and inevitably endows her with this power as well. There are social implications to this power sharing that are not limited to the author who invents the character and the young actor whose rite of passage brings the character to life and to maturity. As I claimed at the outset of this chapter, the Lady's exemplary voice activates and exemplifies the social prospects for ethically and politically articulate female speech in early modern England. Alice Egerton carries into her ordeal the emerging hopes for a truly Reformed culture, and her triumph is exemplary to a nation. By politicizing the discourse of the masque in the way that she speaks the Lady into being, she temporarily but effectively transforms the very discursive and political space in which she speaks. She turns the masque's hermetically sealed fantasy world of aristocratic self-delight into the "public sphere" of early modern liberal society; and she stakes out a place for women to speak and to act in that complex field of social competition and exchange, and political determination.

Maria Magro discerns in the structural features and gender formations of Puritan matrimony as represented in Milton's divorce tracts and *Paradise Lost* evidence to support Jürgen Habermas's account of the emergence of the public and private spheres of early modern bourgeois society.[34] Magro demonstrates how the structural formation of the public sphere, which is reserved for the competitive and acquisitive exercise of "the ethical-civil freedom of the male individual," depends on the simultaneous formation of the private sphere of the household. In the domestic sphere companionate marriage is honored, and female sexuality is recognized, but restricted and domesticated to provide support for the public projects of male self-understanding, competition, and social formation. Magro observes that

> Milton's texts produce a model of femininity which is progressive in its assertion of the positive value of female sexuality, yet ultimately regressive in its assumption that this value rests on a shoring up of male freedom and a gendered public sphere. In a domestic context the sexualized woman provides a site for the development of the male subject's "pure humanity," the ontological corollary of the intimate sphere, and, at the same time, his status as a public man, an individual beset by and operating within the laws of a market economy.[35]

Even as she reads Milton's model as a gender binary one requiring the sequestration of women in the domestic sphere, Magro acknowledges the progressive political dynamic that it generates: "While the gendered public sphere is tied to the ontology of individual male freedom and liberty, the discourse of individual liberty and freedom will prove migratory; post-Restoration female as well as male writers will benefit from it."[36] Milton's *Maske* confirms Magro's description of the progressive impetus of Miltonic texts even as it subverts the rigid gender opposition that organizes the account and challenges her time line. The Lady, decidedly a pre-Restoration speaker, is nevertheless both the prophet of "the discourse of individual liberty and freedom" and the representative of the new humanity who exercises it. Her performance turns the genre of masque as a private, privileged aristocratic entertainment into something that approximates Habermas's bourgeois public sphere: a public symposium on political and ethical value and property.

It is Comus, after all, who seeks to retard the Lady's—and the *Maske*'s—political progress by outlining mutually exclusive public and private spheres for the positioning and exercise of her identity. He proposes to the Lady a position as spectacular trophy woman in the rarefied world of self-regarding aristocratic entertainment and self-indulgence and suggests that her alternative is the restrictive drudgery of domesticity:

> Beauty is Nature's brag, and must be shown
> In courts, at feasts, and high solemnities
> Where most may wonder at the workmanship;
> It is for homely features to keep home,
> They had their name thence; coarse complexions
> And cheeks of sorry grain will serve to ply
> The sampler, and to tease the huswife's wool.
> What need a vermeil-tinctured lip for that,
> Love-darting eyes, or tresses like the morn?
>
> (745–53)

The Lady's vigorous repudiation of Comus (756–79) is not only a triumph of moral character, but a political reconfiguration of the content and the ends of the *Maske*'s discourse and hence a restructuring of the discursive space in which it unfolds. Habermas's public sphere emerges here, at the moment when the Lady rejects the reactionary alternatives proposed by Comus—woman as erotic supermodel or woman as anonymous, silent, and obedient household drone—and asserts herself as a free, socially committed, and socially responsible subject, entitled to and capable of participation in public argument about the disposition of property, the distribution of wealth, and the practice of social justice. Revising even as it substantiates Magro's account, the *Maske* forecasts a public sphere founded not on the restriction of female sexuality and subjectivity to the intimate sphere of domestic concern and home economics, but on women's self-articulating release from patriarchal constraint and challenge to masculinist assumptions. Milton's Lady leads the way to their consequent dynamic and fluid, prophetic and ethical circulation between and negotiation of the claims of both private and public spheres.

This dynamic movement from the private and the lyrical to the public and prophetic is evident whenever the Lady speaks in the

Maske: in her resistance to the entropic power of the Shakespearean soliloquy and discovery of the ground of her own strength in her initial speech (170–229); in the progress of her Echo Song from anxiety to confidence and from timid self-concern to prophetic generosity (230–43); in the defense of her own beleaguered freedom (662–65) and the ferocity of her critical rebukes of Comus (690–705, 756–61); in her clear-sighted articulation of equitable modes of political economy and ecological stewardship (762–79); in the sublime force of her climactic encomium to Virginity (779–99). Her sustained and triumphant argument with Comus provides performative evidence of the integrity of female sexuality, political intelligence, and ethical public commitment. She may be speaking for Milton throughout, but she is also speaking on her own behalf, and on behalf of others lacking her power of voice. The feminizing of political argument and of the rhetorical sublime that is evidenced in the Lady's several speeches introduces something new into the discourse of English literary tradition and of the classical texts on which it is founded and consequently of the culture in formation that fashions its origins and identity on the basis of these traditions.

Recent feminist criticism has forcefully argued that the predominantly male literary discourse of tradition generates itself by the creation of a self-conscious, inspired male voice whose power derives at least in part from the suppression, occlusion, or silencing of female vocality.[37] The strong voice of the Lady—perhaps politically and ethically the most self-consistent, articulate, and powerful female voice in English Renaissance dramatic poetry—achieves its effect not only through Milton's imaginative identification with her, but also through the uncanny sense of all the other voices speaking through her. In a return of the repressed feminine, she recovers the lost and silenced voices of Ovidian heroines, the effaced responses of the innumerable purportedly coy and resistant mistresses of amatory and courtly love poems, and the muted and subjected aspirations of several of her tragic and romantic precursors on the English stage. Historical research into the *Maske*'s domestic and social milieu has shown how the Lady's voice is not only a "literary" voice charged with the vanishing voices of numerous literary characters, but a historically conscious voice that engages and impacts the public sphere, speaking for several "disappeared" women of recent English history, whose stories were implicated in the Egerton family narratives and prospects. By means of the decorous subliminal references appropriate to the *Maske*'s performative occasion, the Lady speaks for the degraded and silenced female relatives of the Egerton family,

Lady Alice's aunt and cousin, maliciously abused by the Earl of Castlehaven and his servants. The Lady also takes up the cry for justice of the serving girl Margery Evans, whose rape in the Ludlow forest and subsequent legal neglect and victimization might have rendered her just one more anonymous and forgotten female victim, had not her persistent claims for legal redress provided the Earl of Bridgewater an early opportunity to exercise his judicial concern for victims of injustice in his own administrative district.[38] When Leah Marcus observes of the Lady's position in the *Maske,* "She has assumed the position of one of the powerless, and her voice becomes their voice,"[39] she might well be speaking of the Lady's identification not only with Margery Evans, but with numerous other powerless figures in literature and history whose suffering invests the Lady's ordeal and whose muted voices are redeemed and regenerated through the Lady's passage into ethical and imaginative maturity.[40]

This reawakening of voice involves what Angus Fletcher, going to the heart of the *Maske*'s poetics, calls "the principle of Echo."[41] Echo, we have seen, is the classical figure whom the Lady evokes and invokes in the time of her peril, lost in the darkness of Comus's tangled wood (230–43). By the time that she has completed her brief and eloquent lyric, the Lady has "translated" the Ovidian nymph from a timid, vulnerable, pining erotic victim into a numinous figure of providential generosity and harmony. This Echo becomes a double figure for the Lady's own vocation of "parley" (241): a Muse who inspires and supervises the Lady's translation of experiential threat and vulnerability into imaginative and prophetic strength and a projection of the Lady's own magnanimous and powerful voice, a voice in which and through which innumerable otherwise vanished voices reawaken, rearticulate themselves, and resonate among the heavenly harmonies to which they give "resounding grace" (243).

Milton engenders a prophetic and sublime voice for the Lady and about the Lady, then, not to return her to the patriarchal oversight of the domestic sphere—a restraining order which would be impossible with a voice like this—but to transform and redeem the very nature of the public sphere. A visionary prototype not only of the Jesus of *Paradise Regained,* but of Blake's emancipatory female heroes Oothoon, Ololon, and Jerusalem, the Lady's resistance to delusory projections of selfhood and desire, and her prophetic recovery of female voices muted and destroyed by those projections, articulates regenerate models of the psychological, the public, and the cosmic spheres at once. The voice of the Lady which Milton scripts and Alice Egerton speaks in 1634 becomes hers in the performance, is in turn amplified and explicated in the textual reechoing of subsequent publications, and provides thereby liberatory prospects and motivation for all who, in witnessing or reading the *Maske,* sustain and magnify its saving project to "awake the courteous Echo" (275) in the interests of human freedom.

7
Girl, Interrupted and the Changing Woman

1

IF THE LADY IN HER RITUAL EXPERIENCE ATTAINS TO SOMETHING LIKE Prophetic strain ("Il Penseroso," 173–74), a skeptic might well ask of the concluding movements of the *Maske* why it is that she requires the intervention and help of others, and why she remains silent. After her triumphant rebuttal and refutation of Comus (799), she remains immobilized, and she speaks not a word, from the time of her rescue, to her release from bondage, to her homecoming. Her seeming passivity and silence are distinct yet interrelated issues that will focus the attention of the final two chapters of this book. First, her captivity and release. The Lady's stasis in Comus's chair is indeed one of the great riddles of Milton's *Maske*. Her enthronement in the chair, subject to Comus's temptation and threat, makes sense as a liminal component typical of rituals of initiation, which frequently include periods of forced restraint and ritual harassment by masked supernatural personae. In constructing his plot, Milton decides to deprive the Lady's brothers of the triumphant release of their sister, and of a decisive triumph over Comus. This puzzle of an incomplete rescue mission is dramatically and thematically consonant with the puzzle of the Lady's paralysis. Milton's psychological tact and comprehension of the logic of female initiation is flawless here: representatives of virtuous male chastity, the brothers are able to drive off the libertine Comus, but the Lady needs a woman's touch to release her from her bondage and complete her initiation. The abortive rescue operation thus divides the structure of the *Maske*'s dramatic center into two parts. These two parts represent two phases of the Lady's initiatory ordeal, and each phase has its presiding supernatural figure. Comus, who plays the role assigned the figure of the "mock bridegroom" in some traditional rites of passage, presides over the first phase of her trial (659–813). Sabrina, invoked by the Attendant Spirit, presides over the second part of the Lady's trial as a tutelary godmother, to mediate the generative mysteries of womanhood to the Lady, and to mobilize her for the social exercise of those mysteries (814–957). A river goddess of flow and fertility, Sabrina exemplifies a once-threatened yet inviolable virginity like the Lady's, transformed into generous and healing maternal power. The Attendant Spirit, as medicine man and master of ceremonies, orchestrates the transition between the two parts of the Lady's trial and provides the framing security of providentially informed choral commentary.

The two parts of the Lady's trial resolve the seeming differences between the Lady's signature virtue, chastity, and the theological virtue of charity.[1] The first part, the debate between Comus and the Lady (659–813), provides occasion for the Lady to reflect on and articulate the productive interinanimations of chastity and virginity as a composite condition of true and vigorous virtue. In the second part, Sabrina releases the Lady from her fixity (814–921) and enlarges the domain of the virtue's exercise by disclosing the intricate mutual identification between chastity and charity. The Lady's virtue thus first constellates itself under the pressure of Comus as a defensive self-centering structure. In the second part of the *Maske*'s initiatory core, Sabrina mobilizes the Lady's virtue into creative, dynamic, expansive, and transformative possibility. Comus sharpens and strengthens chastity as self-knowing resistance to the luxuries of consumption he has to offer. Sabrina sets the Lady's chastity free from its own defenses and initiates her into the productive life of charity. A rigorous "no" to Comus initially immobilizes her, but also clears the Lady's way for the unconditional "yes" of her whole being to the life of charity, of chaste active desire, released by Sabrina's baptismal touch.

Milton patterns the Lady's dilemma on that of Amoret in Spenser's *Faerie Queene*. In Spenser's allegory, Amoret is the twin of the invincible virgin huntress Belphoebe. We need to review Amoret's biography in some detail in order to appreciate Milton's revision of Spenser's scene of erotic bondage and torment. While Belphoebe, adopted by Diana, develops the icy glamour of militant virginity, Amoret is fashioned by the goddess of love to embody the ideal of marital chastity. She grows to maidenhood in the lush vegetative cycles of the earthly paradise, the Garden of Adonis over which Venus presides as goddess of generation (*FQ* 3.6). When she approaches maturity, Amoret goes to finishing school in the Temple of Venus to master the courtly arts of the sensuous woman. Amoret approaches the completion of her social destiny as chaste wife when her destined partner, the complementarily masculine Scudamore, boldly enters the Temple of Venus, claims her as his "glorious spoyle" (*FQ* 4.10.55.9, 4.10.58.3), and forcefully carries her off, weeping and fearful, from the sheltering feminine sanctuary of her adoptive divine mother. But in the very midst of their nuptial celebrations, indeed, in the sportive guise of a wedding masque, Amoret is abruptly whisked off by the enchanter Busyrane "quite away to liuing wight vnknowen" (*FQ* 4.1.3). Busyrane holds her captive in his enchanted castle, where "he tormenteth her most terribly, / And day and night afflicts with mortall paine, / Because to yield him loue she doth deny" (*FQ* 3.11.17.1–3).

When Spenser's hero of chastity, Britomart, infiltrates Busyrane's opulent palace of erotic sadism, she witnesses the horror of Amoret's torture. She observes the Maske of Cupid, whose feature attraction is Amoret, dragged and prodded by Despight and Cruelty, ghastly and nearly drained of life blood, her breast ripped open by a fresh wound and carrying her heart, still steaming with blood, in a silver basin (*FQ* 3.12.19–21). On the subsequent night, when Britomart penetrates the inner sanctum of Busyrane's enchantments, she finds "that same woefull Ladie, both whose hands / Were bounden fast, that did her ill become / And her small wast girt round with yron bands, / Vnto a brasen pillour, by the which she stands" (*FQ* 3.12.30.6–9). Busyrane sits before her, "Figuring straunge characters of his art, / With liuing bloud he those characters wrate, / Dreadfully dropping from her dying hart, / Seeming transfixed with a cruell dart, / And all perforce to make her him to loue" (*FQ* 3.12.31.2–6). Britomart overpowers the enchanter and forces him to undo the charm by reading "those same bloudy lines" backward (*FQ* 3.12.36.7), at which the chain which binds Amoret falls off, the pillar shatters, the luxurious chambers are stripped bare, and the dreadful flames which barred entry to the castle are quenched.

Several critics have explored Amoret's captivity and torture as the victim of a certain idea and art of love, by which both she and Scudamore have been formed as characters. The fantastic world of which Busyrane is master is the world of Renaissance love psychology, with its tropes of love as mock warfare and spiritual torment, and its psychomachia populated by the paired and conflicting emotions and attitudes that afflict and compel lovers. In the Maske of Cupid, these personified figures precede, surround, and follow Amoret as projections of all of her coy strategies and ensuing anxious fears about love in marriage: "Amoret's main tormentors are those very qualities which have preserved her chastity during her courtship, and she is being punished for her long resistance to the power of love. . . . Walking among the maskers, she sees . . . the vengeance of male sexuality on the chastely reticent female."[2] The poet cues us into this psychological projection on her part with his observation about the nightmarish figures who bring up the rear of the Maske: "There were full many moe like maladies, / Whose names and natures I note readen well; / So many moe, as there be phantasies / In wauering wemens wit, that none can tell, / Or paines in loue, or punishments in hell" (*FQ* 3.12.26.1–5).

Britomart, Amoret, Belphoebe, and Florimell are Spenserian splittings in the central books of *The Faerie Queene*. They represent various aspects and possibilities of female chastity, beauty, and desire. Amoret, Belphoebe, and Florimell occupy a somewhat different allegorical position from Britomart in the poem, because they are archetypes: the character and range of responses of each is limited by her conceptual form. Britomart, in contrast, is a human hero whose chastity is a work in progress, shaping itself as individual character through the challenges, experiences, revisions, and corrections she undergoes in her wayfaring. Her resourcefulness and flexibility are manifest, indeed focalized in her traveling disguise as knight errant: she appropriates the attributes of heroic manhood, which endow her with a freedom and mobility equivalent to her near contemporaries, Rosalind and Viola, in the forest of Shakespeare's romances.[3] "She tries to live up to an ideal, which in her quest she may also adumbrate—hence her function in the allegory—but she also has a character which cannot be contained by that or any other closural allegorical significance."[4] Britomart's rescue of Amoret is one of the climaxes of her career and the narrative signal of her integration of several types of virtue in Spenser's Book of Chastity: "Belphoebe is the Heavenly Venus, eschewing earthly love; Amoret is the Earthly Venus, beset by all the dangers love is heir to. Britomart is the human embodiment of both types, passing from the virginity of youth to the chaste married love of maturity."[5] Britomart has the single-mindedness, charismatic force, and militant glamor of Belphoebe as well as the passionate heart and romantic vocation of Amoret. Virginal and ardent at once, a pristine activist subject to the wounds of love, questing for her beloved rather than retreating from and rebuffing love's claims, Britomart, in rescuing Amoret, figuratively prepares for her own tempestuous romantic encounter with her dreamboat Artegall in book 4 of *The Faerie Queene,* the Book of Friendship (*FQ* 4.6).

Milton's Lady is the heir of Britomart in that she too is a composite figure. Elder Brother concisely associates her with the militant virgins Britomart and Belphoebe: "'Tis chastity, my brother, chastity: / She that has that, is clad in complete steel, / And like a quiver'd Nymph with Arrows keen / May trace huge Forests and unharbor'd Heaths, / Infamous Hills and sandy perilous wilds" (420–24). The Lady's ordeal in the palace of Comus affiliates her in turn with Amoret, the captive of Busyrane. Her initial abandonment in the forest also resembles the wandering of the innocent heroine Una of Spenser's first book. The Lady integrates these figures, internalizes and dramatically naturalizes their various agons of chastity. Spenser's allegorical romance is translated into mimetic action and symbolic drama in Milton's *Maske,* whose generic alterations seem both to invoke and to expose the limits of romance in representing moral choice.[6] Although Elder Brother idealizes chastity in Spenserian terms, Milton resists the glamorization of chastity through romance. His Lady internalizes the heroic fortitude, endurance and consistency of Britomart, while reminding us of the hazards of virginity by situating the Lady, like Amoret, in a seriously straitened position. Girls and their admiring younger brothers may dream of knight errantry, of roving about like Britomart, bashing cads and righting wrongs, all in pursuit of a dream lover. But getting boxed in at a party by a charmer who presents himself as easy on the eyes and slick with the flattery, and operates insistently from the conviction that "no" is actually a coy way of suggesting "yes," that is all too common. So Milton constructs the Lady's situation on the basis of Amoret's captivity, but socializes it, naturalizes it, making it a situation of sexual pressure and assault as familiar as last weekend's party.

Milton's Lady asserts a purposeful and invincible character of chastity like Britomart or Belphoebe, yet she finds herself in a captivity like Amoret's. She has been carried off and held captive within the structure of a masque. She has been immobilized by an enchanter who seeks her concession to his desire. She resists his offers, his threats, and his charms, but entrapped as she is, she cannot as yet, and on her own, deliver herself from his assault. As Britomart discovers with Busyrane, it will take his "rod revers'd, / And backward mutters of dissevering power" (816) to release the Lady from her bondage. Pursuing the parallel with Amoret's situation might lead us to construe the Lady's stasis as a symptom of sexual fear, a kind of hysterical paralysis. Irene Tayler makes the case that Blake interpreted the Lady's paralysis this way in his set of illuminations of the *Maske:* "Blake saw the Lady's encounter with Comus as the product of that frightened girl's fantasy: her bondage, the bondage of sexual fears; her release, the release from them."[7] To cultivate such terror is surely an element of Comus's motive. The symbolism and the circumstance—the phallic rod, the mesmerizing power of the enchanter's discourse—seem to favor such a reading. But Comus fails in his efforts at intimidation and seduction. The Lady displays no fear of him, nor of sexuality itself. Tayler, following Blake, assumes that the Lady is bound by her weakness rather than her strength. To account for the Lady's fixture as a sign of sexual fear fails to specify the contrast between what Busyrane represents to Amoret and what Comus represents to the Lady.

Both Busyrane and Comus are artists of desire. They gain their power through their persuasive mystifications of different modes of social organization of sexuality. Busyrane consolidates through his enchantment a deep tradition of courtly love values which valorize adultery, with its obstacles, its risks, its intrigues and disappointments, its compensatory imaginings, as a transgressive, world-defying mode of romantic love. In this tradition, pain is a necessary catalyst of love. Pain purifies desire through trial, intrigue, dispossession. In Spenser's period, such a mode of loving would already have become something of an anachronism, in light of the emerging Reformation culture of bourgeois individualism and social theology of companionate marriage.[8] But Elizabeth I herself, the subliminal model for haughty Belphoebe and the delicately eroticized Faerie Queene of Spenser's fantasy, sponsored to her own advantage and delight a court culture of nostalgic medievalism.[9] Busyrane is one of its dark figments.

Because Amoret went to finishing school in the protective cloister of Venus's temple, it is no wonder that Busyrane is able to captivate her so easily: a slight twist on what she has learned about femininity and sexuality produces the nightmare of love he offers. A master of the love psychology in which Amoret has been nurtured, Busyrane can turn her inside out, so that even her thoughts of resistance feed his power over her. Amoret is manipulated and victimized by the only version of sexual desire and pleasure she has known. Busyrane can rip her heart out and force her to bear it about in a silver chalice because this is how he knows she has been prepared to feel about love. He can write his sadomasochistic romance narrative in her life blood because she has already been formed by the Petrarchan vision of love as suffering. "Lust is the least complex of his perversions," remarks Thomas Roche; "he is the image of love distorted in the mind, distorted by lascivious anticipation or horrified withdrawal. He becomes the denial of the unity of body and soul in true love."[10] Any way that Amoret looks at it, she loses. If she concedes to the opportunity of seduction, she betrays her love. If she resists seduction for the sake of her love, she suffers the unquenchable anguish of unrequited longing. The embodiment of chaste love in marriage, she needs to be delivered from the hold of the stylized self-destructive patterns of traditional courtship, into a social order adequate to respect and sustain such love. "When Britomart rescues Amoret from this place of death, she is ending some five centuries of human experience, predominantly painful."[11]

Comus is a genius of a different age from Busyrane, and his challenge to the Lady is of a different era. Busyrane is old-fashioned, Comus is hip. Busyrane requires dark solitudes and archaic texts and rites to execute his binding spells. Comus thrives on glitter, patter, speed, and special effects. His libertine naturalism flourishes the wit, drive, cynicism, and ruthlessness of an up-and-coming Stuart courtier. Comus pits love against law, natural desire against inhibiting convention, fecundity against order, immediate gratification against repressive temperance. Busyrane appeals to the romantic longing for the pain that is at the very heart of love.[12] Comus promises a world so saturated with delight that there is no possibility of pain. Busyrane casts the nostalgic spell of the dark romance of medievalism. Comus would be great on MTV: he projects the bright, sensation-driven, sensorily overloaded, fragmented sound bites and image bites of the postmodern. Apprenticed in the Inigo Jones era of stagecraft, Comus depends on the technology of special effects to work his spells: "Thus I hurl / My dazzling Spells into the spongy air, / Of power to cheat the eye with blear illusion, / And give it false presentments" (153–56).

The Lady would seem, at first glance, an unlikely candidate for Comus to seduce, since, as she makes clear, she agrees with him about virtually nothing: "[Because] there is not the slightest indication that either Comus or the Lady will be swayed by the other's arguments, their debate takes the form of a dispute between figures whose views are irreconcilably and inalterably opposed."[13] But there is no reason for Comus to suspect serious female resistance to his seduction, since his world view essentially excludes that possibility. As he sees it, a woman, especially an inexperienced one, will either concede passively to his positioning of her as an object of male desire, or, if gifted with more experience, cunning, and ambition, she will consent to the prospect of "mutual and partak'n bliss" (741), which opens the door for her to share in desire's commodification, in the privilege of exploiting others and the world's goods.

But the Lady proves herself free of Amoret's physical and psychological vulnerability. She has been to a different school. She construes the orders of nature, society, and human desire from a radically different standpoint, informed by principles of moderation, equity, justice, and love founded in honest affection between equal partners. She has no prior investment in and displays no mutual interest in the terms of Comus's seduction. She does not participate psychically in the terms of her captivity. In contrast to Amoret's psychologically captivated response to Busyrane, the Lady manifestly and effectively critiques and repudiates the pleasure package Comus has to offer, because she is able to envision and articulate a more compelling and comprehensive alternative. By the end of her account of Nature's temperance and her encomium to virginity (756–99), she holds the upper hand in the rhetorical and psychological contest with her supposed enchanter. Comus himself acknowledges as much (800–805).

2

But although the Lady's resistance to Comus perfectly matches and overmatches his threat, it nevertheless contributes to the outcome he has predicted: "Nay Lady sit; if I but wave this wand, / Your nerves are all chain'd up in Alabaster, / And you a statue; or as *Daphne* was, / Root-bound, that fled *Apollo*" (659–62). The Lady does end up root-bound, but her roots are not where Comus expects them to be, so her bondage is not really a consequence of Comus's power over her. Comus wields an allusion that works against his claim of mastery. Daphne's metamorphosis into the laurel is an equivocal triumph of chastity, frustrating Apollo's desire at the cost of the nymph's humanity.[14] The Lady's temporary paralysis is also a preserver of her chastity and thus, perhaps, evidence that Comus's strategy of enchantment is as self-defeating as the more forthright aggression of his mythological precursor Apollo. Comus cannot get what he wants from the Lady if she has turned to statuary or shrubbery. Daphne's metamorphosis comes miraculously from without, as the fulfillment of her own prayer rather than of the will of her pursuer (*Metamorphoses,* 24). The Lady's analogous circumstance does not answer to the will of her captor, but to a providential will for her well-being. If this is so, her own force of will may be peculiarly implicated in her fixture. For Milton, the Arminian in formation, providence and human volition are mutual participants in the making of the history of the bondage of the human will and of its freedom. Georgia Christopher describes the Lady's entrapment as "a vivid image of the central tenet of Reformation faith—that the Christian is both sinner and justified saint—*simul iustus et peccator*—at once bound and free."[15] Christopher's tropological interpretation encourages us to read the Lady's paralysis as a sign of the bondage of the will, even in the exercise of virtue, and of her ultimate dependency upon providence. Theologically true as this may be, the Lady is not a Lutheran, but a Miltonist. Paradoxically, her manifest captivity is not only a sign of theological limitation but of latent freedom, a freedom achieved and a freedom to come. Her immobility signifies neither Comus's power over her, nor a paralyzing fearfulness, nor what William Kerrigan diagnoses as "a root-bound virtue . . . in bondage to the desire denied," but of unmediated and unmoderated strength, invested with the desire transformed.[16]

Insofar as it is defending itself, the Lady's chastity strengthens itself through entrenchment. Testing its resilience and consolidating and protecting the boundaries of selfhood, it must be static and solid. We have already seen how Elder Brother gives us a clue to this paradox with his mythological account of chastity's strengths. Chaste Diana's "stern frown" (446) is duplicated and detailed in Minerva's demeanor:

> What was that snaky-headed *Gorgon* shield
> That wise *Minerva* wore, unconquer'd Virgin,
> Wherewith she freez'd her foes to congeal'd stone,
> But rigid looks of Chaste austerity
> And noble grace that dash't brute violence
> With sudden adoration and blank awe?
>
> (447–52)

Facing down and freeze-framing the foes of virginity, Minerva's own look turns rigid. Medusa is paralyzed by the very gaze that she fixes on others, and the spooky superimposition of Medusa's monstrous head upon Minerva's shining face in the young scholar's iconography intensifies the suggestion that the immobilizing power of chastity is doubly directed. The exercise of "Chaste austerity" chills and fixes both figures in the icy mutual gaze. The process of image development in this passage supports the psychological point, as life arrests itself in emblematic form, mobility and process congeal to fixity and essence. As a self-completing virtue, chastity may be at risk of setting itself apart and fixing its own enduring status as a living but frozen icon.[17]

The Lady's stasis thus embodies and emblematizes the defensive phase of chastity as the arresting self-direction and concentration of libidinal energy. Lacan can help us understand this fixture. The Lady's refutation of Comus by means of the word and her simultaneous physical paralysis rehearse the formation of a socialized idea of the self, described by Lacan as the insertion of the human subject into the Symbolic order. In Lacan's account, the patriarchally focused Symbolic order interrupts the Imaginary intimacies and exchanges of the mother and child and requires of the maturing child a sacrificial organization of the self and its desires according to the cognitive and ethical structures of the governing culture. The child enters the Symbolic order through the mastery of language, which gives her both greater and lesser control of her world. Language mastery makes the will articulate, expansive, and specific—in effect, it brings the conscious will into focus out of the luminous chaos of imaginary desire—but at the same time makes the will's claims more modest, indeed finite. Through her participation in language, the child confesses the degree to which the world escapes her actual control of it, even as the language she accesses provides a compensatory offer of partial and provisional mastery of the Symbolic representations of the world. As each meaning-bearing element in the Symbolic order of language acquires significance from its differential positioning in the complete ensemble, so emerging identity is paradoxically non-self-centered, because, being structured by and like language, its reference points are beyond the conscious self. The child thus enters the Symbolic order and begins her history in a divided and armored state, aware of both her own distinctness and her limitations, with a Symbolic purchase on the world paid for by the loss of her sense of being at the world's center. Lacan described this starting point for the subject as the assumption of "the armature of an alienating identity, whose rigid structure will mark the subject's entire mental development."[18]

The Lady's rigid posture on Comus's magic throne marks her reenactment of this moment of self-armature in Everychild's career. In her contest with Comus, the Lady proves herself a champion of the Symbolic order, dramatically restaging her own entry into it. The Lady's initiatory ordeal recapitulates the original formation of the subject in childhood, rehearsing the initially defensive posture of a virgin selfhood consolidating and defending its own discrete boundaries. But her performance of this entry at a higher level of integration suggests not the loss and self-division characteristic of the ego-formation of childhood, but mastery of an intact self who thinks of the world as virtually at her command, or rather, at the command of the temperance and chastity to which she has committed herself. The power of the Symbolic order makes itself felt in the *Maske* through the unassailable idealism that provides the Lady the basis of her strength, her self-knowledge, and her identity. The identity that her initiation confers upon the Lady is not what we might expect to be the isolated, crisis-driven, anxious identity of the Protestant ego, but a transpersonal, or as Lacan might say, intersubjective, complex. In contrast to Lacan's ironic model, this intersubjectivity articulates itself not negatively, in terms of alienation, tension, and diminishment of the self, but prospectively, as a radiant and resonant fullness: "The mind finds, that is, the sustaining Other that founds it and authorizes a self-sufficiency that is blameless because it is a sufficiency of perfect dependence."[19] The personalized and personified symbolic structures that the Lady introjects in the course of her initiation become energy sources for self-fashioning, because they are patterns congruent with the dynamic structure of creative love figured forth in the theological antitype of intersubjectivity, the dogma of the Trinity: Father, Son, Spirit: Memory, Understanding, Will: Faith, Hope, Chastity (213–16): Temperance, Chastity, Virginity (767–87).[20]

These internalized virtue clusters promise a dynamic, resilient, and joy-bearing career for the Lady, but at the moment when the temptation is interrupted, they have become potential rather than fully active strengths. If Comus is "much like his Father, but [like] his Mother more" (57), the Lady is perhaps at this point much like her mother, but like her father more.[21] The Lady's immobility in the marble venomed seat, mutely objectified, can be taken in this respect as a parodic mirror of the authority of her own father, Lord Brackley, seated offstage in the chair of state, the symbolic place of the king, for whose own initiation into office the Lady's ordeal has been staged. She has inculcated, and reflects back to the *Maske*'s spectators, the Symbolic order whose hierarchical ordering is patriarchal. But in her repudiation of the enveloping and dissolving version of the primal Mother, figured forth in Circe and in the other goddesses Comus serves (128–35), the Lady has arrived at a stage of identification that's essentially static and defensive, without the sequential flow, the sensory and erotic vibrance, grace, and color that the register of the Imaginary, with its association to the Mother, imparts.[22]

3

Since the Lady has gained the rhetorical advantage and momentum in her rebuff of Comus, one wonders what turn their argument might have taken were it not interrupted. In regard to the *Maske*'s plot, the Lady's immobility suggests that her liminal session in the formation of selfhood is incompletely settled, perhaps disrupted, when her brothers rush on stage with swords drawn. Her "rootbound" condition is an index of unfulfilled possibilities, at least of her own self-deliverance, and possibly of the conversion of Comus: "The roles of the Lady and Comus could be acted so as to suggest that it is she who would seduce him, but to a virtuous life."[23] If such a potential is thwarted by the direction the *Maske*'s plot takes, we might say that the Attendant Spirit's rescue operation is a well-intentioned but ill-timed blunder.

The Attendant Spirit's brief reprimand of the brothers (814–19) specifies the boys' failure to secure Comus's wand, the magic prop they need to release the Lady from captivity. An inheritance not only from Circe but from Busyrane, Comus's precursor in the bondage scenario, the wand is standard-issue equipment for a romance plot like that of Milton's *Maske*. Conventionally enough, it is a sign of phallic power and mystique. Milton's decision to eliminate the wand as a convenient magical instrument for the release of the Lady indicates that her crisis at this stage cannot be resolved by masculine virtue's force or ingenuity. Had Milton scripted the plot to allow the brothers to seize the fetish from Comus, he might have been covertly signaling his hope for the transformation of the masculine sexual ethos, in the Caroline aristocracy, from Neoplatonic idealism and its dark twin, the outlaw libidinism of cavalier erotics, to the frank mutual proprieties of Puritan incarnational materialism. The boys' inability to seize the wand might be taken as an index, in this sense, of Milton's moral realism, his suggestion of the immaturity as yet of such reforming hopes. Perhaps more significantly, had the "rod revers't" (816) been captured and used by the Attendant Spirit and the brothers to dispel the Lady's paralysis, she would still have been, in effect, subject to a male disposition of her crisis and her being, albeit of a more benevolent and sheltering sort than that of the rake Comus. Patriarchal representatives and phallic symbolism would have enacted and controlled the Lady's release from her ritual dormancy into womanhood.

The Attendant Spirit and the brothers are capable of driving out the demonic figure of Comus because they are courteous figures of male chastity particularly well suited to banish predatory and aggressive elements of masculine desire. But they cannot free the lady at this stage of her ritually orchestrated developmental crisis, or communicate to her the body-knowledge requisite for mature engagement with life as a newly grown woman in the social and natural worlds.[24] As an element in the Lady's ordeal of passage, the rescue operation proves to be a male interruption of the mysteries of female initiation, which have their own symbolic and narrative logic. Males can take part in such rites when they have a ritual assignment and role like Comus, the *Maske*'s mock bridegroom. Otherwise, their presence is a disturbance. The patriarchal pattern of a fairy tale may require a hero to rescue the damsel in distress, the Prince to waken Sleeping Beauty or Snow White with a kiss. But the deep structure of Milton's initiatory paradigm, as well as the narrative prefiguration of this episode in Spenser's tale of Amoret, suggest that the sudden male intervention in the Lady's crisis in certain respects complicates it and defers its resolution.

Spenser dramatizes the logic of gender in Amoret's parallel crisis by excluding Scudamore, Amoret's champion, from the rescue of his beloved. Scudamore's helplessness in the rescue of Amoret has to do with his inability to comprehend the risks and the pains of love from the point of view of the woman to whom he is devoted. For he has been fashioned of the same ideological stuff as Amoret, although it is gendered differently. What Amoret perceives as threat, he perceives as appropriate mastery; what Amoret exercises as restraint and defense, he perceives as coy invitation. "Both Scudamore and Amoret are prisoners of a description of love that has become prescriptive—compelled to act roles enshrined in the code of 'courtly love'."[25]

Scudamore's wavering, passionate, impatient behavior indicates that the ambivalent feelings of courtly love are mutual, even among loving couples. He cannot burst through the wall of flame which holds his beloved captive in the House of Busyrane because he himself is part of the problem of her captivity. The wall of flame is a phantasmal projection of the ferocity of Scudamore's desire which keeps Amoret in bondage to her fears of heterosexual love.[26] Spenser renders the irony of Scudamore's frustration after Britomart's lightning-swift passage through the flame:

> Whom whenas *Scudamour* saw past the fire,
> Safe and vntoucht, he likewise gan assay,
> With greedy will, and enuious desire,

7: GIRL, INTERRUPTED AND THE CHANGING WOMAN 239

> And bad the stubborne flames to yield him sway:
> But cruell *Mulciber* would not obay
> His threatfull pride, but did the more augment
> His mighty rage, and with imperious sway
> Him forst (maulgre) his fierceness to relent,
> And backe retire, all scorcht and pitifully brent.
>
> (*FQ* 3.11.26)

The series of adjective-noun phrases describing Scudamore's volcanic emotions—"greedy will," "enuious desire," "threatfull pride," "mighty rage"—are answered and mirrored in the "stubborn flame" and "imperious sway" of the cruel flames. The blurring of the pronominal references "he"/"him"/"his" between the human actor and his elemental adversary reveal that Scudamore is struggling with himself, with his own tempestuous, impatient, and aggressive ardor, captive to his own emotions in love, much as Amoret, in Busyrane's house of pain, is to hers.

By contrast, Britomart's flawless passage into the House of Busyrane, and her subsequent release of Amoret, are enabled by her sympathetic identification with the tormented heroine: "As a woman [Britomart] understands Amoret's attitude toward the physical side of love, and as the exemplar of chastity she is able to make the moral distinction between marriage and adulterous love. Her entry through the wall of flame gives her an intimate knowledge of the House of Busyrane, and her understanding finally allows her to release Amoret from her fears."[27] Dante passes through a purgatorial wall of flame in order to enter the Earthly Paradise, where he at last encounters his beloved Beatrice. In *Purgatorio* 25–27, the flame is double. As barrier, it signifies the fire of lust, the last obstacle to the unimpeded life of sensual and imaginative delight which was the promise of the human body in creation. As *limen,* it is a purifying fire that opens the doors of perception by burning away at last all fallen estimations and excesses of earthbound desiring. So Britomart's passage is similarly double: a purgatorial ordeal, it both tests and purifies her for the waking nightmare of Busyrane's palace. Britomart can enter and endure and overcome because her chaste desire has become so perfected as to dispel the female fear of the male mystique cultivated by the poetics of courtly love.[28]

4

As Amoret's captivity requires female intervention, so does the Lady's. Rites of passage in traditional societies require the initiate to complete her course under the supervision of former initiates. In Milton's *Maske,* the Attendant Spirit recognizes the crisis into which his rescue operation has precipitated the Lady, and calls upon Sabrina, the Goddess of the River (842), as a godmother to rescue her. I use the term "godmother" as a title appropriate to the particular bond formed between the initiate and the mistress of ceremonies who leads her into the next stage of her life.[29] Like her male counterpart, the Attendant Spirit, Sabrina is a textually and mythically overdetermined figure. She serves not only as the tribal sponsor to the Lady, but also as the living personification within the ritual of the goddess whose beneficent presence and whose energy is needed for the girl's passage to womanhood to be efficacious.

This goddess type is not restricted to Milton's pastoral fiction or to its analogues and prototypes in European romantic fiction; knowledge of equivalent figures outside the mythic discourses of Europe can deepen our understanding of Sabrina and sharpen our appreciation of her role in the completion of the Lady's ordeal. In particular, in the figure of Changing Woman, the Cibecue Apache honor a ritual figure closely equivalent to the mythological power invested by the *Maske* in Sabrina:

> As interpreted by Apaches, the primary objective of the puberty ceremonial is to transform the pubescent girl into the mythological figure *istenadleze* ("Changing Woman"). At the request of the presiding medicine man, and "traveling on his chants," the power of Changing Woman enters the girl's body and resides there for four days. During this time, the girl acquires all the desirable qualities of Changing Woman herself, and is thereby prepared for a useful and rewarding life as an adult. . . . Changing Woman is never crippled by old age. As a medicine man explained it: "Changing Woman never gets too old. When she gets to be a certain age, she goes walking towards the east. After a while she sees herself in the distance walking toward her. They both walk until they come together and after that there is only one, the young one. Then she is like a young girl all over again." The power of Changing Woman gives the pubescent girl longevity and the physical capabilities of someone perpetually young. This is the fundamental theme of *nai es* [the puberty ceremony].[30]

With her "maid'n gentleness" and her protective concern for crop and herd and for maidens in "hard-besetting need," (843–57), Sabrina might as well be titled "Changing Woman." Summoned by the Attendant Spirit, who serves in a role like that of the medicine man described here, her relation to the Lady as initiate corresponds to the role played by Changing Woman in Cibecue ceremony. Sabrina embodies the maternal influence and potential whose negative aspects have been ritually articulated, concentrated, and chastened in the refutation and exorcism of the bad mama's boy Comus. The summoning and arrival of Sabrina in the *Maske* bring about the return of the repressed feminine and the healing recovery of the Imaginary within the freshly consolidated Symbolic order.[31]

What suits Sabrina for this ritual task? If the Lady is rehearsing the crisis of Amoret, a Spenserian heroine, it is appropriate for Milton to stage her delivery by summoning another Spenserian heroine. Rising from the depth of Spenser's romance, Sabrina is the latest in the series of "guiltless damsels" (829) whose violation and poetic translation provide the tragic narrative subtext of the Lady's ordeal. She appears not only in immediate response to the Attendant Spirit's invocation, but as a belated epiphany of the heavenly Echo, the providential hope bringer to whom the Lady has appealed in the early stage of her ordeal (230–43). In Milton's version of the story, Sabrina is an archetype of virginity threatened by the jealous violence of a demonic stepmother:

> Whilom she was the daughter of *Locrine*
> That had the Scepter from his father *Brute,*
> She, guiltless damsel, flying the mad pursuit
> Of her enraged stepdam *Guendolen,*
> Commended her fair innocence to the flood
> That stay'd her flight with his cross-flowing course.
> The Water Nymphs that in the bottom play'd,
> Held up their pearled wrists and took her in,
> Bearing her straight to aged *Nereus'* Hall,
> Who piteous of her woes, rear'd her lank head,
> And gave her to his daughters to imbathe
> In nectar'd lavers strew'd with Asphodel,
> And through the porch and inlet of each sense
> Dropt in Ambrosial Oils till she reviv'd
> And underwent a quick immortal change,
> Made Goddess of the River; still she retains
> Her maiden gentleness, and oft at Eve
> Visits the herds along the twilight meadows,
> Helping all urchin blasts, and ill luck signs
> That the shrewd meddling Elf delights to make,
> Which she with precious vial'd liquors heals.
> For which the Shepherds at their festivals

> Carol her goodness loud in rustic lays,
> And throw sweet garland wreaths into her stream
> Of pansies, pinks, and gaudy Daffodils.
>
> (827–51)

Not only Ovid's and Spenser's heroines are echoed and summoned in what James Andrew Clark beautifully calls the "capacious being" of Sabrina.[32] Stella Revard notices the mythological counterpointing accomplished by the Attendant Spirit's allusion to the nymphs Cyrene, Leucothea (875), and Parthenope (879). These nymphs represent optimistic alternatives to the tragic melodramas of Ovidian heroines like Echo, Philomela, and Daphne. Threatened like them with ravishment or death, the chaste steadfastness of these water nymphs issues in happier fates: anticipating Milton's Sabrina, they assume immortal positions as protective and fructifying deities of place and as patrons of city and dynasty.[33] Summing together all these figures, Sabrina fuses Shakespearean heroines as well, joining the pretty pathos of Ophelia's watery submersion in elegiac pastoral (*Hamlet* 4.7.166–83) with the living vitality of the recovered Perdita (*The Winter's Tale* 4.4). One could wish Ophelia, a luckless maiden like Sabrina who commended her fair innocence to the flood, so sweet an outcome to her misery: to be garlanded with posies and honored, like Perdita, as a local incarnation of Proserpina, the Changing Woman of Greco-Roman mythology, herself a ravished maiden made floral goddess of earth's fertility and all its joyous promises.[34]

Crucial to Sabrina's power to "listen and save" (866, 889) is the sacrificial component of her story. Milton revises the story he has received by way of Spenser in order to highlight both Sabrina's innocence and her determination of her own death. In Geoffrey of Monmouth's foundational account of the legend, the powerful Queen Gwendolen, outraged by Locrine's adulterous liaison with Estrildis, raises an army to defeat Locrine. Triumphant, she commands that Estrildis and her child Sabrina be cast into the river. As the Severn, the river bears the daughter's name to "perpetuate the memory of her husband's infamy."[35] In this version of the story, Gwendolen intends for Sabrina to serve as the eternal bearer and reminder of the father's guilt. When Spenser recounts the story in his chronicle of British kings, he notices in passing the pathos of "the sad virgin innocent of all," while keeping his narrative stress on the negative moral example of her father's abuse of power in "disloyall love" (*FQ* 2.10.19) and the crisis in authority and succession precipitated by his adultery. Sabrina serves a minor role in Spenser's dynastic tale. In Milton's *Maske,* as she rises from the river which bears her name, Sabrina also rises from her obscurity in the Spenserian text. By reviving her, Milton accesses and activates a mythological source of power and saving grace that his sage and serious master left half-sunken in the opulent plenitude of his endless work.

By transmitting a version of the story in which Sabrina chooses her own death rather than submitting to a punishment she does not deserve, Milton makes of her a redemptive figure, somewhat like Euripides' Iphigeneia, sacrificially releasing the nation from the cycle of guilt incurred by its ruler and founding father.[36] The "cross-flowing course" of "the flood" (831–32), which stays Sabrina's flight and initiates her apotheosis, the ritual preparation of her body and its anointment with spices, delicately evoke the passion and death of Jesus.[37] The secular ritual of the *Maske* thus veils its representation of sacred sacrifice:

> The conclusion of the *Maske* places the Lady in a rather strictly ordered sacrificial structure. Sabrina, for example, shares the essentially tractable nature of the traditional victim. . . . Through Sabrina the Spirit has linked sacred and profane worlds. Sabrina is not destroyed in the present tense of the drama, because, like Christ, she had been destroyed and reborn in its past tense. Thus the Spirit, like the priest at Mass, re-enacts her death and resurrection in his report of the old legend, while the drama of the *Maske* as a whole plays out roughly this same action through the experience of the Lady.[38]

What guilt is atoned, what redemptive service performed, by the specific sacrificial framework introduced with Sabrina in the *Maske?* To what end, that is, is she offered up, in the context of this Masque of Chastity? Reasoning from effect to cause, we can say that the Lady's release from the spell of Comus, with all that it symbolizes, depends upon Sabrina's prior sacrifice in the face of an analogous threat. What is the ritual logic which links the fate of these two figures, which enables Sabrina to be Changing Woman for the Lady?

Richard Halpern's consideration of this problem is ingenious. Investigating "the ghost of maenadism that haunts the masque" and its potential affiliation with the potentially militant virginity of the Lady, he explains that Sabrina is a scapegoat who provides the saving antidote to man-threatening maenadism: "The evil that she bears off is nothing other than female aggressiveness—that of her almost maenad stepdame—which, in imitation of Christian martyrdom, she wonderfully learns to turn against her own person."[39] Sabrina thus exemplifies a solution to the problem of female sexuality entertained by the *Maske:* that a woman "can become chaste only after she has sacrificed the power over her own sexuality."[40] The Lady whom Sabrina releases from her literal bondage is restored to the figurative bondage of the bourgeois home, currently her father's, eventually her husband's. She need speak no more, Halpern implies, because she is spoken for: the chastity with which Sabrina completes her endowment is "the bourgeois form of social control [which] avoids the extremes of savage virginity and promiscuity."[41]

Halpern provides a telling recognition of the problem of what Sabrina's self-sacrifice stands for. But he misreads it and the *Maske* on at least two counts. His own sense of the fixity of gender categories prevents him from seeing Milton's identification with and investment in the Lady. Thus Halpern can not imagine her as a potential victim of the bacchic horde surrounding Comus, but only as a potential participant. He claims that the "barbarous dissonance" (550, *PL* 7.32) of Comus's host "offers a menace to the male poet and not to the female protagonist. . . . If aggressive virginity characterizes maenadism, then the Lady is already somehow Bacchic."[42] Second, his ideological construction of the *Maske* is at odds with its own explicit and implicit claims: he reads the *Maske* as if it were a conduct book for women, construing the Lady's chastity as a mode of social control and sexual inhibition of women, rather than, as the movement of the *Maske* indicates, a mode of erotic and political enfranchisement and liberation.

Halpern's recognition of Sabrina's status as surrogate victim is a pivotal insight. He acknowledges the key problem created by the association of female sexuality with both victimization and guilt. But he wrongly estimates the resolution of the sacrificial crisis because of his own ideological position. Milton stresses Sabrina's death as a typological and efficacious instance of heroic martyrdom (*PL* 9.32). In commending her fair innocence to the flood (831), Sabrina baptizes her innocence in resistance to violence, rather than capitulating to it as a consequence of imputed fear or guilt. As a scapegoat figure of female victimage, she sums up and translates into a Christological type various tales of victimization spun out by Ovid and alluded to by Milton. At the crucial moment of pathos—the tragic scene of suffering—she willingly embraces her death as a way of preserving her innocence and paradoxically releases other maidens of comparable valor, like the Lady, from analogous fates. She thus translates the female position in the tragic narrative from passive victimization to active heroism. In so doing, she creates a different ending, or at least a different meaning to the ending, of this narrative. Like the translated Echo of the Lady's earlier song (242–43), Sabrina's metamorphosis becomes a figure for providentially directed supernatural change, for transcendental aspiration, in contrast to the dizzying cycle of Comus's dance and what it implies of the enervating flux of Ovidian metamorphosis, the world-bound pathos of energy circling endlessly through a succession of material forms.

Psychologically speaking, this self-offering is not a sacrifice of female sexuality. Rather, it frees female sexuality from the relation to shame and guilt fixed in exegetical and homiletic traditions. Noting that "Puritanism sought to liberate men and women from the oppression of sexual guilt," Juliet Dusinberre diagnoses the complex linking medieval exaltations of virginity in the church and in the cult of courtly love with the conviction "that women are by nature inordinately lustful": "In practical terms a way of keeping the natural concupiscence of women under control is to make the highest virtue of its antithesis: the state of virginity. This protects women from themselves, and it protects men from them. It is an almost Platonic vision of perfection made piquant by the actual daily evidence of imperfection."[43] Sabrina's self-sacrifice symbolically enacts the Reformation's vision of liberation of women from sexual guilt. In contrast to the medieval cult of virginity, Sabrina's self-sacrifice in the interests of virginity has liberatory rather than repressive or quietist consequences. It releases the Lady's exercise of virginity from rigid self-monitoring as an anticipatory exercise in deferring guilt. It opens the way beyond guilt into the active life of chaste desire.

Sabrina's action typologizes Christ's in its expression of perfect innocence and its once-only efficacy:

> But this man, because he continueth ever, hath an unchangeable priesthood. Wherefore he is able also to save them to the uttermost that come unto God by him, seeing he ever liveth to make intercession for them. . . . Who needeth not daily, as those high priests, to offer up sacrifice, first for his own sins, and then for the people's: for this he did once, when he offered up himself. . . . So Christ was once offered to bear the sins of many; and unto them that look for him shall he appear the second time without sin unto salvation. (Hebrews 7:24–28; 9:28)

The Epistle to the Hebrews stresses that the sacrifice of Christ liberates those who look to him from the repetition-compulsion of recurrent insufficient sacrifices for sin. Likewise, Sabrina is a Changing Woman whose self-sacrifice frees the young woman identifying with her from the threat of sexual vulnerability and from the burden of guilt imposed by a long history of cultural suspicion of female sexuality.[44] Proper remembrance and rehearsal of the atoning sacrifice, as it is performed for and by the Lady in the *Maske*'s rite of passage, releases her from self-perpetuating cycles of guilt and fear, and frees her up to live joyfully and youthfully.

Sabrina thus provides an examplary figure of inviolable virginity translated, through trial and sacrifice, into immaculate, protective, magic-bearing maternity. With Sabrina, Milton follows Spenser in anglicizing Ovid, giving local habitation and name to the narrative of feminine transformation. A positive counterpart to Circe and the other goddesses who dominate Comus's imagination of the feminine, Sabrina has been translated through the succession of writers redeeming the legend of her death from guilt-engendering violence.[45] Translated herself, Sabrina is the necessary agent of the Lady's translation, rising out of the depth of her own possibility.[46] As Hélène Cixous writes in a different context of the hidden self-mothering possibility which Milton associates with Sabrina:

> There is hidden and always ready in woman the source; the locus for the other. The mother, too, is a metaphor. It is necessary and sufficient that the best of herself be given to woman by another woman for her to be able to love herself and return in love the body that was "born" to her. Touch me, caress me, you the living no-name, give me my self as myself. . . . Text: my body—shot through with streams of song; I don't mean the overbearing, clutchy "mother" but, rather, what touches you, the equivoice that affects you, fills your breast with an urge to come to language and launches your force; the rhythm that laughs you; the intimate recipient who makes all metaphors possible and desirable; body (body? bodies?), no more describable than god, the soul, or the Other; that part of you that leaves a space between yourself and urges you to inscribe in language your woman's style.[47]

Sabrina, as Cixous evokes it, gives the Lady to herself with her loving touch, returns her to her body and launches her force, leaves a space "between" herself to inscribe her woman's style. Sabrina supplies for the Lady a female imago whose place is dynamically implicated within the Symbolic order, rather than repressed or defused within it. Sabrina's emergence from the water accomplishes for the Lady the purification, anointment, and lubrication of a selfhood whose identity within the Symbolic would otherwise remain primarily defensive and rigid, alienated from her own ardent possibilities. The "equivoice" and "intimate recipient who makes all metaphors possible and desirable," Sabrina completes, seals, and sanctifies the Lady's passage through liminality.

5

If we follow carefully the Lady's initiation as the ritual staging of her erotic maturation, the rising of Sabrina will dispel any lingering suspicions about Milton's conceptualization of chastity as barren, self-sequestering, or a "bourgeois form of social control." Following tradition, Milton installs her as the local deity of the Severn. Because the Severn is a border river of considerable scale and beauty, Sabrina figures forth the creative flow of liminality itself: "she can unlock / The clasping charm and thaw the numbing spell, / If she be right invoked in warbled song" (853–55). In *Areopagitica,* Milton develops the image of Truth as "compared in scripture to a streaming fountain; if her waters flow not in a perpetual progression, they sicken into a muddy pool of conformity and tradition" (*Areopagitica,* 739). Natural observation provides the source for this metaphoric intuition and its allegoric elaborations. A stream is cleansing and musical; wherever you find yourself along a stream, you will find it a perfect expression of flow into natural pattern and into natural music. It is both orderly and processive. It is a living border, bounding territories and communities, joining them and nourishing them, providing means for transport and commerce. Integrating a decontaminated form of the natural fecundity and motion championed by Comus with the trust in nature's inherent orderly self-governance espoused by the Lady, "Sabrina is able to pass on the 'poetic fluency' of *natura naturans* to the staid rationality of *natura naturata.* Here for Milton, as in the 'blissful bowre' of Adam and Eve before they fell, generation coincides with obedience."[48]

Yet Sabrina's origins and fidelities are particularly human. Translated into "Goddess of the River" (842), a *genius loci* as Echo has become (230–43) and Lycidas will be ("Lycidas," 183), Sabrina intimates the possible humanization of nature, as nature itself takes on, in her liminal being, what Blake called "the human form divine."[49] Because she condenses and "translates" Ovid's tragic tales into English poetry and roots them in English soil, Sabrina's legend reminds us that every tale of human beings transformed into natural beings, especially sanctified or tragic ones, deepens the bond between the human and the natural world. As Pythagoras preaches in his lengthy metacriticism of the world of Ovidian changes (*Metamorphoses* 15,

515–32), nothing of the earth is not potentially an erstwhile human. Sabrina personifies this natural piety and natural empathy. She thus serves, in Sears Jayne's interpretation of the *Maske*'s allegory, as an agent of "natural providence": through natural rhythms of regeneration and plenitude, she discloses the grace of God toward humanity.[50] Herself the flowing boundary between the human and the natural, between the natural and the supernatural, a redemptive counterpart to the monstrously prolific Mother Nature of Comus's libertine fantasies (710–36), Sabrina offers an epiphany in human form of the divine in the healing abundance of the natural.

It is not surprising, then, that the Attendant Spirit's prayer of benison for Sabrina exalts her, by translating the wilderness riverscape of the Severn into the stylized pastorals of scripture, redolent with fragrances of biblical sublimity:

> May thy billows roll ashore
> The beryl and the golden ore,
> May thy lofty head be crown'd
> With many a tower and terrace round,
> And here and there thy banks upon
> With Groves of myrrh and cinnamon.
>
> (932–37)

James Andrew Clark observes here the bright and effortless interfusions of the iconography of the Cybele, Magna Mater of pagan myth, with the "thresholds of fragrant experience like that in Solomon's song."[51] Clark alludes to the erotic fullness of the Song of Songs, in which the body of the beloved, fragrant like a garden of cinnamon and myrrh and other spices and fruits, is "a well of living waters, and streams from Lebanon" (Song of Solomon 4:11–15). The biblical scene associated with Sabrina is not only pastoral but hymeneal, evoking, in the allegorical tradition, the mystic marriage of the soul with its true beloved, God. In this marriage, the body will be presented pure and acceptable for the unimaginable delights of spirit.

The fruitfulness of this consummation in turn prefigures the final vision of the Bible, with its promise of apocalyptic fulfillment figured as a visionary wedding between God and his chosen:

> And I saw a new heaven and a new earth: for the first heaven and the first earth were passed away; and there was no more sea. And I John saw the holy city, new Jerusalem, coming down from God out of heaven, prepared as a bride adorned for her husband. . . . And the building of the wall of it was of jasper: and the city was pure gold, like unto

clear glass. And the foundations of the wall of the city were garnished with all manner of precious stones. The First foundation was jasper; the second, sapphire; the third, a chalcedony; the fourth, an emerald; The fifth, sardonyx; the sixth, sardius; the seventh, chrysolite; the eighth, beryl, the ninth, a topaz; the tenth, a chrysoprasus, the eleventh, a jacinth; the twelfth, an amethyst. And the twelve gates were twelve pearls; every several gate was of one pearl; and the street of the city was pure gold, as it were transparent glass. . . . And he shewed me a pure river of water of life, clear as crystal, proceeding out of the throne of God and of the Lamb. In the midst of the street of it, and on either side of the river, was there the tree of life, which bare twelve manner of fruits, and yielded her fruit every month, and the leaves of the tree were for the healing of the nations. (Revelation 21:1–2, 18–21, 22:1–2)

In keeping with both the sprightly flow of the British river and with the rising motion of the *Maske* preparing for its final stages of delight, the Attendant Spirit's song is light and suggestive, not bearing the full heft and dazzling finality of the jewel-encrusted vision of John. But several key features of John's radiant vision are brushstrokes in the Spirit's apocalyptic impressionism: the beryl and the gold, the visionary city, and the "pure river of water of life," which is Sabrina herself, a type of the new Jerusalem, carrying the providential care of God and the foretaste of his glory in the living waters of a Shropshire stream.[52]

With the invocation of Sabrina, then, a new kind of poetry makes its presence felt in the *Maske,* a poetry of "secure delight" and "unreproved pleasures free" ("L'Allegro," 91, 40), of sensory and generative fullness that absorbs and transforms the figural and metrical dynamism displayed by Comus.[53] This poetry celebrates the regenerate senses as portals of discovery of the sublime and the world embraced by the senses as irradiated by a world yet to come. Sabrina's replacement of Comus as supernatural overseer of the Lady's initiation brings about a moral cleansing, claiming, and enlivenment of the chaotic Imaginary world of Comus by the Symbolic coordination, expansion, and sanctification of his imagery of Nature and desire. Through Sabrina's intervention, the Lady's exercise of self-discipline can open into the possibilities of the higher order of pleasure which chastity offers: the virtuous discover full pleasure in life through their wholehearted choice of the good. Chastity reveals itself as a discipline that is both spiritual and physical, issuing in a pleasure that intensifies rather than retards the spiritual life: "The world of the senses is included and not annulled by consecration to the world of the spirit and that discipline forms the basis for the liberation of creative energy rather than the means for its confinement."[54]

Sabrina releases the Lady from her rigorous self-containment through a ritual bath, a symbolic anointing that baptizes her into mature womanhood, a fulfillment and activation of chastity's potential in charity.[55] With her drops "of precious cure," Sabrina touches the Lady's breast, her fingertips, her lips; then she frees her from the "marble venom'd seat / Smear'd with gums of glutinous heat" (916–17), releasing, awakening, and sanctifying her physically and emotionally.[56] Breast, fingers, lips, pelvis: Sabrina releases the bound energy of the Lady's erogenous zones for the active life of chaste desire. Since desire is reborn with the teleological impetus of charity here, the Lady's rediscovered bodily freedom is a spiritual awakening as well, a dawning awareness "through the porch and inlet of each sense" (839) that the body, properly respected and tempered, may turn "by degrees to the soul's essence / Till all be made immortal" (462–63). Sabrina herself embodies the imaginative promise of a body wholly spiritual in form. The Lady incarnates this promise at the moment when the exchange between the two is completed. We recall the description of Changing Woman's identification with the Cibecue girl initiate in *nai es*: "they both walk until they come together and after that there is only one, the young one."[57] This moment of merger and emergence occurs in the *Maske* when Sabrina has completed her ritual anointing: "Sabrina descends, and the Lady rises out of her seat" (s.d. after 921). The simultaneous actions effect a symbolic incarnation. As the Cibecue Apache girl becomes Changing Woman, so the once interrupted Lady now incarnates Sabrina, endowed by the rite with the virtue, magic, strength, generosity, and fertile potentiality carried by the goddess who was once herself a threatened girl.

8
Homecoming Queen

1

SABRINA'S RITUAL BATH AND RELEASE OF THE LADY COMPLETE HER liminal ordeal and set her chastity in motion as charity. The reciprocal motions of Sabrina descending and the Lady rising symbolically merge the two characters and invest the girl with the virtue and the power of the goddess. Milton's Lady is ready to come home. But what is home to her now, and what difference will her initiation make to it? Victor Turner calls the final stage of the traditional rite of passage "reaggregation": "The passage is consummated and the ritual subject . . . reenters the social structure."[1] Turner observes that the return of the initiate and her assumption of adult status and position in society cause change in the society as well as the individual. Still symbolically linked to the supernatural personae she has encountered in the liminal realm and charged with the energies they personify, the initiate refreshes and reenergizes the social order with her otherworldly *numen*. *Communitas* is Turner's term for the transformative surge of community-binding energy that issues from a rite, regenerating social structures and the persons whose lives they organize.[2] So it is that in Milton's *Maske,* the Lady, having endured and matured through Comus's ritual testing, is ready to be restored to family and community, as a woman newly grown and a numinous figure whose presence sanctifies and revitalizes her family and community in its celebratory gathering.

The Cibecue Apache signal the young woman initiate's magic stature in the stage of reaggregation by means of a series of social gestures that indicate their reverence for her as the apotheosis of Changing Woman:

> The Medicine man blesses the pubescent girl by sprinkling a small amount of cattail pollen over her head and shoulders and on the crook of her cane. He then picks up a small basket filled with candy, corn

kernels, and (usually) some coins of low denomination. Standing on the buckskin, directly in front of the girl, he pours these contents over her head. "After he pours it over her head, everything in the baskets gets holy. The girl's power makes all those things holy and good to have." Following the "pouring of the basket," male relatives of the pubescent girl carry the cartons containing candy and fruit through the crowd, encouraging everyone to reach in and take as much as he can. . . . The pubescent girl and her sponsor dance in place, while all adults who so desire line up before the buckskin and repeat for themselves the blessing that inaugurated [the previous] phase. The significance of [this] phase is enormous, for anyone who blesses the girl may at the same time request the power of Changing Woman to grant him a personal wish. . . . For four days after *nai es,* Changing Woman's power continues to reside in the pubescent girl and, acting through her, may be used to cure sickness or bring rain. A Medicine man commented: "At that time she is just like a medicine man, only with that power she is holy. She can make you well if you are sick even with no songs."[3]

The Lady's special social status in the conclusion of Milton's *Maske* is analogous to that of the Cibecue girl initiate. With the healing and mobilizing touch of Sabrina, with what we might call the Changing Woman power released and resident in her, the Lady need not speak, but simply perform the ritual dance and let the healing, fructifying social magic radiate out from her. Her implicit bestowal of blessing to the gathered community completes the *Maske*'s translation of her chastity into its true social form, which is charity: released from her initiatory ordeal, she moves from her static stance of resistance to Comus to a mobile, dynamic dance, from self-protection to self-offering.

The Attendant Spirit announces the impact of the Lady's resocialization as he leads the Lady and her brothers from the "cursed place" (939) of her nocturnal ordeal to

> your Father's residence,
> Where this night are met in state
> Many a friend to gratulate
> His wish't presence, and beside
> All the Swains that there abide,
> With Jigs and rural dance resort.
> We shall catch them at their sport,
> *And our sudden coming there*
> *Will double all their mirth and cheer.*
>
> (947–55; emphasis mine)

The Lady's homecoming coincides with and consummates the harvest festival, doubling its delights. As a Persephone restored from her underworld ordeal, her own social and psychological maturity make her both the presiding spirit and the richest emblem of worldly fruition. The exuberant dance of the swains shows the social order renewing itself through the naturalizing process of ritual. A terrestrial celebration of harvest bounty—"teeming Flocks and granges full" (175)—and of the social harmony and justice anticipated in the rule of the Lady's father, it recollects and rehearses the seasonal rites of fertility to which Enid Welsford traced the origins of the court masque.[4] "Prais[ing] the bounteous *Pan*, / And thank[ing] the gods," yet this time not amiss (176–77), the swains' dance reforms and rejuvenates the dissolute nightcrawling of Comus's crew in the antimasque.

It prepares the ground, in turn, for a higher order of symbolic dance, which the Attendant Spirit also introduces:

> *Back Shepherds, back, enough your play,*
> *Till next Sun-shine holiday:*
> *Here be without duck or nod*
> *Other trippings to be trod*
> *Of lighter toes, and such Court guise*
> *As* Mercury *did first devise*
> *With the mincing* Dryades
> *On the Lawns and on the Leas.*
>
> (958–65)

This announcement seems to resituate the *Maske,* by means of its concluding revels, in the mythological conventions and framework of the Jonsonian masque, with its aristocratic masquers personifying gods and goddesses. Yet the simile structure of the announcement—"*As* Mercury *did first devise* / *With the mincing* Dryades"—reiterates the difference between Milton's and Jonson's ideologies of masquing. The Lady and her brothers, and all those who revel with them, perform *themselves.* They do not pretend to be mythological figures, as Jonson's figures typically do. In the revels that climax Milton's *Maske,* every gracious gesture, conventionally implying a mythologically resonant and ethically coherent universe, is nevertheless a socially recognizable human gesture, whose disposition is toward social renewal and reformation rather than the Neoplatonic escapism of the typical court masque.[5]

In presenting her with her brothers to her parents, the Attendant Spirit interprets the significance of both the preceding initiatory ordeal and of the ensuing dances that will climax the *Maske*'s festivities:

> *Noble Lord, and lady bright,*
> *I have brought ye new delight,*
> *Here behold so goodly grown*
> *Three fair branches of your own.*
> *Heav'n hath timely tri'd their youth,*
> *Their faith, their patience, and their truth,*
> *And sent them here through hard assays*
> *With a crown of deathless Praise,*
>   *To triumph in victorious dance*
> *O'er sensual Folly and Intemperance.*
>
>   (966–75)

Although the *Maske* decorously reattunes itself to the political occasion of Lord Brackley's investiture as Lord President and nominally returns the Lady with her brothers to the security and the authority of their father, it makes its concluding investiture of poetic magic in the Lady. For the moment she is blessed, everything she looks upon is blessed. She is the still point of the turning world of the dance, which the Attendant Spirit explains is itself a tropological and analogical enactment of the soul's triumph over the temptations of the flesh.[6]

The Lady's silence as she emerges from her ordeal and returns to her Father's house may seem to problematize such claims for a triumphal and empowering homecoming. After line 799, she speaks no more. This silence is ambiguous and evocative. Linked to her temporary paralysis in Comus's "marble venom'd seat" (916), it outlasts her release from bondage. Given her decisive proclamation of a higher order of poetry to Comus (779–99), the Lady's silence in response to the events that follow her rhetorical and philosophical triumph seems particularly at odds with conventions of dramatic motivation and response. The historicizing practices of much contemporary criticism tend to interpret the Lady's silence as evidence of Milton's restitution of patriarchal political control over his newly reformed female subject. In such readings, the Lady's silence registers an aesthetic restraining order over the unsettling prophetic fervor with which Milton has endowed the Lady: "After redefining and broadening her boundaries, Milton, in the end, nevertheless suggests that the Lady's individual identity—particularly her sexual identity—is subsumed in the patriarchal family."[7] Her silence is thus an ominous prelude to the Lady's reintegration into the world of her father, which has little room for female prophets, and where a girl is expected to be chaste, silent, and obedient.[8] These political interpretations of the Lady's silence are congruent with psychological explanations of it as a symptom of arrested development. In such accounts, the psychic trauma of the dialogue with Comus has been only incompletely worked through, and the cost of the Lady's restored bodily mobility is a silencing of the self, or at least of self-expression. This approach extends the Lady's temporary immobility into her continuing silence, as a marked residual symptom of the contradictions built into her pursuit and profession of virtue. The Lady's voice, provoked by Comus, is also invested in him, psychically contingent for its strength upon the contrary that he embodies, and so it vanishes with him into the psychic undergrowth of repressed desire.[9]

These assessments have some political and psychological cogency, but I think they misconstrue the occasion, the politics, and the aesthetics of the *Maske*. The Lady does not limp home as a victim in need of intensive therapy or as a willing captive to bourgeois sexual politics led on a silken cord. She returns home *"With a crown of deathless Praise, / To triumph in victorious dance / O'er sensual Folly and Intemperance"* (973–75), fully mobile and radiant, the center of the *Maske*'s regenerative festivities and bestower of its blessings. Historicizing accounts may explain this note of triumph as the way in which the *Maske* mystifies the Lady's subjection to the patriarchal powers that be, but they do so by neglecting or dismissing the notes of autonomy and joy in this annunciation and the way it stages the Lady's triumph as a progressive political triumph, exemplary to a nation. It would be uncharacteristic of Milton to inscribe an ending that implies a muting, compromise, or recantation of his, or his characters', prophetic commitments. In keeping with the prophetic and reforming intentions of Milton's other work, the *Maske* obliges us to consider that the Lady's silent return to her father's house carries with it the prospect not of her passive submission to patriarchal duty, but of the very transformation of the patriarchal household and community, by its festive welcome and inclusion of the female virtue and agency she has won for herself and others "through hard assays" (972).

The silence of the Lady's symbolic status is indeed in keeping with the generic normalization of the *Maske* in its final stages, Milton's belated concession to the masque conventions, which require silence of its aristocratic masquers, a structural shift from antimasque to masque accomplished magically and symbolically rather than dramatically, and ritual revelation of its allegorical conceit in the concluding dances and songs.[10] Not surprisingly for Milton, however, even this apparent return to convention goes against the grain of the great masque prototypes. The lyrics and staging of Ben Jonson's collaborations with Inigo Jones characteristically absorb social reality and identities in the mythic world and the allegorical idea that give the Jonsonian masque its visionary coherence. The concluding movement of the Jonsonian masque dissolves the dramatic wall between masquers and spectators in order to absorb spectators in the vision they have beheld. Masquers and audience alike are released from the actual space and time of the performance occasion and absorbed in the world projected by the performance for the duration of the revels.

Milton's Attendant Spirit, by contrast, leads the Lady and her brothers back to the living world of family and friends. The dances of the masquers and revellers, as we just noted, are stylized but not mythologized. First swains and shepherds perform their country dances (s.d. after 957), then they are succeeded by the more light-footed nobles (961–65). This wholesome sequence of dances strikes a note of social realism atypical of aristocratic masques, albeit one that seems to reinforce the harmonic status quo of class relations idealized by Jonson in his influential encomium "To Penshurst."[11] Less benevolently than such lyrics, masques typically relegate characters associated with the lower classes, their labor, their appetites, and their folly, to the carnivalesque mischief of the antimasque and banish them from the moment of revelatory vision. Milton instead integrates and coordinates the dance of the classes. With the dance of the swains, he represents commoners and peasants in the *Maske*'s climactic festivities, even as the Attendant Spirit whisks them offstage in acknowledgment of the aristocratic imperatives of Milton's commission. Yet the text does not even then allow its noble revellers to escape into mythological fantasy, although it compliments their dances as terrestrial traces of their mythic prototypes, Mercury and the Dryades.[12] This return to Ludlow and its castle effectively dispels, rather than sustains, the myth-world of the Lady's liminal ordeal, even as it socializes the energies and domesticates the wisdom gained there. The *Maske*'s concluding dramatic fictions, although they continue to gesture to a mythologized Beyond, reinforce the vital this-worldliness of the entertainment and of the virtue and the joy to be renewed and celebrated through it.

As deep and wide in its suggestiveness as anything in Milton's work, the Lady's silence is the first of the great dramatic silences in the major poetry. It anticipates and parallels Jesus' silent private return to his mother's house in *Paradise Regained* (*PR* 4.639). It prefigures also "the Seal of silence" (*SA,* 49) or "fort of silence" (*SA,*

236) which symbolized the strength of Samson's innocent conscience in its original covenant to God, as well as the tacit attunement of Samson's regenerate conscience to the rousing motions of the Spirit as he approaches the climax of his tragedy (*SA,* 1381 ff.). It suggests a mysterious, enlivened, and prophetic apprehension like that of Eve's deep redemptive dream, suggestively evoked yet reserved in her final speech to Adam at the end of *Paradise Lost* (*PL* 12.610–15).[13] In Eve's case, as in the mystery of the Lady's silence, Milton's respect for female subjectivity resists intrusive exposition or interpretation. As Eve's reticence about her dream evidences a regenerate humility contemplating the prospect of its own crucial role in salvation history, the Lady's concluding silence speaks her profession of virginity and vocation of chastity as loudly as her words have done. Her silence is deeply eloquent, a sign of power in reserve, of imagination so full of itself that it need not overflow in speech, a sign of poise and readiness, so already in touch with its future that the need to speak of it, or the possibility of speaking of it, is laid to rest.[14]

A sign of dramatic and philosophic tact on Milton's part, the Lady's silence indicates that the more removed mysteries transmitted in the rite of passage are not a matter of public spectacle or interpretation. It could be taken as an iconic representation of ecstatic trance, the attunement of the Lady's "rapt spirits" to "The sublime notion and high mystery / That must be utter'd to unfold the sage / And serious doctrine of Virginity" (785–87).[15] If such is the case, Sabrina's task may have been not to wake a Sleeping Beauty from the safety of erotic dormancy or the chill of hysterical resistance to desire, but more importantly to call her "rapt spirits" back to the flesh, to the terrestrial coordinates of her pilgrimage, as in Donne's "The Ecstasie":

> So must pure Lovers soules descend
> T'affections, and to faculties
> That sense may reach and apprehend,
> Else a great Prince in prison lies.
>
> (65–68)[16]

In this respect, the Lady's silence at her homecoming is a dramatic sign of her achieved chastity's potential, a resting of the "rapt spirit" in a certitude about the self's place and possibilities in the world, whose core is in reserve, unavailable to speech, and whose public quietude is a mark of the soul's integrity. Angus Fletcher explains quite beautifully, "The Lady says not a word—not because the Spirit will not let her, but because it is not logical for her to speak. To speak would be to return to the wasteland of loss."[17] The wasteland of loss is, inevitably enough, the world to which she must return, and in which she must speak, after the *Maske*'s last festal strains fade, and the pageant decorations of Ludlow's Great Hall are struck, and she wakes to her new life in her father's house. But the *Maske* bears the promise, incarnate now in the Lady, that the world to which she returns need not be a wasteland of loss. Like the Cibecue Apache initiate, her transformation promises the renewal and regeneration of the social world to which she returns. "*A Mask* beautifully affirms the capacity of the body in motion to signify":[18] the Lady's final actions intimate this regeneration by means of a sublime miming, a gestural allegory that implies the more removed mysteries of the soul's bliss, which the Attendant Spirit will proceed to describe and explicate in his Epilogue. The *Maske* speaks *for* her, which is different from saying that it silences her. The vision of delight that consummates the *Maske* in dance and song and speech is the dramatic efflorescence of her terrestrial bliss. It testifies to her attainment of a moral and imaginative condition in which the very action of virtue is pleasure giving. Yet what she has to offer family and community are neither private pleasures nor private attainments, but social blessings. In rejoining her community in the revels, the Lady bestows what she has attained of Youth and Joy (1012), Knowledge and Virtue (*An Apology*, 694) upon her gathered family and friends, magnifying their experience of delight and reinvigorating their commitment to the good through the initiatory festivities of worldly *communitas*.[19]

2

Like other initiation rites, the Ludlow *Maske* symbolically designates the maturing body as both a social and a cosmic signifier. "The body," Victor Turner says, "is regarded as a sort of symbolic template for the communication of gnosis, mystical knowledge about the nature of things and how they came to be."[20] The logic of this cultural imprinting of fundamental knowledge depends upon the culturally recurring analogy between body and world. Milton adapted this analogy from the copious and ingenious Renaissance elaborations of the correspondence between microcosm and macrocosm:

[The human body is] the most immediate cosmos with links to the remotest worlds. It is at once a naturally unified, organic whole harmoniously inscribed in the circle of the heavens, and also a dizzying collection of elements, astral bodies, numbers, and natural forces which stand in multiple relations with those entities in the macrocosm. The body is God's metaphor for the world, and the Renaissance poet has no choice but to read it as such and to understand and develop its metaphorical properties.[21]

Because of the built-in reciprocity and reversal in this correspondence, the *Maske*'s ritual organization of the Lady's desire causes change not only in herself but in the world to which she is restored. Of the figure of Christ in *Paradise Lost,* Stanley Fish observes, "He gives form to the universe and to everything in it, including the things in this poem, including the poem itself. In an ultimate sense, *He* is the poem's true form."[22] The same could be said of the Lady's position at the conclusion of the *Maske*. The conventional court masque, we recall, takes its form from the person of the king: "He embodies the mystery of the masque. His is the permanent form of the masque, its life beyond words, a living image, represented. . . . The invention of the masque is translated into the flesh of the king."[23] But the "true form" of Milton's *Maske* is the Lady. Grown from girl to woman, the chaste Lady emblematizes the graciously ordered plenitude of a renewed creation. She is an incarnate idea of order who gives resounding grace (243) to a transformed image of the cosmos.[24]

This translation of the Lady, from girl to woman, and from ethical exemplar to cosmic emblem, can be construed in the gorgeous pastoral eschatology of the paradisal garden that the Attendant Spirit evokes at the end of the *Maske*'s festivities. Concluding the revels, the Epilogue interprets the Lady's social and eschatological significance. I refer to the passage as eschatological because it gestures to the world beyond the Lady's terrestrial and familial homecoming, and it images forth the fulfillment of desire in a new earth and new heaven, in the spatial fullness and eternal presence of a Golden Age setting which is, in the moment of prophetic description, already here.[25] In evoking the feminized otherworldliness of the earthly paradise, the Attendant Spirit intimates that the Lady's body is a this-worldly figure for a redeemed and redemptive sexuality and for the vitally reconfigured cosmos in which it flourishes. If we follow Victor Turner in understanding the initiate's body as "as a sort of symbolic template for the communication of gnosis, mystical knowledge about the nature of things and how they came to be," then Milton's Attendant Spirit, a Mercury figure who is both the psychopomp, the guide of souls, and the interpreter of hermetic enigmas, provides an explication of that gnosis, now incarnate in the Lady, in his great final speech.[26] In this last visionary flourish, Milton, recapitulating and fusing the imaginative sources and stimuli of our longing for terrestrial joy, is already beginning to imagine the earthly paradise of Eden. The impressionistic expectation that climaxes the *Maske* will flower into the full dramatic setting for *Paradise Lost*.[27]

Angus Fletcher remarks of the *Maske* that "its verbal echoing is a radical process, a going to the bottom of language. By recollecting so many poets dead and gone, Milton revives their voices and their ghostly persons."[28] He is also, as we have seen elsewhere, going to the bottom of myth, reviving the ghostly persons and landscapes of the ancient narratives in order to endow this landscape with their sensuous and imaginative richness, and yet implying that his own garden, most lately imagined, is the consummation and the antitype of them all: "*Hesperian* Fables true, / If true, here only, and of delicious taste" (*PL* 4.250–51). Starnes and Talbert note that the Attendant Spirit uniquely identifies the Hesperian gardens with Elysium and the Islands of the Blest, for which "there seems to be no precedent in the ancient poets," but which has its basis in the mythological compendia of Charles Stephanus and Natalis Comes with which Milton was familiar.[29] The perpetual spring, redolent with the fragrances of flowers in abundance, the sweet west wind, the mythologized presences of goddesses of liberality and love, all echo classical visions of a *locus amoenus,* a place of rest, fertility, and joy, the fulfillment of earthly desire. Milton also draws upon Socrates' account in the *Phaedo* of the "True Earth," the fertile, abundant dwelling place of immortal souls, in deep and constant communion with the gods, the elements, and the cosmic order: "[The True Earth] is in the upper air and is a celestial version of the older earthly paradises of the poets—The Isles of the Blest, the Elysian Fields, the Gardens of the Hesperides."[30] These rich sources had in turn been adumbrated in the great Renaissance gardens imagined by Ariosto, Tasso, Marino, and especially Spenser, from whose Garden of Adonis, as many critics have noticed, Milton draws his crucial figure of young Adonis.

Biblical fragrances, "*Nard* and *Cassia's* balmy smells" (991), waft through the garden's "cedarn alleys" (990) as well: the nard perfuming the Bride of the Song of Solomon (1.12, 4.14); the cassia of Exodus (30:24), mixed with other spices for the anointment of the priests of Israel, and making fragrant the garments of the king (Psalm 45:8).[31] The passages from the Song of Solomon and Psalm 45 which evoke these fragrances are lyrics of hymeneal consummation, so

Milton is blending his biblical with his classical sources in a vision of erotic redemption. The Song of Songs metaphorically identifies the earthly paradise with the body of the beloved Bride: "A garden inclosed is my sister, my spouse; a spring shut up, a fountain sealed. Thy plants are an orchard of pomegranates, with pleasant fruits; camphire, with spikenard. Spikenard and saffron: calamus and cinnamon, with all trees of frankincense; myrrh and aloes, with all the chief spices: a fountain of gardens, a well of living waters, and streams from Lebanon" (Song of Solomon 4:11–15).

The topos of the body of the beloved as *hortus conclusus,* a closed garden, a well of living waters, and a fountain of delight, originates in this powerful scene: the image of the fruitful and flower-laden paradise of perpetual spring is "created by the presence of the beloved, of whom it is both the creation and the portrayal."[32]

Who is the Beloved, in the Attendant Spirit's poem? By implication, it is the Lady. In what sense is she the Beloved? The sanctifying erotic evocation of the Song of Solomon emerges first, we have noticed, in the Attendant Spirit's blessing upon Sabrina (922–37). Now, with Sabrina's power and promise incarnate in the Lady, the blessing is hers as well, and the Attendant Spirit's sublime topography is an allegorized projection of her bodily destiny. A still unravished bride of quietness, she is both everywhere and nowhere in the Garden envisioned by the Attendant Spirit.[33] Milton's remarkable adaptation of the body-as-garden topos is to employ it in the celebration of a Lady whose ritual drama has positioned her to be not just the obscure object of desire but the subject and mediator of desire. Her agency and mediation dramatize themselves in the voiceless bodily immediacy of her dance, which, as we have seen, is blessing bestowing. Her significance as the Beloved who motivates virtuous desire resists capture by the objectifying power of textual word or image. Her chastity has decisively resisted its absorption into Comus's patter of libertine naturalism, evading the discursive field where she would be the captive object of a male desire that reifies even as it idealizes female beauty. Because Milton has constructed her as subject *of,* rather than subject *to,* the erotic discourse of the *Maske,* her presence in the scene of erotic innocence and fulfillment that the Attendant Spirit unfolds is all the more powerful because it is subliminal rather than explicit.

Perhaps this is why her relation to the pictorial and mythological fields of the passage is allusive and veiled, implied in the text yet manifest in the dance. Anagogically considered, her erotic destiny is disclosed in the story of Psyche's "wand'ring labors" (1006) on behalf of her love for Cupid,[34] but elements of her story and character are affiliated with the various mythologized females who are the *genii loci* and tutelary spirits of the garden: daughters of Hesperus, Graces, "rosy-bosom'd Hours" (986), Iris (992), even Venus, "th'Assyrian Queen" (1002). Psyche's fulfillment is traditionally allegorized, like the hymeneal duet of the Song of Songs, as a poetic revelation of the mystic marriage of the soul with its true beloved, God. In this marriage, the body will be presented pure and acceptable for the unimaginable delights of spirit. The tropological this-worldly correlate of this spiritual consummation is spelled out by John Rogers: "[The Lady's] own eventual marriage, subtly prefigured in a vision of Cupid and Psyche (ll. 1003–11), articulates a figurative version of what was becoming in seventeenth-century England the normative affirmation of temperate conjugal sexual behavior, the doctrine of 'married chastity.'"[35] Historically sensitive as Rogers's account is, it makes the Lady's social and marital prospects sound much more like duty than fun. But the "allegorical continuum" of the *Maske* does not set up oppositions between earth and heaven, present and future, work and love, duty and delight, concrete and abstract, but unifies them, intensifying the truths of each interpretative frame by framing it with the others.[36] "[We] see the real not behind the apparent but in the apparent," as Rosemond Tuve elegantly puts it.[37] The body is not bruised to pleasure soul, heavenly delight is not a deferred recompense for the drudgery of worldly responsibility, pleasure and virtue are reconciled.[38] If Psyche's marriage to Cupid, the consummating image and event in the Attendant Spirit's speech, is a figure both for the soul's celestial bliss in communion with Christ and for its terrestrial fulfillment in companionate marriage, the delights of marriage are a foretaste of heaven's joys, intensified by anticipation and sanctification; and heaven's joys are enfleshed and humanized by all that human marriage, the crown of creation, "sole propriety / In Paradise of all things common else" (*PL* 4.751–52), promises and realizes.

3

The contrast of these gardens of earthly delight with their parodic type in the tangled night world of Comus and his goddess mother figures is evident. Rosemond Tuve notes that the figure of the Renaissance Circe provides the deep spiritual coherence of the *Maske:* "Upon the great hinge of the Circe-Comus myth Milton's whole invention moves; out of its known connoted meanings the pervasive imagery of light and darkness springs quite naturally."[39] All that Circe had come to represent of sensual abandonment and spiritual disfiguration to Renaissance literati is the challenging contrary from which the Lady's virtue defends, defines, and sharply clarifies itself. In his evocation of an earthly paradise that comprises the several great projections of terrestrial and otherworldly fulfillment of the classical and biblical traditions, the Attendant Spirit paints a counterfigure and counterforce to the Circe-Comus myth, with a comprehensiveness, unity, and imaginary richness unknowable in the Circean bowers of bliss prowled by Comus and his crew of party animals.

Both Circean parody and pastoral prophecy discover their true paradigm in this Neoplatonic vision. The trinity of tutelary virtues to which the Lady testifies and by which she makes her way in the uncertain world of baffled senses—Faith, Hope, and Chastity (213–15)—reappear in the sublime triplicities of Hesperus's "daughters three / That sing about the golden tree" (982–83) and the Graces that "Thither all their bounties bring" (986–87). In Milton's canon, the golden tree prefigures generally the trees with "fruit burnisht with Golden Rind" in Milton's Edenic landscape (*PL* 4.249–51), and particularly "the Tree of Life, / High eminent, blooming Ambrosial Fruit / Of vegetable Gold" (*PL* 4.218–20). If this Hesperian "golden tree" of the *Maske* and the Tree of Life in *Paradise Lost* are typologically implicated in each other, the Attendant Spirit's elimination of the watchful dragon guarding the golden fruits of the Hesperian tree is a sign of paradise regained and of innocence restored, a classical analogue to the release of the cherubim from their sentry duty at the gates in the East of Eden (Genesis 3:24; *PL* 11.118–25, 12.641–44). The "rosy-Bosom'd Hours" (986) pouring forth their gifts along with the Graces intimate the harmonious, beneficent sequence of life maturing to the full ripeness and fruitfulness embodied in the Lady. This is a feminized Paradise, a classicized anticipation of the sanctified visions of delight to be evoked by Milton in *Paradise Lost,* not only in his massive canvas of the unfallen Eden, but in that briefly sketched heavenly scene in which he imagines his Muse conversing with "Eternal Wisdom": "Wisdom thy Sister, and with her [Thou] didst play / In presence of th'Almighty Father, pleas'd / With thy Celestial Song" (*PL* 7.8–11). This feminized paradise is one from which has been exorcised not only the threat of masculine predation represented by Comus, but also the threat of what Blake would call the "shadowy Female will"—that will to power through seduction, enchantment, and dissolution symbolized in the *Maske* by Circe and the Sirens (253) and deified in Hecate, Cotytto, and the lascivious Venus of Comus's rites (124–36).

Milton's indebtedness to Spenser for the central figure of Venus and Adonis is evident and widely acknowledged. Spenser's Garden of Adonis is an earthly paradise of perpetual fertility and generation, yet subject to mutability, "the first seminarie / Of all things that are born to live and die / According to their kinds" (*FQ* 3.6.28–30). It is a place of endlessly creative erotic energy, in which Venus's love for Adonis mythically represents the union of eternal matter, or substance, with changeable form:

> But she her selfe, when ever that she will,
> Possesseth him, and of his sweetnesse takes her fill.
>
> And sooth it seemes they say; for he may not
> For ever die, and ever buried bee
> In baleful night, where all things are forgot;
> All be he subject to mortalitie,
> Yet is eterne in mutabilitie,
> And by succession made perpetuall,
> Transformed oft, and chaunged diverslie:
> For him the Father of all formes they call,
> Therefore needs mote he live, that living gives to all.
> (*FQ* 3.6.46.8–9, 47)

C. S. Lewis describes Venus's loving possession of Adonis as a "continual conquest of death."[40] There are paradoxes and reversals in Spenser's myth, suggestions that his creative synthesis, the new vision created in the poem, is not reducible to the sum of its philosophic or allegorical parts. Adonis in this expository passage is identified as "Father of all formes," and Venus, in her maternal relation to him, manifests herself as eternal divine substance: as *mater* (Latin) of all natural being, hers is the gift of *matter*. Yet Spenser complicates allegoresis by dissolving each partner of the metaphysical dyad into its complement: he also associates the immortal Venus with the heavenly *forms* of Neoplatonism, the beauty of which shape and irradiate the recalcitrant, mutable *matter* of the subcelestial world, personified by Adonis.[41]

The correlations between Venus and Adonis, female and male, eternal and mutable, form and matter, are thus themselves rendered suggestively interchangeable and reversible. This interchange occurs in the very moment and act of sexual generation, to which Spenser's narrator himself testifies, when he declares that although he cannot locate the mythic site of this place of bliss, "well I wote by tryall, that this same / All other pleasant places doth excell . . ." (*FQ* 3.6.29.6–7). He indicates here the experiential source of his myth in the generative joys of sexual love and, possibly, in the generative joys of imaginative creation as well. For a poet's inspired experience of visitation by a muse is very like the account of Venus's joyful possession of Adonis. Like Adonis, the inspired or possessed poet becomes "Father of all formes" in his imagined universe, and as he calls to the mind's eye each form, he is himself co-present in and through it, "by succession made perpetuall, / Transformed oft, and chaunged diverslie" (3.6.47.6–8). Spenser's Garden of Adonis thus represents the vital core of human experience and provides the paradigm of fertility and creativity against which can be measured all the fallen and perverse forms that his poem exposes of exploitative and destructive desire and of its expression in the seductions of art and song.

Milton counts on his readers to supply some of these Spenserian and Neoplatonic associations as he abbreviates and renarrativizes the moment of Venus's brooding over Adonis. But Milton alludes to and absorbs the Spenserian moment while undertaking something quite different. Milton's composition is more painterly than Spenser's and less allegorically explicit. Milton withholds philosophic exposition in order to intensify the pictorial and mythological unity of his paradise. The series of images unfolds as a unified visual field of discrete yet coordinated units, elaborated sequentially in a horizontal movement like the structure of a Renaissance painting or tapestry in which all the elements, simultaneously present, nevertheless invite progressive reading of a cryptic yet inevitable narrative. This emerging narrative implies an allegorical intention and a transcendent unity that exceeds the sum of its visual parts. The pictorial details, structure, and thematic effect of the Attendant Spirit's Epilogue proves to be even closer to that of Botticelli's great painting the *Primavera* than to that of Spenser's Garden of Adonis, or indeed, of any of the literary gardens upon which Milton draws. The Epilogue is, in effect, Milton's *Primavera,* a stylized and allegorically comprehensive sketch of the earthly paradise which intimates the heavenly as well.

Critics have already drawn suggestive parallels between the *Primavera* and the Garden depicted by Milton in the central books of *Paradise Lost.* The following passage has seemed particularly suggestive:

>   The birds their choir apply; airs, vernal airs,
>   Breathing the smell of field and grove, attune

> The trembling leaves, while universal *Pan*
> Knit with the *Graces* and the *Hours* in dance
> Led on the eternal Spring.
>
> (*PL* 4.264–68)

Of this passage, Jeffry Spencer remarks,

> One is struck by the resemblance between the lines above and Botticelli's *Primavera,* which presents a similar tableau of frozen movement in a timeless spring landscape. Like Botticelli, Milton used such a moment of stasis to heighten and universalize his mythic material, until the dance itself represents something ritual and holy, an iconographic embodiment of an eternal present, like the figures on Keats' urn.[42]

Everything Spencer astutely notices here is equally true of Eden's prototype in the *Maske*'s Epilogue, in which Milton orchestrates the same effect of "frozen movement," paradoxically implying both process and permanence. Movement in the Epilogue is initiated but freeze-framed through the crescendo of present active indicative verbs—sing, revels, bring, dwells, fling, waters, blow, shew, drenches, reposes, sits, holds, make—which act like verbs of duration, creating the sense of ever-fresh yet ever-lasting action. This verb pattern creates the sculptural poise of weighty stationing which Keats so much admired and adapted to the purposes of his mature poetry.[43]

Milton also condenses into the Epilogue several features that correspond to Botticelli's painting. The west winds extravagantly flinging hymeneal fragrances about (989) manifest the spring's fructifying power, personified by Botticelli as the western wind-god Zephyr. Milton's Iris corresponds to Botticelli's Flora as the transformed and transforming spirit of awakening vegetation, swathed in a multicolored "purfl'd scarf" (994) textured and rippling like Flora's diaphonous flower-embroidered gown. The "golden tree" (983) of the Epilogue is loaded with the same rich fruits that glow in the arborial upper border of the *Primavera.* The presence in both poem and painting of the three Graces, as they have been treated by interpreters of Botticelli's painting, seems particularly appropriate to the career and destiny of Milton's Lady. Bringing all their bounties to the Garden (986), Milton's Graces serve like Botticelli's as "primitive goddesses of the earth's fruitfulness and liberality,"[44] the very fruitfulness and liberality which the Lady incarnates in the socializing choreography of the *Maske*'s revels. The central and presiding figure, Venus, roots and focalizes the composition and the meaning of both gardens. Although she is horizontally stationed "on the ground" (1001) with her attendant mythological figures, both Milton and Botticelli position her vertically beneath her "fair son" Cupid (1002–6). Finally, if we consider the Attendant Spirit's role in guiding and clarifying our vision of the Beyond, he plays the same role of psychopomp and mystagogue in Milton's Epilogue as Botticelli's mysterious and bemused cloud-stirrer Mercury, who stops the horizontal movement of the eye at the left edge of the *Primavera,* directing it upward and outside the temporal frame, and intimating the cyclical movement of temporal return which begins again with Zephyr's inbursting on the right of the frame.[45]

Edgar Wind's detailed analysis of the Neoplatonic organization of *Primavera* offers a more specific set of suggestions about the Lady's transformed condition and newly presented agency. Wind identifies Botticelli's Graces as *Castitas* (Chastity), *Pulchritudo* (Beauty), and *Voluptas* (Pleasure). *Castitas* is the central figure of their dance, uniting the opposed positions of *Pulchritudo* and *Voluptas*. She bends toward *Voluptas* and meets her gaze, symmetrically mirroring her posture as her hair loosens and begins to cascade down her shoulder, while her stance anchors her in the same ground with *Pulchritudo,* and the curves of their bodies reiterate one another. *Voluptas* and *Pulchritudo* interlace their fingers to form a knot signifying "the Beauty of Passion," which hovers over the head of *Castitas*, while the blindfolded, energetic Cupid overhead is about to release a flaming arrow that appears ready to pierce the nape of her neck. Wind interprets this powerful composition as an initiatory moment: "That this gesture [of interlaced fingers] is made to hover like a crown above the head of Castitas defines the theme of the dance as her initiation. Castitas is the neophyte, initiated into Love by the ministrations of Voluptas and Pulchritudo. . . . as [Castitas] acts the part of the "enraptured" Grace who unites the opposites in her person, the whole dance becomes imbued with her own spirit of chastity which she imparts to her two companions."[46] This is almost precisely the role and character of Milton's initiate Lady in the *Maske*'s revels. Her chastity, resocialized now as a mature grace open to the inspiration of love, imbues the whole dance and its dancers with her spirit.

Yet Venus's posture in the Miltonic garden, as well as her relation to her "fam'd son" (1004), marks Milton's radical departure from his literary prototype in *The Faerie Queene* and his pictorial parallel in the *Primavera*. The Attendant Spirit marks the heightened significance of the depiction of the loving couples Adonis and Venus, Cupid and Psyche, by highlighting it, interrupting his scene painting with a direct address to his readers and auditors: "List, mortals, if your ears be true" (997). We recall that in her profession of virginity (779–99), the Lady withheld expression of the gnosis she attained, because of the insufficiency and distorting apprehension of Comus's ear: "Thou hast nor Ear nor Soul to apprehend / The sublime notion and high mystery / .... Thou art not fit to hear thy self convinc't" (784–85, 792). Now, in the Epilogue, the action of the *Maske* has prepared the listening apprehension of readers and auditors for a previously withheld disclosure. The Attendant Spirit issues this disclosure from the silence of the previously unheard, or inapprehensible. It participates in the already realized knowledge of the initiate Lady. As expression of the deep truth she now embodies, it speaks to the "true" ears of an at last worthy audience.[47]

The Attendant Spirit unveils a mystic diptych of two loving couples, in which the relation between female and male, mortal and divine, is doubly represented:

> Beds of *Hyacinth* and Roses
> Where young *Adonis* oft reposes,
> Waxing well of his deep wound
> In slumber soft, and on the ground
> Sadly sits th'*Assyrian* Queen;
> But far above in spangled sheen
> Celestial *Cupid* her fam'd son advanc't,
> Holds his dear *Psyche* sweet entranc't
> After her wand'ring labors long . . .
>
> (998–1006)

Adonis's fate is quietly prefigured in the beds of Hyacinth, floral emblem of another wounded youth of Ovid's *Metamorphoses*. His healing is already implicit in the image of the Roses on which he also lies, conventional emblems of the energy and splendor of female sexuality. Yet here, since Adonis reposes, "waxing well," upon them, the Roses are like that in Milton's Eden, without thorn (*PL* 4.256). This would be, like Adam and Eve's Bower (*PL* 4.689–705), a fit place for the sexuality of a restored innocence, implied in the floral oxymoron of hyacinths and roses, for Milton suggests that love entails being wounded and being refreshed and made whole.

Yet the moment in the career of Venus and Adonis's love represented here is neither one of rapturous and regenerative possession by the energetic goddess, as in Spenser's paradise—"But she her selfe, when ever that she will, / Possesseth him, and of his sweetnesse takes her fill" (*FQ* 3.6.46.8–9)—nor of tranquil and fructifying beneficence, the quiet bestowal of the revelatory blessing of love, as by the Venus of Botticelli's *Primavera*.[48] Milton's Venus is a figure of loving charity, grieving here over her wounded and reposing beloved, in a composition which resembles a Christian image of the *pietà* of Mary mourning the death of her son.[49] The Christian roles are reversed in this passage, for Milton offers a glimpse of a divine mother mourning over a mortal lover-son. Yet such a literal reversal does not subvert the allegorical parallel, especially in a masque which exercises several gender switches among its series of translations. This Venus is not the wanton sex goddess who sanctions and drives the libertine naturalism of Comus's world of self-consuming desire (124), but "th'*Assyrian* Queen" (1002), oriental Aphrodite in her aspect of Celestial Love, grieving and brooding "on the ground" (1001) over the cost of a mortal love that remains contingent on time and subject to it, yet finally is not overcome by death because of divine love's condescension.[50] In his Proverbs of Hell, Blake declares that "Eternity is in love with the productions of Time."[51] The *pietà* of Venus brooding over the wounded Adonis is Milton's figure for this love, divine charity patiently attendant upon the created order of nature, manifest in its human form, in its vulnerability, its suffering, and its longing for redemption.

If the wounded Adonis in this *pietà* is a pagan type of Christ, the deep wound he suffers stands for the redemptive wound that gathers and transfigures all human suffering into glory. As Milton would have interpreted the Deutero-Isaiac prophecy of the Suffering Servant, "He was wounded for our transgressions, he was bruised for our iniquities; / upon him was the chastisement that made us whole, and with his stripes we are healed" (Isaiah 53:5). If human wholeness and healing issue from this wound, and paradise is regained through it, we can see how the wound of Adonis not only provides the organizing figure for the paradisal gardens of the Epilogue, but also supplies the typological deep structure that organizes and redeems all the instances of tragic suffering remembered by the poem and ritually confronted by the Lady, from Philomela and Echo and the other Ovidian victims, to her redemptive sacrificial prototype in the ritual drama itself, Sabrina.

If the figure of Venus brooding over Adonis authorizes such a typological identification, we can see how inextricable the two panels in this poetic diptych are, for they are dynamically implicated in one another, as Jesus in his suffering and death is necessary to and inseparable from the risen and ascended Christ, who is represented in the *Maske* Epilogue by "Celestial Cupid" (1004). The two loving couples, Venus and Adonis, Cupid and Psyche, are recoupled as contrapuntal images of and references to one another.⁵² Milton's Cupid is of a different order from the Cupids who appear in Spenser's epic romance and Botticelli's *Primavera,* neither of whom appear in their anagogical and celestial aspect. Wind describes Botticelli's figure, on the wing above Venus and ready to fire, as "a passionate, blindfolded Cupid, whose impetuous action supports by contrast the deliberate gesture of [Venus's] hand."⁵³ Spenser frequently represents Cupid in this form, especially in the third book of the *Faerie Queene,* as the vagrant, ubiquitous, arbitrary, irresistible, and cruel force of an impersonal and universal desire. He seems entirely this-worldly, and his heavenly mother has little if any restraining or tempering influence upon him. Highlighted by his sharp contrast to the ethic of romantic marital chastity celebrated by Spenser in the wayfaring hero Britomart, this cruel Cupid represents the torment of love unsatisfied, secretive, manipulative, and adulterous, cultivated by the ideology and poetics of courtly love.⁵⁴

But setting, context, and cumulative associations determine the value and significance of mythological figures in *The Faerie Queene.* When Cupid resorts to his great mother's garden, he lays "his sad darts / Aside, [and] with faire Adonis playes his wanton parts" (3.6.49.8–9). In this setting, without his arrows, "the wingéd boy" is benign and his play is fruitful rather than destructive, verily domesticated by his love for Psyche into a paradigm of faithful marital love (*FQ* 3.6.50). Cupid becomes a figure of "good love" rather than wanton abandonment by putting aside his familiar emblems, his "sad darts" and blindfold. In this aspect Spenser anticipates the resplendent image of Milton's "Celestial Cupid" in the very embrace of his now immortal beloved, although Spenser sets the fulfillment of their love in the paradisal garden of this world, rather than, as Milton, in the ethereal heights beyond. The two poets evoke, yet differently translate, the tradition of Christian allegoresis that read Apuleius's fable of Psyche's quest for and marriage to Cupid as a pagan type of the soul's celestial bliss in marital communion with Christ, disclosed in the Revelation to John (19:6–7). Spenser represents Cupid as the personification of fleshly desire in its various destructive and creative forms and reserves the domain of celestial love for Cupid's mother Venus; he thus represses the anagogical suggestions of Cupid as a figure for divine love. Milton in contrast represses the carnal ambiguities of Spenser's terrestrial Cupid—investing his tempter Comus with them—in order to make his theological allegory clear.

Noting the synonymity between the *Maske*'s "Celestial Cupid" and the epiphany of Amor in "Epitaphium Damonis," from whose arrows "hallowed minds catch fire, and even forms divine" ("Epitaphium Damonis," 197; my translation), John Carey refers to Boccaccio's account of the Psyche fable as a close precedent to Milton's implied meaning:

> Psyche, [Boccaccio] explains, represents the soul, and joined to her is that which preserves the rational element (pure Love). She passes through trials and 'at length she regains the enjoyment of divine bliss and contemplation and is joined to her lover for ever . . . from this love is born Pleasure, which is eternal bliss and joy.' Milton's allegory is near to Boccaccio's: Psyche has attained that release which Venus and Adonis still await.[55]

Carey's suggestive annotation is limited by the dichotomy between natural and celestial love assumed in his final sentence. The "Celestial Cupid," we know from Apuleius's original writing of the fable, has been wounded by his love for Psyche, in effect wounded, like Christ, for Psyche, the human soul. This vulnerability to mortal sorrow and struggle on the part of divine love stands in transcendent counterpoint to the heavenly Venus's love for Adonis, whose wound solicits the answering wound of grief on her part. Although the Attendant Spirit represents these two love affairs at different moments in their careers, and Venus and Adonis "still await" the release into eternal bliss and joy which Psyche enjoys with Cupid, this is not a contrast between earthbound "natural" love, even at its upper limit, and "spiritual" or heavenly love.[56] It is a representation of two different moments in a single indivisible event, intimating emanation, division, and return; or incarnation, passion, and ascension. In the love of Venus and Adonis for one another, and of Cupid and Psyche for one another, pagan Eros and Christian Agape or charity, the hunger of human desire and the selflessness of divine love, become one. This reciprocity of loves, divine and human, spiritual and natural, entails sacrifice yet promises exaltation.

Whereas the Attendant Spirit freeze-frames Venus and Adonis in the moment of his convalescence and her mourning, he evokes the Cupid and Psyche of Apuleius in the rapturous moment of their conjugal embrace, released from their torments and "Emparadis'd in one another's arms" as Adam and Eve will be beheld in Milton's Eden (*PL* 4.506):

> But far above in spangled sheen
> Celestial *Cupid* her fam'd son advanc't,
> Holds his dear *Psyche* sweet entranc't

> After her wand'ring labors long,
> Till free consent the gods among
> Make her his eternal Bride,
> And from her fair unspotted side
> Two blissful twins are to be born,
> Youth and Joy; so *Jove* hath sworn.
>
> (1003–12)

Milton thus highlights the fruitfulness of Cupid and Psyche's embrace by making it simultaneously a procreative moment of erotic consummation and of apotheosis. "Translated" to the judicial and Symbolic domain of the heavenly courts, their desire is socialized and sanctioned, surprisingly, by the "free consent" (1007) of the tributary gods—a parliamentary gesture that signals perhaps a brief, cryptic, but emphatic expression of the young Milton's developing republican sympathies in the long period of Charles I's personal rule—and authorized and legitimated by the Word and the Name of the Father. The oath of Jove that concludes this sequence is both judicial and prophetic. His is the ultimate jurisdiction that validates the marital sanction decided by the assembly of his divine court. His is also the prophetic word that assures that Youth and Joy are "to be born" from the fruitful union of Cupid and Psyche. Both the Attendant Spirit who announces the oath and the young poet who has scripted it claim for the inspired human voice yet once more the full authorizing word of the Father, as we have seen the Lady claim it for herself and Milton in her profession of virginity (779–99).

Yet if Jove seems to have the last word here, it is not without a final fruitful ambiguity. The quick temporal sequencing of these climactic actions—erotic consummation, marital legitimation, birth of offspring, Jove's oath—creates the effect of Jove just barely catching up to the startling transformations of both the terrestrial and the celestial realms wrought by a love so ardently and patiently and chastely pursued. There are two ways of looking at the perfect tense of "so *Jove* hath sworn," which suggests that the final action listed in the sequence has occurred prior to the present tense verbs that lead up to it. It could be read as a sign of Jove's foreknowing and accepting everything that unfolds in the career of Cupid and Psyche's romance, much as the Father foresees and accepts Adam and Eve's fall and all that is to follow from it in the third book of *Paradise Lost.* It could also be read as the revelation of a prevenient grace that has opened the way for all that has come to pass for Cupid and Psyche, as for the Lady in her ordeal. In either case, Jove, belated as he seems to be in his authorizing Word, appears to be both the origin and the end, the formal cause and the final cause, of the work of love, even though the work is still no less the Lady's, and Psyche's, and ours, to do.

Milton follows Apuleius's conclusion fairly closely, to celebrate the socialization, stabilization, and sanctification of erotic delight and fecundity in marriage. But he multiplies the single child, Pleasure, adopted by Spenser from Apuleius (*FQ* 3.6.50.8–9) into the twins Youth and Joy. This doubling creates a third generation of intricately related pairs: Venus-Adonis; Cupid-Psyche; Youth-Joy. Imagining Cupid and Psyche's embrace and the plenitude of delight that issues from it Milton succinctly anticipates not only Eve and Adam's consummation but Raphael's account of the lightness and fullness of angelic sexuality: "if Spirits embrace, / Total they mix, Union of Pure with Pure / Desiring; nor restrain'd conveyance need / As Flesh to mix with Flesh, or Soul with Soul" (*PL* 8.626–29).[57] As has been his practice throughout the *Maske,* Milton's allegoresis is dynamic, reconceiving the mythological tradition for the purposes of social and spiritual transformation. The allegorical twins Youth and Joy are not tepid Puritan personifications of temperance and duty abstracted from desire, but forerunners of Blake's vitalist burning youth, whom he mythologizes as Orc.[58] They are "blissful twins," full of bliss and bliss giving, embodiments of all that is implied linguistically and erotically by the suggestively cognate French term *jouissance,* with its untranslatable signification of playfulness and sexual bliss, the occasion for the rupture of more conditioned and conditional pleasures and for erotic and textual consummation.[59] It is no wonder, then, that the Attendant Spirit closes out his speech with a concluding exhortation to his audience:

> Mortals that would follow me,
> Love virtue, she alone is free,
> She can teach ye how to climb
> Higher than the Sphery chime;
> Or if Virtue feeble were,
> Heav'n itself would stoop to her.
>
> (1018–23)

Once Youth and Joy have been conceived in the virtuous fullness of pure desiring, what more needs to be said of the possibility of human freedom, of the rapture that begets it, and the rapture that it yields?

4

This intimation of a redeemed erotic life, whose promise is exemplified in the silent dance of the newly grown Lady, has a transformative effect on the very picture of heaven into which Cupid and Psyche have ascended. Even more surprising than the massive antithesis between Comus's night world and the Attendant Spirit's paradisal gardens is the Epilogue's apparent contrast to the Prologue's initial vision of otherworldly existence (1–17). The Attendant Spirit, like the Lady he ushers, is going home, and his Epilogue refers us to that home, but it reiterates the setting of the Prologue in a new key and with a more sensuous and complex harmony. Upon the Prologue's suggestion of Plato's True Earth as fleshless patriarchal realm of pure ensphered essences, stably hierarchical, majestic and yet a little frosty, the Attendant Spirit now superimposes this consummate vision of a world of flow and fertility, liquid, colorful, fragrant, and musical, its presiding genii primarily female.

Milton successively revised his drafts of the *Maske* so as to establish and highlight this contrasting superimposition. In the Trinity Manuscript, Milton embedded, in rough draft, a brief description of Hesperian Gardens in the Attendant Spirit's Prologue.[60] Milton canceled this passage in the Trinity Manuscript, and reworked material from it into the Attendant Spirit's Prologue in the Bridgewater performance script. This revised Prologue, performed at Ludlow, anticipated the eventual Epilogue text but cut itself short with the description of the "Beds of Hyacinth and Roses / Where young Adonis oft reposes." The performance Prologue thus introduced the paradisal garden with some of its mythic characters and sweet, luxuriant images, but did not yet suggest the allegory of love that enters the poem with the figures of "th'Assyrian Queen," Cupid and Psyche. Milton subsequently relocated these contents to form the basis of the expanded vision of the 1637 and 1645 Epilogue which we have been considering.[61]

This shift of material from performance Prologue to published Epilogue has several effects. By locating complementary visions of the world beyond the mutable world of appearances in the opening and closing statements of the *Maske,* Milton provides a symmetrical framework and metaphysical balance and closure for his ritual drama.[62] The relocation of the paradisal garden vision from the beginning to the end of the *Maske* and its allegorical expansion also mark Milton's translation of the performance script into a written, and therefore readerly, text. The revels at Ludlow in 1634 *perform* the cosmic harmonies and removed mysteries to be evoked verbally by the Attendant Spirit in the printed text; in its turn, the full text of the Epilogue of 1637 *explicates* the harmonies performed by the masquers. The dances of the 1634 Ludlow revels follow upon and play out the Attendant Spirit's annunciation of the Egerton children's triumphant arrival home "To triumph in victorious dance / O'er sensual Folly and Intemperance" (974–75). "*The dances ended, the Spirit Epiloguizes*" (s.d. after 975): in the printed text, three words—"*the dances ended*"—encompass with a retrospective glimpse the entire period of revelry at Ludlow Castle in which the *Maske*'s 1634 performance reaches its climax in *communitas*. One can imagine revellers at Ludlow in 1634, exhausted by the evening's entertainments and ready to find their ways to bed, too exhausted to be receptive to any further metaphysical instruction and exhortation. They have already danced out its promises. The printed Epilogue fills the textual space and time created by dances that cannot in themselves be textualized.[63] This Epilogue stands in for those revels, a substitute embodiment for the *Maske*'s later readers of the deep truth discovered in the Lady's ritual drama of initiation.

The framing symmetry of printed Prologue and Epilogue also consummates the theme of translation central to the *Maske*. The Prologue materials of the Trinity and Bridgewater manuscripts show us that Milton originally conceived of the Hesperian Gardens as synonymous with the heavenly setting. The same identification of landscape is implicit in the final revision of the *Maske:* "the broad fields of the sky" (979) to which the Spirit intends to fly are identical with the "Regions mild of calm and serene Air" (4), the true Earth and Platonic dwelling place from which he descends in the beginning of the *Maske*. Louis Réau remarks of the topos of the earthly paradise in Christian art, "L'art ne distingue pas le paradis céleste du Paradis terrestre"—art does not distinguish the celestial paradise from the terrestrial paradise—and so it is with Milton's suggestive fusion here.[64] By separating and superimposing the extraterrestrial settings of the Prologue and Epilogue as symmetrical framing structures for the Lady's ritual ordeal, Milton suggests that they are alternative envisionings of the same spiritual setting, the soul's origin and home, which readers must accept and honor in equal measure through the poetic faith tutored by the *Maske*'s mythic imagination. That the Epilogue comes at the end of the drama as a conclusive statement offered to those whose "ears be true" (997) suggests that it offers a more vibrant, particularized, and comprehensive vision of the Beyond to those whose senses, imagination, intellect, and will have participated sympathetically in the initiatory ordeal of the Lady.

As in conventional court masques, cosmos, nature, society, and self converge in a single coherent and comprehensive vision. Drawing from Victor Turner, we might interpret the two parallel and symmetrical visions of Prologue and Epilogue as alternative projections of social and cosmic design in terms of *structure,* that is, the organizing structures that determine and place identity in social relation to others and to the world, and *communitas,* the generative energies released in liminal moments and spaces that motivate, sustain, and revitalize these social identities and relationships. The Prologue stresses rationality, order, law, stability: *natura naturata,* as James Andrew Clark explains. The Epilogue stresses sensation, energy, interaction, fluidity: *natura naturans.*[65] The intense erotic and imaginative energy of this reenvisioned cosmos has been released by the ritual growing of a girl, by the Lady's triumphant initiation. As the Lady's reunion with family and community through the celebratory revels completes her liminal adventure by socializing it, the Spirit's Epilogue brightens, sweetens, and widens the eschatological framing of her experience. Her reentry into the household of her father marks the assumption of the redeemed feminine Imaginary into the Symbolic order, a terrestrial anticipation and incarnation of Psyche's assumption into the celestial realm (1003–11). The *Maske*'s representative of the Symbolic, the Attendant Spirit displays how that order is transformed by its feminization, its structures renewed, refreshed, and sweetly harmonized by the festive spirit of *communitas,* of which the Lady is the radiant harbinger.

5

This translation—of Lady, society, cosmos, and the arts that represent them—has entailed the ritual recognition of and subjection to pain, to suffering, to the possibilities of tragedy. The fates of Echo, Philomela, Daphne, Proserpina, Canens, Orpheus, Oedipus, and Sabrina echo faintly, a final time, through the elegiac suggestion of the wounds of Hyacinth and Adonis, the implied wound of Celestial Cupid and the wandering labors of Psyche. In this wonderful moment, our contemplation of the fullness of paradisal love, including its pain, soars upward toward its final transfiguration and eternal fulfillment. The dragon, once menacingly present in the Trinity Manuscript's cancelled Prologue, has left the golden tree: we peer without guilt, with unguarded eyes, at the site where nature is embraced and transfigured by art, the site where what Blake would name Beulah, nature at its upper limit of erotic pleasure and perfection, becomes Eden, the blazing moment of imagination's embrace of nature in the act of love. This is not Sidney's golden world, in which art perfects nature, but a still green world in which art restores nature and heals it, the moment where, as we recollect from Philomela's story, violated body becomes inviolable voice.

Perhaps the elegiac note of this passage is in part Milton's delicate way of simultaneously sobering and inspiring his audience and his readership for our own reunion with the daily world from which the enchanted liminal space of the *Maske* has temporarily and providentially withdrawn us. "I think / it must be the wound, the wound itself, / which lets us know and love," Galway Kinnell declares in his great *The Book of Nightmares*.[66] "*Moin blessé- / . . . -*I am blessed / Wif dis wound, Ma Kilman," says Philoctéte in Derek Walcott's splendid epic *Omeros*.[67] Love is a deep and irrevocable wounding; only through our wounds can we love; and so wounds, paradoxically, become blessings. Milton discloses this hard but saving wisdom at the end of his Lady's ordeal, in the gorgeous reworking of the generative human core of Spenser's Garden of Adonis: the purchase of true love in the world is dear, but always worth the cost. The tragedies to which our capacity for love leaves us vulnerable can become, through the discipline of chastity and the cultural and imaginative translation it makes possible, the precondition for beauty, for love, for poetry, and for regeneration, for the fullness of good that is suggestively figured in those "blissful twins," Youth and Joy (1010–11).[68]

There are so many ways to try to tell the story of Milton's *Maske,* and I hope that this book has added some new ways, especially by paying attention to the ritual and imaginative experience of its central character, the Lady. The trajectory of desire in the *Maske* originates mythically with the tragic stories of Homer, Sophocles, Euripides, and Ovid, with the devastating yet promissory energies personified in Dionysus. This same trajectory originates historically with the emancipatory expectations of Puritan culture in prerevolutionary England, and biographically with the pressures of growth and change in the youths of the Egerton household, with the shadow of family scandal, and with John Egerton's commission as Lord President to establish justice in England's western frontier. I have drawn from some modern models of psychological and cultural explication in order to account for Milton's dramatization of desire's possible translation into virtue, and of virtue's translation into bliss: Nietzsche to account for its tragic impetus, Lacan and Freud, Kristeva and Cixous to account for its psychological structures and processes, and Turner and Richards and other anthropologists to account for its ritual structure and character types, and for the cultural work that it does. Yet exegetically intriguing and powerful as these several models seem to me to be, they can only take us so far into an explanation of Milton, because of their shared skepticism about the problematics and possibilities of human freedom. Freedom, essential to Milton's invention of the human in the ethical example of his Lady, is severely constrained or illusory in these modern models, which variously describe the formation of the person in terms of subjection to various sorts of determinist imperatives and impersonal forces, whether metaphysical, social, or psychological.[69]

Even as he anticipates these models, Milton transcends them by scripting for the Lady a ritual for the exercise of freedom that does not subject her to mythic, cultural, or psychological necessity, or to tragic pessimism. Lacan describes our initiation into the Symbolic order of language and the society it expresses and enforces as a process of alienation. In Lacan's map, desire alienated by its linguistic socialization follows an asymptotic pattern, in an infinite approach to an infinitely deferred and ultimately impossible completion: the dream of a fully self-present and coherent subject, and its phantom double, a fully realized object of desire.[70] That sense of the asymptote pattern is an element of the Lady's initiation, but it is of a different sort from the ironic design of Lacan's tale of retrospective self-division. The Lady both is and is not yet Psyche. The path marked out for the Lady measures an ever-diminishing gap between the fully mobile, active, imaginative, morally creative and sensually alive subject, and her total fulfillment in the transcendental objective and future promise of the love of God. The aspiration toward that providential closure gives desire its positive impetus and disciplines its way of being in the world. The self fashioned by this career of desire is both centered and in motion, flexible and expansive, capable of a series of moments of self-transcendence of the sort the Lady has ritually experienced in the *Maske,* because it knows and rejoices that its destination and consummation is always beyond.[71]

This expectation of eventual fulfillment allows the Lady as initiate not to succumb to the despair of ever finding satisfaction, however provisional and brief, in anything that the world has to offer. Rightly valued, everything that the world has to offer can become ingredients of virtue and opportunities for charity, which is chastity's way of facing the world: not only a habit of discipline, but the very form of pleasure. Edgar Wind observes of the Florentine Neoplatonists, "The more comprehensive the virtues and the pleasures become, the more largely they are bound to overlap; and when a pleasure or virtue becomes all-embracing—that is, when they reach a perfection achieved only in states of ecstasy—then goodness becomes indistinguishable from bliss."[72] Having learned this, the Lady who as a girl freely, anxiously, yet firmly directed her "chaste footing" (146) into the liminal zone of the *Maske* dances forth from it toward the future, with the soul's wisdom and body's knowledge of a woman actively and ardently prepared to address the world's challenges, temptations, and opportunities with the questing yet disciplined, bliss-giving spirit of youth and joy. She need say nothing more. Loving virtue, she is free. She has arrived, and she, and her father's house, will never be the same. May the freedom and pleasure—the pleasure in freedom, the freedom in pleasure—that Milton scripted for Alice Egerton be so as well for our daughters and granddaughters.

Notes

INTRODUCTION: MILTON'S PORTRAIT OF A LADY

1. Masques for the Stuart princes staged not their accession to their own power, but their subordination to that of their father, enacting "the voluntary subservience of the future monarch to the ruling monarch" (Jean E. Graham, "The Performing Heir in Jonson's Jacobean Masques," *Studies in English Literature* 41, no. 2 [2001]: 381). Graham Parry makes the case that the Jonsonian masques produced at the behest of Prince Henry before his death registered elements of Henry's militant Protestant internationalism, but formally concede to the superior wisdom and majesty of his father James I. See Parry, "The Politics of the Jacobean Masque," in *Theatre and Government under the early Stuarts,* ed. J. R. Mulryne and Margaret Shewring (Cambridge: Cambridge University Press, 1993), 93–100.

2. "Exemplary to a nation" is drawn from Milton's digression on his literary aspirations at the beginning of the second book of *The Reason of Church Government,* in *John Milton: Complete Poems and Major Prose,* ed. Merritt Y. Hughes (New York: Odyssey Press, 1957), 669. References to Milton's poetry and prose in this book, unless otherwise indicated, will be taken from Hughes's edition, and cited parenthetically either by page number, in the instances of Milton's prose, or by line number, in the instances of poems, in the text.

3. Leah S. Marcus, *The Politics of Mirth: Jonson, Herrick, Milton, Marvell, and the Defense of Old Holiday Pastimes* (Chicago: University of Chicago Press, 1986), 198, 173.

4. In addition to *Politics of Mirth,* see also Marcus, "The Milieu of Milton's *Comus:* Judicial Reform at Ludlow and the Problem of Sexual Assault," *Criticism* 25, no. 4 (1983): 293–327.

5. William Kerrigan refers to the *Maske* as a "ceremony of investiture" in *The Sacred Complex: On the Psychogenesis of* Paradise Lost (Cambridge, MA: Harvard University Press, 1983), 51.

6. I will subsequently refer at relevant moments to a number of critical texts assessing the political and religious formations and contexts of the *Maske,* but in referring to the "reformation" of the Lady, let me here acknowledge Linda Gregerson, *The Reformation of the Subject: Spenser, Milton, and the English Protestant Epic* (Cambridge: Cambridge University Press, 1995); Georgia Christopher, *Milton and the Science of the Saints* (Princeton, NJ: Princeton University Press, 1982); Maryann Cale McGuire, *Milton's Puritan Masque* (Athens: University of Georgia Press, 1983); David Norbrook, *Poetry and Politics in the English Renaissance* (London: Routledge & Kegan Paul, 1984); and Kathleen Swaim, "'Myself a True Poem': Early Milton and the (Re)formation of the Subject," *Milton Studies* 38 (2000): 66–95.

7. Angus Fletcher, *The Transcendental Masque: An Essay on Milton's* Comus (Ithaca, NY: Cornell University Press, 1971), 250.

8. Cedric C. Brown, *John Milton's Aristocratic Entertainments* (Cambridge: Cambridge University Press, 1985).

9. It could be argued that Bunyan's target audience is class-bound and therefore that his heroes do not approach the kind of moral universality I am describing. See, however, Sharon Achinstein's remarks about the audience of *Pilgrim's Progress:* "Bunyan, through allegory, appealed to an audience of dissenting souls, writing in code that would be understood by them. The book, however, begs for a wide audience to become part of that distinct group; its message is restricted only by interpretive means, not by social, economic, or political allegiances." *Milton and the Revolutionary Reader* (Princeton, NJ: Princeton University Press, 1994), 179. The same observation about an immediate, class-defined audience and a wider appeal to interpretation and conversion holds for the Spenser of *The Faerie Queene;* and such is also the case for Milton and his *Maske*.

10. W. H. Auden, "In Memory of W. B. Yeats (d. Jan. 1939)," in *Collected Shorter Poems 1927–1957* (New York: Random House, 1975), 142.

11. Catherine Belsey, *John Milton: Language, Gender, Power* (Oxford: Basil Blackwell, 1988), 50. It is too bad that Belsey does not develop this insight in her brief and provocative book, preferring instead to weight her treatment of Milton's management of gender issues with references to Robert Graves's denunciatory *Wife to Mr. Milton* (58–67).

12. Mary Nyquist, "The Genesis of Gendered Subjectivity in the Divorce Tracts and in *Paradise Lost,*" in *Re-Membering Milton: Essays on the Texts and Traditions,* ed. Mary Nyquist and Margaret Ferguson (New York: Methuen, 1988), 101. I use here the term "liberal feminism" as it is posited and critiqued by Nyquist in her essay. The term loosely encompasses several interrelated principles, including equal rights, potentials, opportunities, and responsibilities for women, and companionate egalitarian relations between husbands and wives. For Nyquist and like-minded critics, such principles, motivated by and serviceable to early modern and modern bourgeois organization of social relations, necessarily reinscribe women's subordination to men in both the public and private spheres of modern society. As will be evident in the course of my argument, I take issue with the ideological limitations imposed on this model of feminism, at least as it is projected by Milton in the *Maske*. For further discussion of early English feminism and sexual politics, see also Linda Woodbridge, *Women and the English Renaissance: Literature and the Nature of Womankind, 1540–1620* (Urbana: University of Illinois Press, 1984), and Hilda Smith, *Reason's Disciples: Seventeenth-Century English Feminists* (Urbana: University of Illinois Press, 1982).

13. I have made a parallel examination of and challenge to radical feminist criticism of *Paradise Lost* in "Wrestling with the Angel: *Paradise Lost* and Feminist Criticism," *Milton Quarterly* 20, no. 3 (October 1986): 69–85.

14. Jorge Luis Borges's story "Pierre Menard, Author of *Don Quixote*" in *Ficciones* (New York: A. A. Knopf, 1993), 45–56, provoked this thought experiment. Kathryn Schwarz takes a step in the direction of the thought experiment I propose here, with her insightful comparison of the *Maske* to Margaret Cavendish's wildly melodramatic romance *Assaulted and Pursued Chastity.* This allows her to conceptualize chastity in the two texts without relapsing into gender essentialism in evaluating their authors. Schwarz describes chastity in the two texts as a figure and basis for female autonomy, as "empowered self-restraint" that operates within, yet holds out against and potentially subverts the conventions and limitations of patriarchal ideology. See Schwarz, "Chastity, Militant and Married: Cavendish's Romance, Milton's Masque," *PMLA* 118, no. 2 (2003): 270–85.

15. Ashraf Rushdy provides a powerful and instructive analysis of the double valence of subjectivity in Milton's final works, in *The Empty Garden: The Subject of Late Milton* (Pittsburgh: University of Pittsburgh Press, 1991).

16. Stanley Fish, *How Milton Works* (Cambridge, MA: Harvard University Press, 2001), 166.

17. On "subjectivity" as a discursive formation of English Renaissance drama, see Catherine Belsey, *The Subject of Tragedy: Identity and Difference in Renaissance Drama* (London: Methuen, 1985); and Katharine Eisaman Maus, *Inwardness and Theater in the English Renaissance* (Chicago: University of Chicago Press, 1995). For formation—and disappearance—of the early modern subject in a range of cultural practices in the period, see also Francis Barker, *The Tremulous Private Body: Essays in Subjection* (London: Methuen, 1984), and Christopher Pye, *The Vanishing: Shakespeare, the Subject, and Early Modern Culture* (Durham, NC: Duke University Press, 2000).

18. John Rumrich, *Milton Unbound: Controvery and Reinterpretation* (Cambridge: Cambridge University Press, 1996), 52.

19. Wallace Stevens, "The Well Dressed Man with a Beard," in *The Collected Poems of Wallace Stevens* (New York: Alfred A. Knopf, 1972), 247.

20. "Labyrinth" and "Abyss" are key terms in the account of Calvin's transformation of psychology and theology provided by William J. Bouwsma, *John Calvin: A Sixteenth Century Portrait* (New York: Oxford University Press, 1988).

21. Kathleen Swaim, "'Myself a True Poem,'" 66–95. See also John Guillory's analysis of the Cartesian "cogito" in "Milton, Narcissism, Gender: On the Genealogy of Male Self-Esteem," in *Critical Essays on John Milton,* ed. Christopher Kendrick (New York: G. K. Hall, 1995), 220–28; Francis Barker's comments in *The Tremulous Private Body,* 52–58; and Catherine Belsey: "The inner realm of the Cartesian subject, whose thought is a condition of existence, who exists precisely as consciousness, is a territory explored and peopled in the course of the sixteenth and seventeenth centuries" (*John Milton,* 85).

22. Barker, *Tremulous Private Body,* 62. Catherine Belsey makes a parallel observation: "The subject is what speaks or writes, and it does so in a language which is the inscription of certain knowledges—of a culture. As subjects, we have learnt to signify in a specific society, since signification always precedes us as individuals, and meanings pertain at a specific historical moment" (*Shakespeare and the Loss of Eden: The Construction of Family Values in Early Modern Culture* [London: Macmillan, 1999], 10).

23. Harold Bloom, *Shakespeare: The Invention of the Human* (New York: Riverhead Books, 1998).

24. Marcus, "Milton as Historical Subject," *Milton Quarterly* 25, no. 3 (1991): 120. Marcus pays close attention to the ironies of the frontispiece of Milton's 1645 *Poems,* in which the *Maske* appears as the final poem of the English collection. John K. Hale also analyzes, in considerable detail, the several daring and "unprecedented" features of structure, multiple genres and languages, dating, and rhetoric, of the collection, in "Milton's Self-Presentation in *Poems . . . 1645,*" *Milton Quarterly* 25, no. 2 (1991): 37–48. Both make the case that the volume transforms the idea of the authorial self and his relation to his work. See also the wide-ranging historical and sociological analysis of Milton's authoring of himself as exemplary subject in a period of unprecedented social transformation, in Nancy Armstrong and Leonard Tennenhouse, *The Imaginary Puritan: Literature, Intellectual Labor, and the Origins of Personal Life* (Berkeley and Los Angeles: University of California Press, 1994).

25. Keats, letter to Richard Woodhouse (October 27, 1818), in *Selected Poems and Letters,* ed. Douglas Bush (Boston: Houghton Mifflin, 1959), 279.

26. It is surprising that no attention is paid to the problem of the writer as subject in the *Maske* in the 2000 volume of *Milton Studies* dedicated to postmodern approaches to "the writer in his works." Both Kathleen Swaim and J. Martin Evans write substantive and challenging essays in this volume on varieties of poetic self-representation in the formative texts which Milton organizes into the 1645 *Poems,* but do not take the *Maske* into account. See J. Martin Evans, "The Birth of the Author: Milton's Poetic Self-Construction," *Milton Studies* 38 (2000): 47–65; and Swaim, "Myself a True Poem." John Hale's essay, "Milton's Self-Presentation in *Poems . . . 1645,*" although not included in the 2000 volume of *Milton Studies,* belongs in the company of these essays. Ann Baynes Coiro argues that Milton's later construction of his career in terms of an "overarching plan of vatic power" is not at all self-evident in the period of the composition and first publication of his *Maske.* See Coiro, "Anonymous Milton, or, A *Maske* Masked," *ELH* 71, no. 3 (2004): 609.

27. John Steadman demonstrates the usefulness of a consistent application of the Aristotelian categories of "character" and "thought" in the analysis of character formation in the major poems; see Steadman, "*Ethos* and *Dianoia:* Character and Rhetoric in *Paradise Lost,*" in *Language and Style in Milton,* ed. Ronald David Emma and John T. Shawcross (New York: Frederick Ungar, 1967), 193–202; and *Milton's Epic Characters: Image and Idol* (Chapel Hill: University of North Carolina Press, 1968). My point here is that the same analytic rigor gives structure and consistency to the characters of the *Maske,* but that their schematic conceptual outlines also prefigure the visionary epic characters of Blake.

28. In her adept reading of the Nativity Ode, the companion poems "L'Allegro" and "Il Penseroso," and "Lycidas," Swaim ("Myself a True Poem") shows how Milton's efforts prefigure the variants of subject formation envisioned in contemporary theoretical practice: the "constructed" self of the Ode, the "deferred" selves of "L'Allegro" and "Il Penseroso," the "dialogic" self of "Lycidas." We might supplement Swaim's suggestive work by describing Milton's authorial position in the *Maske* as the "dispersed" subject, or perhaps more accurately as the "schematically dispersed" subject.

29. On the "symptomatic" diagnosis of Milton's identification with the Lady, see especially Kerrigan, *Sacred Complex,* 22–72; and Christopher Kendrick, "Milton and Sexuality: A Symptomatic Reading of *Comus,*" in *Re-Membering Milton,* 43–73. John Shawcross is more historically situated and sympathetic in his account of Milton as "Lady" in *John Milton: The Self and the World* (Lexington: University of Kentucky Press, 1993), 20–54. There are a number of accounts, some more sympathetic to Milton than others, of the way in which the Lady speaks for him. See, among others, Mary Laughlin Fawcett, "'Such Noise as I can Make': Chastity and Speech in *Othello* and *Comus,*" *Renaissance Drama,* n.s. 16 (1985): 159–83; Katharine Eisaman Maus, *Inwardness and Theater;* Mary Loeffelholz, "Two Masques of Ceres and Proserpine: *Comus* and *The Tempest,*" in *Re-Membering Milton,* 25–42; and Michael Lieb, *Milton and the Culture of Violence* (Ithaca, NY: Cornell University Press, 1994), 101–11.

30. William Riley Parker, *Milton: A Biography,* 2 vols. (Oxford: Oxford University Press, 1968), 1:142. Stephen Orgel reiterates this suggestion in "The Case for Comus," *Representations* (Winter 2003): 37.

31. William Blake, "The Marriage of Heaven and Hell," Plate 5, in *The Poetry and Prose of William Blake,* ed. David V. Erdman (Garden City, NY: Doubleday,

1970), 35. Stephen Orgel concurs, rather naively, I think, with this assessment: "[Comus's argument] seems to have engaged Milton's poetic sensibility far more powerfully than anything in the Lady's role, perhaps precisely because, as Shakespeare put it, the truest poetry is the most feigning. . . . Comus's arguments can be argued away, but the rich, sensuous, wonderfully inventive, indeed Shakespearean, poetry is Milton at his best" ("Case for Comus," 35–36).

32. Orgel, "Case for Comus," 29–45.

33. On "Why Milton Matters," see the three essays by that title in *Milton Studies* 44 (2005), by Stanley Fish ("Why Milton Matters; or, Against Historicism," 1–12), Barbara K. Lewalski (13–21), and Joseph Wittreich (22–39).

34. Sir Philip Sidney, "An Apology for Poetry," in *The Critical Tradition,* ed. David Richter (Boston: Bedford Books, 1998), 134–59; Edmund Spenser, "A Letter of the Authors [To Sir Walter Raleigh, Knight]," in *The Faerie Queene,* ed. Thomas P. Roche, Jr. (New York: Penguin Books, 1978), 15.

35. Sidney, "Apology," 138.

36. Ibid., 138.

37. Michael Murrin, *The Veil of Allegory* (New Haven, CT: Yale University Press, 1975), 77.

38. For a succinct account of Althusser's critique of literary and philosophical idealism—including, in Althusser's estimation, the forms of structuralist thought dominating French intellectual life in the 1960s—see Warren Montag, "Louis Althusser (1918–1990) and His Circle," in *The Continuum Encyclopedia of Modern Criticism and Theory,* ed. Julian Wolfreys (New York: Continuum, 2002), 273–79.

39. Louis Althusser, "A Letter on Art in Reply to André Daspre," in *Lenin and Philosophy and Other Essays,* trans. Ben Brewster (New York: Monthly Review Press, 1971), 222–23.

40. James Kavanagh helpfully explicates Althusser here: "Literary work disassembles ideologies, breaking them from their former 'natural' reality, fixing and displaying them on the stage of the text. With this staging, the literary text allows a reader to see, and question, the historical and social specificity of one's assumed sense of self and social reality, to understand it as ideology." See Kavanagh, "That Hive of Subtlety: 'Benito Cereno' and the Liberal Hero," in *Ideology and Classic American Literature,* ed. Sacvan Bercovitch and Myra Jehlen (New York: Cambridge University Press, 1986), 353.

41. For pertinent accounts of the limitations and the contradictions of new historicism, see, among others, Alan Liu, "The Power of Formalism: The New Historicism," *ELH* 56 (1989): 721–71; Catherine Gimelli Martin, "The Ahistoricism of the New Historicism: Knowledge as Power versus Power as Knowledge in Bacon's *New Atlantis,*" in *Fault Lines and Controversies in the Study of Seventeenth-Century English Literature,* ed. Claude J. Summers and Ted-Larry Pebworth (Columbia: University of Missouri Press, 2002), 22–49; Stanley Fish, "The Young and the Restless," and "Milton's Career and the Career of Theory," in *There's No Such Thing as Free Speech and It's a Good Thing, Too* (New York: Oxford University Press, 1994), 243–56, 257–67; and Fish, "Why Milton Matters; Or, Against Historicism," 1–12.

42. "When you're lost enough to find yourself" comes from Robert Frost, "Directive," in *Selected Poems of Robert Frost* (New York: Holt, Rinehart, and Winston, 1966), 252. The saving allegory of the interpretive thread through the labyrinth is inspired by the teaching of my colleague at Sarah Lawrence College, Elfie Raymond.

43. Victoria Kahn, "Virtue and *Virtú* in *Comus,*" in *Machiavellian Rhetoric*

from the Counter-Reformation to Milton (Princeton, NJ: Princeton University Press, 1994), 185–208; Gina Hausknecht, "The Gender of Civic Virtue," in *Milton and Gender,* ed. Catherine Gimelli Martin (Cambridge: Cambridge University Press, 2004), 17–33.

44. Hausknecht, "Gender of Civic Virtue," 32.

45. Alasdair MacIntyre raises the question of what doing moral philosophy (and living a virtuous life) in the post-Enlightenment period entails, in *After Virtue* (Notre Dame, IN: University of Notre Dame Press, 1984), and his critical account broadly informs my discussion here.

46. On Milton's analysis of "cause," see his Ramistic *A Fuller Course in the Art of Logic,* ed. and trans. Walter J. Ong, S.J., and Charles J. Ermatuger, in *Complete Prose Works of John Milton, Volume VIII 1666–1682* (New Haven, CT: Yale University Press, 1982), 222–38.

47. "Wo Es war, soll Ich werden," perhaps more literally translated, "Where It has been, I shall come to be." Sigmund Freud, *New Introductory Lectures on Psychoanalysis,* trans. James Strachey (New York: W. W. Norton, 1965).

48. William Blake, "What is it men in women do require?" in *The Poetry and Prose,* 466.

49. William Kerrigan succinctly and beautifully makes a similar point about *Paradise Lost:* "The dynamics of the sacred complex turn against the oedipal settlement they also preserve, liberating the ego to some degree from its secular submission. . . . The destination was a poem freed from the past, not only as an authentic gift to our culture, but as an act of creation transcending the psychological conditions of its possibility" (*Sacred Complex,* 8).

Chapter 1. "Growing a Girl"

1. Audrey Richards, *Chisungu: A Girl's Initiation Ceremony among the Bemba of Zambia* (London: Routledge, 1988), 125.

2. Ibid., 125.

3. Ibid., 126.

4. Ibid., 128.

5. Mircea Eliade, *Rites and Symbols of Initiation: The Mysteries of Birth and Rebirth,* trans. Willard R. Trask (New York: Harper and Row, 1958), 3.

6. On the genre and development of the masque, see especially Stephen Orgel, *The Illusion of Power* (Berkeley and Los Angeles: University of California Press, 1975); Jonathan Goldberg, *James I and the Politics of Literature: Jonson, Shakespeare, Donne, and Their Contemporaries* (Stanford, CA: Stanford University Press, 1989). For Milton's transformations of the masque, see John G. Demaray, *Milton and the Masque Tradition: The Early Poems, "Arcades," and* Comus (Cambridge, MA: Harvard University Press, 1968); Maryann Cale McGuire, *Milton's Puritan Masque;* Cedric C. Brown, *John Milton's Aristocratic Entertainments;* David Norbrook, *Poetry and Politics;* Leah Sinanoglou Marcus, "Milton's Anti-Laudian Masque," in *Politics of Mirth,* 169–212; Eugene Cunnar, "Milton, Shepherd of Hermas, and the Writing of a Puritan Masque," *Milton Studies* 23 (1987): 33–52; Mindele Anne Treip, "*Comus* and the Stuart Masque Connection, 1632–34," *ANQ: A Quarterly Journal of Short Articles, Notes, and Reviews* 2, no. 3 (July 1989): 83–89; J. Andrew Hubbell, "*Comus:* Milton's Re-formation of the Masque," in *Spokesperson Milton: Voices in Contemporary Criticism,* ed. Charles

W. Durham and Kristin Pruitt McColgan (Selinsgrove, PA: Susquehanna University Press, 1994), 193–205; Lauren Shohet, "Figuring Chastity: Milton's Ludlow *Mask*," in *Menacing Virgins: Representing Virginity in the Middle Ages and Renaissance,* ed. Kathleen Coyne Kelly and Marina Leslie (Newark: University of Delaware Press, 1999), 146–64; Blaire Hoxby, "The Wisdom of Their Feet: Meaningful Dance in Milton and the Stuart Masque," *English Literary Renaissance* 37, no. 1 (2007), 74–99.

7. Welsford, *Court Masque,* 4–5.

8. Ben Jonson, *The Vision of Delight,* 164–68, 189–98, in *Ben Jonson: Selected Masques,* ed. Stephen Orgel (New Haven, CT: Yale University Press, 1970), 156–58. All references to Jonson's masques, unless otherwise indicated, will be to this edition, and cited parenthetically in the text.

9. On the structure of the Stuart masque, see Allardyce Nicoll, *Stuart Masques and the Renaissance Stage* (New York: Harcourt Brace, 1938), and Stephen Orgel, *The Jonsonian Masque* (New York: Columbia University Press, 1981). Leah Marcus shows how the licensed anarchy of the antimasque within the containing structure of the masque made it an ideal performance vehicle for the Stuart strategy of permitting festive and sportive activity as a sign of submission to and reinforcement of royal power: "The Jacobean masque can be regarded as a symbolic enactment of Stuart policy toward holiday topsy-turvydom" (*Politics of Mirth,* 9).

10. The phrase is adapted from Freud, who observes, "The interpretation of dreams is the royal road to a knowledge of the unconscious activities of the mind." *The Interpretation of Dreams,* trans. James Strachey (New York: Avon Books, 1965).

11. Victor Turner, *The Ritual Process: Structure and Anti-Structure* (Chicago: Aldine Publishing Company, 1969), 131–65.

12. These anthropological assessments confirm Mikhail Bakhtin's account of the carnivalesque in *Rabelais and His World,* trans. Helen Iswolsky (Bloomington: Indiana University Press, 1984).

13. William Kerrigan, *Sacred Complex,* 22.

14. For thorough accounts of the social, political, and performance occasions of the *Maske,* see in particular Demaray, *Milton and the Masque Tradition;* Brown, *John Milton's Aristocratic Entertainments;* Marcus, "Milton's Anti-Laudian Masque"; William B. Hunter, Jr., *Milton's* Comus: *Family Piece* (Troy, NY: Whitston Publishing, 1983); and Mindele Anne Treip, "Comus as 'Progress,'" *Milton Quarterly* 20, no. 1 (March 1986): 1–13.

15. On the conformation of character to social role in traditional rites of passages, see Turner, *From Ritual to Theatre,* 115.

16. "As the goal of such a journey, the great hall of Ludlow Castle with its festive assembly points both to the parental home and to heavenly mansions, both to the inaugural celebration and to participation in the supernal community of realized virtue" (Kathleen Swaim, "Allegorical Poetry in Milton's Ludlow Mask," *Milton Studies* 16 [1982]: 172). See also Louise Simons, "'And Heaven Gates Ore My Head': Death as Threshold in Milton's Masque," *Milton Studies* 23 (1987): 53–93.

17. Leah Marcus demonstrates that Milton invokes, only to subvert, the centralizing harmonic integration of social forces and classes typical of the court masque: "The masque separates its audience from the power at the center of government; it does so by creating, over and over again, situations that appear to call for interpretation in terms of the Stuart 'politics of mirth,' but that turn out instead to 'free' judgment so that traditional pastimes and the art of the masque itself no longer

have to be understood as an encoding of Stuart authority" (*Politics of Mirth*, 178–79).

18. Georgia Christopher gives a particularly lucid account of the Lady's consolidation of Reformation faith in *Science of the Saints,* 31–58. The shaping effect of Reformation values on Milton's *Maske* is the subject of McGuire's *Milton's Puritan Masque* and Brown's *John Milton's Aristocratic Entertainments.* John Rogers studies the Lady's profession of virginity as it anticipates the political trope of virginity employed in revolutionary discourses of the civil war and interregnum period. See Rogers, "The Enclosure of Virginity: The Poetics of Sexual Abstinence in the English Revolution," in *Enclosure Acts: Sexuality, Property, and Culture in Early Modern England,* ed. Richard Burt and John Michael Archer (Ithaca, NY: Cornell University Press, 1994), 229–50. Chastity, as Milton embodies the virtue in the character of his Lady, affiliates itself with these developments, in potential resistance to the conception of chastity promoted in conduct books and girls' education, that prescribe women's obedient submission to the interests of father and husband: "Since marriage was the central institution through which women in the early modern patriarchal system were subordinated, the highest priority in their upbringing and training was their future effectiveness and obedience as wives," and chastity was the linchpin of this subordination. Anthony Fletcher, *Gender, Sex, and Subordination in England 1500–1800* (New Haven, CT: Yale University Press, 1995), 375. See also Suzanne W. Hull, *Chaste, Silent and Obedient: English Books for Women 1435–1640* (San Marino, CA: Huntington Library, 1982).

19. Parry, "Politics of the Jacobean Masque," 92. On the collaboration and conflict between Jonson and Jones, see D. J. Gordon, "Poet and Architect: The Intellectual Setting of the Quarrel between Ben Jonson and Inigo Jones," in *The Renaissance Imagination: Essays and Lectures by D. J. Gordon,* ed. Stephen Orgel (Berkeley and Los Angeles: University of California Press, 1980), 77–101; Angus Fletcher, *Transcendental Masque,* 87–115; and John Peacock, "The Stuart Court Masque and the Theatre of the Greeks," *Journal of the Warburg and Courtauld Institutes* 56 (1993): 183–208.

20. Orgel, *Illusion of Power,* 57–58.

21. Orgel, "Introduction" to *Ben Jonson: Selected Masques,* 14. My account of the typical structure of the masque derives from Orgel's scholarship; see also *Illusion of Power* and *Jonsonian Masque.* This paradigm is admittedly too schematic to account for specific variations and elaborations of the masque's symbolic actions. The firm yet flexible antithetical structure of antimasque/masque invented and developed by Jonson dissolves into more elaborate and diffuse intricacies executed by other hands when Jonson fell out of royal favor. In the Caroline period, when Milton composed *Arcades* and the Ludlow *Maske,* Henrietta Maria sponsored masques with loosely structured scenic sequences that drew on continental influences from ballet and early opera. See Welsford, *Court Masque;* Demaray, *Milton and the Masque Tradition,* 59–82; Norbrook, *Poetry and Politics,* 247–57; Hoxby, "Wisdom of Their Feet"; Barbara Lewalski, *Writing Women in Jacobean England* (Cambridge, MA: Harvard University Press, 1993), 15–43; John Peacock, "The French Element in Inigo Jones's Masque Design," in *The Court Masque,* ed. David Lindley (Manchester: Manchester University Press, 1984), 148–68. Milton's *Maske* participates in the Caroline period's loosening experimentation with the form, even as it restores and develops the unified design and ethical rigor of Jonson's texts.

22. See Marcus, *Politics of Mirth,* 1–23, 64–139, for analysis of the political service performed by masques in their dramatization and sublimation of poten-

tially destructive social energies. Freud treated the aesthetic orchestration of anxiety as one of the public functions of art. Freud's account of the dynamics of reading as an individualized set of textual pleasures induced by fiction's power to solicit and sublimate anxiety provides a suggestive paradigm for collective and class-specific aesthetic projects like the *Maske.* See "Creative Writers and Day-Dreaming," trans. James Strachey, in *Criticism: Major Statements,* ed. Charles Kaplan and William Anderson (New York: St. Martin's Press, 1991), 419–28. For Lacan's analytic of the different registers of the Real, the Imaginary, and the Symbolic, see especially Jacques Lacan, *The Language of the Self: The Function of Language in Psychoanalysis,* trans. Anthony Wilden (New York: Dell, 1968). Anthony Wilden's commentary, "Lacan and the Discourse of the Other," is particularly useful in clarifying the differences between the Symbolic and the Imaginary orders, in Lacan's thought; see this essay in *Language of the Self,* especially 161–66, 185–88. For the political application of psychoanalytic theory that stands behind my speculation about social anxieties staged in Stuart masques, see Fredric Jameson, *The Political Unconscious: Narrative as a Socially Symbolic Act* (Ithaca, NY: Cornell University Press, 1981).

23. For more specific analysis of the historical and political backgrounds informing the masques, see Norbrook, *Poetry and Politics,* 175–95; Goldberg, *James I,* 55–65; Barbara Kiefer Lewalski, *Writing Women,* 15–43.

24. Lewalski observes, for instance, the extravagances of the 1609 *Masque of Queenes,* budgeted at one thousand pounds, but with payments amounting to more than three thousand pounds; see *Writing Women,* 338 n. 85.

25. Christopher Hill, *Milton and the English Revolution* (New York: Viking, 1978).

26. See especially Graham Parry, "Politics of the Jacobean Masque." Parry notes that after 1614, having given up writing for the public theatre, "[Jonson's] livelihood depended on the court" (107).

27. Marcus, *Politics of Mirth,* 127. Marcus makes a compelling argument that James was willing to tolerate a degree of implied political and moral criticism on the part of Jonson because of his trust in Jonson's loyalty and delight in his wit; see especially 13, 102. See also Nathaniel Strout's study of how Jonson tries to create an ethical self-reflectiveness, especially among his later audiences and performers, in "Jonson's Jacobean Masques and the Moral Imagination," *Studies in English Literature 1500–1900* 27, no. 2 (1987): 233–47.

28. Jonson, Preface to *Hymenaei, or the Solemnities of Masque and Barriers at a Marriage,* 1–17, in *Selected Masques,* 47–48. Although *Hymenae* (1606) is an early instance of Jonson and Jones's collaboration and thus precedes the open quarrel of their later relationship, the grounds of their disputation is clearly laid out in Jonson's oppositional terms here.

29. John Peacock notices the series of oppositions that organize the passage. Although he does not attend to the way that the oppositions seem to dissolve into each other in this particular instance, Peacock's rich study of the Renaissance discussions, principally among the Italians, of Aristotle's *Poetics,* leads him to conclude that the blurring of the differences and inversion of the hierarchies between the masque's parts that Jonson tried to defend against was "endemic in the whole culture which Jonson himself drew upon in order to produce his neo-classical theory of the masque." See Peacock, "Stuart Court Masque," 194, 197.

30. In her reading of this same passage from the Preface to *Hymenaei,* Joan Faust notices and enlarges upon these ambiguities that "reinforce the connection and interdependence of poetry with the visual." Faust, "*Queenes* and Jonson's

Masques of Mirrors," *Explorations in Renaissance Culture* 28, no. 1 (Summer 2002): 3.

31. Graham Parry's vivid account of the likely conditions of the production of court masques in the banqueting house indicate how Jonson must have realized all that he was up against, despite his Herculean efforts to promote absolutist idealism. See Parry, "Politics of the Jacobean Masque," 113–14.

32. Orgel, *Illusion of Power,* 57.

33. Eliade, *Symbolism, the Sacred, and the Arts,* ed. Diane Apostolos-Cappadona (New York: Crossroads Publishing), 70–71.

34. Goldberg, *James I,* 58–59. See also Hoxby, "Wisdom of Their Feet," 74. Naomi Conn Liebler notices the symbolic correlation between monarch and society in Shakespeare's histories and tragedies, in the social crises of which the royal figures function as "microcosmic kingdoms" (*Shakespeare's Festive Tragedy: The Ritual Foundations of Genre* [London: Routledge, 1995], 15). She points to the correspondences between the tragic disintegration of Shakespeare's monarchs and the ritual degradation of monarchs in traditional societies observed by Victor Turner and René Girard (*Shakespeare's Festive Tragedy,* 123–27).

35. Orgel, *Illusion of Power,* 52.

36. Lewalski argues that the masques composed by Jonson, sponsored by Queen Anne, provide a cultural site for a domestic party of opposition to James's public policies (*Writing Women,* 15–43). Suzanne Gossett's earlier article makes the contrary case that Jonson's masques betray an "attitude toward women, an ambivalence verging on antipathy" (99), and that the more tolerant and promiscuous experimentation in gender blurring in the masque performances with continental influences, patronized by Henrietta Maria, met with not only Puritan resistance but with resistance from "the internal logic of the masque itself" ("'Man-maid, begone!': Women in Masques," *English Literary Renaissance* 18[1988]: 113).

37. In this section of my discussion, I argue a position that respectfully disagrees with several recent intriguing studies of "the Queen's masques." They argue that the authorial power displayed by Queen Anne in the production of the masques, and the political, discursive, and mythic power displayed by her and the other noble women of her court in the masque performance, were substantial and politically significant rather than imaginary and ephemeral. Although Barbara Kiefer Lewalski's *Writing Women* will be my primary reference point, I recommend also Marion Wynne-Davies, "The Queen's Masque: Renaissance Women and the Seventeenth-Century Court Masque," in *Gloriana's Face: Women, Public and Private, in the English Renaissance,* ed. S. P. Cerasano and Marion Wynne-Davies (Detroit: Wayne State University Press, 1992), 79–104; Leeds Barroll, "Inventing the Stuart Masque," in *The Politics of the Stuart Court Masque,* ed. David Bevington and Peter Holbrook (Cambridge: Cambridge University Press, 1998), 121–43; Bernadette Andrea, "Black Skin, the Queen's Masques: Africanist Ambivalence and Feminine Author[ity] in the Masques of *Blackness* and *Beauty,*" *English Literary Renaissance* 29, no. 2 (1999): 246–81; Kathryn Schwarz, "Amazon Reflections in the Jacobean Queen's Masque," *Studies in English Literature* 35 (1995): 293–319, revised as "Stranger in the Mirror: Amazon Reflections in the Jacobean Queen's Masque," in *Tough Love: Amazon Encounters in the English Renaissance* (Durham, NC: Duke University Press, 2000), 109–33; and Lawrence Normand, "Witches, King James, and *The Masque of Queens,* "in *Representing Women in Renaissance England,* ed. Claude J. Summers and Ted-Larry Pebworth (Columbia: University of Missouri Press, 1997), 107–20.

38. Welsford, *Court Masque,* 187; Orgel, "Introduction" to *Ben Jonson: Selected Masques,* 8–9, 13.

39. For Jonson's aesthetic negotiation in his masques of the competing claims of James's pacifist diplomacy, Queen Anne's more overtly pro-Spanish interests, and the Protestant militancy organizing around the maturing Prince Henry, see especially Peter Holbrook, "Jacobean Masques and the Jacobean Peace," in *The Politics of the Stuart Court Masque,* ed. David Bevington and Peter Holbrook (Cambridge: Cambridge University Press, 1998), 67–87.

40. Terry Eagleton, *William Shakespeare* (Oxford: Basil Blackwell, 1987), 2–4.

41. Lawrence Normand notes that this representation of the witches was consistent with the analysis of King James's *Daemonologie* and thus would intrigue the prime witness of the masque and meet with his approval. See Normand, "Witches, King James," 115.

42. Faust, "*Queenes,*" 17.

43. Lewalski, *Writing Women,* 37.

44. Ibid., 38–39. Wynne-Davies makes a comparable point: "the Queen's masque not only challenged the gendered preserves of authorship but questioned the legitimacy of absolute male power as symbolised by the Stuart King" ("Queen's Masque," 80).

45. Lewalski, *Writing Women,* 37. See also Bernadette Andrea, "Black Skin, the Queen's Masques." Andrea's accounts of the masques of *Blackness* and *Beauty* are readily applicable to *The Masque of Queens,* although she makes an especially strong case for the subversive gender and racial shock of Anne's first collaboration with Jonson in *The Masque of Blackness,* in comparison to which the Imaginary spectacle of female power in *Queens* seems decorous and tame. See also Wynne-Davies's account of the Queen's "authorship," in "Queen's Masque," 79–82.

46. Lewalski, *Writing Women,* 36–37.

47. Schwarz, "Amazon Reflections," 294. At this stage of her discussion, Schwarz is alluding more generally to the representational strategies of the several masques sponsored by Queen Anne.

48. These explanatory annotations appear in the edition of *The Masque of Queens* which appears in *Ben Jonson's Plays and Masques,* ed. Robert M. Adams (New York: W. W. Norton, 1979), 337.

49. Ibid., 335.

50. Of course it would hardly have improved diplomatic relations with Spain, whose ambassador Don Fernandez de Girone, was among the invited guests, for the masque to laud the valor, virtue, and autonomy of Elizabeth I. De Girone in fact did not see the masque, although Anne clearly wanted him to. This pragmatic diplomatic motive to repress the memory of Elizabeth in the masque coincides with James's need domestically to minimize the reputation of, and nostalgia for, his strong predecessor. See Wynne-Davies, "Queen's Masque," 85–86.

51. Slavoj Žižek, *The Fragile Absolute—or, Why Is the Christian Legacy Worth Fighting For?* (London: Verso Books, 2000), 65.

52. Kathryn Schwarz also notices the spectral presence of Elizabeth in the power triangle of the queens, and describes Anne, "a queen playing at a goddess's power," as "a place-holder for the more persuasive power of an earlier queen" (Schwarz, "Amazon Reflections," 300). Schwarz claims that the subliminal allusion to Elizabeth invests the nostalgia for her rule into the images of female autonomy and resistance to male sovereignty projected by the masquers. My claim here is just about the opposite: the replacement of the wily and independent Elizabeth by the ultimately self-subordinating Bel-Anna at the pinnacle of the masque's

symbolizing of power is an effort to restabilize the patriarchal hierarchies disrupted by Elizabeth's long rule and the recollection of it.

53. "The masque, for all its Amazonian heroines, celebrates the sovereign and masculine word." Stephen Orgel, "Marginal Jonson," in *The Politics of the Stuart Court Masque,* ed. David Bevington and Peter Holbrook (Cambridge: Cambridge University Press, 1998), 174. See also Orgel, "Jonson and the Amazons," in *Soliciting Interpretation,* ed. Elizabeth Harvey and Katharine Eisaman Maus (Chicago: University of Chicago Press, 1990), 119–39.

54. Sigmund Freud, "Medusa's Head," in *Sexuality and the Psychology of Love,* ed. Philip Rieff (New York: Collier Books, 1963), 212. I study Freud's analysis of the myth more fully in chapter 5, "Girl Power: The Profession of Virginity."

55. Goldberg, *James I,* 88.

56. Ibid.

57. Lewalski, *Writing Women,* 41.

58. McGuire, *Milton's Puritan Masque,* 134–35.

59. Graham Parry observes that the narcissistic wish fulfillment that masques provided for the Caroline court had already become a feature of Jonson's masques in the late period of James's rule: "That outside world was always a source of trouble for King James, who would have liked nothing better than to live in a fortunate isle enjoying his own blessings of union and peace and watching the arts flourish—as long as there was time to hunt" ("Politics of the Jacobean Masque," 113).

60. I should acknowledge that Henrietta Maria's cultural influence, idealized in the masques, was not without political and religious consequences in the court, particularly in the number of conversions to Roman Catholicism by noblewomen within her circle. The queen's Catholic influence provoked anxious suspicion and opposition in the country at large, as expressed most violently in William Prynne's *Histriomastix.* So her superintendence of and participation in masques can be seen not so much as efficacious instances of her power in itself, but as symptoms or evidences of influence that was perceived to be making a difference in society at large. See Erica Veevers, *Images of Love and Religion: Queen Henrietta Maria and Court Entertainments* (Cambridge: Cambridge University Press, 1989).

61. Gossett, "Man-maid, begone!", 111–13. There are certainly other political conflicts staged in the masques performed during the Caroline period, and my brief account of gender experimentation in the genre needs to be read in the context of the political conflicts of the 1630s and the ways in which masques internalized and sought symbolically to stabilize them. Martin Butler provides a chronological analysis of the ultimately unsuccessful efforts of writers of court masques during the period of Charles's personal rule to include elements of reformist criticism within the panegyric requirements of the form. See Butler, "Reform or Reverence? The Politics of the Caroline Masque," in *Theatre and Government under the early Stuarts,* ed. J. R. Mulryne and Margaret Shewring (Cambridge: Cambridge University Press, 1993), 118–56.

62. Mindele Anne Treip demonstrates Milton's familiarity with these contemporary masques in "Stuart Masque Connection," 83–89.

63. Alice Egerton and her older sister Catherine had performed in Aurelian Townshend's *Tempe Restored,* which, remarkably enough, features in its disjointed plot the ethical reformation of the figure of Circe, the mythic mother of Milton's Comus. Thomas and John Egerton danced in Carew's recent production of *Coelum Britannicum,* to which Henry Lawes had contributed. The children were of course costumed performers for Milton's earlier homage to the dowager Countess of

Derby, "Arcades." See Demaray, *Milton and the Masque Tradition,* 54–58, 76–78. Jonson and Jones's charming and spectacular *Oberon,* which honored and starred Prince Henry, performed at court at Christmas in 1611, provides a striking contrast to Milton's adaptation of the drama to the initiation of his young performers. Jonson's masque, we could say, provides a ritual debut for the promising young heir to the throne, but it neither tests nor alters his status or character, and it explicitly defers to his monarch father as "the matter of virtue" (258) and "a god o'er kings" (261). As the embodiment of abstract princely virtue, Henry as Oberon is unassailably static, and yet his virtue is not his own, insofar as he owes it to, and the masque invests it in, his father.

64. Stella Revard, *Milton and the Tangles of Neaera's Hair: The Making of the 1645 Poems* (Columbia: University of Missouri Press, 1997), 153.

65. Marcus, *Politics of Mirth,* 184.

66. On the formation of Milton's political commitments in this period, as evidenced in the *Maske* and other sources, see especially Brown, *Aristocratic Entertainments;* Marcus, "Milton's Anti-Laudian Masque"; Norbrook, *Poetry and Politics;* and Hubbell, "Milton's Re-formation." See also Hill, *Milton and the English Revolution;* Achsah Guibbory, *Ceremony and Community from Herbert to Milton: Literature, Religion, and Cultural Conflict in Seventeenth-Century England* (Cambridge: Cambridge University Press, 1998); and Barbara Lewalski, "How Radical Was the Young Milton?" in *Milton and Heresy,* ed. Stephen B. Dobranski and John P. Rumrich (Cambridge: Cambridge University Press, 1998), 49–72. In her study of Milton's early controversial pamphlets, Janel Mueller does not look back quite so far as to the *Maske,* but her study of the rhetorical and ideological contexts of republican thinking is relevant to this discussion. See Mueller, "Contextualizing Milton's Nascent Republicanism," in *Of Poetry and Politics: New Essays on Milton and His World,* ed. Paul G. Stanwood (Binghamton, NY: Medieval and Renaissance Texts and Studies, 1995), 263–82. On skeptical accounts of the ambivalences and contradictions of Milton's purported early radicalism, see David Loewenstein, "'Fair Offspring Nurs't in Princely Lore': On the Question of Milton's Early Radicalism," *Milton Studies* 28 (1992): 37–48; Annabel Patterson, "'Forc'd Fingers': Milton's Early Poems and Ideological Constraint," in *"The Muses Commonweale": Poetry and Politics in the Seventeenth Century,* ed. Claude J. Summers and Ted-Larry Pebworth (Columbia: University of Missouri Press, 1968), 9–22; Thomas Corns, "Milton before 'Lycidas,'" in *Milton and the Terms of Liberty* (Cambridge: Cambridge University Press, 1999), 23–36.

67. Victoria Kahn, *Machiavellian Rhetoric,* 196. Kahn's analysis of the *Maske* discloses "a conflict between . . . the allegorical and the rhetorical plots of the masque" (197). The "allegorical" model of virtue, as Kahn represents it, is Neoplatonically intact, already complete, static and passively dependent on the grace that sanctions it. The "rhetorical" model of active self-fashioning virtue demonstrates Milton's Arminian commitment to human agency that establishes and authenticates its freedom and substance through trial. Kahn argues that the performative model is implicated in a Machiavellian ideological program of rhetorical efficacy that the allegorical, Neoplatonic model seeks to isolate and critique in the figure of Comus. I do not see these as necessarily antagonistic models in Milton, who dramatizes the realization and authentication of implicit or potential virtue through temptation and action.

68. Marcus's observation about the Attendant Spirit's evocation of the heavens in his Prologue (9–11) coincides with my remarks here about the decentralization

of the source of virtue through the appropriation of conventional royalist tropes: "An audience familiar with masques at court might expect the 'Regions mild of calme and serene aire' to be dominated by the single crown and all-pervasive power of the king, as the bright star representing the monarch dominated the heavens in the final vision of *Coelum Britannicum*. Milton's Attendant Spirit talks instead of many crowns, many thrones available to all of virtue's servants in the afterlife" (*Politics of Mirth*, 182).

69. Fletcher, *Transcendental Masque*, 163.

70. Turner, *Dramas, Fields, and Metaphors*, and *The Forest of Symbols: Aspects of Ndembu Ritual* (Ithaca, NY: Cornell University Press, 1974). This pattern of three stages was first delineated by Arnold van Gennep in *The Rites of Passage*, trans. Monika B. Vizedom and Gabrielle L. Caffee (Chicago: University of Chicago Press, 1960). Some of the specific components mentioned in the following pages are supplied from Richards and Eliade, whose descriptions of ritual coordinate well with this paradigm and provide data from primary rites that suggestively parallel Milton's inventions.

71. Richards, *Chisungu*, 122.

72. Ibid.

73. Turner, *Dramas, Fields, and Metaphors*, 232.

74. Eliade, *Rites and Symbols*, 43.

75. Turner, *Dramas, Fields, and Metaphors*, 273–74.

76. Eliade, *Rites and Symbols*, 47; Richards, *Chisungu*, xxii.

77. John Demaray stresses the symbolic importance of the revels as a climactic social fulfillment of the *Maske*'s "iconographic representation of the dance of virtue and vice in the universe." "The Temple of the Mind: Cosmic Iconography in Milton's *A Mask*," *Milton Quarterly* 21, no. 4 (December 1987): 59.

78. The Lady's request seems informed by St. Paul's assurance, "No temptation has overtaken you that is not common to man. God is faithful, and he will not let you be tempted beyond your strength, but with the temptation will also provide the way of escape, that you may be able to endure it" (1 Corinthians 10:13). In "Without Charity: An Intertextual Study of Milton's *Comus*," *Milton Studies* 34 (1997), Hilda Hollis argues that the prayer, like the Lady's self-presentation in her soliloquy, is evidence of a "problematic self-reliance" (166). Surprisingly, considering her close attention to the *Maske*'s intertextual engagement with Paul's epistles to the Corinthians, Hollis does not notice the equivalence between the Lady's request and this claim that the faithful's self-reliance itself depends on her reliance on God.

79. In the chronology of Milton's work, the Lady's temptation significantly prefigures not only that of Eve in *Paradise Lost* 9, but that of Jesus in *Paradise Regained*, a parallel I develop more fully in chapter 6, "Milton's Lady and Lady Milton: Chastity, Gender, and Prophecy."

80. Most remarkably, see Aemelia Lanyer's defense of Eve in *Salve Deus Rex Judaeorum*, 745–832 (*Major Women Writers of Seventeenth-Century England*, ed. James Fitzmaurice, Josephine A. Roberts, Carol L. Barash, Eugene R. Cunnar, and Nancy A. Gutierrez [Ann Arbor: University of Michigan Press, 1997]). Lanyer's argument exculpates Eve by describing her naiveté; Adam's greater responsibility and greater wisdom makes him the more culpable party. Thus, Lanyer's eloquence on behalf of the recovery of women's rights depends upon her acceptance of prelapsarian inferiority of Eve. See also Rachel Speght's more egalitarian, forceful and witty polemic against the misogynist Joseph Swetnam, in *A Mouzell for Melastomous, the cynicall bayter, and foule mouthed barker against Evahs sex*. Barbara Lewalski studies these important texts in *Writing Women*, 161–69, 230–32. Mary

Nyquist compares Speght's egalitarian feminist polemic to what she interprets as Milton's subordinate positioning of women, in "Genesis of Gendered Subjectivity," 107–109. Desma Polydorou develops Nyquist's critique in greater detail in "Gender and Spiritual Equality in Marriage: A Dialogic Reading of Rachel Speght and John Milton," *Milton Quarterly* 35 (2001): 22–32. For an overview of the controversy over Eve in the Jacobean *querelle de femmes,* see Linda Woodbridge, *Women and the English Renaissance.*

81. James Taafe, "Michaelmas, the 'Lawless Hour,' and the Occasion of Milton's Comus," *English Language Notes* 6 (1968–69): 257–62; William B. Hunter, Jr, "The Liturgical Context of *Comus,*" *English Language Notes* 10 (1972): 11–15, and Hunter, *Milton's* Comus: *Family Piece.*

82. McGuire, *Milton's Puritan Masque,* 76.

83. Jonson rather niftily evades acknowledging here that the masque was revised into the more disjointed *For the Honor of Wales* because it was in fact not well received; see Strout, "Jonson's Jacobean Masques," 242.

84. William Blake, *Marriage of Heaven and Hell,* 34. For Blake, "negations" are morally determined static and mutually self-canceling oppositions; "contraries" are productive antitheses that ceaselessly generate growth and transformation.

85. This description of the social implications of the Lady's initiation is informed by several of the works cited above in note 6, particularly Brown, *John Milton's Aristocratic Entertainments,* and McGuire, *Milton's Puritan Masque.*

86. Joan Faust notes that "in his innovations in and published accounts of the court masque, Jonson manipulated the reflected image not only of James but also of the royal family to guide them through a type of 'mirror stage,' creating and confirming their self-image by presenting a future perfect ideal which includes his own presence" (*"Queenes,"* 12). She cites a passage from Jane Gallop's reading of Lacan to warn that this projected ideal self "is an illusion done with mirrors" (7; Gallop, *Reading Lacan* [Ithaca, NY: Cornell University Press, 1985], 83).

87. Martin Butler, "Reform or Reverence," 152.

88. Barbara Lewalski notices the comparative modesty of the scale of production and the comparative simplicity of character representation in the *Maske* as evidences of its "Puritan religious and political sensibilities" ("Milton's *Comus* and the Politics of Masquing," *Politics of Stuart Court Masque,* 308). Catherine Gimelli Martin composes a vigorous challenge to recent "Puritan" readings of the *Maske,* in "The Non-Puritan Ethics, Aesthetics, and Metaphysics of Milton's Spenserian Masque," *Milton Quarterly* 37, no. 4 (2003): 215–44. Martin stresses the underpinnings of the *Maske*'s ethical and allegorical structures in Spenser's and Francis Bacon's humanist projects, but her rather narrow and rigid construal of "Puritanism" does not take into account the dynamism, complexity, and range of theological ideas and social motivations that the term encompassed in mid-seventeenth-century England.

Chapter 2. Singing Master

1. Victor Turner, *Dramas, Fields, and Metaphors,* 239.

2. Victoria Silver, "Thoughts in Misbecoming Plight: Allegory in *Comus,*" in *Critical Essays on John Milton,* ed. Christopher Kendrick (New York: G. K. Hall, 1995), 51.

3. William B. Hunter, Jr., *Milton's* Comus: *Family Piece,* 37–43.

4. See Kathleen Swaim, "Allegorical Poetry," 170–71.

5. Jean LaFontaine, *Initiation* (New York: Penguin Books, 1985), 87, 123. Victoria Silver is not so sure about the Attendant Spirit's reliability as interpretive guide. She discerns contradictions between the allegorical and the dramatistic elements of the *Maske,* which seem to erode some of the assurances that the Attendant Spirit offers as allegorical expositor of the *Maske*'s actions ("Thoughts in Misbecoming Plight," 47–73).

6. Louis Martz, "The Music of Comus," in *Illustrious Evidence: Approaches to English Literature of the Early Seventeenth Century,* ed. Earl Miner (Berkeley and Los Angeles: University of California Press, 1975), 94. This count of the songs does not include Sabrina's beautiful song (890–901), which is not preserved.

7. LaFontaine, *Initiation,* 187.

8. The performance version of the masque, approximately available to us in the Bridgewater Manuscript, begins with a fourteen line song by the Attendant Spirit excerpted from what would be the beginning of his Epilogue in the print editions. See *A Variorum Commentary on The Poems of John Milton,* vol. 2, part 3, ed. A. S. P. Woodhouse and Douglas Bush (New York: Columbia University Press, 1972), 854; see also the commentary by Louis Martz in "Music of Comus," 94–95. The variant positioning of these lines that link the two heavenly landscapes of the *Maske* will be considered in my treatment of the Epilogue in chapter 8, "Homecoming Queen."

9. Gale H. Carrithers, Jr., "Milton's Ludlow Masque: From Chaos to Community," *English Literary History* 33 (1966): 38.

10. Shohet, "Figuring Chastity," 160.

11. For comparison, see Anne D. Ferry, *Milton's Epic Voice: The Narrator in Paradise Lost* (Chicago: University of Chicago Press, 1983).

12. Angus Fletcher, *The Transcendental Masque.*

13. On the controversy between Jonson and Jones over the relative importance of textual sense and material spectacle, see especially D. J. Gordon, "Poet and Architect," and John Peacock, "Stuart Court Masque." William Riley Parker makes a point about Milton's textualizing of the visual similar to mine, although he makes it in a negative fashion. Contrasting Milton's composition of the *Maske* to Jonson's prolific efforts, he remarks, "Milton's [poetry] (like Shakespeare's for the stage) had to bear the burden of description and compensate, somehow, for the dearth of visual aids to the imagination" (*Milton,* 1, 129).

14. Martin Butler studies the embedded ironies of *Coelum Britannicum,* centering on the speeches of the railing god figure Momus, yet concludes, "Although Momus problematises the certainties of the Caroline masque and enables the ethical framework which polices royal power to be foregrounded more assertively than was customary, his disparagement does not finally displace the legitimating functions of the form. . . . He is clearly amused by the inflated claims of Caroline kingship, but he can hardly be said to be opposed to its survival." ("Reform or Reverence?", 140–41).

15. "*Comus* has received high critical praise because, unlike almost all other masques in the seventeenth century, it unifies and captures in words other theatrical arts—scenic spectacle, dialogue, and particularly lyrical song—and through them conveys forceful and often subtle symbolic and didactic meanings." John Demaray, "Temple of the Mind," 59–60.

16. Roger Wilkenfeld contrasts the verbal and dramatic density of the *Maske* to the succession of spectacular scenes that require the poet's supplementary explication in the textual versions of Jonson's masques. Wilkenfeld remarks that Milton

"could present readers with a 'clean' literary text of his poem precisely because he had used his emblematic imagery with such a masterful economy." See "The Seat at the Center: An Interpretation of *Comus*," *English Literary History* (1966): 171.

17. On allegory's veiling of truth, and the process of its interpretation, see especially Murrin, *Veil of Allegory.*

18. See Swaim, "Allegorical Poetry," 190. It will be evident to any reader familiar with Swaim's fine essay that I am deeply indebted to her for the direction that this chapter takes.

19. See also Philip Schwyzer's account of the politics of the Sabrina legend in Michael Drayton's *Polyobion,* in "Purity and Danger on the West Bank of the Severn: The Cultural Geography of *A Masque Presented at Ludlow Castle,* 1634," *Representations* 60 (Autumn 1997): 22–48.

20. Fletcher, *Transcendental Masque,* 193.

21. Shohet, "Figuring Chastity," 157. On the problematics of pinning down an exclusive allegorical meaning of Haemony, see the *Variorum Milton,* vol. 2, part 3, 932–38. Sabrina seems to be somewhat less controversial, most critics recognizing the baptismal elements of her release of the Lady and developing variations on Woodhouse's foundational discussions of the *Maske,* in which Sabrina mediates "divine grace" in the order of nature. However, William A. Oram, developing a proposal of Richard Neuse, links Sabrina to repressed elements of bodily life in the Lady and suggests that Sabrina embodies the "dark forces of the unconscious life of nature . . . when they have received their 'natural' Christian orientation." See Oram, "The Invocation of Sabrina," *Studies in English Literature* 24 (1984): 129; and Neuse, "Metamorphosis and Symbolic Action in *Comus*," *English Literary History* 34, no. 1 (1967): 56. I will give further attention to Sabrina in Chapter 7, "Girl, Interrupted and the Changing Woman." On the problematics of interpretation of symbolism in the poem, see Stanley Fish, "Problem Solving in *Comus*," in *Illustrious Evidence: Approaches to English Literature of the Early Seventeenth Century,* ed. Earl Miner (Berkeley and Los Angeles: University of California Press, 1975), 115–31.

22. Fish observes of the various problems of the *Maske,* "when an explanation is found, it does not disambiguate" the significance of the object, person, or event in question. See "Problem Solving," 126. My disagreement with Fish has to do with his claim that once "the lesson of the double perspective" (126)—temporal and eternal, sensory and spiritual, accidental and essential—has been mastered, the interpretive effort that the poem encourages—and rewards—is drained of importance. Indeed, from Fish's perspective, interpretation would seem to ensnare the reader in the inessential and accidental.

23. Louis Martz suggests that Haemony may be interpreted as poetry itself, in "Music of Comus": "Is it the 'sacred song' that gives one power to penetrate disguises, guard from evil, and rescue from enchantment?" (108). See also Swaim, "Allegorical Poetry," 13; and Heather Dubrow,"The Masquing of Genre in *Comus." Milton Studies* 44 (2005): 72.

24. Nancy Lindheim's smart reading of the Haemony passage "grounds" the meaning of Haemony in this-worldly properties that are not canceled or forgotten by abstracted allegorical readings: "Discussions of haemony that speak exclusively of its allegorical valence run counter to the poesis it embodies." Lindheim, "Pastoral and Masque at Ludlow," *University of Toronto Quarterly* 67, no. 3 (Summer 1998): 659. Lindheim's study of the way in which pastoral elements of

the *Maske* resist the Neoplatonic ascent of its allegory coordinates with Victoria Silver's critique of allegory's inadequacies in "Thoughts in Misbecoming Plight."

25. The crisis of knowledge that motivates the soul-searching of *Lycidas* iterates this same process of textual recovery, only in a more explicitly tragic key. Linda Gregerson describes the formation of saving knowledge in that poem: "The narrator's present grief re-presents and re-processes the secure accumulation of his earlier learning and builds out of that trauma a higher synthesis that makes a future possible. . . . In its pursuit of answers, *Lycidas* acts out the dependency of cognition upon re-cognition" (*Reformation of the Subject,* 150).

26. Hollis summarizes eucharistic readings of Haemony as Christ's blood in "Without Charity," 170. It follows that Sabrina's release of the Lady from her bondage occurs through baptism (170–71).

27. I think specifically of the Father's ethical self-limitation in regard to human freedom as he declares it in *Paradise Lost* 3.124–28; and of his announcement of the metaphysical self-limitation that allows for the creation of a universe out of his substance yet ontologically separate from him (*PL* 7.168–73). This insight was impressed on me by a remarkable essay by Sarah Lawrence undergraduate Kate Frey.

28. Beth Bradburn, studying bodily metaphors and functions in the *Maske* in relation to medical and physiological treatises in the early modern period, observes of this passage, "Metaphorically, then, the Lady generates the smell that eventually heals her." See Bradburn, "Bodily Metaphor and Moral Agency in *A Masque:* A Cognitive Approach," *Milton Studies* 43 (2004): 30.

29. Noting that Thyrsis's name puns on the Bacchic *thyrse,* or wand, Fletcher argues that "Comus, the demonic parody of Dionysian virtue, only pretends to possess the power of benign transformation. Thyrsis, however, has this power" (*Transcendental Masque,* 165–66). Thyrsis's honorific account of the Lady's singing projects this power upon her upon her as well. We could deconstruct his accolade by noting that the power it attributes to the Lady's voice is not so much inherent in the voice itself, but an auditory effect conjured by the description of it. That is, the Attendant Spirit, ever faithful to his instructive task, teaches us how to listen to and to think about the Lady's song. But it is, after all, the Lady's singing that inspires his account. I prefer to read the two vocal performances—the Echo Song and Thyrsis's account of it—as a remarkable duet, creative and interpretive, mutually constitutive, that evidences the very power of music that both pieces celebrate.

30. John Keats, "Ode to a Nightingale," *John Keats: Selected Poems and Letters,* 205–7.

31. Elisabeth A. Frost succinctly notes that the Attendant Spirit "appears as that figure whose superior knowledge guides the young people through this moral trial. After recounting the histories of the various participants—himself, Comus, and the Lady—he serves as a bridge between specatators and masquers, furnished with both the omniscience of a divine observor and the means to participate in the unfolding drama." Frost, "The Didactic *Comus:* Henry Lawes and the Trial of Virtue," *Comitatus* 22 (1991): 90–91.

32. Milton's biographers are generally agreed that Henry Lawes obtained the commission for Milton to script the *Maske,* as he had previously done with *Arcades,* to honor the Dowager Countess of Derby. See Barbara Lewalski, *The Life of John Milton: A Critical Biography* (Oxford: Blackwell Publishers, 2002), 58; John Shawcross, *John Milton: The Self and the World* (Lexington: University of Kentucky Press, 1993), 28; William Riley Parker, *Milton,* 1, 140. Biographers also

concur that the revisions and reorderings of the poem for the performance script approximated by the Bridgewater Manuscript were probably also overseen by Lawes.

33. Franklin R. Baruch, "Milton's *Comus:* Skill, Virtue, and Henry Lawes," *Milton Studies* 5 (1973): 292. I make this claim about the heuristic authority of Lawes as Attendant Spirit while mindful of Victoria Silver's admonition that "the Spirit is . . . a dubious guide to how things mean" ("Thoughts in Misbecoming Plight," 54). I agree with Silver that the seeming allegorical security provided by the Attendant Spirit's explications of characters, events, and objects is frequently inadequate to account for the existential crises of the *Maske*'s plot. But I think that the Attendant Spirit's commentary is intended not to foreclose and settle meaning of these crises for his students (us among them), but to exemplify and encourage modes of imaginative comprehension that, while drawing on interpretive traditions to understand life situations, also make something new of them.

34. Swaim, "Allegorical Poetry," 169.

35. Fletcher, *Transcendental Masque,* 16.

36. Marcus, *Politics of Mirth,* 181.

37. Lewalski, *Life of John Milton,* 58.

38. Ibid., 67; Shawcross, *John Milton,* 314 n. 7.

39. Shawcross, *John Milton,* 59, 70, 189. Lewalski provides a similar estimation of the timing of the several poems: "I think it likely that 'Ad Patrem' was written in the final weeks of 1637 or early 1638, just after publication of *A Maske* and *Lycidas,* or in immediate expectation of their appearance" (*Life of John Milton,* 71). On the basis of her study of the commissioning and the early publication and reception of the *Maske,* Ann Baynes Coiro provides a cautionary estimation of the consolidation of confidence and dedication to prophetic vocation that I am claiming for Milton's composition and early publication of the *Maske.* Noting that Milton's acceptance of the commission from the Bridgewater family indicated his willingness to consider the customary path of the poet to recognition by way of aristocratic patronage, that the original publication of the *Maske* in 1637 was anonymous, and that its author was even suspected to be the Cambridge wit, dramatist, and poet Thomas Randolph, Coiro argues that "in 1634 and in 1637 (and in some ways, even in 1645), Milton's *A Maske Presented at Ludlow Castle* is still the work of an idealistic and ambitious young dramatist, not of a revolutionary prophet with his singing robes around him" ("Anonymous Milton," 621–22).

40. Lewalski neatly sums up the critical estimation of Lawes's achievement: "Lawes along with some others in his generation produced settings that eschewed harmony and counterpoint in favor of recitative and declamatory song, accommodating musical stress and quantity to verbal values so as to set off the poet's words and sense" (*Life of John Milton,* 201). Angus Fletcher explores the parallels to, and possible influences of, Italian opera and music theory on Milton and Lawes's conception of the *Maske* in particular and English music of the period more generally (*Transcendental Masque,* 175–86).

41. This collaboration can be instructively contrasted to the tense rivalry between Ben Jonson and Inigo Jones. Although Jones was not a musician, in Jonson's neo-Aristotelian conception of the masque, Jones's stagecraft was linked with music and dance as ornamental and transitory elements of the genre, in contrast to the poet's essential and lasting work of verse, plot, and character construction. See John Peacock, "Stuart Court Masque," 184–87.

42. Percy Bysshe Shelley, "A Defence of Poetry," in *Shelley's Poetry and*

Prose, ed. Donald H. Reiman and Sharon B. Powers (New York: W. W. Norton, 1977), 508.

43. Shawcross, *John Milton,* 237.
44. Nietzsche, *Birth of Tragedy,* 98.
45. Marcus, *Politics of Mirth,* 181.
46. If we compare the Attendant Spirit's relationship to the Lady, the *Maske*'s protagonist, to the several appearances of his epic precursor, Hermes-Mercury, we find the classical messenger more direct, precise, and even brisk in his management of his duties toward the hero in need. In the *Odyssey,* Hermes appears three times, as divine courier and psychopomp: to demand of Kalypso that she take the leash off Odysseus and provide him the wherewithal for his final journey homeward; to prepare Odysseus for his confrontation with Circe; and to lead the souls of the executed suitors to the underworld. In Virgil's creative revision of Odysseus's erotic entanglements, Mercury appears in the *Aeneid* with the abrupt and uncompromising command that Aeneas shake off the effeminate slackness of his affair with Dido and get under way toward the fulfillment of his divinely ordained mission. In each of these cases, the god appears directly and undisguised, issues a demand or provides necessary information in a businesslike way, and then leaves the messy business of mortals to be dispatched as efficiently as possible; he clears the way for decisive action. Milton's Attendant Spirit adopts more of the tutelary strategies of intervention that Homer had assigned for Athena as Telemachus's and Odysseus's guide and support, appearing in disguise and providing detailed on-the-spot coaching for the dilemma ahead, then leaving the risk and the accomplishment in the mortal's hands and will. Yet despite his concern for the Lady's safety, the Attendant Spirit never appears directly to her or provides resources and instruction for her as she approaches her own ordeal of erotic captivity and temptation.
47. Silver, "Thoughts in Misbecoming Plight," 48.
48. Stephen Orgel has fun tallying up the Attendant Spirit's miscues and inadequacies to the tasks at hand in "Case for Comus," 32–33. But he does not seem to follow through with an adequate explanation, in part because he wants to problematize the moral opposition between Comus and the Attendant Spirit. Orgel joins Victoria Silver in his suspicions about the Attendant Spirit, but his suspicions have to do with what he takes to be the contradictions of patriarchy, whereas Silver's have to do with what she explains as the contradictions of allegorical representation.
49. Samuel Johnson lays down the gauntlet with his observations that "as a drama it is deficient. The action is not probable." Johnson proceeds to critique nondramatic inconsistencies in speech and dialogue as "inelegantly splendid, and tediously instructive" (*Lives of the English Poets,* ed. G. B. Hill [Oxford: Clarendon Press, 1905], 1:167–69). Among modern critics, E. M. W. Tillyard notes the improbabilities of action and inconsistencies in style (*Milton* [London: Chatto & Windus, 1966], 66–75); and Don Cameron Allen more ferociously critiques the poem on every level as "a Failure in Artistic Compromise" (*The Harmonious Vision: Studies in Milton's Poetry* [Baltimore: Johns Hopkins University Press, 1954], 24–40).
50. See, among others, Demaray, *Milton and the Masque Tradition;* Brown, *John Milton's Aristocratic Entertainments;* McGuire, *Milton's Puritan Masque;* and Treip, "Stuart Masque Connection," 83–89.
51. William A. Oram notes the oddity of the *Maske*'s seemingly unstable structure prior to the invocation of Sabrina: "The first eight hundred lines of the masque stress its uncertainties formally by an avoidance of closure. Scenes are not re-

solved: they are suspended or interrupted." Oram argues that this makes the transformation scene of Sabrina's arrival all the more spectacular and sublime ("Invocation of Sabrina," 122). Elisabeth Frost neatly resolves some of the evidences of uncertain structure in the *Maske* by dividing the structure into two parts: "The first is devoted almost entirely to a discussion of virtue and its relation to choice, reason, and trial, while the second, beginning with the invocation of Sabrina, involves magic and spells, focusing on song, dance, and lyric verse." In this way, Frost argues, Milton demonstrates the saving complementarity of reason and the arts of imagination in the education of the children in virtue. See "Didactic Comus," 88–89.

52. McGuire, *Milton's Puritan Masque*, 67.
53. Brown, *John Milton's Aristocratic Entertainments*, 57.
54. Silver, "Thoughts in Misbecoming Plight," 70.
55. A feminist rejoinder to this claim would be that Milton himself is of course the male who controls and manipulates the mysteries of the Lady's initiation. My hope is that the larger argument of this book will demonstrate that Milton scripts a text for the Lady's freedom rather than her subjection and that Milton invests his own interests in the voice and the acts of the Lady, so that, insofar as he enters the *Maske* as a spectral presence among the performers, it is primarily in identification with the character of the Lady.
56. LaFontaine, *Initiation*, 118.
57. Ibid., 14–15.

Chapter 3. Tragedy in Translation

1. See Christopher Kendrick, "Milton and Sexuality," 58–59; Michael Wilding, "Milton's 'A Masque Presented at Ludlow Castle, 1634': Theatre and Politics on the Border," *Milton Quarterly* 21, no. 4 (December 1987): 35–51; Philip Schwyzer, "Purity and Danger," 22–48.
2. See Marcus, "Milieu of Milton's *Comus*," 293, 319–21.
3. Taafe, "Michaelmas," 257–62; Hunter, "Liturgical Context," 11–15.
4. Heather Dubrow notes Milton's fascination with "the mental geography of ominous borderlands," particularly generic and political ones, in "Masquing of Genre," 79.
5. Turner, *Dramas, Fields, and Metaphors*, 232.
6. Eliade, *Rites and Symbols*, 36–37.
7. Turner, *Dramas, Fields, and Metaphors*, 233.
8. Swaim, "Allegorical Poetry," 181.
9. Insofar as the *Maske* provides the social occasion and cultural passage for the fifteen-year-old Alice, the Lady, into the status of marriageability, sexuality necessarily enters the field of her concern as both a physiological and a social pressure. The attending anxiety and uncertainty would perhaps be deepened by a paradox noted by the anthropologist Patty Jo Watson in discussing this paper with me: although the children of the noble classes in the medieval and early modern periods typically married earlier than middle-class and upper-class children do presently, their physical maturation occurred later than it does now.
10. John Leonard's rigorous critique of William Kerrigan's Freudian analysis of the Lady's "root-bound virtue" (in *Sacred Complex*, 55) stands as a warning against excessively sexualizing readings of her plight. See Leonard, "Saying 'No'

to Freud: Milton's *A Mask* and Sexual Assault," *Milton Quarterly* 25 (1991): 129–40. My argument is not, like Kerrigan's, about what her desire denied does to the Lady (paralyze her), but what the Lady does with her desire acknowledged (strengthen and define herself).

11. Eliade, *Rites and Symbols*, 3.
12. Turner, *Dramas, Fields, and Metaphors*, 273–74.
13. The case for the philosophic consistency at the expense of the dramatic credibility of the dialogues in the *Maske*, with a consequent thinning out of character, is made by John Demaray, *Milton and the Masque Tradition;* and George William Smith, Jr., "Milton's Revisions and the Design of *Comus*," *English Literary History* 46, no. 1 (Spring 1979): 56–80.
14. When Milton allows soliloquy the dark meandering undertow of Jacobean drama, it is to construct his most Shakespearean and unredeemable—and therefore fascinating—character, Satan. In *Paradise Lost,* dramatic soliloquy is a signal flag of fallenness, the sign of the character's alienation from the God-given dialogic structures of creation that constitute and enlarge identity in the epic. When Eve and Adam turn inward to converse with themselves (*PL* 9.744, 9.895), we know that they are in trouble. David Robertson insightfully studies the self-creating processes of Miltonic soliloquies in "Soliloquy and Self in Milton's Major Poems," in *Of Poetry and Politics: New Essays on Milton and His World,* ed. Paul G. Stanwood (Binghamton, NY: Medieval and Renaissance Texts and Studies, 1995), 59–77. Robertson's description of the resistance to and transformation of panic, doubt, and despair in the soliloquies of Mary and of Jesus in *Paradise Regained* coordinates with my argument, implying that the Lady is an early type, in Milton's literary career, of their heroic self-reckoning.
15. This moment of visionary recognition anticipates a crucial moment in English Romantic lyricism, when the poet in Keats's "Ode to Psyche" declares to the goddess: "thy lucent fans, / Fluttering among the faint Olympians, / I see, and sing, by my own eyes inspired" (41–43). *Selected Poems*, 204.
16. "'Form' is the remarkable key word, since chastity is a design, the divine principle which Spenser had celebrated in the third book of *The Faerie Queene,* in the myth of Adonis and his gardens" (Fletcher, *Transcendental Masque,* 169).
17. Swaim, "Allegorical Poetry," 176, 184–85.
18. Martz, *Poet of Exile,* 8.
19. Turner, *Dramas, Fields, and Metaphors,* 274.
20. Several instructive essays engage Milton's original treatment of Ovidian myths of endangered women. See Kathleen Wall, "*A Mask Presented at Ludlow Castle:* The Armor of Logos," in *Milton and the Idea of Woman,* ed. Julia M. Walker (Urbana: University of Illinois Press, 1988), 52–65; Mary Loeffelholz, "Two Masques," 25–42; and Joseph M. Ortiz, "'The Reforming of Reformation': Theatrical, Ovidian, and Musical Figuration in Milton's *Mask,*" *Milton Studies* 44 (2005): 84–111. See also Richard DuRocher's foundational study, *Milton and Ovid* (Ithaca, NY: Cornell University Press, 1985), and Lynn Enterline's recent study of sexual violence and poetic voice in Ovid and his influence on Petrarch and Shakespeare, in *The Rhetoric of the Body from Ovid to Shakespeare* (Cambridge: Cambridge University Press, 2000).
21. Swaim, "Allegorical Poetry," 182.
22. Leonard Barkan discusses the pathology and vocal reflectivity of Echo in *The Gods Made Flesh: Metamorphosis and the Pursuit of Paganism* (New Haven, CT: Yale University Press, 1986), 48. Noelle Caskey provides a Jungian review and synthesis of contemporary analyses of anorexia that is useful in reflecting on

Ovid's Echo, in "Interpreting *Anorexia Nervosa,*" in *The Female Body in Western Culture: Contemporary Perspectives,* ed. Susan Rubin Suleiman (Cambridge, MA: Harvard University Press, 1986), 175–89.

23. George Sandys, *Ovid's Metamorphoses English'd, Mythologized, and Represented in Figures,* ed. Karl K. Hulley and Stanley T. Vandershall (Oxford, 1632; repr., Lincoln: University of Nebraska Press, 1970), 156. Further references and quotations from Sandys' edition will be cited as *OME* parenthetically in the text.

24. As noted earlier, this analysis of the *Maske* periodically draws upon the psychoanalytic typology of the Imaginary and the Symbolic orders developed by Jacques Lacan, particularly in *The Language of the Self.* For the sake of this discussion, admittedly oversimplifying Lacan's account, I note that the subject's involvement in the Imaginary order, associated with the visual field and the ever-changing regions of erotic fantasy and self-image, derives from the preoedipal relation to the mother; the subject's insertion into the Symbolic order, associated with language and the order of social law, comes out of the child's recognition of and confrontation with the father.

25. Stephen Orgel signals the danger here: "[I]t is difficult to see it as anything but a subversive moment, introducing self-absorption and a dangerous vanity into the purity of the Lady's character. . . . [S]he is surrounded with—or creates for herself—a world of versions of the self, of solipsism" ("Case for Comus," 38–39). Ronald Corthell thoughtfully studies both the dangers and the potentials of the narcissistic elements in the Lady's self-imaging and relation to the males who surround her in "Go Ask Alice: Daughter, Patron, and Poet in *A Mask Presented at Ludlow Castle,*" *Milton Studies* 44 (2005): 117–20.

26. William Blake, "The Book of Thel," in *Complete Poetry and Prose,* 4–8.

27. Louise Simons discusses the irony of Comus's materialization as an instance of "a system of false echoes, which Milton uses to cheat the ear of the unwary auditor." Simons, "'And Heaven Gates Ore My Head,'" 68–69.

28. C. L. Barber, "*A Mask Presented at Ludlow Castle:* The Masque as a Masque," in *The Lyric and Dramatic Milton,* ed. Joseph H. Summers (New York: Columbia University Press, 1965), 53.

29. See, e.g., the parodic scene involving Echo in Jonson's *Cynthia's Revels,* 1.2–3, in *Ben Jonson, IV,* ed. C. H. Herford, and Percy and Evelyn Simpson (Oxford: Clarendon Press, 1932), 48–53; the monitory echo in John Webster's *The Duchess of Malfi* i (5.3.1–43), in *Drama of the English Renaissance, II: The Stuart Period,* ed. Russell A. Fraser and Norman Rabkin (New York: Macmillan, 1976), 475–515; the providential echo of George Herbert's "Paradise" and "Heaven," in *George Herbert and Henry Vaughan,* ed. Louis L. Martz (Oxford: Oxford University Press, 1986), 119, 171.

30. John Hollander, *The Untuning of the Sky: Ideas of Music in English Poetry 1500–1700* (Princeton, NJ: Princeton University Press, 1961), 323. Angus Fletcher develops a typically suggestive consideration of the literary aspects of "the principle of Echo" in *Transcendental Masque,* 198–209.

31. Swaim, "Allegorical Poetry," 194.

32. Fletcher, *Transcendental Masque,* 203.

33. For a brief account of the Bridgewater and Trinity Manuscript versions of the last line of the Lady's song and their implications, see Milton *Variorum,* vol. 2, part 3, 894.

34. "Unexpressive" is a key word for the celestial music inapprehensible to mortal ears in the Nativity Ode, 116; and in "Lycidas," 176.

35. Kathleen Swaim observes of the associative identifications in the *Maske,*

"All the female figures are in fact forms of the same psyche—Psyche herself (1005) is the final one—and figure forth the Lady's psyche as masques and allegories generally represent ideas and spiritual action" ("Allegorical Poetry," 182). Simons, among others, notes that the Lady's homecoming in the *Maske* allegorically prefigures her celestial destination ("'And Heaven Gates,'" 91).

36. DuRocher, *Milton and Ovid*, 50.
37. Barkan, *Gods Made Flesh*, 247.
38. Ibid., 245.
39. Fletcher, *Transcendental Masque*, 203.
40. John Demaray makes the case that the threat posed by Comus to the Lady is insignificant because of the symbolic ritual oppositions of the masque structure and the fixed mind of the Lady (*Milton and the Masque Tradition*, 89–90). But Milton's development of the *Maske* in the direction of ethical drama requires its audience and readership to take the danger embodied in Comus seriously.
41. On various Renaissance strategies of interpretation of classical myths, see Jean Seznec, *The Survival of the Pagan Gods: The Mythological Tradition and Its Place in Renaissance Humanism and Art*, trans. B. F. Sessions (Princeton, NJ: Princeton University Press, 1972); Edgar Wind, *Pagan Mysteries in the Renaissance* (New York: W. W. Norton, 1968); DeWitt T. Starnes and Ernest William Talbert, *Classical Myth and Legend in Renaissance Dictionaries: A Study of Renaissance Dictionaries in Their Relation to the Classical Learning of Contemporary English Writers* (Westport, CT: Greenwood Press, 1973).
42. See Barkan, *Gods Made Flesh*, 94–136, on medieval and Renaissance revisionary exegeses of Ovid.
43. Milton's objections to passive acceptance of received wisdom and authoritative opinion are too frequent and too consistent to enumerate. The great declaration on behalf of freedom of thought is, of course, *Areopagitica* (Hughes, 716–49). His critique of "implicit faith" and insistence on liberty in scriptural interpretation appears in the prologue of *De Doctrina Christiana* (Hughes, 901–3).
44. DuRocher, *Milton and Ovid*, 19.
45. For overviews of Milton's education in and invention with classical mythology, see Davis P. Harding, *Milton and the Renaissance Ovid* (Urbana: University of Illinois Press, 1946); Douglas Bush, *Mythology and the Renaissance Tradition in English Poetry* (New York: W. W. Norton, 1963), 260–97; and DuRocher, *Milton and Ovid*.
46. T. S. Eliot, *The Waste Land*, 97–103, in *The Waste Land and Other Poems* (New York: Harcourt Brace, 1987), 54.
47. Jonathan Goldberg, *Voice Terminal Echo: Postmodernism and English Renaissance Texts*, (New York: Methuen, 1986), 135. Lynn Enterline analyzes the gender differentiation that occurs in Ovid's recurring versions of the moment when the poetic voice originates from a violated body: "One of several kinds of violation—rape, metamorphosis, death—are nonetheless required of beautiful female forms if male voices are to be raised in song" (*Rhetoric of the Body*, 91). Enterline stresses, however, that Ovid's poem cultivates voices that resist and destabilize its ostensible efforts to privilege "the male rhetoric of vocal animation" (*Rhetoric of the Body*, 79). In the case of this topos in Milton's *Maske*, I think that Milton works against male gendering of the poetic voice in several ways, including his own projective identification with the Lady, his subversion of the specious poetic and rhetorical values articulated by the libertine Comus, and his dramatization of the Lady as exemplary poet who recovers and "translates" the lost voices of Ovidian heroines like Echo and Philomela.

48. Lieb, *Culture of Violence,* 9.

49. Sophocles, *Oedipus at Colonus,* trans. Robert Fitzgerald, in *The Oedipus Cycle,* trans. and ed. Dudley Fitts and Robert Fitzgerald (New York: Harcourt, Brace, and World, 1969). Citations from this translation appear parenthetically by page numbers in the text.

50. On Sabrina as a figure representing and exemplifying justice as a tutelary figure for the Earl of Bridgewater, see Marcus, "Milieu of Milton's *Comus,*" 293–327. Philip Schwyzer examines Milton's adaptation of the Sabrina legends to the celebration of English nationalism in "Purity and Danger," 22–48. Aeschylus's *Eumenides* dramatizes Athena's "translation" of the Furies, from primordial goddesses avenging crimes of blood against kin to beneficent powers protecting the institutions of rational human justice in Athens.

Chapter 4. Double Trouble

1. Turner, *Dramas, Fields, and Metaphors,* 239.
2. Richards, *Chisungu,* 122.
3. R. H. Singleton studies the influence of Puteanus's *Comus* on Milton's *Maske* in "Milton's *Comus* and the *Comus* of Erycius Puteanus," *PMLA* 68 (1943): 949–57. More recently, Ross Leasure studies the relation of the *Maske* to Puteanus, with particular attention to homoerotic threat, in "Milton's Queer Choice: Comus as Castlehaven." *Milton Quarterly* 36, no. 2 (May 2002): 63–86. Although the direct influence of Jonson's Comus in *Pleasure Reconciled to Virtue* upon Milton's conception is debatable, since Jonson's masque was not published and publicly available until 1640, John Demaray suggestively notes both characters "share the same dedication to libertine wantonness" (*Milton and the Masque Tradition,* 87). Despite the absence of positive documentary evidence, is hard to believe that Milton, given his literary ambition and his favorable connection to Henry Lawes, the court insider deeply involved in masquing culture, would be ignorant of Jonson's invention.
4. McGuire, *Milton's Puritan Masque,* 42.
5. Leonora Leet Brodwin makes the interesting argument that Comus is so moved by the Lady's song to Echo that he intends to "reclaim his own better nature from its profligate indulgence through marriage to her. . . . He tempts her to renounce not premarital chastity for promiscuity but the ideal of virginity for that of marriage" (Brodwin, "Milton and the Renaissance Circe," *Milton Studies* 6 [1974]: 48–50). This strikes me as a charming but far-fetched premise in light of Comus's sinister behavior both before and after his testimony to her song (244–65), but it is ironically consonant with what I consider Comus's ritual role as a "mock bridegroom."
6. Pauline Réage, *The Story of O,* trans. Sabine d'Estrée (New York: Ballantine Press, 1973); Stanley Kubrick, dir., *Eyes Wide Shut* (1999).
7. Christopher Kendrick suggestively interprets the Lady's fixed silence in her chair as a sign of Milton's displacement of her father's, and thus the king's, presiding authority ("Milton and Sexuality," 58–61).
8. On Jonson's neoclassical theoretical and dramaturgical influences, see Peacock, "Stuart Court Masque," 183–208. Peacock neatly demonstrates that, strangely enough, tragedy, in its Aristotelian codification, provided the structural

blueprint and theoretical basis for the Stuart masque as Ben Jonson formulated and defended it.

9. Lieb, *Culture of Violence,* 9.

10. Friedrich Nietzsche, *The Birth of Tragedy and The Case of Wagner,* trans. Walter Kauffman (New York: Random House, 1967). All references to *The Birth of Tragedy* are to this edition and are cited parenthetically as *BT* in the text.

11. Richard Halpern, "Puritanism and Maenadism in *A Mask,*" in *Rewriting the Renaissance: The Discourses of Sexual Difference in Early Modern Europe,* ed. Margaret Ferguson, Maureen Quilligan, and Nancy J. Vickers (Chicago: University of Chicago Press, 1986), 90.

12. René Girard, *Violence and the Sacred,* trans. Patrick Gregory (Baltimore: Johns Hopkins University Press, 1977), 162–63.

13. Other crucial poetic sites evidencing Milton's anxieties about bacchic threats of dismemberment include "Lycidas," 58–63, and *Paradise Lost* 7.32–39. See Lieb, *Culture of Violence,* 46–51.

14. "[*Sparagmos*] is the tearing apart of a live animal victim; [*omophagia*] is the eating of an animal's raw and warm flesh, thus ingesting the god, who is reborn inside one. In that act, which is always described in the ancient texts as one of joy, the animal was felt to be Dionysos himself, from whom his worshippers took sudden godlike ecstasy and strength." Robert Bagg, "Introduction," *The Bakkhai by Euripides* (Amherst: University of Massachusetts Press, 1978), 2. Nancy Lindheim suggests the relevance of Euripides' *Hippolytus* to the Lady's story: Hippolytus prefigures the Lady as a beautiful youth devoted to chastity in a way that figures, in Lindheim's interpretation, as a dangerous self-regard ("Pastoral and Masque," 653–54). We might extend Lindheim's account to observe how Hippolytus's fate resembles that of Pentheus: his indifference and resistance to the claims of a god of desire (Venus) eventuates in his tragic destruction.

15. Nietzsche's account of the dismemberment and regeneration of Dionysus derives from the Orphic interpretation of the myth; see M. S. Silk and J. P. Stern, *Nietzsche on Tragedy* (Cambridge: Cambridge University Press, 1987), 175–78. A suggestive correspondence to Nietzsche's allegory appears in the allegorization of Ovid by George Sandys, who acknowledges that Bacchus was regarded by his devotees as "the father of generation" (*OME,* 153). Sandys elaborates an analogous explanation of Circe, Bacchus's partner in Milton's genealogical myth, in terms of a cosmic process of disintegration and renewal (653–54).

16. Nietzsche notices the reconciliation of the two powers as "the most important moment in the history of the Greek cult" (*BT,* 39). The Pythia's prologue in Aeschylus's *Eumenides* links Phoebus and Dionysus as presiding spirits in the Apollinian shrine at Delphi (Aeschylus, *The Oresteia,* trans. Robert Fagles [New York: Bantam Books, 1975], 255–56). Apollo and Dionysus were the most powerful of the gods honored in ancient Thebes, and in the deme of Ikarion "Dionysos was closely associated with the Pythian Apollo" (Marcel Detienne, *Dionsysos at Large,* trans. Arthur Goldhammer [Cambridge, MA: Harvard University Press, 1989], 18, 30). See also Andrew Stewart, "Dionysos at Delphi: The Pediments of the Sixth Temple of Apollo and Religious Reform in the Age of Alexander," in *Macedonia and Greece in Late Classical and Hellenistic Times,* ed. Beryl Barr-Sharrar and Eugene Borza (Washington, DC: National Gallery of Art, 1982), 211.

17. T. S. Eliot, "Burnt Norton," in *Four Quartets* (New York: Harcourt Brace Jovanovich, 1971), 14.

18. Silk and Stern, *Nietzsche on Tragedy,* 175.

19. Kathleen Swaim, "Lycidas and the Dolphins of Apollo," *Journal of English and Germanic Philology* 72, no. 8 (July 1973): 340–49.

20. As a heavenly messenger, the Attendant Spirit anticipates Raphael in *Paradise Lost* as a Mercury figure; see Swaim, "Allegorical Poetry," 170–71. Yet Mercury and Apollo are themselves suggestively doubled. Mercury as Apollo's brother performs services on his behalf, and in effect speaks for him, most notably in the prologue to Euripides' *Ion.*

21. Matthew Steggle, "'The Tragical Part': Milton's Masque and Euripides," *Classical and Modern Literature* 20, no. 1 (2000): 18–36; William Riley Parker, *Milton's Debt to Greek Tragedy in* Samson Agonistes (Hamden, CT: Archon Books, 1963), 295–96.

22. Swaim, "Allegorical Poetry," 170.

23. Robert Hoopes, *Right Reason in the English Renaissance* (Cambridge, MA: Harvard University Press, 1962).

24. Bagg, "Introduction," 7–8.

25. This mythoclastic strategy parallels on a large scale the "creative iconoclasm" which Lana Cable studies in *Carnal Rhetoric: Milton's Iconoclasm and the Poetics of Desire* (Durham, NC: Duke University Press, 1995). Milton disrupts what Cable would call "the affective and cognitive complacency" (38) encouraged by conventional allegoresis and so requires his readers—including the Lady as reader of her own circumstance—actively to reconstruct the meaning of the myths, and thereby "change the terms of our engagement with the world" (38). Joseph Ortiz analyzes Milton's disruption of conventional allegorical interpretations of Ovid in the *Maske,* in order to test the adequacy of rigorous Puritan antitheatrical doctrine; but Ortiz claims, in contrast to my argument here, that these disruptions serve the destabilizing interests of Comus, the master theatrical artist. See Ortiz, "'The Reforming of Reformation,'" 90–96.

26. Milton's Samson will be another carrier of his culture's hopes who is pulled into the Dionysian vortex of tragedy, but the trajectory of his tragic career as hero follows more closely on that described by Nietzsche. This note will sketch some pertinent comparisons between the *Maske* as Milton's "virtual tragedy" and the full-blown tragedy of *Samson Agonistes,* with its explicit deployment of Greek prototypes and Aristotelian structures. Samson certainly is the Dionysian type of hero described by Nietzsche, displaying "the mask of a fighting hero, and entangled, as it were, in the net of the individual will" (*BT,* 73). The *Maske*'s structure indeed bears closer analogies to Greek tragic prototypes, anticipating *Samson Agonistes* in this respect, than to Jacobean and Caroline drama. It observes unities of plot, time, and place; it includes soliloquies, deploys stichomythia (277–90), and restricts dialogue to two characters in any given scene. It observes the framing structures of tragedy in the opening and closing speeches of the Attendant Spirit, and alternates, to some degree, dramatic dialogue with choral commentary.

The Lady prefigures the tragic Samson in several respects: her political status as exemplary to a nation; her bondage and subjection to an opposing power that oscillates between seduction and sparagmatic threat; her clarification and solidification of self-knowledge through the dialectical challenge of her adversary; her liberating access to an interiority opening secretly toward the divine but withheld from the immediate experience of other characters and the public audience; her achievement, in the eyes of her family and her society, of everlasting praise. Whereas the Lady becomes in effect the *antitype* whose figure and story complete and translate the stories of the various tragic victims who prefigure her, Samson is an anticipatory *type* of Christ (and, Nietzsche would say, of Dionysus), although whether he is a negative or positive type remains a matter of critical debate.

27. In the agonistic hero Heracles, persecuted relentlessly by his stepmother Hera, Philip Slater discloses a paradigm of the conflicted relation between mothers and sons in classical Athens and its crucial impact on cultural and political expression, including tragedy. *The Glory of Hera: Greek Mythology and the Greek Family* (Boston: Beacon Press, 1968), 337–96. A number of tragic episodes of myth highlight the violent tension between mother and child as the driving force of tragedy. In Euripides' *Ion,* for instance, Creusa nearly destroys her own son Ion through tragic misrecognition; in the background of this crisis, staged at Delphi—the seat of the divinatory powers of both Apollo and Dionysus—lies Creusa's original attempt to destroy the infant Ion through exposure. Euripides's Medea destroys her children in agonized retaliation against Jason's faithlessness. In Ovid, the tragedy of Philomela and Procne's slaughter of Procne's innocent son Itys is played out under the mass hysteria of Bacchic celebration. In the *Oresteia,* Aeschylus dramatizes the reversal of this violence of mother against child in Orestes' ritual murder of his mother Clytemnestra, an action compelled and sponsored by Apollo. In their contrasting treatments of *Electra,* Sophocles and Euripides refocused the matricidal plot on the figure of Orestes' grieving and furious sister. John Rumrich notices the pattern of conflicted and violent mother-son relationships in tragedy, and its linkage to the intensity of the bond between Comus and Circe; see Rumrich, *Milton Unbound,* 82.

28. For overview of the significance of the Circe myth in Milton's *Maske,* see especially Brodwin, "Milton and the Renaissance Circe," 21–83; and Rosemond Tuve, *Images and Themes in Five Poems by Milton* (Cambridge, MA: Harvard Press, 1957), 130. Consistent with the Renaissance allegorizations of her, Erich Neumann analyzes Circe as the "young witch" formation of the Goddess archetype, who lures people to the transformation and disintegration of the psyche: she is one of the negative manifestations of primordial goddesses in whom "the character of enchantment leading to doom is dominant." See Neumann, *The Great Mother: An Analysis of the Archetype,* trans. Ralph Mannheim (Princeton, NJ: Princeton University Press, 1973), 81, 288.

29. Inigo Jones, notes for Aurelian Townshend, *Tempe Restored,* in *Court Masques: Jacobean and Caroline Entertainments, 1605–1640,* ed. David Lindley (Oxford: Oxford University Press, 1995), 163.

30. On the relation of *Comus* to *Tempe Restored,* see especially Demaray, *Milton and the Masque Tradition,* 79–83, and Treip, "Stuart Masque Connection," 83–89.

31. Brodwin shows that the Homeric myth afforded Renaissance writers a more complex set of temptations than the standard allegory of sensual entrapment. Brodwin's close analysis of the Circe episode in *Odyssey* 10 reveals that, beyond the sensual embrutement of his men, Circe threatens Odysseus with a potential "unmanning" through sexual self-indulgence and a spiritual enervation through idle "carefree joy" (24–25). As Brodwin demonstrates, Comus's menu of pleasure combines and intermixes these several types of temptation (46–54).

32. Sir Thomas Browne, *Religio Medici,* in *Seventeenth-Century Verse and Prose, Volume One: 1600–1660,* ed. Helen C. White, Ruth C. Wallerstein, Ricardo Quintana, and A. B. Chambers (New York: Macmillan, 1971), 346.

33. Eliade, *Rites and Symbols,* 36–37.

34. Leah Marcus demonstrates that Comus's invitation to revelry would serve the interests of the Crown and of Archbishop Laud's Church, by promoting "inno-

cent" festivities of the sort encouraged by the reissuing of the *Book of Sports* in 1633. See Marcus, "Milton's Anti-Laudian Masque," 169–212.

35. Rosemond Tuve observes that in Comus's vision, the universal process of existence is purposeless: "the vast skiey system is nothing but one grand and idiotic whirligig" (*Images and Themes,* 144).

36. Yeats, "Sailing to Byzantium," *Collected Poems,* 191.

37. Fredric Jameson argues that polarization of experiential complexities is a feature of the Imaginary register in Lacan's account of the psyche; as will be seen, this corresponds to my own assessment of Comus's entrapment in and promotion of the Imaginary. See Jameson, "Imaginary and the Symbolic," 338–95.

38. William Shakespeare, *A Midsummer Night's Dream,* ed. Wolfgang Clemen (New York: Signet, 1963). Subsequent reference to *A Midsummer Night's Dream,* cited parenthetically as *MND* in the text, will be to this edition. William Shakespeare, *Hamlet,* ed. Edward Hubler (New York: Signet, 1963). Each text treats the status of its supernatural spirits ambiguously. Although Oberon insists that "we are spirits of a different sort" than the nightbound spirits of evil (3.2.388), both the Faeries of *A Midsummer Night's Dream* and Hamlet's father's Ghost confine themselves to nocturnal activity.

39. Oram nicely analyzes the prosody and effects of this passage: "The closest passage to this one in Milton's earlier verse is the exaggerated, parodic exordium of *L'Allegro;* in both there is a pleonastic over-statement, a heavy-handedness which contrasts with the language of the rest of the work. . . . The passage is a special effect in the language of the masque, a stylistic mimicry in exaggeratedly crude verse of a mind dominated by its own uncontrolled desires" ("Invocation of Sabrina," 127).

40. On ex officio outbursts of rural lawlessness during Michaelmas festivities, see James Taaffe, "Michaelmas,' 257–62. On Milton's critical opposition to the official toleration and encouragement of "holiday sports" by the regime of Charles I, see Leah Marcus, *Politics of Mirth,* 169–212.

41. See Allen Mandelbaum, trans., *The Metamorphoses of Ovid* (New York: Harcourt Brace, 1993), 215–21. Medea's invocation of Hecate is preparatory and essential to the grisly blood rites of her black magic.

42. Oram provides an incisive treatment of the invocation of Cotytto as a perverse and dangerous fertility ritual that parodically prefigures the salvific summons to Sabrina in the *Maske*'s transformation scene. See "Invocation of Sabrina," 126–27. The "Teeth Mother" is Robert Bly's designation of the Terrible Mother of Neumann's archetypal analysis. See Neumann, *Great Mother,* 147–73; and Robert Bly, "The Teeth Mother Naked at Last," in *Sleepers Joining Hands* (New York: Harper and Row, 1973).

43. Nancy Lindheim notices this ecological breakdown, in "Pastoral and Masque," 651.

44. Fletcher, *Transcendental Masque,* 245–46.

45. Kerrigan, *Sacred Complex,* 53.

46. Good starting points for an overview of the nature of Nature in Milton's poetry are William G. Madsen, "The Idea of Nature in Milton's Poetry," in *Three Studies in the Renaissance: Sidney, Jonson, Milton,* Yale Studies in English 138 ed. Richard B. Young et. al. (New Haven, CT: Yale University Press), 181–283; and more recently, Diane Kelsey McColley, "Beneficent Hierarchies: Reading Milton Greenly," in *Spokesperson Milton: Voices in Contemporary Criticism,* ed. Charles W. Durham and Kristin P. McColgan (Selinsgrove, PA: Susquehanna University Press, 1994), 231–48. For the conceptualization of Nature in Milton's

Maske, see A. S. P. Woodhouse's foundational argument, "The Argument of Milton's *Comus,*" *University of Toronto Quarterly* 11 (1941–42): 46–71; Joan Bennett, "Virgin Nature in *Comus*" *Milton Studies* 23 (1987): 21–32; and James Andrew Clark, "Milton *Naturans,* Milton *Naturata:* The Debate Over Nature in *A Maske Presented at Ludlow,*" *Milton Studies* 20 (1984): 3–25. Relevant also is Barbara Lewalski's essay, "Innocence and Experience in Milton's Eden," in *New Essays on Paradise Lost,* ed. Thomas Kranidas (Berkeley and Los Angeles: University of California Press, 1969), 80–117. Lewalski beautifully describes how Adam and Eve's ongoing efforts to transform the bourgeoning virgin wilderness into the garden space of Eden corresponds to the dynamic cultivation of selfhood and relationship that makes them human and images of the Creator.

47. Carrithers observes, "[Comus] views the whole cosmos in consumer-technocratic terms, and sees no ruling Father but only a weltering race between appetites and the occasions and fruits of appetite" "Milton's Ludlow Mask," 36).

48. See Anthony Wilden's commentary on Lacan's Imaginary and Symbolic, in *Language of the Self,* especially 161–66, 185–88. See also Fredric Jameson, "Imaginary and the Symbolic"; and Joseph H. Smith, *Arguing with Lacan: Ego Psychology and Language* (New Haven, CT: Yale University Press, 1991), 95–106, 119–22.

49. Lacan, *Language of the Self,* 31.

50. Jameson, "Imaginary and the Symbolic," 378.

51. Carol Scheidenhelm succinctly observes, "Although Comus enters in to the society of the Other and interacts with its members, Lacan would consider him dysfunctional because of Comus' refusal to accept the authority of the language of the Other." Scheidenhelm, "'Heav'n Hath Timely Tri'd [Her] Youth': Self-Knowledge Through Language in Milton's *Comus,*" *Renaissance and Reformation/Renaissance et Réforme* 27, no. 3 (1992), 60.

52. Homer, *The Odyssey of Homer,* trans. Richmond Lattimore (New York: Harper & Row, 1967).

53. For an analysis of the melancholy that haunts Menelaos's magnificent palace and its relation to the temptation of immortal ease, see William Anderson, "Calypso and Elysium," in *Essays on the Odyssey,* ed. Charles Taylor (Bloomington: Indiana University Press, 1963), 73–86.

54. George William Smith, Jr., makes the case that Comus is not a very competent seducer because Milton's revisions of the *Maske* de-emphasize the temptation element in Comus's exchange with the Lady in order to sharpen the differences between them into a debate. See "Milton's Revisions," 56–80.

55. James Andrew Clark notes Comus's adaptation to his own purposes of Despayre's seduction of the Redcrosse Knight, in "Milton *Naturans,* Milton *Naturata,*" 26.

56. Brown, *John Milton's Aristocratic Entertainments,* 64–65.

57. Turner, *Forest of Symbols,* 105–6.

58. Ibid., 106.

59. Brown, *John Milton's Aristocratic Entertainments,* 73, 88.

60. Eugene Cunnar argues that "the male myth of a sexual Golden Age provided seventeenth-century poets with a means to construct fantasies designed to secure their power over women as it alleviated male sexual anxieties." See "Fantasizing a Sexual Golden Age in Seventeenth-Century Poetry," in *Renaissance Discourses of Desire,* ed. Claude J. Summers and Ted-Larry Pebworth (Columbia: University of Missouri Press, 1993), 204. For the emergence of challenging female voices in the tradition of erotic lyric, see, in the same volume, Achsah Guibbory,

"Sexual Politics/Political Sex: Seventeenth-Century Love Poetry," 206–22; and Arlene Steibel, "Subversive Sexuality: Masking the Erotic in Poems by Katherine Philips and Aphra Behn," 223–36. Behn's comic "The Disappointment" is a particularly amusing deflation of libertine sexual presumption. Although Philips's *encomia* to female friendship and Behn's parodies of masculine eroticism provide vigorous female alternatives to the male sex-talk of which Comus is a master, they nevertheless operate within the presumptions and conventions of the courtly rhetoric of desire and the cavalier rhetoric of friendship that Milton's Lady repudiates.

61. See Bennett, "Virgin Nature in *Comus*," 25. At this stage in the argument of the *Maske*, the Lady represents, according to James Andrew Clark, "nature *naturata*," nature conceived as the stable, self-regulating rationally ordered system of creation ("Milton *Naturans*, Milton *Naturata*," 8–9). This vision of nature is informed by the Aristotelian mean of temperance, as explained by J. Martin Evans in "From Temperance to Abstinence: The Argument of *Comus* Revisited," in *"All in All": Unity, Diversity, and the Miltonic Perspective*, ed. Charles W. Durham and Kristin A. Pruitt (Selinsgrove, PA: Susquehanna University Press, 1999), 224–31.

62. Like Herbert's "British Church," the Lady's Nature declines the flash and allure of the more provocative maternal figures that mesmerize Comus and his crew, but it can be said of her, "A fine aspect in fit array, / Neither too mean, nor yet too gay, / Shows who is best." George Herbert, "The British Church," in *George Herbert and the Seventeenth-Century Religious Poets,* ed. Mario A. Di Cesare (New York: W. W. Norton, 1978), 44. One might also discern a prototype of the Lady's Nature in Spenser's Mercie, "well knowne ouer all, / To be both gratious, and eke liberall" (*FQ* 1.10.34.4–5), the matron, nurse, and tutor of the House of Holiness where the Redcrosse Knight is restored to spiritual health.

Chapter 5. Girl Power

1. See Woodhouse's crucial essay, "Argument of Milton's *Comus,*" 46–71.

2. We can compare Milton's addenda to the performance text of the *Maske* to Jonson's notes to the published texts of his masques, as an explication of what was implied and understood in the performance. But instead of claiming the hermeneutic privilege of author, as Jonson does, Milton embeds the explication into the text as a dramatically appropriate commentary and lets his character speak for herself—and, as we shall see, for himself.

3. Controversy over the virginal female body in the masque does not originate with Milton, but begins early in the Jacobean period. Marie Loughlin studies the ways in which Ben Jonson and Thomas Campion, in their respective marriage masques, attempt to inscribe the problematic virginal bodies of the masquing brides into the normative designs of marital chastity and of a regime anxious to consolidate its authority in the union of the realms of England and Scotland and to dispel nostalgia for the reign of the Virgin Queen. See Loughlin, "'Love's Friend and Stranger to Virginitie': The Politics of the Virginal Body in Ben Jonson's *Hymenaei* and Thomas Campion's *The Lord Hay's Masque*," *English Literary History* 63, no. 4 (1996): 833–49. Milton's revival of the theme of virginity and linkage of it to the theme of the political and moral autonomy of the individual might be taken as a radical revision of Jonson's and Campion's uneasy poetic settlements in the interests of the Crown.

4. Kerrigan, *Sacred Complex,* 35.

5. John Rogers, *The Matter of Revolution: Science, Poetry, and Politics in the Age of Milton* (Ithaca, NY: Cornell University Press, 1996), 82.
6. Fletcher, *Transcendental Masque*, 215.
7. The phrase "a condition of complete simplicity" is drawn from T. S. Eliot's "Little Gidding" (253), in *Four Quartets,* 59.
8. Kathryn Schwarz, "Chastity, Militant and Married," 274. Schwarz's analysis nicely problematizes the assumption that chastity is a less enigmatic and problematic model than virginity for patriarchal cultures attempting to define and regulate female sexuality.
9. See Fletcher: "If chastity is a stylistic virtue and virginity an absolute physical and metaphysical fact, the two occupy different places in the biography of the individual. If both then differ temporally, chastity may be said to lead to an awareness of the world outside oneself, while virginity leads to an interior knowledge of one's inner self" (*Transcendental Masque,* 225–26).
10. More fully developed treatments of mutuality and equality in Milton's representation of the first marital partnership can be found in Diane Kelsey McColley, *Milton's Eve* (Urbana: University of Illinois Press, 1983), and my "Wrestling with the Angel." Mary Nyquist provides a robust critique of what she sees as the bourgeois liberalism of this position, in "Genesis of Gendered Subjectivity"; see also Desma Polydorou, "Gender and Spiritual Equality," 22–32. Gina Hausknecht's study of gender in Milton's prose complements my account of gender in his poetics by showing how Milton's disposition toward masculinist essentialism and to a marital hierarchy founded on it is destabilized in the prose by his strong commitment to the exercise of rational liberty, a social virtue that is characterized as "masculine," but not restricted to the male sex. See Hausknecht, "Gender of Civic Virtue," 17–33.
11. Rogers, "Enclosure of Virginity," 229–50.
12. On the reformation of sexual ethics and its literary consequences, see William and Malleville Haller, "The Puritan Art of Love," *Huntington Library Quarterly* 5 (1942): 235–72; William Haller, "'Hail Wedded Love,'" *English Literary History* 13 (1946): 79–97; Juliet Dusinberre, *Shakespeare and the Nature of Women* (New York: Harper and Row, 1975); Steven Ozment, *The Age of Reform, 1250–1550: An Intellectual and Religious History of Late Medieval and Reformation Europe* (New Haven, CT: Yale University Press, 1980). Seventeenth-century English conduct books for women and documentary evidence of marriage settlements provide evidence for the conservative social function of female chastity in securing patriarchal authority and property in family relations. My argument in this book and particularly in this chapter is that Milton resists this ideological pressure by conceiving the Lady's chastity as the dynamic source of a freedom that is at once imaginative, spiritual, and political. For research into the formation of chaste women of the aristocratic and bourgeois classes, see Fletcher, *Gender, Sex, and Subordination,* and Hull, *Chaste, Silent, and Obedient.*
13. Christopher, *Science of the Saints,* 40.
14. Lauren Shohet notices that one of the revisionary surprises of the *Maske* is the way in which "a chaste Lady eloquently defends the principle of Chastity, traducing the conventional link between chastity and silence" ("Figuring Chastity," 146). John Rogers recognizes the prophetic tenor of the addendum to the Lady's speech. Rogers argues that it erupts as a radical and generically indecorous contrast to the socially harmonizing virtue of conjugal chastity and thus recedes into an implied but "unrealized potential" of the *Maske*'s narrative ("Enclosure of Virginity," 231–32). In *The Matter of Revolution,* Rogers handles the thematics of chas-

tity and virginity in the *Maske* somewhat differently and, in my estimation, less satisfactorily. Other critics who have analyzed the radical political implications of the encomium to virginity include Maureen Quilligan, *Milton's Spenser and the Politics of Reading* (Ithaca, NY: Cornell University Press, 1983); and Richard Halpern, "Puritanism and Maenadism," 88–105. Both these critics discern in the Lady's rhetoric a potential threat to the patriarchal order that underwrites the *Maske*. In their readings, the *Maske*'s silencing of the Lady and submission of her to the Attendant Spirit's rescue operation implicitly subdue this threat and restore the Lady to her appropriate place.

15. B. J. Sokol, "'Tilted Lees', Dragons, *Haemony,* Menarche, Spirit, and Matter in *Comus,*" *Review of English Studies,* n.s., 16 (1990): 309–24.

16. Arthur E. Barker, *Milton and the Puritan Dilemma, 1641–1660* (Toronto: University of Toronto Press, 1942), 339.

17. Rogers, "Enclosure of Virginity," 233.

18. For speculation about Milton's personal investment in the doctrine of virginity, and identification with the Lady, see Kerrigan, *Sacred Complex,* especially 20–21, 48–56; E. M. W. Tillyard, *Milton,* rev. ed. (London: Chatto and Windus, 1966), 318–26; John Shawcross, *John Milton,* 20–54; Katharine Eisamann Maus, "Womb of His Own," in *Inwardness and Theater,* 182–209. John Leonard meticulously critiques scholarly generalizations about Milton's personal "cult of celibacy" in "Milton's View of Celibacy," 188–201.

19. See Angus Fletcher: "By adding this peroration, Milton develops the range of his fable and framework. For while in this fable virginity assumes chastity, chastity does not require virginity. Virgin being transcends the chaste. In his final reworking of the text Milton suddenly throws the whole of the *Maske* into relief by clarifying this transcendence" (*Transcendental Masque,* 212).

20. Ibid., 212.

21. Ibid., 239.

22. "Dreams with an intestinal stimulus throw light in analogous fashion on the symbolism involved in them, and at the same time confirm the connection between gold and faeces which is also supported by copious evidence from social anthropology." Sigmund Freud, *The Interpretation of Dreams,* trans. James Strachey (New York: Avon Books, 1965), 439.

23. Camille Paglia, *Sexual Personae: Art and Decadence from Nefertiti to Emily Dickinson* (New York: Random House, 1991), 182, 176, 179.

24. Lacan, *Language of the Self,* 31.

25. See Loeffelholz, "Two Masques"; Kendrick, "Milton and Sexuality"; and Orgel, "Case for Comus."

26. This argument about intersubjectivity and the sources of Prospero's magic was presented more fully in my account of "Prospero's Potent Art" (paper, Forum on Shakespeare and Gender, annual convention of the Modern Language Association, New York, December 30, 1986).

27. C. L. Barber, "The Family in Shakespeare's Development: Tragedy and Sacredness," in *Representing Shakespeare: New Psychoanalytic Essays,* ed. Murray M. Schwartz and Coppélia Kahn (Baltimore: Johns Hopkins University Press, 1980), 195.

28. I am observing here how Milton defuses the incest motif derived from his adaptation of Miranda's plight in *The Tempest,* not implying that inordinate incestuous motivations circulated through the Earl of Bridgewater's household. Barbara Breasted makes the case that the *Maske* served a reputation-purifying function for

the Egerton family as it recovered from the recent sexual scandal studied in detail in her "*Comus* and the Castlehaven Scandal," *Milton Studies* 3 (1971): 201–24.

29. Kendrick, "Milton and Sexuality," 59.

30. Norbrook, *Poetry and Politics,* 264. Orgel claims that any freedom that the Lady might seem to stake out for herself, particularly in her marriage choice, is illusory, because of the imperatives of the patriarchal aristocracy that control her experience ("Case for Comus," 40).

31. Carol Scheidenhelm reads the Lady's refusal to disclose her doctrine as a defensive ruse: "The Lady denies a rhetorical response because she is unable to internalize her understanding of the doctrine of Virginity. She understands the concept intuitively but is unable to put her knowledge into speech, defending her silence with the claim that Comus is not worthy of an explanation" ("'Heav'n Hath Timely Tri'd [Her] Youth,'" 65). This is an interesting claim, but I think it is at odds with the effect of the speech, on Comus and on the audience; the Lady communicates decisively that she knows what she is not talking about.

32. Ernst Robert Curtius, *European Literature and the Latin Middle Ages,* trans. Willard R. Trask (New York: Harper and Row, 1963), 159–62.

33. Kerrigan, *The Sacred Complex,* 30.

34. Jean E. Graham identifies the Lady's rhetorical figure as "*praeteritio,* an ironic refusal to speak," as denominated by Henry Peacham; or the parallel structure of "*paralepsis,* or the passager," defined by Puttenham. Neither these figures nor *occupatio* seem to me to define the Lady's strategy, since in each of these figures, an apparent gesture of refusal to speak ironically leads to a disclosure of what was to be withheld. See Graham, "Virgin Ears: Silence, Deafness, and Chastity in Milton's *Maske,*" *Milton Studies* 36 (1998), 5.

35. A more ample treatment of "The Apparition" can be found in my essay, "Love as a Spectator Sport in John Donne's Poetry," in *Renaissance Discourses of Desire,* eds. Claude J. Summers and Ted-Larry Pebworth (Columbia, MO: University of Missouri Press, 1993), 46–62.

36. *John Donne's Poetry,* ed. A. L. Clements (New York: W. W. Norton and Co., 1966), 27.

37. Kathleen Wall, "*A Mask Presented at Ludlow Castle:* The Armor of Logos," 52–63.

38. See Lacan's ruminations on the "full Word [parole plein]" and the "empty Word [parole vide]" in *The Language of the Self,* especially 9–29, 55–61.

39. Ibid., 58.

40. On the role of the phallus as a signifier in the formation of the subject, see especially Jacques Lacan, "On a question preliminary to any possible treatment of psychosis," in *Ecrits,* trans. Alan Sheridan (New York: W. W. Norton & Co., 1977), 179–225. See also Anthony Wilden's commentary, "Lacan and the Discourse of the Other," *Language of the Self,* especially 161–66, 185–88.

41. Lacan, "On a question preliminary," 198–99.

42. Paglia, *Sexual Personae,* 80.

43. Several recent studies have examined what they take to be either Milton's or Elder Brother's misreading of Ovid's account of the Medusa myth. See Julia M. Walker, "The Poetics of Antitext and the Politics of Milton's Allusions," *Studies in English Literature* 37 (1997): 160–61; Rumrich, *Milton Unbound,* 78; John Leonard, "'Thus They Relate, Erring': Milton's Inaccurate Allusions," *Milton Studies* 38 (2000): 113–17. I do not find anything in Elder Brother's idealizing misprision that is out of line with the ingenious and flexible practices of typical Renaissance allegorization.

44. Of the voyeuristic pictorial indulgences in Spenser, Camille Paglia writes, "*The Faerie Queene* makes cinema out of the west's primary principle: to see is to know; to know is to control. The Spenserian eye cuts, wounds, rapes" (*Sexual Personae,* 173).

45. Neumann, *Great Mother.*

46. Rumrich, *Milton Unbound,* 78.

47. Jonson, *Masque of Queens,* 351, in *Selected Masques,* 93.

48. J. Laplanche and J.-B. Pontalis, "Sublimation," in *The Language of Psychoanalysis,* trans. Donald Nicholson-Smith (New York: W. W. Norton, 1973), 433.

49. Laplanche and Pontalis, "Narcissism," 255–57. See also John Guillory's excellent "Milton, Narcissism, Gender: On the Genealogy of Male Self-Esteem," in *Critical Essays on John Milton,* ed. Christopher Kendrick (New York: G. K. Hall, 1995), 195–233. In brief, Guillory traces Milton's disposition to represent "narcissism" as a potentially feminine and feminizing disability, sublimated into "self-esteem" as a male virtue, subtly thereby reinforcing conventional gender typologies. Guillory examines primarily the prose tracts and *Paradise Lost.* I think that consideration of the Lady's translation of narcissism into virtue and of Milton's projective identification with her would require some revision of his argument.

50. St. Augustine, *Confessions,* trans. R. S. Pine-Coffin (London: Penguin Books, 1980), 233.

51. Sigmund Freud, "The Medusa's Head," in *Sexuality and the Psychology of Love,* trans. Philip Rieff (New York: Collier Books, 1963), 212–13.

52. The binary opposition of homosexual/heterosexual is inadequate to describe the complex systems of sexual practice, both authorized and outlawed, and the nuanced varieties of gender and class identification, in classical Greece, Augustan Rome, or Renaissance England. So my characterization of the "normative" heterosexualities of Rome and England is a provisional generalization meant to acknowledge the authorizing and outlawing disposition of the "official" cultures of these periods, and thereby to problematize Freud's assertion. See, among others, Michel Foucault's *The History of Sexuality,* 3 vols. (New York: Random House, 1978–84); Ramsay MacMullen, "Roman Attitudes to Greek Love," *Historia* 31 (1982), 484–502; Jonathan Goldberg, *Sodometries: Renaissance Texts, Modern Sexualities* (Stanford, CA: Stanford University Press, 1992); Bruce Smith, *Homosexual Desire in Shakespeare's England* (Chicago: University of Chicago Press, 1991).

53. Freud, "Medusa's Head," 212.

54. Ibid.

55. Kristeva, *Powers of Horror: An Essay on Abjection,* trans. Leon Roudiez (New York: Columbia University Press, 1982), 13–14.

56. The warning, the flashing eyes, and the floating hair are from Coleridge, "Kubla Khan," 49–50, in *Coleridge: Selected Poetry and Prose,* ed. Elizabeth Schneider (New York: Holt, Rinehart, and Winston, 1951), 116.

57. My understanding of tragedy's relation to its sponsoring deity has developed out of conversations with my colleague Michael Davis and the classes on tragedy that he teaches at Sarah Lawrence College.

58. Paglia, *Sexual Personae,* 83.

59. Katharine Eisaman Maus analyzes the signifying potential of the Lady's body for Milton's representation of his own creativity in "Womb of His Own," 200–209.

60. In "Enclosure of Virginity," John Rogers demonstrates that the Lady's encomium to virginity presages the political usage of the trope of virginity by writers

and preachers in the revolutionary period of the mid-seventeenth century. See also Georgia Christopher, who observes "Milton is attempting to preserve the virginity of the concept of faith against any contamination from works, even loving ones" (*Science of the Saints,* 38).

Chapter 6. Milton's Lady and Lady Milton

1. John Shawcross argues that the composition of *Lycidas* in November, 1637, is the decisive moment when Milton acknowledges that his vocation will be poetry. Although I would argue with Shawcross's minimization of vocational hints and longings in earlier poems, particularly the Nativity Ode and Sonnet 7, my claim that Milton stages his own initiation into poetic maturity in the *Maske* is compatible with Shawcross's claims about "Lycidas." The near coincidence of the fully elaborated, first published version of the *Maske* and the completion and publication of "Lycidas," as well as their contiguity as the last English texts in the 1645 *Poems* suggest that these are vocational breakthrough poems for Milton. See Shawcross, *John Milton,* 68–70.

2. René Descharmes, *Flaubert before 1857,* 103; cited by Albert Thibaudet, "*Madame Bovary,*" trans. Paul de Man, in Gustave Flaubert, *Madame Bovary,* ed. and trans. Paul de Man (New York: Norton Critical Editions, 1965), 371. See also, in the same volume, Jean-Paul Sartre's suggestive analysis of Flaubert's identification with Emma Bovary, "Flaubert and *Madame Bovary:* Outline of a New Method," trans. Hazel Barnes, 302–8.

3. The locus classicus for modern academic polemics on Milton's purported misogyny remains Sandra Gilbert and Susan Gubar's influential *The Madwoman in the Attic: The Woman Writer and the Nineteenth-Century Literary Imagination* (New Haven, CT: Yale University Press, 1979). Gilbert and Gubar draw the activating phrase for their critique, "Milton's bogey," from Virginia Woolf, *A Room of One's Own* (New York: Harcourt Brace, 1989), 114.

4. A parallel argument is offered by Ronald Corthell: "*A Mask* creates a cross-gendered fantasy of empowerment that inverts or at least suspends conventional hierarchies within patriarchy and patronage by transposing daughters, fathers, poets, and patrons as signifiers of cultural authority" ("Go Ask Alice," 111–12).

5. Kendrick, "Milton and Sexuality," 43. John Leonard clears the way for my essay with his closely argued exegetical refutation of the claim, first proposed by James Holly Hanford, and still influencing critics like Kendrick and William Kerrigan, that Milton staked his early poetry on a vow of celibacy. See Leonard, "Milton's View of Celibacy," 188–201.

6. Kendrick, "Milton and Sexuality," 62–63.

7. Kerrigan, *Sacred Complex,* 26.

8. For development of the incarnation theme in the language and imagery of the Nativity Ode, see my essay, "Doctrine as Deep Structure in Milton's Early Poetry," in *A Fine Tuning: Studies of the Religious Poetry of Herbert and Milton,* ed. Mary A. Maleski (Binghamton, NY: Medieval and Renaissance Texts & Studies, 1989), 187–203.

9. Kendrick, "Milton and Sexuality," 63.

10. Gina Hausknecht's analysis of "the gender of civic virtue" in Milton's prose tracts coordinates with my study of virtue and gender here. Hausknecht concludes that nothing in Milton's arguments excludes women from the rational

"masculine" exercise of freedom of intellect and will in the public sphere: "The space opened up for gender does not preclude assumptions based on sex but it does indicate that those assumptions are not totalizing. It allows for a rational Eve in *Paradise Lost.* In Comus it gives a teenage girl the moral and intellectual stamina not only to resist temptation bodily but to reject it with 'seasonable and well grounded speaking' (*CPW* 2:585)" ("Gender of Civic Virtue," 32).

11. John Leonard cites Calvin's *Institutes* 4.12.28 to indicate that this category reversal has precedents in Reformation doctrine: "*species secunda virginitatis, est matrimonii casta dilectio* ('the second kind of virginity is the chaste love of marriage')." *John Milton: The Complete Poems,* ed. John Leonard (New York: Penguin Putnam, 1998), 680. Mary Laughlin Fawcett notes Milton's reference to this same passage from the *Institutes,* in her "'Such Noise as I can Make,'" 164.

12. Guillory, *Poetic Authority,* 77.

13. Rumrich, *Milton Unbound,* 73.

14. Preceding and standing behind these recent historically and culturally specific reconsiderations of chastity and virginity is Angus Fletcher's nuanced reflection in *Transcendental Masque,* 209–26.

15. John Rogers, "Enclosure of Virginity," 238–39. See also Halpern, "Puritanism and Maenadism," 88–105, and Kendrick, "Milton and Sexuality," 47.

16. Kendrick, "Milton and Sexuality," 55. Michael Lieb observes of the Lady, "she is, in fact, the female counterpart of the archetypal poet" (*Culture of Violence,* 106).

17. Abraham Heschel, *The Prophets,* vol. 1 (New York: Harper & Row, 1969), 3–27. William Kerrigan traces the prophetic style and trajectory of Milton's career in *The Prophetic Milton* (Charlottesville: University Press of Virginia, 1974).

18. Lieb, *Culture of Violence,* 52.

19. Hubbell, "Milton's Re-Formation," 196–97.

20. Shawcross, *John Milton,* 50–51.

21. Kerrigan, *Sacred Complex,* 50–51.

22. Maus, *Inwardness and Theater,* 191.

23. Ibid., 207–8.

24. Lieb, *Culture of Violence,* 110–11.

25. Shawcross, *John Milton,* 40.

26. Feminist readings are rightly fascinated by the speechlessness and seeming passivity of the Lady after her debate with Comus and the intervention by the Attendant Spirit and her brothers. They tend to agree that Milton's intention in the final movements of the *Maske* is to put his spunky and eloquent Lady back on the leash of feminine silence and submission and hand the leash back to her father. See, for instance, Mary Laughlin Fawcett's argument that the problem of female vocality in *Othello* and *Comus* is resolved when "in both works the chastity-speech theme is appropriated by the male artist" ("'Such Noise as I can Make,'" 163). Mary Loeffelholz's study of Milton's indebtedness to Shakespeare, Spenser, and Ovid for the female characters who underwrite his myth reads this intertextual practice as a literary instance of the cultural exchange of women ("Two Masques," 33–34). Although, surprisingly, Elizabeth Harvey gives only passing attention to Milton, she develops an argument that strongly pertains to his voice and the Lady's. She argues that "transvestite ventriloquism" (the construction of female personae by male writers) "is an appropriation of the feminine voice, and . . . it reflects and contributes to a larger cultural silencing of women" (*Ventriloquized Voices,* 12).

27. This is not to imply that women were incidental figures in Stuart court

masques; see chapter 1, "'Growing a Girl': The Masque of Passage," and the critical and historical texts noted there. Both Anne of Denmark and Henrietta Maria commissioned and performed in masques, and major female power players of the court joined them. But women's patronage and visible prominence in masques, rather than interrogating or subverting the royalist and patriarchal premises of the genre, ultimately reinforced them.

28. "Ad Patrem" has been suggestively linked, thematically and chronologically, to the *Maske* by several editors and critics. See the review of chronology in *The Poems of John Milton,* ed. John Carey and Alastair Fowler (New York: W. W. Norton, 1968), 148. See also John Shawcross's several statements of correlation between the anxieties expressed in "Ad Patrem" and the publication of the *Maske:* "With the publication of 'Comus,' if the suggested dating of 'Ad Patrem' is accurate, Milton was able not only to show that his study and retired life have been meaningful, but also that questions of sexual morality have been answered" (*John Milton,* 59; also 70, 189). My point, that Milton's female persona in the *Maske* provides an imaginative release from filial anxieties, does not depend upon a chronological correlation between the two poems, although such a correlation provides welcome support to the point.

29. Aeschylus, *The Eumenides,* 751–53, in *The Oresteia,* trans. Robert Fagles.

30. Freud, "Medusa's Head," 212–13.

31. Georgia Christopher, *Science of the Saints,* 38.

32. Hélène Cixous, "The Laugh of the Medusa," trans. Keith Cohen and Paula Cohen, *Signs: Journal of Women in Culture and Society 1,* no. 4 (1976): 884.

33. William Blake, "What is it men in women do require," in *The Poetry and Prose,* 466.

34. Jürgen Habermas, *The Structural Transformation of the Public Sphere: An Inquiry into a Category of Bourgeois Society,* trans. Thomas Burger and Frederick Lawrence (Cambridge: MIT Press), 1989.

35. Maria Magro, "Milton's Sexualized Woman and the Creation of a Gendered Public Sphere," *Milton Quarterly* 35, no. 2 (May 2001): 98.

36. Ibid., 104.

37. Lynn Enterline develops this argument in her study of Ovid and his successors in *Rhetoric of the Body.* Elizabeth D. Harvey studies the various ways in which male poets colonize the female voice through what she calls "gendered ventriloquism," in *Ventriloquized Voices.* The direction of such argument makes the innovative work of Renaissance poets a formation of early modern gender identity, but of course on male terms: constructing female characters and female voices is not an imaginative exercise in empathetic identification with the other, but an ideological exercise in speaking for, and thereby silencing, the other. On a parallel track, Katharine Eisaman Maus studies the emergence of the early modern subject, through the construction of an "inwardness" fantasized in various ways by male poets about the interior spaces of the female body, analogizing their own creative processes to those corporeal mysteries, and thereby mystifying them. See Maus, *Inwardness and Theater.* Such readings, informed and sophisticated as they are, seem to me to reproduce the gendered essentialism that they critique in the projects of various male poets. That is, they presume that male poets are essentially excluded, by reason of biological destiny and cultural conditioning, from the experience, and therefore from the interpretation, and the expression, of what it is to be a woman: never the twain shall meet.

38. In *"Comus* and the Castlehaven Scandal," Barbara Breasted brings the notorious Castlehaven scandal of the early 1630s to bear on modern interpretations of

the theme of chastity in the *Maske.* In "Milton's *Comus:* The Irrelevance of the Castlehaven Scandal," *Milton Quarterly* 21, no. 4 (December 1987): 24–34, John Creaser argues that neither the Egerton family nor their tactful young author would have wanted to raise the spectre of that scandal explicitly at the celebratory occasion of the earl's installation. But Creaser also acknowledges that the scandal was likely to be part of the recent memory of everyone present at the *Maske,* and therefore hard to dissociate from its thematics, and that the Lady's defense of "the freedom of my mind" (663) might be construed as a retrospective challenge to anyone pernicious enough to suspect the integrity of Countess Anne and her daughter Elizabeth, the victims of Castlehaven's abuse (31–32). In "Milieu of Milton's *Comus,"* and subsequently in "Earl of Bridgewater's Legal Life," Leah Marcus brings to critical light the case of Margery Evans, whose victimization in the real world prefigured the ritual experience of the Lady.

39. Marcus, "Earl of Bridgewater's Legal Life," 20.

40. Harold Bloom's description of the trope *apophrades*—"the return of the dead"—identifies the figurative strategy by which the Lady's poetic voice comes into its strength. But there is a significant feminizing revision of Bloom's own patriarchal "revisionary ratio" here, in that the reawakened voices who echo through the Lady's speech, stronger in the belated poet's conjuring and iteration of them, are not those of "strong" poetic father figures, but of "weak" and largely silenced daughter figures. See Bloom, *The Anxiety of Influence* (New York: Oxford University Press, 1997), 139–55.

41. Fletcher, *Transcendental Masque,* 198–209.

Chapter 7. Girl, Interrupted

"Girl, Interrupted" is the title of Susanna Kaysen's novel, *Girl, Interrupted* (New York: Vintage Books, 1994); "Changing Woman" is drawn from Keith Basso's study of female initiation in *The Cibecue Apache* (New York: Holt, Rinehart, and Winston, 1970).

1. The history of responses to the Lady's substitution of the "unblemish't form of Chastity" (215) for charity, as the third of the theological virtues, nearly constitutes the history of modern criticism of the *Maske* itself.

2. Thomas Roche, *The Kindly Flame: A Study of the Third and Fourth Books of Spenser's Faerie Queene* (Princeton, NJ: Princeton University Press, 1964), 75–76; see also Susanne Lindgren Wofford, "Gendering Allegory: Spenser's Bold Reader and the Emergence of Character in *The Faerie Queene* III," *Criticism* 30 (1988): 1–21.

3. See Kathryn Schwarz's study of Britomart's transvestitism in *Tough Love,* 137–74.

4. Wofford, "Gendering Allegory," 20.

5. Roche, *Kindly Flame,* 102–3.

6. Wofford neatly makes a comparable point about the tension in Spenser's text between the fixture of allegory and the character dynamic of Britomart: "Spenser isolates one aspect of his art and represents it in the figure of Busyrane, while Britomart in her victory is associated with another incipient aspect of his own technique, one which, at this moment in the dialectic, points the way out of allegory" (19). See also Heather Dubrow's study of Milton's ambivalence toward romance in "Masquing of Genre," 63–70.

7. Irene Tayler, "Say First! What Mov'd Blake? Blake's *Comus* Designs and *Milton*," in *Blake's Sublime Allegory,* ed. Stuart Curran and Joseph Anthony Wittreich (Madison: University of Wisconsin Press, 1973), 235.

8. On the courtly love traditions, and their impact on Spenser, see Roche, *Kindly Flame;* Isabel MacCaffrey, *Spenser's Allegory: The Anatomy of Imagination* (Princeton, NJ: Princeton University Press, 1976); C. S. Lewis, *Allegory of Love: A Study of Medieval Tradition* (New York: Oxford University Press, 1958); and Lewis, *Spenser's Images of Life,* ed. Alastair Fowler (Cambridge: Cambridge University Press, 1967).

9. Roy Strong, *The Cult of Elizabeth: Elizabethan Portraiture and Pageantry* (London: Thames and Hudson, 1977).

10. Roche, *Kindly Flame,* 83; see also Wofford, "Gendering Allegory," 19.

11. Lewis, *Allegory of Love,* 297.

12. Shelley's praise of the troubadors and Petrarch, "whose verses are as spells, which unseal the inmost enchanted fountains of the delight which is in the grief of love," suggests that they are Busyrane's more benign precursors ("A Defence of Poetry," 497).

13. Demaray, *Milton and the Masque Tradition,* 89–90.

14. Ovid, *The Metamorphoses,* trans. Allen Mandelbaum, 20–25. Subsequent references to this version will be cited parenthetically in the text.

15. Georgia Christopher, *Science of the Saints,* 52. Studying patristic and Reformation reflection about the problems of involuntary physical arousal like nocturnal emissions, Debora Shuger draws conclusions similar to Christopher's about the Lady's plight. See Shuger, "'The Bliss of Dreams': Theology in Milton's *Maske*," *Hellas, A Journal of Poetry and the Humanities* 7, 2 (Fall/Winter 1996): 139–53.

16. Kerrigan, *Sacred Complex,* 55. In his exacting critique of psychoanalytic interpretations of the *Maske,* Kerrigan's in particular ("Saying 'No' to Freud," 129–40), John Leonard insists that we test our interpretations against the straightforward recognition that the Lady is bound by Comus's magic and threatened by his predatory sexuality, not by her own repressed desire. Although I take Leonard's admonition to heart, I proceed with this analysis with the assumption that there is a psychic content to the Lady's paralysis, although not the neurotic one which conventional theories of repression like Kerrigan's describe.

17. See Stanley Fish, *How Milton Works,* 183–84, for a comparable account of the Lady's fixity. Stephen Orgel describes the Lady's rigid unresponsiveness as evidence of "the inhumanity of virtue" ("Case for Comus," 39).

18. Lacan, "The mirror stage as formative of the function of the I as revealed in psychoanalytic experience," in *Ecrits: A Selection,* trans. Alan Sheridan (New York: W. W. Norton, 1977), 4. In contrast to my earlier use of the masculine pronoun to describe the preoedipal child, I use the feminine pronoun in this sequence not only as a way of acknowledging the Lady's representative role in reiterating this crucial sequence of character formation, but also because differentiation of gender occurs as one of the "alienating" components of assimilation to the Symbolic order.

19. Fish, *How Milton Works,* 166.

20. In *De Trinitate,* St. Augustine provides the foundational account of the triplicate orders of creation, and of the human soul, as images of the Trinitarian structure of the Deity. See *Augustine: Later Works,* trans. John Burnaby (London: SCM Press, 1955).

21. Fish, *How Milton Works,* 172–73.

22. My discussion here parallels that of Oram, who argues that "in rejecting

Comus [the Lady] rejects her own physical nature which shows itself, most obviously, in her power of movement" ("Invocation of Sabrina," 131). Oram slightly oversimplifies the situation by identifying Comus with the Lady's own "lower nature," "irrational, appetitive part of herself," and "bodily instincts," rather than with a certain (and self-destructive) way of looking at and using nature, appetite, and instinct. In saying No to the libertine Comus, the Lady has not yet learned how to say Yes to her newly awakened bodily life, but that is different from claiming that she has rejected or denied it.

23. Fletcher, *Transcendental Masque*, 216.
24. Ronald Corthell makes similar observations about the inaccessibility of the Lady's experience to the custodial males of her family; see "Go Ask Alice," 122.
25. MacCaffrey, *Spenser's Allegory*, 112.
26. Roche, *Kindly Flame*, 77.
27. Ibid., 83–84.
28. Kathryn Schwarz's fascinating account of Britomart's successes in performing masculinity dovetails with my reading here. Schwarz shows how Britomart's cross-dressed knighthood, adopting the ensemble of "masculine" signifiers without being confined or defined by them, proves more efficacious in the demonstration of "masculine" virtue than the efforts of her male counterparts. The gendered essentialism underwriting the mystique of chivalric heroism leaves male knights both physically and psychologically more vulnerable to defeat and loss. See Schwarz, *Tough Love*, 149–52.
29. The Bemba people of Zambia would recognize Sabrina as a cultural parallel to *nacimbusa*, an elder woman figure whose experience, status, and knowledge of the mysteries suit her to supervise, instruct, and protect the initiates in the crucial stages of their passage (Richards, *Chisungu*, 57–58). Other traditional cultures confer corresponding ritual tasks and dignities upon the godmother figure. The Okiek of the Kenyan highlands call her *matireenik* (Corrine Ann Krantz, *Affecting Performance: Meaning, Movement, and Experience in Okiek Women's Initiation* [Washington, DC: Smithsonian Institution Press, 1994], 139–40); the Cibecue Apache call her *nai esn* (Basso, *Cibecue Apache*, 56–58).
30. Basso, *Cibecue Apache*, 64–65. Another suggestive parallel to Sabrina appears among some riverine peoples of Nigeria, who look to a figure very like Sabrina, the water goddess whom they call Mammywata, for health, well-being, peace, and fertility. Sabrina is the ethnically mixed offspring of the Briton Locrine and Estrildis, daughter of the Hun Humber. Mammywata is likewise a hybrid cultural invention, a biracial figure who is the child of a colonialist father and an African mother. She dwells alone, in river settings, "perpetually combing her thick hair, symbol of fertility." Although she is childless, "Mammywata is figured as performing a maternal function in the society at large" (Chikwenye Okenyo Ogunyemi, *Africa Wo/Man Palava: The Nigerian Novel by Women* [Chicago: University of Chicago Press, 1996], 31, 33). Mammywata has particular pertinence to the cultivation of the female psyche: "Usually alone, Mammywata loves reflecting on herself, stressing her introspective nature, individuality, and self-sufficiency. Since she dwells in water well stocked with mirrors, she constantly looks at her own reflection. This intense, female, self-directed gaze replaces the customary, demeaning male gaze; the look inward uplifts woman" (Ogunyemi, *Africa Wo/Man Palava*, 33). Mammywata's type of solitary introspective serenity, a positive narcissism translated to readiness for compassion's opportunities, radiant with potential energy for healing, transforming, and fertility, is beautifully evoked in the Attendant Spirit's invocatory song to Sabrina, "sitting / Under the glassy, cool,

translucent wave, / In twisted braids of Lilies knitting / The loose train of thy amber-dropping hair" (860–63). Ronald Corthell's reflections on the mystique of female narcissism are pertinent to this powerful attribute of Sabrina and analogous figures ("Go Ask Alice," 116–18).

31. Studying closely the classical prototypes set in play by Milton's mythmaking, Stella Revard notes that "it is not until the feminine deity rises from the nurturing water that the Lady is truly released. With Sabrina and her attendant nymphs the power of the feminine enters the *Mask.*" My argument is somewhat different here: "the power of the feminine" has already been dangerously present in the figure of Comus, Circe's child and devotée of the profane Venus (124), Cotytto (129), and Hecate (135). Revard observes that protective mother figures of classical myth, Cyrene and Thetis, anticipate Sabrina in their intervention on behalf of an imperiled child; and that the goddess Artemis, to whom the nymph Cyrene is devoted, "is not just a goddess of virginity, but a deity who guides young women through all the stages of their life from maidenhood to marriage to motherhood." See Revard, "Sabrina and the Classical Nymphs of Water," in *Milton and the Tangles of Neaera's Hair,* 129, 131, 135. Joseph Ortiz provides a sobering counterpoint to these optimistic stories in his study of the less fortunate nymph Scylla, whose horrific fate and monstrous transformation, alluded to by Comus, become ironically intertwined with Comus's threat to the Lady. See Ortiz, "'Reforming of Reformation,'" 91–93.

32. Clark, "Milton *Naturans,* Milton *Naturata,*" 19.

33. Revard, "Sabrina and the Classical Nymphs," 130–56.

34. For an archetypal reading of the Proserpina myth and the relation of the Eleusinian Mysteries which celebrate it to processes of psychological maturation and integration see C. G. Jung and C. Kerényi, *Essays on a Science of Mythology: The Myths of the Divine Child and the Divine Maiden,* trans. R. F. C. Hull (New York: Harper and Row, 1963). For treatment of the Proserpina motif in the *Maske,* see Mary Loeffelholz, "Two Masques," 25–42.

35. *Variorum* vol. 2, part 3, 958.

36. See especially Iphigenia's heroic speech in Euripides's *Iphigenia at Aulis:* "I am resolved to die. And I will do it gloriously. I have put all mean thoughts out of my heart. . . . All these things I shall achieve by my death, and my name, as the liberator of Hellas, shall be blessed" (348, in *Ten Plays by Euripides,* trans. Moses Hadas and John McLean [New York: Bantam Books, 1963]. Philip Schwyzer contemporizes the nationalist symbolism of Sabrina's role by examining its context in seventeenth-century debates about England's relation to the western and Welsh territories in the greater political entity of Britain. Schwyzer documents that the legendary St. Winifred would have been a more authentic local "healing maiden of the water" (38). But as a Catholic sponsor of traditional rural festivity, she would have problematized the *Maske*'s idealization of English virtue and support for English hegemony in the larger union ("Purity and Danger," 38–39).

37. The Christological parallels of Sabrina's story provide narrative support for Woodhouse's explanation that Sabrina participates in the Lady's ordeal as a manifestation of divine grace. Woodhouse, "The Argument of Milton's *Comus,*" *University of Toronto Quarterly* 11 (1941–42): 46–71, and "*Comus* Once More," *University of Toronto Quarterly* 19 (1949–50): 218–23.

38. Fletcher, *Transcendental Masque,* 240.

39. Richard Halpern, "Puritanism and Maenadism," 96.

40. Ibid., 96.

41. Ibid., 100. Halpern's conclusion is a standard feminist and new historicist

reading in its assessment of the Lady's achieved chastity as a "bourgeois form of social control" of women.

42. Ibid., 91–92. See, in contrast, Michael Lieb's treatment of the recurring motif of Dionysian violence in Milton's work, in *Culture of Violence,* especially his treatment of Milton's identification with the Lady on 101–6.

43. Juliet Dusinberre, *Shakespeare and the Nature of Women,* 72–73.

44. Jeanie Grant Moore observes that "an undercurrent of distrust of women lies just beneath the surface. Even though the outcome of the temptation is a foregone conclusion, the need for a lady's virtue to be proven publicly at all casts a shadow on the picture of perfection." See Moore, "The Two Faces of Eve: Temptation Scenes in *Comus* and *Paradise Lost,*" *Milton Quarterly* 36, no. 1 (March 2002): 5. Moore's claims seem to be at odds with Milton's insistence on the necessity of the test of virtue, whether exercised by man or woman.

45. *Variorum* vol. 2, part 3, 957–59.

46. Sears Jayne observes that "Sabrina, though Heaven gave her to the Lady, may be termed the Lady's own, as may all the natural powers of the soul" ("Subject of Milton's Ludlow Masque," 102).

47. Heléne Cixous, "Laugh of the Medusa," 881–82.

48. Clark, "Milton *Naturans,* Milton *Naturata,*" 23.

49. Blake, "The Divine Image," in *The Poetry and Prose,* 12. "The humanization of nature and the naturalization of the human heart" are central themes of Harold Bloom's *The Visionary Company: A Reading of English Romantic Poetry* (Garden City, NY: Doubleday, 1961).

50. Jayne, "Subject of Milton's Ludlow Masque," 102.

51. Clark, "Milton *Naturans,* Milton *Naturata,*" 23.

52. Cedric Brown notes that the fruitful prosperity associated with Sabrina overflows the specifics of her rescue of the Lady, to figure forth a spirit of apocalyptic nationalism: "In what is said about Sabrina Milton made an affective visionary celebration of a whole land, something touching, beyond the Arcadian, the apocalyptic" (*John Milton's Aristocratic Entertainments,* 126).

53. In addition to Clark, "Milton *Naturans,* Milton *Naturata,*" see Annabel Patterson, "'L'Allegro,' 'Il Penseroso' and *Comus:* The Logic of Recombination," *Milton Quarterly* 9, no. 3 (1975): 75–79.

54. Balachandra Rajan, *The Lofty Rhyme: A Study of Milton's Major Poetry* (Coral Gables, FL: University of Miami Press, 1970), 39.

55. The ritual bath is a common feature of rites of initiation, perhaps signifying purification after the girl's initial experience of menses (Richards, *Chisungu,* 122). See also B. J. Sokol, "'Tilted Lees,'" 309–24, for a suggestive account of the *Maske*'s implicit ritual "celebration of the menarche" (323). Although Hilda Hollis is too severe a critic of the necessary self-defensiveness of the Lady's advocacy of chastity, she does acknowledge that in the resolution of the *Maske* plot, "chastity is not undermined by charity but is completed by it" ("Without Charity," 169).

56. In "'The Bliss of Dreams,'" Debora Shuger correlates those "gums of glutinous heat" with patristic and Reformation puzzling over the phenomenon of nocturnal emissions and the questions raised about guilt and sin in instances of involuntary physical arousal. This kind of psychosexualized reading was nicely rebutted by Leonard in his previous critique of Kerrigan: "We cannot infer guilt in the Lady from Comus's spillages" (Leonard, "Saying No," 130). James W. Broaddus also understands those "gums" as emissions from the Lady, contextualizing his analysis by reference both to Britomart's romantic career and to the Renaissance physiology that informs it (Broaddus, "'Gums of Glutinous Heat' in Mil-

ton's *Mask* and Spenser's *Faerie Queene*," *Milton Quarterly* 37, no. 4 [2003], 205–14). Although Broaddus treats these emissions as healthy signs of female emotional and erotic development rather than as signs of theological problems, I think that the tonality of the passage, with its connotations of entrapment and pollution, and the dramatic circumstances, suggest that the gums are a part of Comus's strategem and a mark of his discourtesy and indecency, rather than evidence of involuntary excitement and physiological response on the Lady's part. Beth Bradburn offers an intriguing resolution to this conundrum by suggesting that "the gums may be read as a kind of human resin, a fragrant secretion of the Lady's body." If they represent "a form of radical moisture" that actually seals off the virtuous person from possible pollution, they would form a kind of residue protecting the Lady from the venom of Comus's seat ("Bodily Metaphor and Moral Agency in A Masque: A Cognitive Approach," *Milton Studies* 43 [2004], 30–31). Although I am not quite convinced, I find this account attractive because it accepts the "gums" as a secretion from the Lady while understanding them as a sign of her bodily and spiritual integrity rather than as a sign of her being divided against herself.

57. Basso, *Cibecue Apache*, 64–65.

CHAPTER 8. HOMECOMING QUEEN

1. Turner, *Dramas, Fields, and Metaphors*, 232.
2. Turner, *Ritual Process*, 131–65.
3. Basso, *Cibecue Apache*, 67–68.
4. Welsford, *Court Masque*, 8. On the promise of justice associated with the Earl of Bridgewater's new tenure as Lord President of Wales and the West Marches, see Marcus, "Milieu of Milton's *Comus*," 293–327.
5. Blair Hoxby observes, "In the main dance there is no royalty to watch or dance. The earl is represented as neither more nor less than a magistrate and a father before whom his children dance as themselves. In so doing, they instantiate their inner virtue, reveal their native nobility, and display their good upbringing" ("Wisdom of Their Feet," 95).
6. Yeats's "A Dialogue of Self and Soul" ends with the Self's declaration, "When such as I cast out remorse / So great a sweetness flows into the breast / We must laugh and we must sing, / We are blest by everything, / Everything we look upon is blest" (*The Collected Poems*, 232; see also section 4 of "Vacillation," 246). "The still point of the turning world" is from T. S. Eliot's "Burnt Norton": "At the still point of the turning world. Neither flesh nor fleshless; / Neither from nor towards; at the still point, there the dance is, / But neither arrest nor movement" ("Burnt Norton," 61–63, in *Four Quartets*, 15).
7. Julie H. Kim, "The Lady's Unladylike Struggle: Redefining Patriarchal Boundaries in Milton's *Comus*," *Milton Studies* 35 (1997): 19. See also Stephen Orgel's peremptory account of Lady Alice Egerton's inevitable and total subjection to the will of her father in the crucial matter of marital choice ("Case for Comus," 40–42).
8. There have been several variations on this interpretation. Christopher Kendrick, for example, notes the radical potential of the bourgeois Puritan social forces embodied in the Lady, but describes this potential as ultimately self-disabling ("Milton and Sexuality," 43–73). Richard Halpern, as we have seen, traces affilia-

tions between the Lady's profession of virginity and the threat of a maenadism that must be dispelled ("Puritanism and Maenadism," 88–105). In John Rogers's account, the silencing of the Lady submits her to the exigencies of both genre and class and leaves the discursive and political power of the trope of virginity "an unrealized potential" of the *Maske* ("Enclosure of Virginity," 229–50). Mary Laughlin Fawcett makes the case that the *Maske* appropriates the power of speech from the Lady in whom it is initially invested, in the interests of Milton's own claims to poetic authority ("'Such Noise as I can Make,'" 159–83). See Suzanne W. Hull, *Chaste, Silent, and Obedient,* for social evidence for these historicizing interpretations.

9. William Kerrigan's psychoanalytic commentary on the Lady's paralysis would obtain for her continuing silence as well: "Hers is a root-bound virtue, caught in a reaction-formation to oedipal temptation. It is not free. It is in bondage to the desire denied" (*Sacred Complex,* 55).

10. Elisabeth A. Frost notes the structural normalization of the *Maske* after the driving out of Comus, in "Didactic *Comus,*" 87–103.

11. Questioning the portrait of the young Milton as an emerging radical, Annabel Patterson notices the conventional agrarian conservatism of this passage, as well as similar notes struck in "L'Allegro," in "'Forc'd Fingers,'" 9–22. See also David Loewenstein, "'Fair Offspring Nurs't in Princely Lore,'" 27–48. Hugh Jenkins studies the impact of the country-house poem on the *Maske,* in "Milton's *Comus* and the Country House-Poem," *Milton Studies* 32 (1996): 169–88.

12. Mindele Anne Treip notices the courteous allusion to the recent court masques *Coelum Britannicum* and *Albion's Triumph,* whose mythic characters included Mercury, in "Stuart Masque Connection," 85.

13. On the implications of Eve's silence, see my essay, "Sorting the Seeds: The Regeneration of Love in *Paradise Lost,*" *Milton Studies* 28 (1991): 180.

14. Jean Graham has noted the spiritual ambiguity and generic propriety of the Lady's silence as an ambiguous preserve of her integrity. See Graham, "Virgin Ears," 10–15.

15. Sears Jayne proposes that we read the Lady's immobile and silent condition in a Neoplatonic allegorical frame, as the first stage of a divine ecstasy. See Jayne, "Subject of Milton's Ludlow Masque," 176 ff. In Jayne's Neoplatonic analysis, the Lady's release by Sabrina, representing *mens,* the Divine Mind, completes her ecstasy by allowing her to rise from the world of the flesh to union with God. I agree with other critics who see Sabrina's intervention as a restoration and redemption of the bodily life, which of course prefigures the consummation of human desiring in the life to come. See, for instance, Oram, "Invocation of Sabrina," 135–36.

16. John Donne, "The Ecstasie," in *John Donne's Poetry.*

17. Fletcher, *Transcendental Masque,* 250.

18. Hoxby, "Wisdom of Their Feet," 76.

19. The Lady incarnates and prefigures the visionary Psyche of the *Maske*'s Epilogue, from whose "unspotted side" Youth and Joy are "to be born" (1005–12). When Milton reiterates the Psyche myth in *An Apology against a Pamphlet,* he names the twin offspring of Psyche as Knowledge and Virtue, identifying them in effect as ethical correlatives of the *Maske*'s Youth and Joy. For the aspiring poet who twins himself as the embattled reformer, these doubled sets of twins are indistinguishable from one another; and so his Lady's final gestures of festive rejuvenation are also exercises in moral renewal for her community.

20. Victor Turner, *Forest of Symbols,* 107.

21. Leonard Barkan, *Nature's Work of Art: The Human Body as Image of the World* (New Haven, CT: Yale University Press, 1975), 50–51. See also Hoxby, "Wisdom of Their Feet," 78; E. M. W. Tillyard, *The Elizabethan World Picture* (New York: Vintage Books, n.d.), 91–94; and Turner, *Forest of Symbols:* "The cosmos may in some cases be regarded as a vast human body" (107).

22. Stanley Fish, "Discovery as Form in *Paradise Lost*," in *New Essays on Paradise Lost*, ed. Thomas Kranidas (Berkeley and Los Angeles: University of California Press, 1971), 12.

23. Jonathan Goldberg, *James I*, 58–59.

24. "Idea of order" is drawn from Wallace Stevens's "The Idea of Order at Key West." As I reread Stevens's great poem with the Lady in mind, I find the consonance between the two texts, and their female singers, haunting and beautiful:

> It was her voice that made
> The sky acutest at its vanishing.
> She measured to the hour its solitude.
> She was the single artificer of the world
> In which she sang. And when she sang, the sea,
> Whatever self it had, became the self
> That was her song, for she was the maker. Then we,
> As we beheld her striding there alone,
> Knew that there never was a world for her
> Except the one she sang and, singing, made.

Stevens, *Collected Poems*, 129–30. Compare the Attendant Spirit's evocation of the "soft and solemn-breathing sound" of the Lady's Echo Song: "I was all ear, / And took in strains that might create a soul / Under the ribs of Death" (555–62). Elizabeth Drury of Donne's *Anniversaries*, another visionary maiden whose "progress from this world to the next" is of cosmic and salvific significance, anticipates Milton's Lady as such an incarnate "idea of order."

25. John Arthos refers to the Platonic "eschatology" of the Epilogue in "The Realms of Being in the Epilogue of *Comus*," *Modern Language Notes* 76 (1961): 321. A. Bartlett Giamatti notes the ways in which the poetic and exegetical traditions of the earthly paradise embedded eschatological expectation. In his great Fourth Eclogue, "Virgil has adapted the traditional Golden Age vision for prophetic purposes, and it is small wonder that Christians regarded this Eclogue as a forecast of Christ. Henceforth the Golden Age will be utilized for a time in the future as well as an image of the past." Giamatti, *The Earthly Paradise and the Renaissance Epic* (New York: W. W. Norton, 1966), 24.

26. Kathleen Swaim notes the Attendant Spirit's role as a Hermes figure in the *Maske*, citing Edgar Wind's account of Hermes's role in Renaissance Neoplatonism:

> Not only was Mercury the shrewdest and swiftest of the gods, the god of eloquence, the skimmer of clouds, the psychopompos, the leader of the Graces, the mediator between mortals and gods bridging the distance between earth and heaven; to humanists Mercury was above all the "ingenious" god of the probing intellect, sacred to grammarians and metaphysicians, the patron of lettered inquiry and interpretation to which he had lent his very name . . . , the revealer of secret or "Hermetic" knowledge, of which his magical staff became a symbol. In a word, Hermes was the divine mystagogue.

Swaim, "Allegorical Poetry," 171; Edgar Wind, *Pagan Mysteries*, 122.

27. John Rumrich observes of the conclusion of the *Maske*, "the Lady resists

acquiescence in a natural world that would efface her spiritual singularity and seeks instead the lofty autonomy described in the Attendant Spirit's epilogue" (*Milton Unbound,* 94). It will be evident from my reading of the revels and the Epilogue that I could not disagree more. Although "lofty autonomy" is a good phrase to characterize the tone and setting of the Attendant Spirit's Prologue, it is hard to find any data in the vibrant, sensuous Epilogue to support this description. Stanley Fish falls back on the same dualism in observing that the Lady's virtue "places her in a relationship of opposition to her own skin. . . . the topos [of eternal soul trapped in a mortal body] becomes uncomfortable when it is literalized in the form of a woman who must continually suppress every impulse that might otherwise move her" (*How Milton Works,* 183). Surprisingly, after a wonderful account of dance as the harmonic incarnation of spirit and the participatory evidence of the soul's attunement with the divine, Fish would have us neglect that the Lady ever gets off Comus's gummy chair to be the principal dancer of the revels. As an elegant corrective to these dualisms, see Hoxby: "The final dance of Milton's *Mask* beautifully affirms that the body in motion can express the dispositions of the mind and the passions of the soul" ("Wisdom of Their Feet," 96).

28. Fletcher, *Transcendental Masque,* 203.

29. Starnes and Talbert, *Classical Myth and Legend* 310. Hunter notices the association of the mythic islands of the west, as evoked in Plutarch's *Moralia,* with the islands of Anglesey and Man in the sea to the north and west of Wales, islands to which the Bridgewater family "had strong ties" (*Milton's* Comus, 39–41).

30. B. A. Wright, *TLS* (Aug. 4, 1935), 367.

31. Milton *Variorum* vol. 2, part 3, 981. Catherine I. Cox studies not only the *Maske*'s incorporation of images of the Song of Songs, but also the ways in which the Lady's role and destiny parallel those of the Song's Bride; see "The Garden Within: Milton's Ludlow Masque and the Tradition of Canticles," *Milton Studies* 31 (1994): 23–44.

32. Charles Dempsey, *The Portrayal of Love: Botticelli's* Primavera *and Humanist Culture at the Time of Lorenzo the Magnificent* (Princeton, NJ: Princeton University Press, 1992), 151.

33. "Thou still unravished bride of quietness" opens Keats's "Ode on a Grecian Urn" (*Selected Poems and Letters,* 207).

34. Swaim, "Allegorical Poetry," 182.

35. Rogers, "Enclosure of Virginity," 230. Marie H. Loughlin supplements this doctrinal directive with evidence from medical and anatomy texts that describe "virginal desire" as "that which produces and confirms lawful heterosexual intercourse as comprising a woman's naturally- and divinely-ordained goal" (Loughlin, "'Love's Friend,'" 836). Milton's deployment of the Psyche myth could be seen, in Loughlin's terms, as a mythological reinforcement of this medical and social agenda.

36. Swaim, "Allegorical Poetry," 173.

37. Tuve, *Images and Themes,* 116.

38. My sense of place here is affected by Yeats's "Among School Children": "Labor is blossoming or dancing where / The body is not bruised to pleasure soul, / Nor beauty born out of its own despair, / Nor blear-eyed wisdom out of midnight oil" (*Collected Poems,* 214).

39. Tuve, *Images and Themes,* 135.

40. C. S. Lewis, *Spenser's Images of Life,* 56.

41. Venus is associated with eternal forms in the description of "her heavenly hous, / The house of goodly formes and faire aspects, / Whence all the world de-

rives the glorious / Features of beautie, and all shapes select, / With which high God his workmanship hath deckt . . ." (*FQ* 3.6.12.1–5).

42. Jeffry Spencer, *Heroic Nature: Ideal Landscape in English Poetry from Marvell to Thompson* (Evanston, IL: Northwestern University Press, 1973), 112.

43. "Milton in every instance pursues his imagination to the utmost. . . . But in no instance is this sort of perseverance more exemplified than in what may be called his stationing or statu[a]ry. He is not content with simple description, he must station,—thus here [*PL* 7.422–23] we not only see how the Birds 'with clang despised the ground,' but we see them 'under a cloud in prospect.'" This notation occurs in Keats's copy of Milton. On the "ideal of dynamic poise" in Keats's poems, strengthened by his reading of Milton, see Walter Jackson Bate, *John Keats* (Cambridge, MA: Harvard University Press, 1963), 246–47.

44. Dempsey, *Portrayal of Love,* 35.

45. John Demaray frames the imagery of the Epilogue by reference to the visually spectacular imagery of the court masques that Milton is reverbalizing and reforming in the Ludlow *Maske* ("Temple of the Mind," 60–61).

46. Wind, *Pagan Mysteries,* 118–19.

47. It is typical of the metaphysical and aesthetic wit of the *Maske* that this signal, keyed to "true" *auditors,* appears first in the *printed* text of 1637, thus rendering itself accessible to readers in the "unexpressive notes" (Nativity Ode, 116) of writing.

48. Wind, *Pagan Mysteries,* 119–20; Dempsey, *Portrayal of Love,* 157–58. Dempsey reads the look and the gesture of Botticelli's Venus as directed toward a spectator made worthy by love: "Set before our eyes are not merely the accidental appearances of the beloved's beauty, but the image of love itself, Venus surrounded by all the manifold effects and attributes of her fecund grace, the fully perfected idea of love as it was in fact truly represented in the heart of the beloved even before this could have been known" (158).

49. As a fertility god whose death and resurrection are associated with the renewal of spring, Christianity's Easter season, Adonis is a pagan type of Christ. Art historians have noted the pietà motif in several of Nicolas Poussin's paintings, in particular his "Venus with the Dead Adonis" (Musée des Beaux-Arts, Caen). This painting's composition remarkably mirrors that of another Poussin painting of the late 1620s, "Lamentation over the Dead Christ" (Bayerisch Etaatsgemaldesammllunger, Munich). The posture of Poussin's Christ with his "pronated arm" closely resembles that of Poussin's mortally wounded Adonis, although the directional movements of the paintings are reversed. Although Richard Verdi suggests that the female parallel to Venus in the lamentation over Christ is the distraught Magdalene, the "swooning virgin," Christ's mother Mary more closely parallels the curve of Venus over the fallen Adonis. Richard Verdi, *Nicolas Poussin 1594–1665,* with an essay by Pierre Rosenberg (London: Zwemmer and The Royal Academy of Arts, 1995), 154–55, 307.

50. In *Complete Poems and Collected Prose,* Merritt Y. Hughes cites Pausanias for the identification of Venus in her apparition as "Assyrian Queen," "Worshipped as a heavenly divinity (rather than as the goddess of earthly passion)" (113). The editors of the *Variorum* dispute this identification by noting that Venus's apparently earthbound love is contrasted to the true heavenly love achieved by Cupid and Psyche, "far above in spangled sheen" (1003; *Variorum* vol. 2, part 3, 984–85). John Carey notes that "Venus and Adonis are types of natural love," identified by the mythographers with earth and the sun, in the generative rhythm of the sun's waning in winter and procreative restoration in spring; but that Mil-

ton's location of them in "the Elysian fields of the moon" locates them in a "transitional state," anticipating the final separation of soul and mind, and blissful return of the mind to its origins (*Poems of John Milton,* 227). As will be seen from my reading of the reciprocities between the pairs of Venus and Adonis and Cupid and Psyche, I think that Milton is pressuring the dualism of conventional allegoresis by a double movement that links divine and human, celestial and natural, female and male realms inextricably.

51. William Blake, "The Marriage of Heaven and Hell," in *Poetry and Prose,* 35.

52. Nancy Lindheim refers to the pairing of Venus and Adonis with Cupid and Psyche as a "mythological diptych," yet she reads the two pairs oppositionally, with the anagogical significance of the Cupid and Psyche allegory contrasting the cyclical and time-bound limitations of the naturalistic eros symbolized by Venus and Adonis ("Milton's Garden of Adonis: The Epilogue to the Ludlow Masque," *Milton Studies* 35 [1997]: 30, 36). John Rumrich similarly observes, "The figure of Adonis stands for the natural cycle of life and death that Milton's Lady aspires to transcend" (*Milton Unbound,* 93).

53. Wind, *Pagan Mysteries,* 119–20.

54. Lewis, *Spenser's Images,* 31.

55. Carey, *Poems of John Milton,* 227–28.

56. In making this claim, I am challenging not only Carey but the standard critical contrast made between the loving couples in Epilogue, that the Venus and Adonis pair represent love as it is bound to time, flesh, and the cycles of nature, while the celestial Cupid and Psyche pair represent divine and spiritual love that transcends these tragic limitations. See, for instance, Rumrich, *Milton Unbound,* 93; and Nancy Lindheim's recent excellent studies: "Milton reinterprets the sequence of Spenser's myths from Venus and Adonis to Cupid and Psyche in order to contrast the endless, sad, cyclical configuration of time as understood by classical civilization with the linear promise of Christianity" (Lindheim, "Pastoral and Masque at Ludlow," 664; see also Lindheim, "Milton's Garden of Adonis," 30, 36).

57. The erotic intensities of the heterosexual couples in the Epilogue problematize Richard Rambuss's contention that "Milton's recasting of [devotional topics] not only drains them of much of their potential for erotic cathexis, [it] also strikingly decorporealizes them." Richard Rambuss, *Closet Devotions* (Durham, NC: Duke University Press, 1998), 134. Bruce Boehrer depends on Rambuss's article in his treatment of the hymeneal festivities that climax "Lycidas" (and "Epitaphium Damonis") as evidence of Milton's "conflicted sense of matrimony: one that desires the estate and imagines it as coextensive with spiritual salvation and yet simultaneously rejects feminine sexuality as disruptive to the poet's vocation and offers no specific place for women in its climactic vision of heavenly wedlock" (Boehrer, "'Lycidas': The Pastoral Elegy as Same-Sex Epithalamium," *PMLA* 117, no. 2 [March 2002]: 233).

58. Orc is represented in Blake's splendid engraving, "Glad Day," which Harold Bloom describes thus: "Blake's Orc dances on tiptoe, a superbly Renaissance figure, with both arms flung out and the light bursting from him. His eyes are flashing, and his floating hair is rich with light. He both reflects the sunlight and radiates light to it, and he treads underfoot the serpent and the bat as he dances." Bloom observes, "Orc is the human imagination trying to burst out of the confines of nature, but this creative thrust in him is undifferentiated from merely organic energy. . . . He means new life and sexual renewal, which appear in the periodic

overthrow of literary conventions as well as of restrictive social and religious forms" (*Visionary Company,* 13, 12).

59. Roland Barthes, *The Pleasure of the Text,* trans. Richard Miller (New York: Hill and Wang, 1975).

60. The passage begins after line 4, "In Regions mild of calm and serene Air":

> amidst the Hesperian gardens, on whose bancks {where the banks}
> bedew'd wth nectar, & celestiall songs
> aeternall roses grow {yeeld, blow, blosme} & hyacinth
> & fruits of golden rind, on whose faire tree
> the scalie-harnest {watchfull} dragon ever keeps
> his uninchanted {never charmed} eye, & round the verge
> & sacred limits of this blisfull {happie} Isle
> the jealous ocean that old river winds
> his farr-extended armes till wth steepe fall
> halfe his wast flood ye wide Atlantique fills
> & halfe the slow unfadom'd Stygian poole {poole of styx}
> but soft I was not sent to court yor wonder
> with distant worlds & strange removed clim
> {I doubt me gentle mortalls these may seeme
> strange distances to heare & unknowne climes}
> yet thence I come and fro thence behold
> above the smoake & stirre of this dim spot . . .

This manuscript draft is taken from the Milton *Variorum* vol. 2, part 3, 856.

61. S. E. Sprott provides a detailed presentation of the manuscripts and revisions by Milton in *John Milton, "A Maske": The Earlier Versions* (Toronto: University of Toronto Press, 1973). See also the earlier study by John Diekhoff, "The Text of 'Comus,' 1634–45," *PMLA* 52, no. 3 (1937): 705–27. Nancy Lindheim provides a clear brief account of the positioning of the Hesperian Gardens material in Milton's successive drafts of the *Maske* ("Milton's Garden of Adonis," 23–24).

62. We recall here Nietzsche's critical remarks about the metaphysical security created by Euripides' prologues and epilogues (*BT,* 85).

63. "It [the Epilogue] is perhaps more emblematic than purely descriptive, seeking to translate the final dance (a masque gesture) into a verbal idea" (Lindheim, "Pastoral and Masque at Ludlow," 661).

64. Louis Réau, *Iconographie de l'art chrétien,* (Paris, PUF: 1955–59), vol. 2, part 2, 750, cited by Roland M. Frye in his discussion of Milton's depiction of Eden and its relation to Heaven in *Paradise Lost* (*Milton's Imagery and the Visual Arts: Iconographic Tradition in the Epic Poems* [Princeton, NJ: Princeton University Press, 1978], 193).

65. Clark, "Milton *Naturans,* Milton *Naturata,*" 9, 23.

66. Galway Kinnell, *The Book of Nightmares* (Boston: Houghton Mifflin, 1971), 58.

67. Derek Walcott, *Omeros* (New York: Farrar, Straus, and Giroux, 1990), 18.

68. Coinciding with my own reading here, Lauren Shohet quite beautifully explains the vulnerability that makes community and communion possible, in the final sentence of her essay: "Vulnerability in the *Mask* figures not only the potential to bond with others in creating a chaste community, but also the openness to communion with God that is imaged in other sources as the marriage of Christ and his bride: the supremely significant, feminized human soul" ("Figuring Chastity," 164).

69. John Rumrich critiques the modern critical "invention" of a Milton commit-

ted to the didactic transmission of different forms of determinist Christian orthodoxies and critiques as well the reinscription of this determinism in recent new historicist accounts of Milton. Rumrich provides an alternative portrait of a heretical Milton committed uncompromisingly to the exercise of human freedom, "a poet of indeterminacy who found ways to incorporate the uncertain and the evolving into his most highly realized works of literary art: a poetics of *becoming*" (*Milton Unbound,* 31).

70. "I identify myself in language, but only by losing myself in it like an object. What is realized in my history is not the past definite of what was, since it is no more, or even the present perfect of what has been in what I am, but the future anterior of what I shall have been for what I am in the process of becoming" (Jacques Lacan, *Language of the Self,* 63). See also Marshall Grossman's treatment of the construction of Adam's subjectivity in his articulation of the experience of lack, in "The Rhetoric of Feminine Priority and the Ethics of Form in *Paradise Lost*," *English Literary Renaissance* 33 (2003): 424–43.

71. Lana Cable's analysis of the iconoclastic momentum of Milton's "carnal rhetoric" describes a similar trajectory of self-transcendence in the metaphorical passages of Milton's major prose and *Samson Agonistes.* Although Cable does not discuss the *Maske* in her study, the concluding sentence of her book makes eloquent sense of the Lady's once and future career: "Milton equips the human imagination with a paradigm for *sustaining* (as opposed to 'spending') its most precious asset and condition for survival: the ontological longing of transformative desire" (*Carnal Rhetoric,* 196).

72. Wind, *Pagan Mysteries,* 71.

Bibliography

Achinstein, Sharon. *Milton and the Revolutionary Reader.* Princeton, NJ: Princeton University Press, 1994.

Aeschylus. *The Oresteia.* Translated by Robert Fagles. New York: Bantam Books, 1975.

Alcorn, C. Fred. *The Psychoanalytic Theory of Greek Tragedy.* New Haven, CT: Yale University Press, 1992.

Allen, Don Cameron. *The Harmonious Vision: Studies in Milton's Poetry.* Baltimore: Johns Hopkins University Press, 1954.

Althusser, Louis. *Lenin and Philosophy and Other Essays.* Translated by Ben Brewster. New York: Monthly Review Press, 1971.

Anderson, William. "Calypso and Elysium." In *Essays on the Odyssey,* edited by Charles Taylor, 73–86. Bloomington: Indiana University Press, 1963.

Andrea, Bernadette. "Black Skin, the Queen's Masques: Africanist Ambivalence and Feminine Author(ity) in the Masques of *Blackness* and *Beauty.*" *English Literary Renaissance* 29, no. 2 (Spring 1999): 246–81.

Apuleius. *The Golden Ass.* Translated by Jack Lindsay. Bloomington: Indiana University Press, 1962.

Aristotle. *Poetics.* Translated by Leon Golden. In *The Critical Tradition: Classic Texts and Contemporary Trends,* edited by David H. Richter, 42–64. Boston: Bedford Books, 1998.

Armstrong, Nancy, and Leonard Tennenhouse. *The Imaginary Puritan: Literature, Intellectual Labor, and the Origins of Personal Life.* Berkeley and Los Angeles: University of California Press, 1994.

Arthos, John. "The Realms of Being in the Epilogue of *Comus.*" *Modern Language Notes* 76 (April 1961): 321–24.

Auden, W. H. *Collected Shorter Poems 1927–1957.* New York: Random House, 1975.

Augustine. *Augustine: Later Works.* Translated by John Burnaby. London: SCM Press, 1955.

———. *Confessions.* Translated by R. S. Pine-Coffin. London: Penguin Books, 1980.

Bakhtin, Mikhail. *Rabelais and His World.* Translated by Helen Iswolsky. Bloomington: Indiana University Press, 1984.

Barber, C. L. "*A Mask Presented at Ludlow Castle:* The Masque as a Masque." In *The Lyric and Dramatic Milton,* edited by Joseph H. Summers, 35–63. New York: Columbia University Press, 1965.

———. "The Family in Shakespeare's Development: Tragedy and Sacredness." In *Representing Shakespeare: New Psychoanalytic Essays,* edited by Murray M.

Schwartz and Coppélia Kahn, 188–202. Baltimore: Johns Hopkins University Press, 1980.

Barkan, Leonard. *The Gods Made Flesh: Metamorphosis and the Pursuit of Paganism.* New Haven, CT: Yale University Press, 1986.

———. *Nature's Work of Art: The Human Body as Image of the World.* New Haven, CT: Yale University Press, 1975.

Barker, Arthur E. *Milton and the Puritan Dilemma, 1641–1660.* Toronto: University of Toronto Press, 1942.

Barker, Francis. *The Tremulous Private Body: Essays in Subjection.* London: Methuen, 1984.

Barroll, Leeds. "Inventing the Stuart Masque." In *The Politics of the Stuart Court Masque,* edited by David Bevington and Peter Holbrook, 121–43. Cambridge: Cambridge University Press, 1998.

Barthes, Roland. *The Pleasure of the Text.* Translated by Richard Miller. New York: Hill and Wang, 1975.

Baruch, Franklin R. "Milton's *Comus:* Skill, Virtue, and Henry Lawes." *Milton Studies* 5 (1973): 289–308.

Basso, Keith. *The Cibecue Apache.* New York: Holt, Rinehart, and Winston, 1970.

Bate, Walter Jackson. *John Keats.* Cambridge, MA: Harvard University Press, 1963.

Belsey, Catherine. *John Milton: Language, Gender, Power.* Oxford: Basil Blackwell, 1988.

———. *Shakespeare and the Loss of Eden: The Construction of Family Values in Early Modern Culture.* London: Macmillan, 1999.

———. *The Subject of Tragedy: Identity and Difference in English Renaissance Drama.* London: Methuen, 1985.

Bennett, Joan. "Virgin Nature in *Comus.*" *Milton Studies* 23 (1987): 21–32.

Berry, Philippa, and Jayne Elisabeth Archer. "Reinventing the Matter of Britain: Undermining the State in Jacobean Masques." In *The Politics of the Stuart Court Masque,* edited by David Bevington and Peter Holbrook, 119–34. Cambridge: Cambridge University Press, 1998.

Blake, William. *The Poetry and Prose of William Blake.* Edited by David V. Erdman. Garden City, NY: Doubleday, 1970.

Bloom, Harold. *The Anxiety of Influence.* New York: Oxford University Press, 1997.

———. *Shakespeare: The Invention of the Human.* New York: Riverhead Books, 1998.

———. *The Visionary Company: A Reading of English Romantic Poetry.* Garden City, NY: Doubleday, 1961.

Bly, Robert. *Sleepers Joining Hands.* New York: Harper and Row, 1973.

Boehrer, Bruce. "'Lycidas': The Pastoral Elegy as Same-Sex Epithalamium." *PMLA* 117, no. 2 (March 2002): 222–36.

Borges, Jorge Luis. *Ficciones.* Translated by Emecé Editores and edited by Anthony Kerrigan. New York: Knopf, 1993.

Bouwsma, William J. *John Calvin: A Sixteenth Century Portrait.* New York: Oxford University Press, 1988.

Bradburn, Beth. "Bodily Metaphor and Moral Agency in *A Masque:* A Cognitive Approach." *Milton Studies* 43 (2004): 19–34.

Breasted, Barbara. "*Comus* and the Castlehaven Scandal." *Milton Studies* 3 (1971): 201–24.

Broaddus, James W. "'Gums of Glutinous Heat' in Milton's *Mask* and Spenser's *Faerie Queene.*" *Milton Quarterly* 37, no. 4 (2003): 205–14.

Brodwin, Leonora Leet. "Milton and the Renaissance Circe." *Milton Studies* 6 (1974): 21–83.

Brown, Cedric C. *John Milton's Aristocratic Entertainments.* Cambridge: Cambridge University Press, 1985.

Browne, Sir Thomas. *Religio Medici.* In *Seventeenth-Century Verse and Prose, Volume One: 1600–1660,* edited by Helen C. White, Ruth C. Wallerstein, Ricardo Quintana, and A. B. Chambers, 335–54. New York: Macmillan, 1971.

Bush, Douglas. *Mythology and the Renaissance Tradition in English Poetry.* New York: W. W. Norton, 1963.

Butler, Martin. "Reform or Reverence? The Politics of the Caroline Masque." In *Theatre and Government under the Early Stuarts,* edited by J. R. Mulryne and Margaret Shewring, 118–56. Cambridge: Cambridge University Press, 1993.

Cable, Lana. *Carnal Rhetoric: Milton's Iconoclasm and the Poetics of Desire.* Durham, NC: Duke University Press, 1995.

Carrithers, Gale H., Jr. "Milton's Ludlow Masque: From Chaos to Community." *English Literary History* 33 (1966): 23–42.

Caskey, Noelle. "Interpreting *Anorexia Nervosa.*" In *The Female Body in Western Culture: Contemporary Perspectives,* edited by Susan Rubin Suleiman, 175–89. Cambridge, MA: Harvard University Press, 1986.

Christopher, Georgia. *Milton and the Science of the Saints.* Princeton, NJ: Princeton University Press, 1982.

Cixous, Hélene. "The Laugh of the Medusa." Translated by Keith Cohen and Paula Cohen. *Signs: Journal of Women in Culture and Society* 1, no. 4 (1976): 875–93.

Clark, James Andrew. "Milton *Naturans,* Milton *Naturata:* The Debate Over Nature in *A Mask Presented at Ludlow.*" *Milton Studies* 20 (1984): 3–25.

Coiro, Ann Baynes. "Anonymous Milton, or, *A Maske* Masked." *ELH* 71, no. 3 (2004): 609–29.

Coleridge, Samuel Taylor. *Coleridge: Selected Poetry and Prose.* Edited by Elizabeth Schneider. New York: Holt, Rinehart, and Winston, 1951.

Corns, Thomas N. "Milton before 'Lycidas.'" In *Milton and the Terms of Liberty,* 23–36. Cambridge: Cambridge University Press, 1999.

Corthell, Ronald. "Go Ask Alice: Daughter, Patron, and Poet in *A Mask Presented at Ludlow Castle.*" *Milton Studies* 44 (2005): 111–28.

Cox, Catherine I. "The Garden Within: Milton's Ludlow Masque and the Tradition of Canticles." *Milton Studies* 31 (1994): 23–44.

Creaser, John. "Milton's *Comus:* The Irrelevance of the Castlehaven Scandal." *Milton Quarterly* 21, no. 4 (December 1987): 24–34.

Cunnar, Eugene. "Fantasizing a Sexual Golden Age in Seventeenth-Century Poetry." In *Renaissance Discourses of Desire,* edited by Claude J. Summers and Ted-Larry Pebworth, 179–205. Columbia: University of Missouri Press, 1993.

———. "Milton, the Shepherd of Hermas, and the Writing of a Puritan Masque." *Milton Studies* 23 (1987): 33–52.

Curtius, Ernst Robert. *European Literature and the Latin Middle Ages.* Translated by Willard R. Trask. New York: Harper and Row, 1963.

Demaray, John G. *Milton and the Masque Tradition: The Early Poems, "Arcades," and* Comus. Cambridge, MA: Harvard University Press, 1968.

———. "The Temple of the Mind: Cosmic Iconography in Milton's *A Mask.*" *Milton Quarterly* 21, no. 4 (1987): 59–76.

Dempsey, Charles. *The Portrayal of Love: Botticelli's* Primavera *and Humanist Culture at the Time of Lorenzo the Magnificent.* Princeton, NJ: Princeton University Press, 1992.

Detienne, Marcel. *Dionysos at Large.* Translated by Arthur Goldhammer. Cambridge, MA: Harvard University Press, 1989.

Diekhoff, John. "The Text of 'Comus,' 1634–45." *PMLA* 52, no. 3 (1937): 705–27.

Donne, John. *John Donne's Poetry.* Edited by A. L. Clements. New York: W. W. Norton, 1966.

Dubrow, Heather. "The Masquing of Genre in *Comus.*" *Milton Studies* 44 (2005): 62–83.

DuRocher, Richard. *Milton and Ovid.* Ithaca, NY: Cornell University Press, 1985.

Dusinberre, Juliet. *Shakespeare and the Nature of Women.* New York: Harper & Row, 1975.

Eagleton, Terry. *William Shakespeare.* Oxford: Basil Blackwell, 1987.

Eliade, Mircea. *Myth, Dreams, and Mysteries: The Encounter Between Contemporary Faiths and Archaic Realities.* Translated by Phillip Mairet. London: Harvil Press, 1960.

———. *Rites and Symbols of Initiation: The Mysteries of Birth and Rebirth.* Translated by Willard R. Trask. New York: Harper and Row, 1958.

———. *Symbolism, the Sacred, and the Arts.* Edited by Diane Apostolos-Cappadona. New York: Crossroad Publishing, 1977.

Eliot, T. S. *Four Quartets.* New York: Harcourt Brace, 1971.

———. "Tradition and the Individual Talent." In *The Critical Tradition: Classic Texts and Contemporary Trends,* edited by David Richter, 498–503. Boston: Bedford Books, 1998.

———. *The Waste Land and Other Poems.* New York: Harcourt Brace, 1958.

Enterline, Lynn. *The Rhetoric of the Body from Ovid to Shakespeare.* Cambridge: Cambridge University Press, 2000.

Euripides. *The Bakkhai by Euripides.* Translated by Robert Bagg. Amherst: University of Massachusetts Press, 1978.

———. *Ten Plays by Euripides.* Translated by Moses Hadas and John McLean. New York: Bantam Books, 1963.

Evans, J. Martin. "The Birth of the Author: Milton's Poetic Self-Construction." *Milton Studies* 38 (2000): 47–65.

———. "From Temperance to Abstinence: The Argument of *Comus* Revisited." In *"All in All": Unity, Diversity, and the Miltonic Perspective,* edited by Charles W. Durham and Kristin A. Pruitt, 124–31. Selinsgrove, PA: Susquehanna University Press, 1999.

Faust, Joan. "*Queenes* and Jonson's Masques of Mirrors." *Explorations in Renaissance Culture* 21, no. 1 (Summer 2002): 1–29.

Fawcett, Mary Laughlin. "'Such Noise as I can Make': Chastity and Speech in *Othello* and *Comus*." *Renaissance Drama*, n.s., 16 (1985): 159–83.

Ferry, Anne D. *Milton's Epic Voice: The Narrator in Paradise Lost.* Chicago: University of Chicago Press, 1983.

Fish, Stanley. "Discovery as Form in *Paradise Lost*." In *New Essays on* Paradise Lost, edited by Thomas Kranidas, 1–14. Berkeley and Los Angeles: University of California Press, 1971.

———. *How Milton Works.* Cambridge, MA: Harvard University Press, 2001.

———. "Inaction and Silence: The Reader in *Paradise Regained*." In *Calm of Mind: Tercentenary Essays on* Paradise Regained *and* Samson Agonistes *in Honor of John S. Diekhoff*, edited by Joseph Anthony Wittreich, Jr., 25–47. Cleveland: Press of Case Western Reserve University, 1971.

———. "Milton's Career and the Career of Theory." In *There's No Such Thing as Free Speech and It's a Good Thing, Too,* 257–67. New York: Oxford University Press, 1994.

———. "Problem Solving in *Comus*." In *Illustrious Evidence: Approaches to English Literature of the Early Seventeenth Century,* edited by Earl Miner, 115–31. Berkeley and Los Angeles: University of California Press, 1975.

———. *Surprised by Sin: The Reader in* Paradise Lost. London: Macmillan, 1967.

———. "The Young and the Restless." In *There's No Such Thing as Free Speech and It's a Good Thing Too,* 243–56. New York: Oxford University Press, 1994.

———. "Why Milton Matters; or, Against Historicism." *Milton Studies* 44 (2005): 1–12.

Fitzmaurice, James, Josephine A. Roberts, Carol L. Barash, Eugene R. Cunnar, and Nancy A. Gutierrez, editors. *Major Women Writers of Seventeenth-Century England.* Ann Arbor: University of Michigan Press, 1997.

Flaubert, Gustave. *Madame Bovary.* Edited and translated by Paul de Man. New York: Norton Critical Editions, 1965.

Fletcher, Angus. *The Transcendental Masque: An Essay on Milton's* Comus. Ithaca, NY: Cornell University Press, 1971.

Fletcher, Anthony. *Gender, Sex, and Subordination in England 1500–1800.* New Haven, CT: Yale University Press, 1995.

Foucault, Michel. *The History of Sexuality.* 3 vols. New York: Random House, 1978–84.

Fraser, Russell A., and Norman Rabkin, eds. *Drama of the English Renaissance, II: The Stuart Period.* New York: Macmillan, 1976.

Freud, Sigmund. "Creative Writers and Day-Dreaming." Translated by James Strachey. In *Criticism: Major Statements,* edited by Charles Kaplan and William Anderson, 419–28. New York: St. Martin's Press, 1991.

———. *The Interpretation of Dreams.* Translated by James Strachey. New York: Avon Books, 1965.

———. *New Introductory Lectures on Psychoanalysis.* Translated by James Strachey. New York: W. W. Norton, 1965.

———. *Sexuality and the Psychology of Love.* Edited by Philip Rieff. New York: Collier Books, 1963.

Frost, Elisabeth A. "The Didactic *Comus:* Henry Lawes and the Trial of Virtue." *Comitatus* 22 (1991): 87–103.

Frost, Robert. *Selected Poems of Robert Frost.* New York: Holt, Rinehart, and Winston, 1966.

Frye, Roland M. *Milton's Imagery and the Visual Arts: Iconographic Tradition in the Epic Poems.* Princeton, NJ: Princeton University Press, 1978.

Gallop, Jane. *Reading Lacan.* Ithaca, NY: Cornell University Press, 1985.

Gardner, Helen. "Milton's 'Satan' and the Theme of Damnation in Elizabethan Tragedy." In *Milton: Modern Essays in Criticism,* edited by Arthur E. Barker, 205–17. New York: Oxford University Press, 1975.

Giamatti, A. Bartlett. *The Earthly Paradise and the Renaissance Epic.* New York: W. W. Norton, 1966.

Gilbert, Sandra, and Susan Gubar. *The Madwoman in the Attic: The Woman Writer and the Nineteenth-Century Literary Imagination.* New Haven, CT: Yale University Press, 1979.

Girard, René. *Violence and the Sacred.* Translated by Patrick Gregory. Baltimore: Johns Hopkins University Press, 1977.

Goldberg, Jonathan. *James I and the Politics of Literature: Jonson, Shakespeare, Donne, and Their Contemporaries.* Stanford, CA: Stanford University Press, 1989.

———. *Sodometries: Renaissance Texts, Modern Sexualities.* Stanford, CA: Stanford University Press, 1992.

———. *Voice Terminal Echo: Postmodernism and English Renaissance Texts.* New York: Methuen, 1986.

Gordon, D. J. "Poet and Architect: The Intellectual Setting of the Quarrel between Ben Jonson and Inigo Jones." In *The Renaissance Imagination: Essays and Lectures by D. J. Gordon,* edited by Stephen Orgel, 77–101. Berkeley and Los Angeles: University of California Press, 1975.

Gossett, Suzanne. "'Man-maid, begone!': Women in Masques." *English Literary Renaissance* 18 (1988): 96–113.

Graham, Jean. "The Performing Heir in Jonson's Jacobean Masques." *Studies in English Literature* 41, no. 2 (2001): 381–98.

———. "Virgin Ears: Silence, Deafness, and Chastity in Milton's *Maske.*" *Milton Studies* 36 (1998): 1–17.

Greenblatt, Stephen. *Learning to Curse: Essays in Early Modern Culture.* New York: Routledge, 1990.

———. *Renaissance Self-Fashioning: From More to Shakespeare.* Chicago: University of Chicago Press, 1980.

Gregerson, Linda. *The Reformation of the Subject: Spenser, Milton, and the English Protestant Epic.* Cambridge: Cambridge University Press, 1995.

Grossman, Marshall. *"Authors to Themselves": Milton and the Revelation of History.* Cambridge: Cambridge University Press, 1987.

———. "The Rhetoric of Feminine Priority and the Ethics of Form in *Paradise Lost.*" *English Literary Renaissance* 33 (2003): 424–43.

Guibbory, Achsah. *Ceremony and Community from Herbert to Milton: Literature, Religion, and Cultural Conflict in Seventeenth-Century England.* Cambridge: Cambridge University Press, 1998.

———. "Sexual Politics/Political Sex: Seventeenth-Century Love Poetry." In *Renaissance Discourses of Desire,* edited by Claude J. Summers and Ted-Larry Pebworth, 206–22. Columbia: University of Missouri Press, 1993.

Guillory, John. "Milton, Narcissism, Gender: On the Genealogy of Male Self-Esteem." In *Critical Essays on John Milton,* edited by Christopher Kendrick, 195–233. New York: G. K. Hall, 1995.

———. *Poetic Authority: Spenser, Milton, and Literary History.* New York: Columbia University Press, 1983.

Habermas, Jürgen. *The Structural Transformation of the Public Sphere: An Inquiry into a Category of Bourgeois Society.* Translated by Thomas Burger and Frederick Lawrence. Cambridge: MIT Press, 1989.

Hale, John K. "Milton's Self-Presentation in *Poems . . . 1645.*" *Milton Quarterly* 25, no. 2 (1991): 37–48.

Haller, William. "'Hail Wedded Love.'" *English Literary History* 13 (1946): 79–97.

Haller, William, and Malleville Haller. "The Puritan Art of Love." *Huntington Library Quarterly* 5 (1942): 235–72.

Halpern, Richard. "Puritanism and Maenadism in *A Mask.*" In *Rewriting the Renaissance: The Discourses of Sexual Difference in Early Modern Europe,* edited by Margaret Ferguson, Maureen Quilligan, and Nancy J. Vickers, 88–105. Chicago: University of Chicago Press, 1986.

Hanford, James Holly. *A Milton Handbook.* New York: Appleton-Century-Crofts, 1970.

Harding, Davis P. *Milton and the Renaissance Ovid.* Urbana: University of Illinois Press, 1946.

Harvey, Elizabeth. *Ventriloquized Voices: Feminist Theory and English Renaissance Texts.* London: Routledge, 1992.

Hausknecht, Gina. "The Gender of Civic Virtue." In *Milton and Gender,* edited by Catherine Gimelli Martin, 17–33. Cambridge: Cambridge University Press, 2004.

Heschel, Abraham. *The Prophets.* 2 vols. New York: Harper & Row, 1969.

Hill, Christopher. *Milton and the English Revolution.* New York: Viking, 1978.

Holbrook, Peter. "Jacobean Masques and the Jacobean Peace." In *The Politics of the Stuart Court Masque,* edited by David Bevington and Peter Holbrook, 67–87. Cambridge: Cambridge University Press, 1998.

Hollis, Hilda. "Without Charity: An Intertextual Study of Milton's *Comus.*" *Milton Studies* 34 (1997): 159–78.

Holy Bible. Authorized King James Version. Cleveland: World Publishing Company, n.d.

Homer. *The Odyssey of Homer.* Translated by Richmond Lattimore. New York: Harper & Row, 1967.

Hoopes, Robert. *Right Reason in the English Renaissance.* Cambridge, MA: Harvard University Press, 1962.

Hopkins, Gerard Manley. *A Hopkins Reader.* Edited by John Pick. Garden City, NY: Doubleday Image Books, 1966.

Hoxby, Blair. "The Wisdom of Their Feet: Meaningful Dance in Milton and the Stuart Masque." *English Literary Renaissance* 37, no. 1 (2007): 74–99.

Hubbell, J. Andrew. "*Comus:* Milton's Re-Formation of the Masque." In *Spokesperson Milton: Voices in Contemporary Criticism,* edited by Charles W. Durham and Kristin Pruitt McColgan, 193–205. Selinsgrove, PA: Susquehanna University Press, 1994.

Hull, Suzanne W. *Chaste, Silent and Obedient: English Books for Women 1435–1640.* San Marino, CA: Huntington Library Press, 1982.

Hunter, William B., Jr. "The Liturgical Context of *Comus.*" *English Language Notes* 10 (1972): 11–15.

———. *Milton's* Comus: *Family Piece.* Troy, NY: Whitston Publishing, 1983.

Jakobson, Roman. "Closing Statement: Linguistics and Poetics." In *Style in Language,* edited by Thomas A. Sebeok, 350–77. Cambridge: M. I. T. Press, 1966.

Jameson, Fredric. "The Imaginary and the Symbolic in Lacan: Marxism, Psychoanalytic Criticism, and the Problem of the Self." *Yale French Studies* 55–56 (1977): 338-95.

———. *The Political Unconscious: Narrative as a Socially Symbolic Act.* Ithaca, NY: Cornell University Press, 1981.

Jayne, Sears. "The Subject of Milton's Ludlow Masque." In *Milton: Modern Essays in Criticism,* edited by Arthur E. Barker, 88–102. New York: Oxford University Press, 1975. 88–102.

Jenkins, Hugh. "Milton's *Comus* and the Country-House Poem." *Milton Studies* 32 (1996): 169–88.

Johnson, Samuel. *Lives of the English Poets.* Edited by G. B. Hill. 3 vols. Oxford: Clarendon Press, 1905.

Jung, C. G., and C. Kerényi. *Essays on a Science of Mythology: The Myths of the Divine Child and the Divine Maiden.* Translated by R. F. C. Hull. New York: Harper and Row, 1963.

Kahn, Victoria. *Machiavellian Rhetoric from the Counter-Reformation to Milton.* Princeton, NJ: Princeton University Press, 1994.

Kavanagh, James H. "That Hive of Subtlety: 'Benito Cereno' and the Liberal Hero." In *Ideology and Classic American Literature,* edited by Sacvan Bercovitch and Myra Jehlen, 352–83. New York: Cambridge University Press, 1986.

Keats, John. *Selected Poems and Letters.* Edited by Douglas Bush. Boston: Houghton Mifflin, 1959.

Kendrick, Christopher. "Milton and Sexuality: A Symptomatic Reading of *Comus.*" In *Re-Membering Milton: Essays on the Texts and Traditions,* edited by Mary Nyquist and Margaret W. Ferguson, 43–73. New York: Methuen, 1988.

Kerrigan, William. "The Articulation of the Ego in the English Renaissance." In *The Literary Freud: Mechanisms of Defense and the Poetic Will,* edited by Joseph H. Smith, 261–308. New Haven, CT: Yale University Press, 1980.

———. "The Heretical Milton: From Assumption to Mortalism." *English Literary Renaissance* 5 (1975): 125–66.

———. *The Prophetic Milton.* Charlottesville: The University Press of Virginia, 1974.

———. *The Sacred Complex: On the Psychogenesis of* Paradise Lost. Cambridge, MA: Harvard University Press, 1983.

Kim, Julie H. "The Lady's Unladylike Struggle: Redefining Patriarchal Boundaries in Milton's *Comus.*" *Milton Studies* 35 (1997): 1–20.

Klein, Joan Larsen. "The Demonic Bacchus in Spenser and Milton." *Milton Studies* 21 (1985): 93–118.

Krantz, Corrine Ann. *Affecting Performance: Meaning, Movement, and Experience in Okiek Women's Initiation.* Washington, DC: Smithsonian Institution Press, 1994.

Kristeva, Julia. *Powers of Horror: An Essay on Abjection.* Translated by Leon Roudiez. New York: Columbia University Press, 1982.

Kubrick, Stanley, director. *Eyes Wide Shut.* Los Angeles: Warner Home Video, 2000.

Lacan, Jacques. *Ecrits: A Selection.* Translated by Alan Sheridan. New York: W. W. Norton, 1977.

———. *The Language of the Self: The Function of Language in Psychoanalysis.* Translated by Anthony Wilden. New York: Dell, 1968.

LaFontaine, Jean. *Initiation.* New York: Penguin Books, 1985.

Laplanche, J., and J.-B. Pontalis. *The Language of Psycho-Analysis.* Translated by Donald Nicholson-Smith. New York: W. W. Norton, 1973.

Leasure, Ross. "Milton's Queer Choice: Comus as Castlehaven." *Milton Quarterly* 36, no. 2 (May 2002): 63–86.

Leonard, John. "Milton's View of Celibacy: A Reconsideration of the Evidence." In *Of Poetry and Politics: New Essays on Milton and His World,* edited by Paul G. Stanwood, 188–201. Binghamton, NY: Medieval and Renaissance Texts and Studies, 1995.

———. "Saying 'No' to Freud: Milton's *A Mask* and Sexual Assault." *Milton Quarterly* 25 (December 1991): 129–40.

———. "'Thus They Relate, Erring': Milton's Inaccurate Allusions." *Milton Studies* 38 (2000): 96–121.

Lewalski, Barbara Kiefer. "How Radical was the Young Milton?" In *Milton and Heresy,* edited by Stephen B. Dobranski and John P. Rumrich, 49–72. Cambridge: Cambridge University Press, 1998.

———. "Innocence and Experience in Milton's Eden." In *New Essays on Paradise Lost,* edited by Thomas Kranidas, 80–117. Berkeley and Los Angeles: University of California Press, 1969.

———. *The Life of John Milton: A Critical Biography.* Oxford: Blackwell Publishers, 2002.

———. "Milton's *Comus* and the Politics of Masquing." In *The Politics of the Stuart Court Masque,* edited by David Bevington and Peter Holbrook, 296–320. Cambridge: Cambridge University Press, 1998.

———. "Why Milton Matters." *Milton Studies* 44 (2005): 13–21.

———*Writing Women in Jacobean England.* Cambridge, MA: Harvard University Press, 1993.

Lewis, C. S. *Allegory of Love: A Study of Medieval Tradition.* New York: Oxford University Press, 1958.

———. "A Note on Comus." *Review of English Studies* 8 (1932): 170–76.

———. *Spenser's Images of Life.* Edited by Alastair Fowler. Cambridge: Cambridge University Press, 1967.

Lieb, Michael. *Milton and the Culture of Violence.* Ithaca, NY: Cornell University Press, 1994.

Liebler, Naomi Conn. *Shakespeare's Festive Tragedy: The Ritual Foundations of Genre.* London: Routledge, 1995.

Lindheim, Nancy. "Milton's Garden of Adonis: The Epilogue to the Ludlow Masque." *Milton Studies* 35 (1997): 21–41.

———. "Pastoral and Masque at Ludlow." *University of Toronto Quarterly* 67, no. 3 (Summer 1998): 639–68.

Lindley, David, ed. *Court Masques: Jacobean and Caroline Entertainments, 1605-1640.* Oxford: Oxford University Press, 1995.

Liu, Alan. "The Power of Formalism: The New Historicism." *ELH* 56 (1989): 721–71.

Loeffelholz, Mary. "Two Masques of Ceres and Proserpine: *Comus* and *The Tempest.*" In *Re-Membering Milton: Essays on the Texts and Traditions,* edited by Mary Nyquist and Margaret W. Ferguson, 25–42. New York: Methuen, 1988.

Loewenstein, David. "'Fair Offspring Nurs't in Princely Lore': On the Question of Milton's Early Radicalism." *Milton Studies* 28 (1992): 37–48.

Loughlin, Marie. "'Love's Friend and Stranger to Virginitie': The Politics of the Virginal Body in Ben Jonson's *Hymenaei* and Thomas Campion's *The Lord Hay's Masque.*" *English Literary History* 63, no. 4 (1996): 833–49.

MacCaffrey, Isabel. *Spenser's Allegory: The Anatomy of Imagination.* Princeton, NJ: Princeton University Press, 1976.

MacIntyre, Alasdair. *After Virtue.* Notre Dame, IN: University of Notre Dame Press, 1984.

MacMullen, Ramsay. "Roman Attitudes to Greek Love." *Historia* 31 (1982): 484–502.

Magro, Maria. "Milton's Sexualized Woman and the Creation of a Gendered Public Sphere." *Milton Quarterly* 35, no. 2 (May 2001): 98–112.

Madsen, William G. "The Idea of Nature in Milton's Poetry." In *Three Studies in the Renaissance: Sidney, Jonson, Milton,* Yale Studies in English 138, edited by Richard B. Young *et al.,* 181–283. New Haven, CT: Yale University Press.

Marcus, Leah Sinanoglou. "The Earl of Bridgewater's Legal Life: Notes toward a Political Reading of *Comus.*" *Milton Quarterly* 21, no. 4 (December 1987): 13–23.

———. "The Milieu of Milton's *Comus:* Judicial Reform at Ludlow and the Problem of Sexual Assault." *Criticism* 25, no. 4 (1983): 293–327.

———"Milton as Historical Subject." *Milton Quarterly* 25, no. 3 (1991): 120–27.

———. *The Politics of Mirth: Jonson, Herrick, Milton, Marvell, and the Defense of Old Holiday Pastimes.* Chicago: University of Chicago Press, 1986.

———. "Valediction: In which, the Scene Closed up and the Revels Ended, the Masquers Take Their Leave." In *The Politics of the Stuart Court Masque,* edited by David Bevington and Peter Holbrook, 321–26. Cambridge: Cambridge University Press, 1998.

Martin, Catherine Gimelli. "The Ahistoricism of the New Historicism: Knowledge as Power versus Power as Knowledge in Bacon's *New Atlantis.*" In *Fault Lines and Controversies in the Study of Seventeenth-Century English Literature,* edited by Claude J. Summers and Ted-Larry Pebworth, 22–49. Columbia: University of Missouri Press, 2002.

———. "The Non-Puritan Ethics, Aesthetics, and Metaphysics of Milton's Spenserian Masque." *Milton Quarterly* 37, no. 4 (2003): 215–44.

Martz, Louis, ed. *George Herbert and Henry Vaughan.* Oxford: Oxford University Press, 1986.

———. "The Music of *Comus.*" In *Illustrious Evidence: Approaches to English Literature of the Early Seventeenth Century,* edited by Earl Miner, 93–113. Berkeley and Los Angeles: University of California Press, 1975.

———. *Poet of Exile: A Study of Milton's Poetry.* New Haven, CT: Yale University Press, 1980.

Maus, Katharine Eisaman. *Inwardness and Theater in the English Renaissance.* Chicago: University of Chicago Press, 1995.

McColley, Diane Kelsey. "'All in All': The Individuality of Creatures in *Paradise Lost.*" In *"All in All": Unity, Diversity, and the Miltonic Perspective,* edited by Charles W. Durham and Kristin A. Pruitt, 21–38. Selinsgrove, PA: Susquehanna University Press, 1999.

———. "Beneficent Hierarchies: Reading Milton Greenly." In *Spokesperson Milton: Voices in Contemporary Criticism,* edited by Charles W. Durham and Kristin P. McColgan, 231–48. Selinsgrove, PA: Susquehanna University Press, 1994.

———. *Milton's Eve.* Urbana: University of Illinois Press, 1983.

McGuire, Maryann Cale. *Milton's Puritan Masque.* Athens: University of Georgia Press, 1983.

Meyerhoff, Barbara. "Rites of Passage: Process and Paradox." In *Celebration: Studies in Festivity and Ritual,* edited by Victor Turner, 109–35. Washington, DC: Smithsonian Institution Press, 1982.

Milton, John. *John Milton: Complete Poems and Major Prose.* Edited by Merritt Y. Hughes. New York: Odyssey Press, 1957.

———. *John Milton: The Complete Poems.* Edited by John Leonard. New York: Penguin Putnam, 1998.

———. *"A Maske": The Earlier Versions.* Edited by S. E. Sprott. Toronto: University of Toronto Press, 1973.

———. *The Poems of John Milton.* Edited by John Carey and Alastair Fowler. London and New York: Longman Group and W. W. Norton, 1972.

Montag, Warren. "Louis Althusser (1918–1990) and His Circle." In *The Continuum Encyclopedia of Modern Criticism and Theory,* edited by Julian Wolfreys, 273–79. New York: Continuum, 2002.

Moore, Jeanie Grant. "The Two Faces of Eve: Temptation Scenes in *Comus* and *Paradise Lost.*" *Milton Quarterly* 36, no. 1 (March 2002): 1–19.

Mueller, Janel. "Contextualizing Milton's Nascent Republicanism." In *Of Poetry and Politics: New Essays on Milton and His World,* edited by Paul G. Stanwood, 263–82. Binghamton, NY: Medieval and Renaissance Texts and Studies, 1995.

Murrin, Michael. *The Veil of Allegory.* New Haven, CT: Yale University Press, 1975.

Neumann, Erich. *The Great Mother: An Analysis of the Archetype.* Translated by Ralph Mannheim. Princeton, NJ: Princeton University Press, 1972.

Neuse, Richard. "Metamorphosis and Symbolic Action in *Comus.*" *English Literary History* 34, no. 1 (1967): 49–64.

Nicoll, Allardyce. *Stuart Masques and the Renaissance Stage.* New York: Harcourt Brace, 1938.

Nietzsche, Friedrich. *The Birth of Tragedy and The Case of Wagner.* Translated by Walter Kaufman. New York: Random House, 1967.

Norbrook, David. *Poetry and Politics in the English Renaissance.* London: Routledge & Kegan Paul, 1984.

Normand, Lawrence. "Witches, King James, and *The Masque of Queens.*" In *Representing Women in Renaissance England,* edited by Claude J. Summers and Ted-Larry Pebworth, 107–20. Columbia: University of Missouri Press, 1997.

Nyquist, Mary. "The Genesis of Gendered Subjectivity in the Divorce Tracts and in *Paradise Lost.*" In *Re-Membering Milton: Essays on the Texts and Traditions,* edited by Mary Nyquist and Margaret Ferguson, 99–127. New York and London: Methuen, 1988.

Ogunyemi, Chikwenye Okenyo. *Africa Wo/Man Palava: the Nigerian Novel by Women.* Chicago: University of Chicago Press, 1996.

Oram, William A. "The Invocation of Sabrina." *Studies in English Literature* 24 (1984): 121–39.

Orgel, Stephen. "The Case for Comus." *Representations* (Winter 2003): 29–45.

———. *The Illusion of Power: Political Theater in the English Renaissance.* Berkeley and Los Angeles: University of California Press, 1975.

———. "Jonson and the Amazons." In *Soliciting Interpretation,* edited by Elizabeth Harvey and Katharine Eisaman Maus, 119–39. Chicago: University of Chicago Press, 1990.

———. *The Jonsonian Masque.* New York: Columbia University Press, 1981.

———. "Marginal Jonson." In *The Politics of the Stuart Court Masque,* edited by David Bevington and Peter Holbrook, 144–75. Cambridge: Cambridge University Press, 1998.

Ortiz, Joseph M. "'The Reforming of Reformation': Theatrical, Ovidian, and Musical Figuration in Milton's *Mask.*" *Milton Studies* 44 (2005): 84–111.

Ovid. *The Metamorphoses of Ovid.* Translated by Allen Mandelbaum. New York: Harcourt Brace, 1993.

Ozment, Steven. *The Age of Reform, 1250–1550: An Intellectual and Religious History of Late Medieval and Reformation Europe.* New Haven, CT: Yale University Press, 1980.

Paglia, Camille. *Sexual Personae: Art and Decadence from Nefertiti to Emily Dickinson.* New York: Random House, 1991.

Parker, William Riley. *Milton: A Biography.* 2 vols. Oxford: Oxford University Press, 1968.

———. *Milton's Debt to Greek Tragedy in* Samson Agonistes. Hamden, CT: Archon Books, 1963.

Parry, Graham. "The Politics of the Jacobean Masque." In *Theatre and Government under the Early Stuarts,* edited by J. R. Mulryne and Margaret Shewring, 87–117. Cambridge: Cambridge University Press, 1993.

Patterson, Annabel. "'Forc'd Fingers': Milton's Early Poems and Ideological Constraint." In *"The Muses Commonweale": Poetry and Politics in the Seventeenth Century,* edited by Claude J. Summers and Ted-Larry Pebworth, 9–22. Columbia: University of Missouri Press, 1988.

———. "'L'Allegro,' 'Il Penseroso' and *Comus:* The Logic of Recombination." *Milton Quarterly* 9, no. 3 (1975): 75–79.

Peacock, John. "The French Element in Inigo Jones's Masque Design." In *The Court Masque,* edited by David Lindley, 148–68. Manchester: Manchester University Press, 1984.

———. "The Stuart Court Masque and the Theatre of the Greeks." *Journal of the Warburg and Courtauld Institutes* 56 (1993): 183–208.

Polydorou, Desma. "Gender and Spiritual Equality in Marriage: A Dialogic Reading of Rachel Speght and John Milton." *Milton Quarterly* 35 (2001): 22–32.

Porter, James I. *The Invention of Dionysus: An Essay on* The Birth of Tragedy. Stanford, CA: Stanford University Press, 2000.

Pye, Christopher. *The Vanishing: Shakespeare, the Subject, and Early Modern Culture.* Durham, NC: Duke University Press, 2000.

Quilligan, Maureen. *Milton's Spenser: The Politics of Reading.* Ithaca, NY: Cornell University Press, 1983.

Radzinowicz, Mary Ann. *Toward* Samson Agonistes: *The Growth of Milton's Mind.* Princeton, NJ: Princeton University Press, 1978.

Rajan, Balachandra. *The Lofty Rhyme: A Study of Milton's Major Poetry.* Coral Gables, FL: University of Miami Press, 1970.

Rambuss, Richard. *Closet Devotions.* Durham, NC: Duke University Press, 1998.

Réage, Pauline. *The Story of O.* Translated by Sabine d'Estrée. New York: Ballantine Press, 1973.

Réau, Louis. *Iconographie de l'art chrétien.* 3 vols. Paris: PUF, 1955–59.

Revard, Stella. *Milton and the Tangles of Neaera's Hair: The Making of the 1645 Poems.* Columbia: University of Missouri Press, 1997.

Richards, Audrey. *Chisungu: A Girl's Initiation Ceremony among the Bemba of Zambia.* London: Routledge, 1988.

Robertson, David. "Soliloquy and Self in Milton's Major Poems." In *Of Poetry and Politics: New Essays on Milton and His World,* edited by Paul G. Stanwood, 59–77. Binghamton, NY: Medieval and Renaissance Texts and Studies, 1995.

Roche, Thomas. *The Kindly Flame: A Study of the Third and Fourth Books of Spenser's* Faerie Queene. Princeton, NJ: Princeton University Press, 1964.

Rogers, John. "The Enclosure of Virginity: The Poetics of Sexual Abstinence in the English Revolution." In *Enclosure Acts: Sexuality, Property, and Culture in Early Modern England,* edited by Richard Burt and John Michael Archer, 229–50. Ithaca, NY: Cornell University Press, 1994.

———. *The Matter of Revolution: Science, Poetry, and Politics in the Age of Milton.* Ithaca, NY: Cornell University Press, 1996.

Rumrich, John. *Milton Unbound: Controversy and Reinterpretation.* Cambridge: Cambridge University Press, 1996.

Rushdy, Ashraf. *The Empty Garden: The Subject of Late Milton.* Pittsburgh: University of Pittsburgh Press, 1991.

Sandys, George. *Ovid's Metamorphoses English'd, Mythologized, and Represented in Figures.* Edited by Karl K. Hulley and Stanley T. Vandershall. Oxford, 1632; repr., Lincoln: University of Nebraska Press, 1970.

Sartre, Jean-Paul. "Flaubert and *Madame Bovary:* Outline of a New Method." Translated by Hazel Barnes. In Gustave Flaubert, *Madame Bovary,* edited and translated by Paul de Man, 302–8. New York: Norton Critical Editions, 1965.

Scheidenhelm, Carol. "'Heav'n Hath Timely Tri'd [Her] Youth': Self-Knowledge Through Language in Milton's *Comus.*" *Renaissance and Reformation/Renaissance et Réforme* 27, no. 3 (1992): 59–67.

Schwarz, Kathryn. "Amazon Reflections in the Jacobean Queen's Masque." *Studies in English Literature* 35 (1995): 293–319.

———. "Chastity, Militant and Married: Cavendish's Romance, Milton's Masque." *PMLA* 118, no. 2 (2003): 270–85.

———. *Tough Love: Amazon Encounters in the English Renaissance.* Durham, NC: Duke University Press, 2000.

Schwyzer, Philip. "Purity and Danger on the West Bank of the Severn: The Cultural Geography of *A Masque Presented at Ludlow Castle,* 1634." *Representations* 60 (Autumn 1997): 22–48.

Seznec, Jean. *The Survival of the Pagan Gods: The Mythological Tradition and Its Place in Renaissance Humanism and Art.* Translated by B. F. Sessions. Princeton, NJ: Princeton University Press, 1972.

Shakespeare, William. *Hamlet.* Edited by Edward Hubler. New York: Signet, 1963.

———. *Macbeth.* Edited by Sylvan Barnet. New York: Signet, 1963.

———. *A Midsummer Night's Dream.* Edited by Wolfgang Clemen. New York: Signet, 1963.

———. *The Tempest.* Edited by Robert Langbaum. New York: Signet, 1963.

———. *The Winter's Tale.* Edited by Frank Kermode. New York: New American Library,1963.

Shawcross, John. "Certain Relationships of the Manuscripts of *Comus.*" *Publications of the Bibliographical Society of America* 54 (1960): 38–56.

———. *John Milton: The Self and the World.* Lexington: University of Kentucky Press, 1993.

Shelley, Percy Bysshe. *Shelley's Poetry and Prose.* Edited by Donald H. Reiman and Sharon B. Powers. New York: W. W. Norton, 1977.

Shohet, Lauren. "Figuring Chastity: Milton's Ludlow *Mask.*" In *Menacing Virgins: Representing Virginity in the Middle Ages and Renaissance,* edited by Kathleen Coyne Kelly and Marina Leslie, 146–64. Newark: University of Delaware Press, 1999.

Shuger, Debora. "'The Bliss of Dreams': Theology in Milton's *Maske.*" *Hellas, A Journal of Poetry and the Humanities* 7, no. 2 (Fall/Winter 1996): 139–53.

Shullenberger, William. "Doctrine as Deep Structure in Milton's Early Poetry." In *A Fine Tuning: Studies of the Religious Poetry of Herbert and Milton,* edited by Mary A. Maleski, 187–203. Binghamton, NY: Medieval and Renaissance Texts & Studies, 1989.

———. "Love as a Spectator Sport in John Donne's Poetry." In *Renaissance Discourses of Desire,* edited by Claude J. Summers and Ted-Larry Pebworth, 46–62. Columbia, MO: University of Missouri Press, 1993.

———. "Prospero's Potent Art." Paper presented at the Forum on Shakespeare and Gender, annual convention of the Modern Language Association. New York, December 30, 1986.

———. "Sorting the Seeds: The Regeneration of Love in *Paradise Lost.*" *Milton Studies* 28 (1991): 163–84.

———. "Wrestling with the Angel: *Paradise Lost* and Feminist Criticism." *Milton Quarterly* 20, no. 3 (October 1986): 69–85.

Sidney, Philip. "An Apology for Poetry." In *The Critical Tradition,* edited by David Richter, 134–59. Boston: Bedford Books, 1998.

Silk, M. S., and J. P. Stern. *Nietzsche on Tragedy.* Cambridge: Cambridge University Press, 1987.

Silver, Victoria. "Thoughts in Misbecoming Plight: Allegory in *Comus.*" In *Critical Essays on John Milton,* edited by Christopher Kendrick, 47–73. New York: G. K. Hall, 1995.

Simons, Louise. "'And Heaven Gates Ore My Head': Death as Threshold in Milton's Masque." *Milton Studies* 23 (1987): 53–93.

Singleton, R. H. "Milton's *Comus* and the *Comus* of Erycius Puteanus." *PMLA* 68 (1943): 949–57.

Slater, Philip. *The Glory of Hera: Greek Mythology and the Greek Family.* Boston: Beacon Press, 1968.

Smith, Bruce. *Homosexual Desire in Shakespeare's England.* Chicago: University of Chicago Press, 1991.

Smith, George William, Jr. "Milton's Revisions and the Design of *Comus.*" *English Literary History* 46, no. 1 (Spring 1979): 56–80.

Smith, Hilda. *Reason's Disciples: Seventeenth-Century English Feminists.* Urbana: University of Illinois Press, 1982.

Smith, Joseph H. *Arguing with Lacan: Ego Psychology and Language.* New Haven, CT: Yale University Press, 1991.

Sokol, B. J. "'Tilted Lees', Dragons, *Haemony,* Menarche, Spirit, and Matter in *Comus.*" *Review of English Studies,* n.s., 16 (1990): 309–24.

Sophocles. *The Oedipus Cycle.* Translated and edited by Dudley Fitts and Robert Fitzgerald. New York: Harcourt, Brace, and World, 1969.

Spencer, Jeffry. *Heroic Nature: Ideal Landscape in English Poetry from Marvell to Thompson.* Evanston, IL: Northwestern University Press, 1973.

Spenser, Edmund. *The Faerie Queene.* Edited by Thomas P. Roche, Jr. New York: Penguin Books, 1978.

Sprott, S. E., ed. *John Milton, "A Maske": The Earlier Versions.* Toronto: University of Toronto Press, 1973.

Starnes, DeWitt T., and Ernest William Talbert. *Classical Myth and Legend in Renaissance Dictionaries: A Study of Renaissance Dictionaries in Their Relation to the Classical Learning of Contemporary English Writers.* Westport, CT: Greenwood Press, 1973.

Steadman, John. "*Ethos* and *Dianoia:* Character and Rhetoric in *Paradise Lost.*" In *Language and Style in Milton,* edited by Ronald David Emma and John T. Shawcross, 193–202. New York: Frederick Ungar, 1967.

———. *Milton's Epic Characters: Image and Idol.* Chapel Hill: University of North Carolina Press, 1968.

———. *The Wall of Paradise: Essays on Milton's Poetics.* Baton Rouge: Louisiana State University Press, 1985.

Steggle, Matthew. "'The Tragical Part': Milton's Masque and Euripides." *Classical and Modern Literature* 20, no. 1 (2000): 18–36.

Steibel, Arlene. "Subversive Sexuality: Masking the Erotic in Poems by Katherine Philips and Aphra Behn." In *Renaissance Discourses of Desire,* edited by Claude J. Summers and Ted-Larry Pebworth, 223–36. Columbia: University of Missouri Press, 1993.

Stevens, Wallace. *The Collected Poems of Wallace Stevens.* New York: Alfred A. Knopf, 1972.

Stewart, Andrew. "Dionysos at Delphi: The Pediments of the Sixth Temple of Apollo and Religious Reform in the Age of Alexander." In *Macedonia and Greece in Late Classical and Hellenistic Times,* edited by Beryl Barr-Sharrar and Eugene Borza, 205–28. Washington, DC: National Gallery of Art, 1982.

Strong, Roy. *The Cult of Elizabeth: Elizabethan Portraiture and Pageantry.* London: Thames and Hudson, 1977.

Strout, Nathaniel. "Jonson's Jacobean Masques and the Moral Imagination." *Studies in English Literature, 1500–1900* 27, no. 2 (1987): 233–47.

Swaim, Kathleen. "Allegorical Poetry in Milton's Ludlow Mask." *Milton Studies* 16 (1982): 167–99.

———. "Lycidas and the Dolphins of Apollo." *Journal of English and Germanic Philology* 72, no. 8 (July 1973): 340–49.

———. "'Myself a True Poem': Early Milton and the (Re)formation of the Subject." *Milton Studies* 38 (2000): 66–95.

Taaffe, James. "Michaelmas, the 'Lawless Hour,' and the Occasion of Milton's *Comus.*" *English Language Notes* 6 (1968–69): 257–62.

Tanner, John. *Anxiety in Eden: A Kierkegaardian Reading of* Paradise Lost. New York: Oxford University Press, 1993.

Tayler, Irene. "Say First! What Mov'd Blake? Blake's *Comus* Designs and *Milton.*" In *Blake's Sublime Allegory,* edited by Stuart Curran and Joseph Anthony Wittreich, 233–58. Madison: University of Wisconsin Press, 1973.

Thickstun, Margaret Olofson. *Fictions of the Feminine: Puritan Doctrine and the Representation of Women.* Ithaca, NY: Cornell University Press, 1988.

Tillyard, E. M. W. *The Elizabethan World Picture.* New York: Vintage Books, n.d.

———. *Milton.* London: Chatto and Windus, 1966.

Todorov, Tzvetan. "Primitive Narrative." In *The Poetics of Prose,* translated by Richard Howard, 53–65. Ithaca: Cornell University Press, 1977.

Townshend, Aurelian. *Tempe Restored.* In *Court Masques: Jacobean and Caroline Entertainments, 1605–1640,* edited by David Lindley, 165–75. Oxford: Oxford University Press, 1995.

Treip, Mindele Anne. "*Comus* as 'Progress.'" *Milton Quarterly* 20, no. 1 (1986): 1–13.

———. "*Comus* and the Stuart Masque Connection, 1632–34." *ANQ: A Quarterly Journal of Short Articles, Notes and Reviews* 2, no. 3 (July 1989): 83–89.

———. "Descend from Heav'n Urania": *Milton's* Paradise Lost *and Raphael's Cycle in the* Stanza della Segnatura. ELS Monograph Series No. 35. Victoria, B.C.: English Literary Studies, 1985.

Turner, Victor. *Dramas, Fields, and Metaphors.* Ithaca, NY: Cornell University Press, 1974.

———. *The Forest of Symbols: Aspects of Ndembu Ritual.* Ithaca, NY: Cornell University Press, 1970.

———. *From Ritual to Theatre: The Human Seriousness of Play.* New York: PAJ Publications, 1982.

———. *The Ritual Process: Structure and Anti-Structure.* Chicago: Aldine, 1969.

Tuve, Rosemond. *Images and Themes in Five Poems by Milton.* Cambridge, MA: Harvard University Press, 1962.

Van Gennep, Arnold. *The Rites of Passage.* Translated by Monika B. Vizedom and Gabrielle L. Caffee. Chicago: University of Chicago Press, 1960.

Veevers, Erica. *Images of Love and Religion: Queen Henrietta Maria and Court Entertainments.* Cambridge: Cambridge University Press, 1989.

Verdi, Richard. *Nicolas Poussin 1594–1665.* With an essay by Pierre Rosenberg. London: Zwemmer and The Royal Academy of Arts, 1995.

Virgil. *The Aeneid.* Translated by Robert Fitzgerald. New York: Vintage, 1990.

Wall, Kathleen. "*A Mask Presented at Ludlow Castle:* The Armor of Logos." In *Milton and the Idea of Woman,* edited by Julia M. Walker, 52–65. Urbana: University of Illinois Press, 1988.

Walker, Julia M. "The Poetics of Antitext and the Politics of Milton's Allusions." *Studies in English Literature* 37 (1997): 151–71.

Welsford, Enid. *The Court Masque.* London: Cambridge University Press, 1927.

Wilding, Michael. "Milton's 'A Masque Presented at Ludlow Castle, 1634': Theatre and Politics on the Border." *Milton Quarterly* 21, no. 4 (December 1987): 35–51.

Wilkenfeld, Roger. "The Seat at the Center: An Interpretation of *Comus.*" *English Literary History* (1966): 170–97.

Wind, Edgar. *Pagan Mysteries in the Renaissance.* New York: W. W. Norton, 1968.

Wittreich, Joseph. "Why Milton Matters." *Milton Studies* 44 (2005): 22–39.

Wofford, Susanne Lindgren. "Gendering Allegory: Spenser's Bold Reader and the Emergence of Character in *The Faerie Queene* III." *Criticism* 30 (1988): 1–21.

Woodbridge, Linda. *Women and the English Renaissance: Literature and the Nature of Womankind, 1540–1620.* Urbana: University of Illinois Press, 1984.

Woodhouse, A. S. P. "The Argument of Milton's *Comus.*" *University of Toronto Quarterly* 11 (1941–42): 46–71.

———. "*Comus* Once More." *University of Toronto Quarterly* 19 (1949–50): 218–23.

Woodhouse, A. S. P., and Douglas Bush, eds. *A Variorum Commentary on the Poems of John Milton.* Vol. 2, part 3. New York: Columbia University Press, 1972.

Woolf, Virginia. *A Room of One's Own.* New York: Harcourt Brace, 1989.

Wynne-Davies, Marion. "The Queen's Masque: Renaissance Women and the Seventeenth-Century Court Masque." In *Gloriana's Face: Women, Public and Private, in the English Renaissance,* edited by S. P. Cerasano and Marion Wynne-Davies, 79–104. Detroit: Wayne State University Press, 1992.

Yeats, William Butler. *The Collected Poems of W. B. Yeats.* New York: Macmillan, 1973.

Žižek, Slavoj. *The Fragile Absolute—or, Why Is the Christian Legacy Worth Fighting For?* London: Verso Books, 2000.

Index

Achebe, Chinua: *Things Fall Apart,* 109
Achinstein, Sharon, 281 n. 9
"Ad Patrem," 99–100, 102, 218, 298 n. 39, 317 n. 28
Aeschylus: *The Eumenides,* 218, 304 n. 50, 305 n. 16; *Oresteia,* 307 n. 27
allegory, 34, 46, 206, 281 n. 9, 296 n. 17, 299 n. 48, 307 nn. 28 and 31; and the court masque, 49, 54, 57, 68, 122, 156; in Jonson's *The Masque of Queens,* 61; and Milton's critique of or resistance to allegoresis in *A Maske,* 37, 43, 68, 69, 86–88, 105, 122, 136, 138, 146, 153–54, 156, 193–94, 219, 262, 265, 296–97 n. 24, 306 n. 25, 327–28 n. 50; and Nietzsche, 148, 305 n. 15; Sandys's, 135–36, 138, 200, 305 n. 15; Spenser's, 31, 136, 227, 229, 264, 265, 294 n. 88, 318 n. 6; uses of in *A Maske,* 36, 84, 86–87, 104, 119, 154, 193–94, 247–48, 258, 261, 262, 265, 269, 270, 274, 292 n. 67, 294 n. 88, 295 n. 5, 296 n. 21, 296–97 n. 24, 298 n. 33, 302–3 n. 35, 313 n. 43, 324 n. 15, 328 n. 52. *See also* typology
Allen, Don Cameron, 299 n. 49
Althusser, Louis, 32, 284 nn. 38, 39, and 40
Andrea, Bernadette, 289 n. 37, 290 n. 45
Anne, Queen, 36, 60, 62–66, 79, 144, 289 n. 37, 290 nn. 39, 45, 47, and 50, 290–91 n. 52, 316–17 n. 27
anthropology, 21, 35, 48, 113, 278
antimasque, 35, 49, 50, 53–54, 57, 256, 286 n. 9, 287 n. 21; in *A Maske,* 69, 70, 72, 106, 110, 113, 114, 117, 143, 158, 162, 253, 255; in *The Masque of Queens,* 60–61, 162

antinomianism, 28, 29, 78, 117
Apollo, 38, 144, 148–54, 307 n. 27
Apology for Smectymnuus, An (*Apology against a Pamphlet, An*), 25, 40, 204, 205–9, 258, 324 n. 19
Apuleius, 270–71, 273
Arcades, 143, 287 n. 21, 291–92 n. 63, 297–98 n. 32
Areopagitica, 25–26, 44, 75–76, 79, 80, 94, 117, 179, 182, 195, 247, 303 n. 43
Ariosto, Ludovico, 260
Aristotle: *Poetics,* 145, 288 n. 29, 304–5 n. 8
Armstrong, Nancy, 282 n. 24
Arthos, John, 325 n. 25
Auden, W. H.: "In Memory of W. B. Yeats (d. Jan. 1939)," 18, 281 n. 10
Augustine, Saint: *Confessions,* 198, 314 n. 50; *De Trinitate,* 319 n. 20

Bacchus/Dionysus, 38, 83, 96, 142, 145–55, 161, 173, 192, 200, 277, 297 n. 29, 305 nn. 13–16, 306–7 n. 26, 307 n. 27, 322 n. 42
Bacon, Francis, 294 n. 88
Bagg, Robert, 305 n. 14, 306 n. 24
Bakhtin, Mikhail, 286 n. 12
Barber, C. L., 128, 186–87
Barkan, Leonard, 301–2 n. 22, 303 nn. 37, 38, and 42, 325 n. 21
Barker, Arthur, 180, 312 n. 16
Barker, Francis, 282 nn. 17, 21, and 22
Barroll, Leeds, 289 n. 37
Barthes, Roland, 329 n. 59
Baruch, Franklin R., 298 n. 33
Basso, Keith, 318 n, 320 n. 30, 323 n. 57, 323 n. 3
Bate, Walter Jackson, 327 n. 43

348

INDEX

Beaumont, Francis: *The Maid's Tragedy,* 162
Behn, Aphra: "The Disappointment," 309–10 n. 60
Belsey, Catherine, 281 n. 11, 282 nn. 17, 21, and 22
Bemba, 38, 48, 51–52, 70, 74, 142, 320 n. 29
Bennett, Joan, 308–9 n. 46, 310 n. 61
Bible, 25, 30, 35, 40, 77–78, 83, 85, 92, 112, 128, 129–31, 178, 205, 206–8, 210–13, 215, 220, 245, 248–49, 260–61, 263, 269, 270, 293 n. 78, 326 n. 31
Blake, William, 26, 35, 149, 224, 230–31, 263, 277, 283 n. 27; "The Book of Thel," 126; "The Divine Image," 247; "Glad Day," 273, 328–29 n. 58; *The Marriage of Heaven and Hell,* 28, 78, 269, 294 n. 84; "What is it men in women do require?" 45, 220, 285 n. 48, 317 n. 33
Bloom, Harold, 24–25, 282 n. 23, 318 n. 40, 322 n. 49, 328–29 n. 58
Bly, Robert, 308 n. 42
Boehrer, Bruce, 328 n. 57
Borges, Jorge Luis: "Pierre Menard, Author of *Don Quixote,*" 281 n. 14
Botticelli, Sandro: *Primavera,* 265–67, 269, 270, 327 n. 48
Bouwsma, William J., 282 n. 20
Bradburn, Beth, 297 n. 28, 322–23 n. 56
Breasted, Barbara, 312–13 n. 28, 317–18 n. 38
Bridgewater, 1st Earl of (John Egerton; also Lord Brackley), 69, 187, 304 n. 50, 323 nn. 5 and 7, 326 n. 29; as civilizing agent and judicial authority, 16, 111–12, 224, 253, 277, 323 n. 4; installation as Lord President of the Council of Wales and the West Marches of, 15, 17, 51, 68, 103, 104, 236, 254, 277, 317–18 n. 38
Broaddus, James W., 322–23 n. 56
Brodwin, Leonora Leet, 304 n. 5, 307 nn. 28 and 31
Brontë sisters, 109
Brown, Cedric, 169, 172, 281 n. 8, 287 n. 18, 292 n. 66, 294 n. 85, 299 n. 50, 300 n. 53, 322 n. 52
Browne, Sir Thomas: *Religio Medici,* 307 n. 32
Brydges, Elizabeth, 317–18 n. 38
Bunyan, John: *Pilgrim's Progress,* 17, 281 n. 9
Bush, Douglas, 303 n. 45
Butler, Martin, 291 n. 61, 294 n. 87, 295 n. 14

Cable, Lana, 306 n. 25, 330 n. 71
Calvin, John, 282 n. 20; *Institutes,* 316 n. 11
Cambridge University, 100; Christ's College, 27, 215
Campion, Thomas, 310 n. 3
capitalism, 164, 168
Carew, Thomas: *Coelum Britannicum,* 16, 66, 68, 87–88, 98, 291–92 n. 63, 292–93 n. 68, 295 n. 14, 324 n. 12
Carey, John, 271, 317 n. 28, 327–28 n. 50, 328 n. 56
carnivalesque, 49, 54, 60, 120, 256, 286 n. 12
Carrithers, Gale, 86, 295 n. 9, 309 n. 47
Caskey, Noelle, 301–2 n. 22
Castlehaven, Countess of (Anne Tuchet, née Stanley), 224, 317–18 n. 38
Castlehaven, 2nd Earl of (Mervyn Tuchet), 224, 312–13 n. 28, 317–18 n. 38
Catholicism, 23, 54, 291 n. 60, 321 n. 36
cavalier poets, 35, 88, 237, 309–10 n. 60
Cavendish, Margaret: *Assaulted and Pursued Chastity,* 281 n. 14
Changing Woman, 41, 240–42, 243, 245, 250, 251–52
charity, 227, 250, 251, 252, 269, 271, 318 n. 1, 322 n. 55
Charles I, King, 15, 36, 66–67, 68, 79, 94, 144, 272, 291 n. 61, 308 n. 40; *Book of Sports* (1633 reissue), 307–8 n. 34
chastity, 17, 37, 90, 91, 98, 105, 114, 115, 124, 125, 127, 150, 167, 235–36, 238, 243–45, 251, 254, 257, 261, 267, 281 n. 14, 301 n. 16, 305 n. 14,

317–18n. 38, 321–22n. 41; as dynamic source of social freedom, transformation, and pleasure, 39, 43, 47, 52–53, 67, 79, 117–21, 141, 176–77, 203, 206–9, 212–13, 227, 244, 249–50, 252, 277, 278–79, 287n. 18, 311n. 12; exchanged for theological charity, 227, 250, 251, 252, 318n. 1, 322n. 55; married, 22, 177–78, 180, 182, 185, 186, 208, 215, 227–29, 232, 239, 262, 310n. 3, 311–12n. 14, 316n. 11; militant iconography of, 39–40, 193–98, 201, 217–19, 228–30, 234, 239, 243; and Milton's personal celibacy, 180, 204, 208, 215–17, 312n. 18, 315n. 5; and Milton's transformation of gender hierarchy, 203, 207–8, 215–20; and Nature's order, 173, 175, 233, 247; and poetics, rhetoric, and prophecy of the Lady and Milton, 39–40, 141, 153, 175–76, 178–81, 187, 188, 190–93, 201–18, 220, 233, 254, 277, 311–12n. 14; and/vs. virginity, 175–94, 196–99, 201–2, 203–4, 206, 208–10, 214–15, 217, 219, 223, 227, 230, 233, 235–36, 241, 243, 257, 287n. 18, 310n. 3, 311nn. 8 and 9, 311–12n. 14, 312nn. 18 and 19, 313n. 31, 314–15 n. 60, 316n. 14, 323–24n. 8, 326n. 35
chisungu, 46–47, 51–52, 70, 74, 142
Christopher, Georgia, 179, 234, 280n. 6, 287n. 18, 314–15n. 60, 317n. 31, 319n. 15
Cibecue Apache, 41, 42, 240–41, 250, 251–52, 258, 318n, 320n. 29, 323n. 3
Circe, 38, 39, 40, 83, 89, 113, 125, 126, 129, 145, 147, 155–57, 161–66, 168, 173, 191, 196, 206, 236, 246, 262–63, 291–92n. 63, 299n. 46, 305n. 15, 307nn. 27, 28, and 31, 321n. 31
civil war/English revolution, 80, 205, 209, 211, 287n. 18
Cixous, Hélène, 219, 246, 278, 317n. 32, 322n. 47
Clark, James Andrew, 242, 248, 276, 308–9n. 46, 309n. 55, 310n. 61, 322n. 48, 322n. 53
Coiro, Ann Baynes, 283n. 26, 298n. 39
Coleridge, Samuel Taylor: "Kubla Khan," 314n. 56
Comes, Natalis, 260
Corns, Thomas, 292n. 66
Corthell, Ronald, 302n. 25, 315n. 4, 320n. 24
Counter-Reformation, 179
courtly love, 41, 223, 228, 231–32, 238, 239, 245, 270, 319n. 8
Cox, Catherine I., 326n. 31
Creaser, John, 317–18n. 38
crisis poems, 21
Cunnar, Eugene, 285n. 6, 309–10n. 60
Curtius, Ernst Robert, 313n. 32

dance, 18, 49, 50, 54, 58, 59, 60, 61, 74–75, 158–59, 176, 245, 253–55, 258, 261, 267, 274–75, 293n. 77, 298n. 41, 323n. 5, 325–26n. 27
Dante Alighieri: *Divine Comedy,* 189; *Inferno,* 109, 112; *Purgatorio,* 239
Davis, Michael, 314n. 57
death, 36, 77, 95, 96, 126, 129, 160–61
De Doctrina Christiana, 303n. 43
de Girone, Don Fernandez, 290n. 50
Demaray, John G., 285n. 6, 286n. 14, 287n. 21, 291–92n. 63, 293n. 77, 295n. 15, 299n. 50, 301n. 13, 303n. 40, 304n. 3, 307n. 30, 319n. 13, 327n. 45
Dempsey, Charles, 326n. 32, 327n. 44, 327n. 48
Derby, Dowager Countess of (Alice Egerton, formerly Stanley, née Spencer), 99, 143, 291–92n. 63, 297–98n. 32
Descartes, René, 23
Detienne, Marcel, 305n. 16
Diekhoff, John, 329n. 61
Diodati, Charles, 204, 205
Donne, John, 21; *Anniversaries,* 325n. 24; "The Apparition," 190, 313n. 35; "The Ecstasie," 257, 324n. 16
Drayton, Michael: *Polyobion,* 296n. 19
Drury, Elizabeth, 325n. 24

INDEX

Dubrow, Heather, 296 n. 23, 300 n. 4, 318 n. 6
DuRocher, Richard, 136, 301 n. 20, 303 nn. 36, 44, and 45
Dusinberre, Juliet, 245, 311 n. 12, 322 n. 43

Eagleton, Terry, 290 n. 40
Egerton, Alice: and marriageability and virginity, 179–82, 187–88, 300 n. 9, 323 n. 7; performance in previous masques of, 16, 291–92 n. 63; as singer in *A Maske,* 95, 129; transformed and initiated in *A Maske,* 15–17, 42, 47, 48, 68, 70, 78–80, 97, 108, 165, 179, 181, 187, 220, 224, 279, 300 n. 9
Egerton, Catherine, 291–92 n. 63
Egerton, John (father of Alice). *See* Bridgewater, 1st Earl of
Egerton, John (brother of Alice; Lord Brackley; Elder Brother), 32, 37, 39–40, 41, 52, 68, 70, 72, 73–74, 84–85, 88–92, 94–99, 103–10, 113, 114, 125, 126–28, 134–35, 150, 152, 157, 165, 176, 181, 183, 185, 187, 193–97, 199, 201, 217, 226, 230, 237–38, 252–54, 256, 275, 277, 291–92 n. 63, 313 n. 43, 316 n. 26
Egerton, Thomas (brother of Alice; Second Brother), 32, 37, 41, 52, 68, 72, 73–74, 84–85, 88–92, 94–95, 97–98, 103–10, 113, 114, 125, 126–28, 134–35, 150, 152, 157, 165, 176, 183–84, 187, 194–95, 226, 237–38, 252–54, 256, 275, 277, 291–92 n. 63, 316 n. 26
ego, 26, 28, 41, 44–45, 162, 168, 236, 285 n. 49
Elegy 6, 40, 204–5
Eliade, Mircea, 46, 113, 116, 157, 285 n. 5, 289 n. 33, 293 nn. 70, 74, and 76, 300 n. 6, 301 n. 11, 307 n. 33
Eliot, T. S.: "Burnt Norton," 149, 254, 305 n. 17, 323 n. 6; "Little Gidding," 176, 311 n. 7; *The Waste Land,* 137–38, 303 n. 46
Elizabeth I, Queen, 64–66, 231, 290 n. 50, 290–91 n. 52, 310 n. 3, 319 n. 9

emblems/emblem books, 119–20, 169, 234, 253, 259, 270, 295–96 n. 16, 329 n. 63
empiricism, 47
England: and European diplomacy, 54, 60, 63, 290 nn. 39 and 50; foundational myths of, 83, 304 n. 50, 320 n. 30; gathering conflict in, 55, 79–80, 112; nostalgia for Elizabeth I in, 64–65, 290–91 n. 52, 310 n. 3; the private self in, 52; royalist ideology in, 35–36, 47, 49–50, 53, 55, 59–68, 94; and union of Britain, 310 n. 3, 321 n. 36. *See also* civil war/English revolution; republicanism
Enterline, Lynn, 301 n. 20, 303 n. 47, 317 n. 37
epic, 87, 89, 112, 136, 139, 204, 283 n. 27
"Epitaphium Damonis," 74, 270–71
Euripides, 151, 243, 277, 329 n. 62; *The Bacchae,* 146, 147, 150, 153, 154, 155, 210, 305 n. 14; *Electra,* 307 n. 27; *Hippolytus,* 305 n. 14; *Ion,* 306 n. 20, 307 n. 27; *Iphegenia at Aulis,* 243, 321 n. 36; *Medea,* 307 n. 27
Evans, J. Martin, 283 n. 26, 310 n. 61
Evans, Margery, 224, 317–18 n. 38

Faust, Joan, 288–89 n. 30, 294 n. 86
Fawcett, Mary Laughlin, 283 n. 29, 316 nn. 11 and 26, 323–24 n. 8
feminism, 19–21, 40, 217, 223, 281 nn. 12 and 13, 293–94 n. 80, 300 n. 55, 316 n. 26, 321–22 n. 41
Ferry, Anne D., 295 n. 11
fertility/generativity, 35, 49, 50, 59, 70, 134, 140, 160, 162, 169, 181–83, 227, 250, 253, 260, 265, 273, 274, 308 n. 42, 320–21 n. 30
Fish, Stanley, 21, 259, 284 nn. 33 and 41, 296 nn. 21 and 22, 319 nn. 17, 19, and 21, 325–26 n. 27
Flaubert, Gustave: *Madame Bovary,* 203, 315 n. 2
Fletcher, Angus, 17, 89, 105, 129, 134, 161, 182, 224, 257–58, 260, 280 n. 7, 287 n. 19, 295 n. 12, 297 n. 29, 298 nn. 35 and 40, 301 n. 16, 302 nn. 30 and

32, 311 nn. 6 and 9, 312 nn. 19, 20, and 21, 316 n. 14, 320 n. 23, 321 n. 38
Fletcher, Anthony, 287 n. 18, 311 n. 12
Fletcher, John: *The Maid's Tragedy*, 162
Foucault, Michel, 44, 314 n. 52
Fowler, Alastair, 317 n. 28
France, 63
Freud, Sigmund, 23, 24, 44–45, 65, 155, 161, 183, 192, 198–99, 201, 217, 278, 285 n. 47, 286 n. 10, 287–88 n. 22, 291 n. 54, 300–301 n. 10, 312 n. 22, 314 n. 52, 53, and 54
Frost, Elisabeth A., 297 n. 31, 299–300 n. 51, 324 n. 10
Frost, Robert: "Directive," 32, 284 n. 42
Frye, Roland M., 329 n. 64
Fuller Course in the Art of Logic, A, 285 n. 46

Gallop, Jane, 294 n. 86
Geoffrey of Monmouth, 91, 242
Giamatti, A. Bartlett, 325 n. 25
Gilbert, Sandra, 315 n. 3
Girard, René, 289 n. 34, 305 n. 12
Goldberg, Jonathan, 58, 65–66, 138, 285 n. 6, 288 n. 23, 289 n. 34, 303 n. 47, 314 n. 52, 325 n. 23
Gordon, D. J., 287 n. 19, 295 n. 13
Gossett, Suzanne, 67, 289 n. 36, 291 n. 61
Graham, Jean E., 280 n. 1, 313 n. 34, 324 n. 14
Graves, Robert, 281 n. 11
Gregerson, Linda, 280 n. 6, 297 n. 25
Grossman, Marshall, 330 n. 70
Gubar, Susan, 315 n. 3
Guibbory, Achsah, 292 n. 66, 309–10 n. 60
Guillory, John, 282 n. 21, 314 n. 49, 316 n. 12

Habermas, Jürgen, 221–22, 317 n. 34
Hale, John K., 282 n. 24, 283 n. 26
Haller, Malleville, 311 n. 12
Haller, William, 311 n. 12
Halpern, Richard, 146, 243–44, 305 n. 11, 311–12 n. 14, 316 n. 15, 321–22 nn. 39–42, 323–24 n. 8
Hanford, James Holly, 315 n. 5
Harding, Davis P., 303 n. 45
Hardy, Thomas, 109
Harvey, Elizabeth, 316 n. 26, 317 n. 37
Hausknecht, Gina, 43, 284–85 nn. 43 and 44, 311 n. 10, 315–16 n. 10
Hawthorne, Nathaniel: *The Scarlet Letter,* 109; "Young Goodman Brown," 109
Henrietta Maria, Queen, 36, 66–67, 79, 144, 287 n. 21, 289 n. 36, 291 n. 60, 316–17 n. 27
Henry, Prince (d. 1612), 15, 63, 280 n. 1, 290 n. 39, 291–92 n. 63
Herbert, George, 21; "The British Church," 310 n. 62; "Heaven," 302 n. 29; "Paradise," 302 n. 29
Heschel, Abraham, 316 n. 17
Hill, Christopher, 288 n. 25, 292 n. 66
history, 25, 31, 32, 75, 77, 130, 257
Holbrook, Peter, 290 n. 39
Hollander, John, 128, 129, 302 n. 30
Hollis, Hilda, 293 n. 78, 297 n. 26, 322 n. 55
Homer, 39, 83, 85, 205, 277; *Odyssey,* 90, 91, 104, 156–57, 162, 165–66, 299 n. 46, 307 n. 31, 309 nn. 52 and 53
Hoopes, Robert, 306 n. 23
Hoxby, Blaire, 285–86 n. 6, 287 n. 21, 289 n. 34, 323 n. 5, 324 n. 18, 325 n. 21, 325–26 n. 27
Hubbell, J. Andrew, 285–86 n. 6, 292 n. 66, 316 n. 19
Hughes, Merritt Y., 327–28 n. 50
Hull, Suzanne W., 287 n. 18, 311 n. 12, 323–24 n. 8
humanism, 30–32, 103, 137, 151, 156, 219, 294 n. 88
Hunter, William B., Jr., 286 n. 14, 294 n. 81, 294 n. 3, 300 n. 3, 326 n. 29

"Il Penseroso," 93, 134, 226, 283 n. 28
Imaginary, 45, 54, 56, 65, 72, 79–80, 83, 125, 126, 133, 141, 164–65, 169, 170, 173, 174, 201, 218, 235, 236,

INDEX

241, 249, 276, 287–88 n. 22, 290 n. 45, 302 n. 24, 308 n. 37, 309 n. 48
individualism, 22, 52, 170, 231
initiation: Eliade on, 46; of the Lady, 15–18, 20, 27, 36, 37, 41, 42, 47, 53, 68, 70–74, 75, 82, 105, 108, 109–11, 113, 122, 142, 161, 174, 226, 235, 236, 238–41, 247, 251, 258, 259, 268, 275–76, 278, 294 n. 85, 322 n. 55; of Milton into poetic and political maturity, 27, 203, 217–18, 315 n. 1
interregnum, 209, 287 n. 18

James I, King, 15, 36, 60, 62–66, 94, 144, 280 n. 1, 288 n. 27, 290 n. 50, 291 n. 59, 294 n. 86; *Daemonologie*, 290 n. 41
Jameson, Fredric, 287–88 n. 22, 308 n. 37, 309 nn. 48 and 50
Jayne, Sears, 248, 322 nn. 46 and 50, 324 n. 15
Jenkins, Hugh, 324 n. 11
Johnson, Samuel: *Lives of the English Poets,* 299 n. 49
Jones, Inigo, 16, 53, 55–57, 87, 155, 232, 256, 287 n. 19, 288 n. 28, 291–92 n. 63, 295 n. 13, 298 n. 41
Jonson, Ben, 18, 31, 49, 122, 253, 256, 287 nn. 19 and 21, 288 nn. 26–29, 289 n. 36, 290 n. 39, 291 n. 59, 294 n. 86, 295–96 n. 16, 304–5 n. 8, 310 nn. 2 and 3; emphasis on written texts of masques and instructive power of poetry by, 53, 55–58, 87–88, 288 nn. 28 and 29, 288–89 n. 30, 295 n. 13, 298 n. 41; and female power deriving from the king, 59–68, 289 nn. 31 and 36, 290–91 n. 52. Works: *Cynthia's Revels,* 302 n. 29; *Hymenaei,* 56–57, 288 nn. 28 and 29, 288–89 n. 30; *Masque of Beauty,* 59, 290 n. 45; *Masque of Blackness,* 59, 290 n. 45; *Masque of Queens,* 59, 60–66, 162, 197, 290 n. 41, 45, and 50, 290 nn. 45 and 50, 290–91 n. 52; *Oberon,* 291–92 n. 63; *Pleasure Reconciled to Virtue,* 42, 60, 78, 143, 294 n. 83, 304 n. 3; "To Penshurst," 256; *The Vision of Delight,* 49, 286 n. 8
Jung, Carl, 85, 321 n. 34

Kahn, Victoria, 43, 69, 284–85 n. 43, 292 n. 67
Kavanagh, James, 284 n. 40
Kaysen, Susanna: *Girl, Interrupted,* 318 n
Keats, John, 26, 35, 266, 283 n. 25, 327 n. 43; "Ode on a Grecian Urn," 261, 326 n. 33; "Ode to a Nightingale," 96, 297 n. 30; "Ode to Psyche," 301 n. 15
Kendrick, Christopher, 188, 204, 283 n. 29, 300 n. 1, 304 n. 7, 312 n. 25, 315 nn. 5 and 9, 316 nn. 15 and 16, 323–24 n. 8
Kerényi, C., 321 n. 34
Kerrigan, William, 51, 163, 176, 189, 190, 204, 214, 217, 234, 280 n. 5, 283 n. 29, 285 n. 49, 300–301 n. 10, 312 n. 18, 315 n. 5, 316 nn. 17 and 21, 319 n. 16, 322–23 n. 56, 324 n. 9
Kierkegaard, Søren, 23
Kim, Julie H., 323 n. 7
King, Edward, 100
Kinnell, Galway: *The Book of Nightmares,* 277, 329 n. 66
Krantz, Corrine Ann, 320 n. 29
Kristeva, Julia, 199, 278, 314 n. 55
Kubrick, Stanley: *Eyes Wide Shut,* 144

labyrinth/maze, 23, 32–34, 42, 44, 72–73, 76, 83, 109, 112–15, 128, 158, 165, 282 n. 20, 284 n. 42
Lacan, Jacques, 54, 56, 79, 164, 184, 192, 235–36, 278, 287–88 n. 22, 294 n. 86, 302 n. 24, 308 n. 37, 309 nn. 48, 49, and 51, 312 n. 24, 313 nn. 38–41, 319 n. 18, 330 n. 70
LaFontaine, Jean, 295 nn. 5 and 7, 300 nn. 56 and 57
"L'Allegro," 159, 211, 249, 283 n. 28, 308 n. 39, 324 n. 11
Lanyer, Aemelia: *Salve Deus Rex Judaeorum,* 293–94 n. 80
Laplanche, J., 314 nn. 48–49
Laud, William (Archbishop of Canterbury), 159, 210, 212, 307–8 n. 34
Lawes, Henry, 36–37, 69, 72, 84, 89, 97–102, 108, 143, 152, 291–92 n. 63,

297–98 n. 32, 298 n. 33, 298 n. 40, 304 n. 3
Leasure, Ross, 304 n. 3
Leonard, John, 300–301 n. 10, 312 n. 18, 313 n. 43, 315 n. 5, 316 n. 11, 319 n. 16, 322–23 n. 56
Lewalski, Barbara K., 62–63, 284 n. 33, 287 n. 21, 288 nn. 23 and 24, 289 nn. 36 and 37, 291 n. 57, 292 n. 66, 293–94 n. 80, 294 n. 88, 297–98 n. 32, 298 nn. 37, 38, and 39, 298 n. 40, 308–9 n. 46
Lewis, C. S., 264, 319 nn. 8 and 11, 326 n. 40, 328 n. 54
libertinism, 35, 38, 41, 69, 143, 144, 167, 169, 172, 177, 182, 183, 226, 232–33, 261, 269, 303 n. 47, 304 n. 3, 309–10 n. 60
Lieb, Michael, 138, 146, 211, 215, 283 n. 29, 305 n. 13, 316 nn. 16, 18, and 24, 322 n. 42
Liebler, Naomi Conn, 289 n. 34
liminality, 38, 71–77, 82, 97, 110–14, 117, 119–22, 142, 146, 154, 157, 170, 185, 187, 226, 237, 247, 251, 256, 276, 277, 279
Lindheim, Nancy, 296–97 n. 24, 305 n. 14, 308 n. 43, 328 nn. 52 and 56, 329 nn. 61 and 63
literacy, 24, 51
Liu, Alan, 284 n. 41
Loeffelholz, Mary, 283 n. 29, 301 n. 20, 312 n. 25, 316 n. 26, 321 n. 34
Loewenstein, David, 292 n. 66, 324 n. 11
Loughlin, Marie, 310 n. 3, 326 n. 35
Ludlow Castle, 15, 72, 80–81, 84, 91, 102–3, 110, 111, 113, 256, 258, 274–75, 286 n. 16
"Lycidas," 27, 74, 100, 130, 189, 209, 247, 283 n. 28, 297 n. 25, 298 n. 39, 302 n. 34, 305 n. 13, 315 n. 1

MacCaffrey, Isabel, 319 n. 8, 320 n. 25
MacIntyre, Alasdair, 285 n. 45
MacMullen, Ramsay, 314 n. 52
Madsen, William G., 308–9 n. 46
Magro, Maria, 221, 222, 317 nn. 35 and 36

Marcus, Leah, 25, 68–69, 224, 280 nn. 3 and 4, 282 n. 24, 285 n. 6, 286 n. 9, 286 n. 14, 286–87 n. 17, 287–88 n. 22, 288 n. 27, 292 n. 66, 292–93 n. 68, 298 n. 36, 299 n. 45, 300 n. 2, 304 n. 50, 307–8 n. 34, 308 n. 40, 317–18 nn. 38 and 39
Marino, Giambattista, 260
marriage, 22, 46, 177–78, 180, 182, 185, 186, 208, 215, 219, 221, 227–29, 231–32, 239, 262, 272, 273, 287 n. 18, 304 n. 5, 310 n. 3, 311 nn. 10 and 12, 311–12 n. 14, 313 n. 30, 316 n. 11, 323 n. 7, 328 n. 57
Martin, Catherine Gimelli, 284 n. 41, 294 n. 88
Martz, Louis, 295 nn. 6 and 8, 296 n. 23, 301 n. 18
Marx, Karl, 44
Maske, A (*Comus*): anxiety regarding internal disorder and libertine court/aristocratic corruptions in, 38, 69, 143–44, 164, 169, 171–72, 210, 237; Attendant Spirit as ideal poet and guide in, 27, 28, 36–37, 72, 83–89, 91–94, 97–98, 101–2, 108, 151–52, 227, 240–41, 259–60, 267, 295 n. 5, 297 nn. 29 and 31, 298 n. 33, 299 n. 46–48, 325 n. 26; Bridgewater Manuscript of, 175, 274–75, 295 n. 8, 297–98 n. 32, 302 n. 33; class prerogative in, 17, 69, 79, 95, 106–8, 123, 168–69, 180, 194, 220, 221, 255–56, 323 n. 5; and Comus's bipolarity and parentage, 38–39, 83, 126, 144, 145–68, 173, 191–92, 236, 262–63, 305 n. 15, 307 nn. 27 and 31, 321 n. 31; and Comus's eroticism and rhetoric, 20, 28–29, 39, 41, 43–44, 77, 80, 83, 87, 89, 94, 105, 114–16, 120–21, 126, 127, 142–45, 147, 157–62, 165–72, 175, 180, 182–83, 188, 203, 219, 222, 230–33, 261, 269, 283–84 n. 31, 303 nn. 40 and 47, 304 nn. 3 and 5, 307 n. 31, 309 n. 54, 309–10 n. 60, 319 n. 17; dramatic plot, argument, and characterization in, 26–27, 68, 105–7, 111, 123, 226, 230, 299 n. 49;

Echo Song in, 24, 36, 37–38, 84, 95–96, 107, 124–41, 153, 197–98, 211, 223, 241, 245, 297 n. 29, 302 n. 33, 304 n. 5, 325 n. 24; Egerton's installation as occasion for performance of, 15, 17, 51, 68, 69, 103–4, 236, 254, 277, 280 n. 5, 286 n. 13, 317–18 n. 38; and the emerging, autonomous Puritan self or early modern subject, 18–19, 21–26, 27, 30, 35, 38, 39, 47–48, 52, 70, 78–79, 107, 111, 118–19, 123, 147, 154, 170, 172–74, 202, 220–22, 282 nn. 17, 21, and 22; and example for the nation or universality of the Lady's achievement as kind of Everyman, 16, 17–18, 19, 75–78, 220, 254, 280 n. 2, 306–7 n. 26; and family scandal, 223–24, 277, 312–13 n. 28, 317–18 n. 38; first publication of in 1637 and literary addendum for, 20, 75, 81, 99–100, 175, 179–81, 203, 206, 274–75, 298 n. 39, 310 n. 2, 311–12 n. 14, 327 n. 47; Haemony in, 36, 89, 90–93, 296 nn. 21 and 23, 296–97 n. 24, 297 n. 26; homecoming of the Lady and her brothers in, 41–42, 52, 73–75, 81, 110, 203, 226, 251–58, 275–76, 279; intertextuality, textual reinterpretation by the Lady, and "translation" in, 17, 25, 35, 37–38, 45, 89, 91, 92, 124–41, 154, 187, 198, 200, 210, 223, 245–47, 259, 269, 270, 272, 276, 277, 303 n. 47, 306–7 n. 26; and Jesus' ordeal as framework for the Lady's, 211–14. 224, 293 n. 79; Lady's introductory soliloquy in, 24, 37, 114–23, 223; Lady's silence in, 22, 40–42, 226, 252, 254–58, 274, 304 n. 7, 311–12 n. 14, 313 n. 34, 316 n. 26, 318 n. 40, 323–24 n. 8, 324 nn. 9, 14 and 15; masculine plot for the brothers in, 106–8, 114, 226, 230, 237–38; as a masque released from the authority of the king, 17, 18, 19, 36, 37, 47, 68–70, 78, 103–4, 188, 259, 286–87 n. 17, 292–93 n. 68, 304 n. 7; Milton's identification with characters in, 19, 26–28, 40, 99, 101–2, 151, 203, 206, 208, 209, 214, 217–20, 244, 283 nn. 28 and 29, 300 n. 55, 303 n. 47, 312 n. 18, 314 n. 49, 314 n. 59, 317 n. 28; performativity of, 15, 16, 17, 35–36, 39, 251–54, 257–58, 274–75; and prophetic voice, 19–20, 28, 130–31, 203–6, 208, 210–12, 217–18, 220–24, 226, 254, 255, 259, 272, 311–12 n. 14; and the public sphere, 16, 20, 28, 39, 40–41, 212–13, 221–22, 224, 306–7 n. 26, 317 nn. 34–36; reconfiguring ideal of womanhood and use of female as moral agent or subject in, 16–17, 19–21, 27–28, 36, 37, 40–41, 69–70, 78, 80, 107, 108, 172–73, 181, 187, 191–92, 202, 203, 217–18, 220–24; Sabrina's role in, 36, 41–42, 73, 80, 82–83, 89–93, 104, 105, 106, 128, 130, 140, 142, 143, 154, 161, 219, 226–27, 240–50, 251, 252, 257, 261, 269, 276, 296 n. 21, 297 n. 26, 299–300 n. 51, 304 n. 50, 308 n. 42, 320 n. 29, 320–21 n. 30, 321 nn. 31, 33, 36, and 37, 322 nn. 46 and 52, 324 n. 15; situated in 1645 *Poems,* 20, 27, 75, 274, 282 n. 24, 298 n. 39, 315 n. 1; Trinity Manuscript of, 274–76, 302 n. 33, 329 nn. 60 and 61; visionary Epilogue to, 20, 42, 45, 75, 81, 87–88, 92, 98, 151, 187, 249, 258, 259–76, 295 n. 8, 324 n. 19, 325 n. 25, 325–26 n. 27, 327 n. 45, 328 nn. 56 and 57, 329 n. 63. *See also* allegory; antimasque; chastity; initiation; mythology; ritual/rite of passage; symbolism; virtue

masque, 285–86 n. 6, 286–87 n. 17, 287–88 n. 22, 288 n. 23, 291 nn. 59 and 61, 327 n. 45; archaic ritual origins of, 48–50, 253; and celebrating aristocratic virtue, 18, 35, 42, 53–55, 57, 69, 78–79, 88, 106; and celebrating king as source of power, 15, 17–18, 35–37, 47, 49–50, 53–56, 58–61, 66–67, 70, 78, 79–80, 94, 103, 144,

259, 280 n. 1, 286 n. 9, 289 n. 31, 295 n. 14, 316–17 n. 27; convention of presenter in, 82, 102, 108; erotic imagination of, 142–45, 310 n. 3; and female virtue and power deriving from the king in the "queen's masques," 36, 59–68, 79, 144, 289 nn. 36 and 37, 290–91 n. 52, 316–17 n. 27; hybridity of, 145–46, 304–5 n. 8; inclusion of audience in, 53–54, 58–59, 73, 110–11, 256; Jonsonian conventions and ethics of, 18, 31, 49, 53, 55–58, 65–66, 87–88, 122, 253, 255–56, 287 n. 21, 288 nn. 27–29, 289 nn. 31 and 36, 290 n. 39, 298 n. 41, 304–5 n. 8; and marking occasions, 15; professional players vs. aristocratic masquers in, 57, 59, 67–68, 97; spectacular, costly excess of, 55, 288 n. 24; stages/structure of the, 35–36, 48, 51, 53, 70, 236, 286 n. 9, 287 n. 21; triumphalist outcomes of, 153. *See also* antimasque; revels

Maus, Katharine Eisaman, 214, 282 n. 17, 283 n. 29, 312 n. 18, 314 n. 59, 316 n. 22, 317 n. 37

McColley, Diane Kelsey, 308–9 n. 46, 311 n. 10

McGuire, Maryann Cale, 78, 106, 280 n. 6, 285 n. 6, 287 n. 18, 291 n. 58, 294 n. 85, 299 n. 50, 304 n. 4

medievalism, 41, 178–79, 231–32

Medusa, 39–40, 65, 195–201, 217–19, 234, 313 n. 43

Milton, John (father of writer), 36, 99–101

Milton, John: and authorial projections and identifications with characters, 19, 25–28, 40, 89, 99, 101, 151, 203–4, 206, 208, 209, 214, 217–19, 244, 282 n. 24, 283 nn. 26, 28, and 29, 300 n. 55, 303 n. 47, 312 n. 18, 314 n. 49, 314 n. 59, 317 nn. 28 and 37; and conflict with father over poetry and music, 36, 99–102, 218, 317 n. 28; as "Lady of Christ's," 21, 27, 215–17, 219; political commitments of, 15–16, 18–19, 35–36, 69, 78–79, 208–9, 272, 292 n. 66; and tragedy and loss, 22; viewed as patriarchal, masculinist writer, 19, 21, 27–28, 40, 203, 254, 293–94 n. 80, 300 n. 55, 311 n. 10, 315 n. 3; withdrawal for study of, 100. *See also titles of individual works*

Minerva/Athena, 39–40, 155, 194–201, 217–20, 234, 299 n. 46, 304 n. 50

Montag, Warren, 284 n. 38

Montague, Walter: *The Shepherd's Paradise,* 67

Moore, Jeanie Grant, 322 n. 44

morality play, 23

Mueller, Janel, 292 n. 66

Murrin, Michael, 284 n. 37, 296 n. 17

music, 36, 50, 59, 61, 74–75, 85, 89, 95, 96–102, 108, 128–30, 135, 147, 149, 150, 152, 158, 208, 247, 274, 297 n. 29, 298 nn. 40 and 41, 302 nn. 30 and 34

mythology, 36, 134–39, 153–54, 156, 275, 303 nn. 41 and 45, 307 n. 27, 321 n. 34; Attendant Spirit as custodian and explicator of uncanny world of, 85, 89, 94, 152; and Botticelli, 265–67, 269, 270; Comus and traditions of, 94, 145; dispelling of, 256; Elder Brother's use of, 193–95, 217–19, 234, 313 n. 43; and formative personal myths for Milton, 146, 206; and idealism of the masque, 97; and Jonson's rationale for absolutism, 55, 65–66, 78, 253, 288 n. 26; legitimation of Earl of Bridgewater/patriarchy through, 103, 108; and liminal, supernatural figures, 82; Milton's and the Lady's reconfigurations of 17, 34–35, 37–38, 48, 68–69, 124, 130, 134, 136, 146, 152–54, 173, 242–43, 253, 260, 261–62, 265, 269, 273, 306 n. 25, 327 n. 49, 328 n. 56; Nietzsche's reading of, 146–49, 152–53; and representation of the Imaginary order, 164–65, 173; and Sabrina as overdetermined figure, 240–43, 320 nn. 29 and 30, 321 n. 31; Spenser's use of, 41, 264–65, 267, 268,

270, 273, 326–27 n. 41, 328 n. 56; as unconscious of the masque, 48, 50, 161. *See also* Ovid

Nativity Ode. *See* "On the Morning of Christ's Nativity"
nature, 36, 49–50, 59, 90–93, 95, 113, 122, 160–61, 163–64, 168, 169, 171, 173, 175, 233, 247–49, 276–77, 308–9 n. 46, 310 nn. 61 and 62, 319–20 n. 22, 322 n. 49, 328 n. 56
Neoplatonism, 31, 36, 67, 68, 85, 105, 136, 151, 237, 253, 263, 264, 267, 292 n. 67, 296–97 n. 24, 324 n. 15, 325 n. 26. *See also* Plato/Platonism
Neumann, Erich, 195, 307 n. 28, 308 n. 42, 314 n. 45
Neuse, Richaard, 296 n. 21
new historicism, 19, 21, 29–30, 32, 284 n. 41, 321–22 n. 41, 323–24 n. 8, 329–30 n. 69
Nicholl, Alardyce, 286 n. 9
Nietzsche, Friedrich, 35, 278; *The Birth of Tragedy,* 38, 96, 146–54, 305 nn. 10, 15, 16, and 18, 306–7 n. 26, 329 n. 62
Nigeria, 320–21 n. 30
Nonconformists, 16
Norbrook, David, 280 n. 6, 285 n. 6, 287 n. 21, 288 n. 23, 292 n. 66, 313 n. 30
Normand, Lawrence, 289 n. 37, 290 n. 41
Nyquist, Mary, 281 n. 12, 293–94 n. 80, 311 n. 10

Of Education, 31
Ogunyemi, Chikwenye Okenyo, 320–21 n. 30
"On the Morning of Christ's Nativity," 26, 27, 92, 159, 189, 204, 205, 283 n. 28, 302 n. 34, 315 nn. 1 and 8, 327 n. 47
Oram, William A., 296 n. 21, 299–300 n. 51, 308 nn. 39 and 42, 319–20 n. 22, 324 n. 15
Orgel, Stephen, 29, 57, 283 n. 30, 283–84 n. 31, 284 n. 32, 285 n. 6, 286 n. 9, 287 n. 21, 290 n. 38, 291 n. 53, 299 n. 48, 302 n. 25, 312 n. 25, 313 n. 30, 319 n. 17, 323 n. 7
Ortiz, Joseph M., 301 n. 20, 306 n. 25, 321 n. 31
Ovid, 35, 65, 277, 303 nn. 42, 44, and 45; *Metamorphoses,* 38, 96, 124–39, 146, 150, 154, 159, 195, 198–200, 218, 223, 224, 233, 242, 244–45, 246, 268, 269, 277, 301 n. 20, 301–2 n. 22, 303 n. 47, 305 n. 15, 306 n. 25, 307 n. 27, 308 n. 41, 313 n. 43, 316 n. 26, 317 n. 37
Ozment, Steven, 311 n. 12

Paglia, Camille, 184, 313 n. 42, 314 nn. 44 and 58
pamphlets/pamphlet wars, 77, 172, 205, 208, 209, 221, 292 n. 66, 293–94 n. 80
Paradise Lost, 89, 128, 244, 265–66, 285 n. 49, 305 n. 13, 314 n. 49, 327 n. 43, 330 n. 70; authorial selfhood in, 25, 28, 101, 138–39; Christ in, 259, 325 n. 22; Death in, 160–61; and divine creativity, 86–87; Eve tempted in, 77–78, 134–35, 143, 169, 293 n. 79; Eve's redemptive dream in, 257; God the Father in, 94, 101, 107, 297 n. 27; Nature and Eden in, 163, 247, 260, 263, 265–66, 268, 271, 308–9 n. 46, 329 n. 64; prayer in, 76, 138–39; Raphael as guide in, 86, 87, 104, 189, 273, 306 n. 20; resisting tragedy in, 22; Satan in, 24, 29, 60–61, 69, 143, 169, 301 n. 14; soliloquy in, 24, 301 n. 14; and the two sexes, chastity, and marriage, 59, 177–78, 215, 221, 247, 268, 271, 273, 311 n. 10, 315–16 n. 10; universality of Adam and Eve as moral agents in, 17, 107
Paradise Regained, 22, 29, 112, 119, 124, 170, 213, 214, 224, 256, 293 n. 79, 301 n. 14
Parker, William Riley, 283 n. 30, 295 n. 13, 297–98 n. 32, 306 n. 21
Parry, Graham, 280 n. 1, 287 n. 19, 288 n. 26, 289 n. 31, 291 n. 59
pastoral, 27, 42, 67, 83, 84, 95, 98, 108,

112, 128, 132, 134, 210, 240, 242, 248, 259, 296–97 n. 24
patriarchy, 19, 28, 29, 30, 36, 48, 69, 102–4, 107, 108, 158, 165, 181, 183, 186–88, 191–92, 199, 201, 203, 209, 218, 219, 222, 224, 236, 237–38, 254, 255, 274, 281 nn. 11–13, 287 n. 18, 289 nn. 36 and 37, 290–91 n. 52, 299 n. 48, 311 nn. 8 and 12, 311–12 n. 14, 313 n. 30, 315 n. 4, 318 n. 40
patronage, 99, 144, 298 n. 39, 315 n. 4
Patterson, Annabel, 292 n. 66, 322 n. 53, 324 n. 11
Peacock, John, 287 nn. 19 and 21, 288 n. 29, 295 n. 13, 298 n. 41, 304–5 n. 8
personification, 82, 91, 97, 119, 121, 161, 228, 236, 270, 273
Petrarch/Petrarchan mode, 143, 169, 231, 301 n. 20, 319 n. 12
Philips, Katherine, 309–10 n. 60
Pirandello, Luigi, 16
Plato/Platonism, 83, 86, 103, 120, 245, 274, 325 n. 25. *See also* Neoplatonism
Plutarch: *Moralia,* 326 n. 29
Poems of Mr. John Milton (1645), 20, 27, 75, 101, 274, 282 n. 24, 283 n. 26, 298 n. 39, 315 n. 1
poetry, power of, 29, 30–32, 35, 36, 41, 55–57, 62, 85, 89, 91–94, 98–102, 108, 120, 129–31, 149, 172, 173
Polydorou, Desma, 293–94 n. 80, 311 n. 10
Pontalis, J.-B., 314 nn. 48–49
postmodernism, 31, 43–44, 283 n. 26
Poussin, Nicholas: "Lamentation over the Dead Christ," 327 n. 49; "Venus with the Dead Adonis," 327 n. 49
print culture, 24
Prolusion 6, 31, 216, 218
Prolusion 7, 93–94
Protestantism, 23, 30, 55, 121, 151, 169, 179, 182, 219, 236, 280 nn. 1 and 6, 290 n. 39. *See also* Reformation
Prynne, William: *Histriomastix,* 67, 291 n. 60

Puritanism, 16, 22, 47, 55, 67, 78–79, 111, 123, 154, 172–73, 178, 211, 220, 221, 237, 245, 273, 277, 289 n. 36, 294 n. 88, 306 n. 25, 323–24 n. 8
Puteanus, Erycius: *Comus,* 304 n. 3
Pye, Christopher, 282 n. 17

Quilligan, Maureen, 311–12 n. 14

Rajan, Balachandra, 322 n. 54
Rambuss, Richard, 328 n. 57
Randolph, Thomas, 298 n. 39
Réage, Pauline: *The Story of O,* 144, 304 n. 6
Reason of Church Government, The, 16, 75, 280 n. 2
Réau, Louis, 275, 329 n. 64
Reformation, 17, 22, 52, 75, 153, 170, 179, 182, 207, 209, 212–13, 219, 220, 231, 234, 245, 280 n. 6, 287 n. 18
regression, 39, 125–27, 161–63, 168, 170, 173
republicanism, 22, 69, 78–79, 272, 292 n. 66
Revard, Stella, 68, 242, 292 n. 64, 321 nn. 31 and 33
revels, 20, 35, 53, 58, 70, 74–75, 80–81, 115, 142, 162, 253–58, 259, 266, 274–75, 293 n. 77, 325–26 n. 27
Richards, Audrey, 46, 278, 285 nn. 1–4, 293 nn. 70–72, 304 n. 2, 322 n. 55
ritual/rite of passage: elders' role in, 51, 82, 84, 108, 117; in *A Maske,* 15, 17–19, 27, 34, 36, 37, 38, 41–42, 47, 48–49, 51, 52, 70–76, 80, 82, 84, 85, 94, 97, 105–6, 107, 109–11, 116–17, 122, 123, 138, 142, 147, 152–54, 160, 161, 167, 170, 171, 173, 175–76, 181, 187, 203, 220, 226, 237–41, 243, 247, 250, 251, 257, 267, 274–78, 320 n. 29; and origins of the masque, 48–50, 253, 285 n. 7, 323 n. 4; reaggregation moment of, 41–42, 71, 73–74, 110, 251; and the ritual antagonist or "mock bridegroom," 38, 71, 73, 82, 142, 167, 226, 238, 293 n. 71, 304 nn. 2 and 5; three stages of, 71, 110, 293 n. 70; in tradi-

INDEX 359

tional or premodern societies, 35, 38, 46–48, 51–52, 58, 82, 107–8, 109–10, 122, 142, 226, 239–40, 251, 286 n. 15, 320 n. 29. See also *chisungu;* initiation; liminality
Robertson, David, 301 n. 14
Roche, Thomas, 232, 318 nn. 2 and 5, 319 n. 8, 320 nn. 26 and 27
Rogers, John, 209, 262, 287 n. 18, 311 nn. 5 and 11, 311–12 n. 14, 312 n. 17, 314–15 n. 60, 316 n. 15, 323–24 n. 8, 326 n. 35
romance, 230–32, 237, 281 n. 14, 318 n. 6
Rumrich, John, 21–22, 196, 209, 282 n. 18, 307 n. 27, 313 n. 43, 314 n. 46, 316 n. 13, 325–26 n. 27, 328 nn. 52 and 56, 329–30 n. 69
Rushdy, Ashraf, 282 n. 15

Samson Agonistes, 22, 24, 26, 170, 212, 256–57, 306–7 n. 26, 330 n. 71
Sandys, George: *Ovid's Metamorphoses English'd . . . ,* 126, 131–38, 146, 150, 192, 195–200, 302 n. 23
Scheidenhelm, Carol, 309 n. 51, 313 n. 31
Schopenhauer, Arthur, 146
Schwarz, Kathryn, 63, 281 n. 14, 289 n. 37, 290 n. 47, 311 n. 8, 318 n. 3, 320 n. 28
Schwyzer, Philip, 296 n. 19, 300 n. 1, 304 n. 50, 321 n. 36
self-fashioning, 24, 25, 37, 53, 89, 119, 168, 173, 236, 278, 292 n. 67
Severn River, 83, 91, 242–43, 247, 248, 249
sexuality, 15, 19, 38–39, 40, 42, 105, 115, 116–17, 125, 138, 140–41, 142, 176–89, 194, 196–98, 201, 219–20, 221–23, 229–31, 243, 245–46, 254, 255, 259, 264–65, 268, 271, 273, 300 n. 9, 311 n. 8, 314 n. 52, 319 nn. 15 and 16, 328 n. 57. *See also* chastity
Seznec, Jean, 303 n. 41
Shakespeare, William: and female heroines and sexuality, 185–87, 218, 229, 242, 316 n. 26; and ghosts, 159, 308 n. 38; monarchs in, 61, 94, 118, 163, 289 n. 34; and Ovidian violence, 301 n. 20; and pastoral, 112, 242; and romantic comedies, 58, 68; and soliloquies, subjectivity, and character development, 22–26, 28, 35, 114, 118–19, 123, 223, 301 n. 14; and sprites, 83, 158, 159; and tragedy, 24, 61, 118–19, 163, 289 n. 34; and the visual, 295 n. 13; and witches, 60–61, 115. Works: *As You Like It,* 185, 218, 229; *Hamlet,* 23, 25, 118, 119, 123, 159, 242, 282 n. 23, 308 n. 38; *1 & 2 Henry IV,* 25; *Macbeth,* 60–61, 65, 115, 118, 119, 123, 163; *A Midsummer Night's Dream,* 83, 158, 159, 163, 308 n. 38; *Othello,* 22, 118, 119, 316 n. 26; *The Tempest,* 83, 94, 185–87, 312 n. 26, 312–13 n. 28; *Twelfth Night,* 185, 218, 229; *The Winter's Tale,* 185, 242
Shawcross, John, 100, 101, 102, 213, 215, 297–98 n. 32, 298 nn. 38 and 39, 312 n. 18, 315 n. 1, 317 n. 28
Shelley, Percy Bysshe: "A Defence of Poetry," 101, 319 n. 12
Shohet, Lauren, 86, 89, 285–86 n. 6, 311–12 n. 14, 329 n. 68
Shuger, Debora, 319 n. 15, 322–23 n. 56
Shullenberger, William, 281 n. 13, 311 n. 10, 312 n. 26, 313 n. 35, 315 n. 8, 324 n. 13
Sidney, Sir Philip, 277; "An Apology for Poetry," 31
Silk, M. S., 305 nn. 15 and 18
Silver, Victoria, 105, 294 n. 2, 295 n. 5, 296–97 n. 24, 298 n. 33, 299 n. 48, 300 n. 54
Simons, Louise, 286 n. 16, 302 n. 27, 302–3 n. 35
Singleton, R. H., 304 n. 3
Slater, Philip, 307 n. 27
Smith, Bruce, 314 n. 52
Smith, George William, Jr., 301 n. 13, 309 n. 54
Smith, Hilda, 281 n. 12
Smith, Joseph H., 309 n. 48

Socrates, 102; *Phaedo,* 260
Socratic rationalism, 150–53
Sokol, B. J., 312 n. 15, 322 n. 55
soliloquy, 22, 24, 37, 118–19, 122, 124, 223, 301 n. 14
Sonnet 7, 214, 315 n. 1
Sonnet 13, 101
Sophocles, 38, 277; *Electra,* 307 n. 27; *Oedipus at Colonus,* 139–40, 154
Spain, 63, 290 nn. 39 and 50
Spanish Armada, 64
Specht, Rachel: *A Mouzell for Melastomous . . . ,* 293–94 n. 80
Spencer, Jeffry, 266, 327 n. 42
Spenser, Edmund, 35, 39, 99, 136, 246, 294 n. 88, 316 n. 26, 319 n. 8, 328 n. 56; *The Fairie Queene,* 17, 31, 41, 89, 109, 144, 157, 167, 183–85, 194–96, 209, 227–33, 237–39, 241–43, 260, 264–65. 267, 268, 270, 277, 281 n. 9, 301 n. 16, 309 n. 55, 310 n. 62, 314 n. 44, 318 nn. 2–6, 319 n. 12, 320 n. 28, 322–23 n. 56, 326–27 n. 41; "A Letter of the Authors [To Sir Walter Raleigh, Knight]," 31
Sprott, S. E., 329 n. 61
Starnes, DeWitt T., 260, 303 n. 41
Steadman, John, 283 n. 27
Steggle, Matthew, 306 n. 21
Steibel, Arlene, 309–10 n. 60
Stephanus, Charles, 260
Stern, J. P., 305 nn. 15 and 18
Stevens, Wallace, 35; "The Idea of Order at Key West," 325 n. 24; "The Well Dressed Man with a Beard," 22, 282 n. 19
Stewart, Andrew, 305 n. 16
Strong, Roy, 319 n. 9
Strout, Nathaniel, 288 n. 27, 294 n. 83
subject, early modern, 19, 21–30, 35, 43, 47–48, 52, 111, 170, 220, 282 nn. 16, 17, 21, 22, and 24, 283 n. 28
sublime, 22, 26, 139, 153, 154, 181, 189, 205, 223, 224, 249, 258, 261, 263, 299–300 n. 51
Swaim, Kathleen, 280 n. 6, 282 n. 21, 283 nn. 26 and 28, 286 n. 16, 295 n. 4, 296 nn. 18 and 23, 298 n. 34, 300 n. 8,
301 nn. 17 and 21, 302 n. 31, 302–3 n. 35, 306 nn. 19, 20, and 22, 325 n. 26, 326 nn. 34 and 36
Swetnam, Joseph, 293–94 n. 80
Symbolic order, 42, 45, 54, 56–57, 79–80, 101, 133, 141, 164–65, 192, 201, 218, 235–36, 241, 246, 249, 272, 276, 278, 287–88 n. 22, 302 n. 24, 309 nn. 48–50, 319 n. 18
symbolism: in court masques, 47, 50, 54; of Haemony and Sabrina, 90–92, 245, 250, 251, 296 n. 21; of the Lady's liminal zone, 111–13; and the Lady's reenactment of Philomela, 138; of Lawes, 97; in *A Maske* generally, 47, 48, 187, 255, 258, 295 n. 15, 296 n. 21; in *The Masque of Queens,* 64, 65; and Milton's poetic inheritance, 34; and phallic symbols and sexual fear, 201, 230–31, 237; of the revels, 20; and rites of passage 46, 48, 82, 113, 187, 258

Taafe, James, 294 n. 81, 300 n. 3, 308 n. 40
Talbert, Ernest William, 260, 303 n. 41
Tasso, Torquato, 260
Tayler, Irene, 230–31
Tennenhouse, Leonard, 282 n. 24
Tillyard, E. M. W., 299 n. 49, 312 n. 18, 325 n. 21
Townshend, Aurelian: *Albion's Triumph,* 66, 324 n. 12; *Tempe Restored,* 66, 67, 68, 155, 291–92 n. 63, 307 n. 30
tragedy, 21, 22, 38, 118–19, 123–24, 132, 137–39, 141, 145–151, 153–55, 173, 257, 278, 297 n. 25, 304–5 n. 8, 306–7 n. 26, 307 n. 27, 314 n. 57
Treip, Mindele Anne, 285 n. 6, 286 n. 14, 291 n. 62, 299 n. 50, 307 n. 30, 324 n. 12
Turner, Victor, 50, 71, 72–75, 113, 117, 170, 171, 251, 258, 259, 276, 278, 286 nn. 11 and 15, 289 n. 34, 293 n. 70, 301 n. 19, 304 n. 1, 324 n. 20, 325 n. 21
Tuve, Rosemond, 262–63, 308 n. 35, 326 nn. 37 and 39

typology, 25, 75, 77, 135, 173, 178, 212, 244, 245, 263, 269

Uganda, 33–34
uncanny, 61, 85, 89, 110–12, 115, 134, 185, 201, 220, 223
unconscious, 24, 48, 50, 61, 114, 118, 153, 161

van Gennep, Arnold, 293 n. 70
Veevers, Erica, 291 n. 60
Verdi, Richard, 327 n. 49
Virgil, 85; *Aeneid,* 104, 299 n. 46; Fourth Eclogue, 325 n. 25
virginity. *See under* chastity
virtue, 21, 34, 43–45, 60, 155, 229, 237, 284–85 n. 43, 285 n. 44, 292 n. 67, 293 n. 77, 322 n. 44; aristocratic, 18, 53, 57, 61, 79; and the Attendant Spirit, 97, 152; and the brothers, 106–7; as existential stance in Milton, 35; and the feminine in the "queen's masques," 36, 59, 62, 64–66; the Lady's embodiment and translation of, 37, 39, 42–45, 68–70, 78–79, 117, 156, 213, 236, 251, 255, 258, 262, 263, 273, 278–79, 314 n. 49, 315–16 n. 10; royal, 15, 35–36, 292–93 n. 68. *See also* chastity

Walcott, Derek: *Omeros,* 277, 329 n. 67
Wales, 15, 51, 99, 111–12, 321 n. 36, 323 n. 4, 326 n. 29
Walker, Julia M., 313 n. 43
Wall, Kathleen, 190, 301 n. 20, 313 n. 37

Watson, Patty Jo, 300 n. 9
Webster, John: *The Duchess of Malfi,* 119, 123, 302 n. 29
Welsford, Enid, 49, 253, 286 n. 7, 287 n. 21, 290 n. 38, 323 n. 4
Whitehall, 102
Wilden, Anthony, 287–88 n. 22, 309 n. 48
Wilding, Michael, 300 n. 1
Wilkenfeld, Roger, 295–96 n. 16
Wind, Edgar, 267, 270, 279, 303 n. 41, 325 n. 26, 327 n. 48, 330 n. 72
Wittreich, Joseph, 284 n. 33
Wofford, Susanne Lindgren, 318 nn. 2, 4, and 6, 319 n. 10
Woodbridge, Linda, 281 n. 12, 293–94 n. 80
Woodhouse, A. S. P., 175, 296 n. 21, 308–9 n. 46, 310 n. 1, 321 n. 37
Woolf, Virginia: *A Room of One's Own,* 315 n. 3
Wordsworth, William, 26
Wright, B. A., 326 n. 30
Wynne-Davies, Marion, 289 n. 37, 290 nn. 44 and 45

Yeats, W. B., 35; "Among School Children," 262, 326 n. 38; "A Dialogue of Self and Soul," 254, 323 n. 6; "Sailing to Byzantium," 158, 308 n. 36

Zambia, 38, 46, 142
Žižek, Slavoj, 65, 290 n. 51